The Other Digital China

The Other Digital China

Nonconfrontational Activism
on the Social Web

Jing Wang

Harvard University Press

Cambridge, Massachusetts
London, England
2019

Second printing

Library of Congress Cataloging-in-Publication Data
Names: Wang, Jing, 1950– author.
Title: The other digital China : nonconfrontational activism
on the social web / Jing Wang.
Description: Cambridge, Massachusetts : Harvard University Press, 2019. |
Includes bibliographical references and index.
Identifiers: LCCN 2018057417 | ISBN 9780674980921
Subjects: LCSH: Internet and activism—China. | Social media—China. |
Social change—China. | China—Social conditions—2000–
Classification: LCC HM851 .W357 2019 | DDC 302.23/1— dc23
LC record available at https://lccn.loc.gov/2018057417

To the change makers and dreamers in China

Contents

Introduction

Walking Around the Obstacles

Most people with a corporate mind-set can think only of e-commerce, smart cities, and creative industry parks whenever the term "digital China" is invoked. *The Other Digital China: Nonconfrontational Activism on the Social Web* engages with the civic side of things but strives to go beyond the familiar terrain of online surveillance by foregrounding the multiple agents of change in contemporary China. Among them, the most dedicated but the least visible are grassroots nongovernmental organizations (NGOs) whose voice is rarely heard in mainstream media. Chinese NGOs are modern-day unsung heroes pivotal to the survival of the underprivileged in rural and urban China. Their existence is often obscured by our fixation with Chinese censors, as if people living in the Middle Kingdom have only two choices—being brainwashed or becoming dissidents. "How can there be real NGOs in an authoritarian country?" is a predictable response whenever I launch a discussion about Chinese NGOs. It is high time to bring into the spotlight those invisible agents at a time when hopes for a Chinese civil society seem to have receded. They are agents that have mastered the art of making change in a country where the concept of "social good" might sound rhetorical if we were to focus too intently on the censors' rules. Is contemporary China, notorious for its centralization, a seamlessly controlled web as the conventional wisdom would like us to believe? The reality is far more complex. It is best captured in a characteristic Chinese mind-set—rules are meant to be bent, if not resisted. The savviest practitioners of this wisdom are the tens of thousands

1

of grassroots NGOs that are skirting political obstacles day in and day out, not walking through them.

The Other Digital China: Nonconfrontational Activism on the Social Web is devoted to the digital practices emerging from China's multiple sectors at a transformative moment, thanks partly to the arrival of social media and web 2.0 technology, and partly to the Communist Party's new commitment to the policy of *zhengshe fenkai* (separation of government from society). This is the best of times for patriots who celebrate the ascendance of China to global center stage and perhaps the worst of times as President Xi Jinping keeps a tighter hold on dissent than ever before. Either way, one is compelled to ask: Whither goes a social sector that constitutes the backbone of civil society at the juncture of the Chinese Communist Party's (CCP) decision to "innovate social governance" (*shehui zhili chuangxin*)—a grand vision requiring a hearty three-way cooperation between weak civic organizations, the hegemonic state, and a timid public? No less urgent is a parallel question: What practices are arising from Chinese activists' and citizens' encounter with social media? Both questions inevitably lead to a third one: What kind of the "social" could be emerging after Xi consolidated power on a historic scale?

The second generation of the web (known as Web 2.0) has truly revolutionized the ways people communicate with each other. Since the launch of Sina Weibo in 2009, microblogging has spread quickly in China. By the first quarter of 2018, over 1.4 billion Chinese were monthly active users of Sina's competitor—mobile messaging app WeChat ("2018 nian Zhongguo Weixin" 2018). How have the grassroots NGOs coped with the popularization of social media? Today, if you are a social media influencer—a free agent, so to speak—functioning independently of nonprofit organizations, you can start a networked fundraising campaign effortlessly. And if you are a social media savvy company like Tencent.com, Sina.com, or Alibaba.com, you can make a direct impact on philanthropy, thereby skipping foundations and NGOs. Not surprisingly, both the free agents' action and the corporate approach have posed a daunting challenge to Chinese grassroots NGOs. Free agents and corporate China, each in its own *modus operandi,* have created memorable social-media-for-social-good campaigns that successfully mobilized the public to engage in activism en masse. Those two new groups of actors are increasingly ubiquitous, and they outpaced NGOs in achieving social goals and serving public interests. What does it mean when the nonprofits, which historically held a monopoly on doing social good, are no longer society's prescribed or preferred ways of fulfilling social goals? This question points to a prevalent trend that is reshaping philanthropy all over the world and is by no means unique to China.[1] But in a country where unofficial civic organizations are so disenfranchised, one has to wonder if this emerging phenomenon is something to celebrate or worry about?

This book maps out the ecosystem, with all its benign and portentous outgrowths, of a new brand of activism, which we may call social media activism, nicknamed "activism 2.0"—social actions that are triggered through peer-to-peer networking between weak ties and mobilized via viral communications to build virtual support communities *at scale*. I chronicle the multifaceted ways that Chinese grassroots NGOs and other civic actors use social media tools and open platforms to produce social good. Like it or not, those navigating in the terrain of social action enabled by Web 2.0 technology have no singular identity. They include not only traditionally defined nonprofit actors, but also visionary free agents, the corporate social responsibility sector, socially concerned change makers in software developer communities and maker labs, and other types of young entrepreneurs who share aspirations for creating a kinder China. Together, actors from diverse sectors are forming an invisible coalition and bringing incremental change to society. NGOs are no longer the only players in Chinese civic life.

I track the transformation of activism in China at a moment when social media has gone mainstream. Three major questions run through the entire book. First, how are various change agents using social media to do social good? Second, what are the demographic footprints of those engaged in social media activism? Third, what are the key trends that are converging to facilitate the emergence of an activism 2.0 culture in China? These trends include the rise of the ideology of "microcharity" (*wei gongyi*) and "everybody a philanthropist" (*renren ke gongyi*), "tech-4good" as a cool trend gaining momentum among young software developers and interaction designers based in first- and second-tier cities, and no less important, the ascendance of "social innovation" (*shehui chuangxin*) and maker movements both as innovation policy and social practice, which drew the entrepreneurial post-1980s and post-1990s generations into a national start-up fever. All those developments span the early 2010s and the end of the decade. They highlight the ways in which social action, cultural discourse, policy decisions, maker projects, university volunteer programs, and corporate citizenship initiatives are intersecting at a particular historical moment to bolster the foundation of a new order of information and communication technology (ICT) powered activism.

Subsequent chapters will address each of those trends. Mapping the terrain has to start with two primary inquiries: Who are the players in activism 2.0? What does the ecosystem of social media enabled activism look like in China today? In the old media environment, NGOs and community activists were the major players. But the whole ecosystem changed with the entry of social media because it brought in, on a massive scale, three new groups of social actors—free agents (of which the majority are university students and graduates), the commercial sector, and IT company-based software developers and designers who share a passion for making interactive nonprofit technology. My purpose in mapping this emerging field is to illustrate that in China today, producing social good doesn't just involve NGOs and foundations. Free agents, the corporate sector, and techies are also actively invested in shaping the ecosystem of social media activism.

I mentioned earlier the emergence of **free agents** in the new media era. They can tap into their own expansive, and sometimes global, network to launch a social campaign all by themselves. In China, free agent and celebrity journalist Deng Fei made a name for himself by starting the Free Lunch for Children campaign on his microblog. Similar examples abound among Chinese millennials, which raises the question of the impact of demographic change on the production of social good. Today, not only are young generations less tied to any particular organizational form and more open to creating their own social networks to advance their social missions and services, they also have a stronger faith than the previous generations in the capacity of new media technology to solve social problems. Chapter 4 treats this demographic phenomenon, which is as prevalent in the US and Western Europe as in China, fleshing out the culture and practice of global millennial philanthropy.

Apart from free agents, today's change making initiatives also include **CSR (corporate social responsibility)** driven philanthropy—corporate activities that utilize social media to trigger mass activism online. The classic example is Ecotonoha, a Japanese IT company's CSR program that enabled netizens to nurture virtual trees collectively with the ultimate goal of curbing global warming. Virtual leaves were planted online, and real trees were planted offline accordingly. Indeed, CSR2.0 campaigns have mushroomed everywhere; China is no exception. Forward-looking corporations are earnest practitioners of participatory social campaigns, a global phenomenon discussed in Chapters 3 and 4. In China, IT companies like Tencent.com and Sina.com compete with each other in shaping the culture of "social media for social good," which drives many cynics to ask: What is there to gain or lose when companies are turned into do-gooders? What happens when (social) cause marketing is turning into crowdsourced projects? Are mass collaborations enabled by social media actually advancing social good or is it just a new PR attempt, or even a new face of the corporate exploitation of mass-sourced labor?

Techies and interaction designers are the third new group of social actors treated in Chapter 5. By the end of 2013, socially concerned programmers and interaction designers employed in transnational and domestic Chinese IT companies started forming groups, clubs, and communities in first-tier cities. Leveraging the tremendous energy emanating from those niche groups, NGO2.0, a grassroots nongovernmental organization I founded in China, initiated a civic hackathon program, bringing together nonprofits, programmers, interaction designers, and product managers to create solutions to the problems encountered by participating NGOs. Since November 2015, our civic hackathons have produced prototypes of mobile apps and other collaborative design solutions that assist NGOs in managing their projects more efficiently. This is a burgeoning trend that needs careful documentation, not least because it also dovetails with the subculture of creative entrepreneurship in China (Chapters 2 and 5).

Numerous examples can also be cited that relate to the social media practice of the **nongovernmental organizations** themselves—the fourth group of change agents treated in this book. My favorite example is a best practice provided by Greening Han River, a Hubei-based organization. Inspired by the digital training workshop NGO2.0 held in 2010, they did an experiment—using microblogging on Google Buzz to do a live broadcast of water testing of the polluted Han River. Those of us affiliated with my nonprofit organization followed the water testing team on social media, station by station, around the clock, to share the findings of the water testing in real time. The day-long virtual connectedness was quite remarkable, given we all lived in different parts of China! Since the mid-2010s, innovative NGOs like Greening Han River and many Chinese foundations have frequently explored experiential advocacy, learning from the lessons provided by experiential marketing. Chapter 3 is filled with case studies of activism 2.0 spearheaded by both for-profit and nonprofit organizations. Indeed, social media has torn down the boundary separating for-profit and nonprofit communication strategies. The crossover seems inevitable as more and more resource-starved NGOs are considering the option of evolving into social enterprises, a trend occurring at the same time as big corporations are launching private foundations at an ever-faster speed. Out of this mutual crossover, new forms of activism are emerging on social media platforms.

I have enumerated multiple social nodes and multiple social actors that dot the new ecosystem of activism 2.0 in China today. None of them fits squarely into the profile of confrontational activists prescribed in Western liberal cultures. Walking around obstacles and navigating tactfully between what is lawful and what is illegitimate, Chinese agents are making social change inch by inch on their own terms under the surveillance of the authoritarian regime. In a field dominated by liberal thinking that equates action with resistance and social change with street revolutions, it is time that nonconfrontational activism is introduced in a book format, conceptualized, and fully documented with case studies. If this category of activism is brought to light and the simple binarism of domination versus resistance counteracted, we can begin to highlight the question of the agency of change makers in authoritarian countries. Chapter 1 zeroes in on the proposition of nonconfrontational activism, starting with a literature review of the existing scholarship related to the subject while enumerating various strategies of gaming the system practiced by Chinese nonconfrontational activists.

This book grew out of an emerging field—social media enabled action research. I ask: What happens to old-school participatory action research (PAR) when it intersects not only with digital media but also with social media? Methodologically, I am interested in exploring not only the evolution of PAR in Western and Southern hemispheres (including Cuba and Latin America) but also the Chinese experimentation with it that began in 1977 at the start of the post-Mao period and spanned across two fields—education and social work—in subsequent decades. Chapter 6 provides an overview of the developments of PAR in both English and Chinese writings. Instead of affiliating myself directly with PAR, I take a step back and ask what insights can be gained from understanding a research tradition theoretically committed to undermining dualism but which falls short of overcoming the divide separating rationalized, dispassionate "research" from the passionate but weakly theorized "action."

Surely, writing about action research in a scholar's study has its limits, for the imbalance of theory and praxis would be too conspicuous for a research topic privileging action and emphasizing *mens et manus* (mind and hand). What gave impetus to the genesis of *The Other Digital China* is not merely scholarship, for the playground of my ideas extends from the library to the field. My pursuit of an activist agenda—as the founder and secretary-general of a Chinese NGO—precedes the scholarly one. This book can thus be seen as a frontline testimony of a change agent personally involved in shaping Web 2.0 culture and practice in China's nonprofit sector since 2009.

An Introduction to NGO2.0

Between fall 2008 and summer 2009, I spent my sabbatical year in China and laid down the foundation for NGO2.0, a project originally designed to enhance the digital and social media literacy of grassroots NGOs in China's western and central provinces. Little did I know that this project would grow into a nonprofit organization based in Shenzhen and Beijing half a decade later. In 2009, Web 2.0 was a concept completely foreign to the nonprofit sector and a suspicious term in the eyes of Chinese censors. Throughout the early 2010s, my teammates and I took pains to find creative ways of deflecting the disciplinary blows dealt by hostile local governments—setbacks not severe enough for me to call it quits. Soon, the politics around social media were relaxed for the better as internet giants Sina.com and Tencent.com began exploiting Web 2.0 technology in their experiments with a new brand of peer-to-peer philanthropy (details provided in Chapter 3). The government followed suit, slowly but steadily promoting the idea of philanthropy 2.0. But it was not until 2015 when Premier Li Keqiang started trumpeting the discourse of "Internet Plus" (*hulianwang jia*)—digitalization of the industrial sector—did the culture and practice of ICT-powered activism became legitimate. Using digital and social media to do civic work is now tolerable, if not as fully acceptable, to the regime as business 2.0 ventures.

For ten years NGO2.0 witnessed the twists and turns of internet governance policy. We stumbled along, lying low and perfecting the walk around changing obstacles. In August 2014, we received a license to run as a full-fledged nonprofit organization specializing in social media and nonprofit technology. In April 2016, we published *Internet Plus Public Good: Playing with New Media* (*Hulianwang jia gongyi: Wanzhuan xin meiti*), a Chinese collection of Web 2.0 training materials we developed for grassroots NGOs (Wang and Zhou 2016). Thanks to an indefatigable team and a decade of support from the Ford Foundation in Beijing, I succeeded in shepherding NGO2.0 from concept to phenomenon.

From 2009 to 2019, more than 1,600 NGOs completed our training program. They learned to utilize digital tools and social media platforms to create spreadable content, collaborate online, run their organizations transparently, crowdfund online, recruit volunteers and donors, do advocacy campaigns, and use human-centered design methodology to craft technological solutions to the problems they were tackling. As the project evolved, we also helped NGOs build collaboration with cross-sector partners, among them, the CSR sector. To accomplish that specific goal, we rolled out a crowdsourced philanthropy map, an online platform that connects grassroots NGOs and CSR managers across provinces and across NGO issue areas. More than 4,700 NGOs entered voluntarily as registered members of the map (www.ngo20map.com), and another 20,000 NGOs are featured there as crawled data. Details about the partnership mechanism of this map are discussed in Chapters 3 and 6.

Parallel to this map is a second crowdsourced product we developed—a field guide to software for NGOs (http://tools.ngo20.org/)—a toolbox complete with nonprofit usage scenarios outlined for each social media tool and platform showcased in the guide. To facilitate the user's search for relevant entries in the field guide, we provide a system of categorization built on three principles: the technological literacy of the user, the role of the user in his or her organization, and specific organization needs (for example, online collaboration, digital marketing, volunteer and project management, CRM software, data visualization, online survey, streaming and cloud service, website building, and search engine optimization).

No less valuable are the two virtual NGO networks we set up on QQ and WeChat that connect our past workshop trainees. During the first three years of the founding of NGO2.0, I spent four hours daily using QQ, an instant messaging platform, to converse with young grassroots workers, build friendships, listen to their troubles, provide moral support, and brainstorm about solutions to the social problems they were facing. It was those long morning and late evening heart-to-heart marathon chats that motivated me to do more than just hold social media literacy workshops.

With the passage of time, and driven by my strong desire to help grassroots organizations to find resources, NGO2.0 morphed into a cross-sector platform, assisting grassroots NGOs in developing collaboration with local businesses, local techie communities, and local universities—the social actors I enumerated earlier. Some of those attempts were successful and some were not. But we were persistent in our mission of mobilizing local resources to solve local problems. During our growth from a project into an organization, not only have we evolved into a nationwide support-type NGO, I was also exposed, bit by bit, to a gradually unfolding, captivating picture of activism 2.0 culture, in which diverse groups of change makers—NGO2.0's multisectoral collaborators—leverage the network effect afforded by Web 2.0 technology to make change in a country where rampant problems of poverty, injustice, and inequality challenge its GDP-driven status as a developed country. What goes into *The Other Digital China* is thus partly research and partly field observations gained from my own experiences of working in the Chinese nonprofit sector as the founder and secretary-general of NGO2.0.

I did not turn into an activist overnight and pick up research on social action and social media on a whim. Many colleagues present and past wondered about my current endeavor because it departed sharply from my previous scholarly engagements (to name a few, comparative literature, modern and contemporary Chinese cultural and intellectual history, popular culture studies, and advertising research). To answer this nagging question, I turn to 1950s Taiwan.

In 1949, my parents left their extended families in the mainland and retreated to Taiwan with Chiang Kai-shek's Nationalist government. They arrived in Taipei empty handed, and for more than a decade and half, we lived in a squatter house. When I was old enough for schooling, my parents sent me to a newly built private school. I stayed there until I was twelve, sharing the same classes with the sons and daughters of Nationalist dignitaries and well-to-do Mandarin families migrated from the mainland, the offspring of the political and cultural establishment of the 1950s and 1960s Taipei. As a young girl, I experienced what social class meant even though I couldn't process the meaning of "class" intellectually. The days and years went by slowly as I endured discriminations of various kinds.

Experiences during our formative years stay with us, defining who we are and what we do later in life. My natural empathy with the underprivileged needs no theoretical cultivation. Childhood memories continued to mold my class consciousness and led me to the second trigger for the birth of NGO2.0, a moment that came much later and rather unexpectedly in

2006. Working as a devoted volunteer to establish the China branch of Creative Commons—an open content movement launched in the US and built on a set of open digital licenses—I had my first close encounter with a Web 2.0 practice and learned what it could do to help those who do not possess media capital. In the spring of that year, Lawrence Lessig, the mastermind of Creative Commons (henceforth CC), went to Beijing to attend the inaugurating ceremony of CC China Mainland. I was in the audience when he made an exuberant, congratulatory statement saying that CC's global user community exploded with the increase of 1.3 billion Chinese users overnight. That remark made an indelible impact on my mind not only because Lessig swept aside, unwittingly, the issue of the digital divide running rampant in developing countries but also because it dawned on me, for the first time in my academic career, that perhaps I could help tackle, in however small ways, the problem of digital literacy for the disadvantaged in China. A seed of activism was sown in 2006, but it would take another two years for me to launch NGO 2.0.

In 2008 when I took my sabbatical in China, Chinese nonprofit practitioners were not fully aware of the implications of digital media to their work, not to mention getting ready for the impending onslaught of microblogging in the wake of Sina.com's launch of its popular Weibo platform. For most nonprofits, going digital meant nothing more than building a website. Peer-to-peer media outlets and viral communication were unheard of. Although the government touted the success of its Village to Village Project that provides universal services including access to the internet in over 87 percent of rural China, NGOs in second-, third-, and fourth-tier cites were clueless about how to navigate online and create digital content. Even those located in first-tier cities were not advanced enough to learn how to maximize their presence on the social web for support and engagement. As a volunteer of Creative Commons, I couldn't help asking myself: What use are CC licenses for those living in developing countries if they don't even know how to create content online? And what's the point of preaching to NGOs the benefits of digital buildup on the static traditional web when social media are providing open, decentralized, and cost-free tools and platforms? Why hire a techie to build a Noah's Ark when you can use WordPress or SXL.cn to do the same? Why waste paper printing documents when you can use Pinboard, Evernote, or other social bookmarking tools to store the content in digital folders for viewings anytime and anywhere? Why bother making phone calls to find out everybody's availability when you can use Zuduijun, a WeChat app, or Doodle? Why agonize over everybody's messy schedules for an offline group meeting when you can do it on Ding Talk, Skype, or make a WeChat call? The list goes on and on.

The larger context for NGO2.0's origin is clear, and to cut a long story short, I left Cambridge, Massachusetts, and arrived in Beijing in the summer of 2008. It took me a few months to scout the ground and identify viable collaborators.[2] The MIT brand name went a long way in helping me set things up. Half a year later I created a project aimed at helping Chinese NGOs to learn how to create digital, spreadable content, and no less important, teaching them how to leapfrog from the Web 1.0 to 2.0 thinking and practice.

For those unfamiliar with either term, I will describe briefly what distinguishes the first from the second generation of the Web. If we characterize the earlier Web as *readerly* and centralized, which manifests a top-down and one-to-many communication mechanism, the arrival of Web 2.0 technology changes the power hierarchy of sender and receiver. The new technology now empowers the people by turning the Web into decentralized, *writerly,* and interactive networks where communication takes place from node to node (i.e., many-to-many) in an infinitely expanding fashion. Most important, we have all become content creators and distributors. With the proliferation of We (are the) Media, collective intelligence is now open-sourced and available to all, easy to access and harness. And suddenly, boundaries are torn down and intermediaries are disposable. Uber, Airbnb, and other forms of sharing economy that infiltrate our daily lives are the most visible manifestations of Web 2.0 technologies at work.[3]

Back to the Chinese context, the arrival of Web 2.0 technology freed NGOs that had previously no media outlets from a communication bottleneck. Needless to say, it is an urgent task for them to learn how to navigate the social web. NGO2.0 came into existence in response to that need. Although itself an excellent case study of social media activism, NGO2.0 does not constitute the centerpiece of this book. Instead, it provides nothing more than an entry point to my examination of the emerging ecosystem of activism 2.0. Entering this thematic proper requires a quick overview of both the negative and constructive forces at work. The crisscross of those competing forces makes the future of the Chinese social sector difficult to assess. Crises are lurking everywhere and yet in a typical

Chinese fashion, countermeasures abound for each and every crisis. More importantly, the numerous change agents of contemporary China (NGOs, university professors, foundation leaders, earnest CSR visionaries, and even enlightened individuals in the CCP) are all skilled practitioners of nonconfrontational activism. Winning the battle without conflict and in spite of censorship, they have carved out a legitimized space for action. Finally, there is an additional *actant* to reckon with—social media—which plays an important role in empowering the weak social sector. In the following, I will examine each of those forces at work. First, what happens to NGOs when they are thrust into new media environment?

In the Wind Tunnel, Even Pigs Are Flying!

Fast forward to 2016. Chinese nonprofit organizations were at a crossroads. According to the statistics released by China Internet Network Information Center (CNNIC) (2016), Chinese internet users reached 710 million toward the end of the year, and approximately 646 million people were smart phone users. More than 56 percent of the entire population were online shoppers (Alibaba Research Center 2015, 6).[4] If the digital is already ushering in a new way of engaging with consumers and netizens in developed countries, the digital revolution in China is moving at an even faster pace as cities compete with one another to climb up the digital ladder with ever-expanding technological architecture and infrastructural upgrades. We are witnessing the mutually amplifying forces of accelerated adoption and accelerated innovation, which thrust the entire country into a metaphorical wind tunnel where pigs and other wingless creatures are blasted into the sky and forced to soar involuntarily. This is a sight unsettling to some, especially to NGO practitioners who aren't digitally ready and social media savvy. Being forced to fly sums up the enormous pressure the entire nonprofit sector was put under. In a nutshell, adapt or die.

Optimists saw a scenario of happy flying pigs. Indeed, social media gives those suffering from communication deficit a voice and access to the public. Breaking out of the censors' narrative control is the first step toward strengthening media representation for NGOs themselves and the underprivileged constituents they serve. Although it is difficult to connect open communication infrastructure with actual social movements on the ground, one should never underestimate the incremental impact that long-term media action can shift public dialogue and build momentum for policy advocacy. After all, more and more NGOs are taking advantage of the growing trend that has been propelling the 2,987 deputies of China's National People's Congress to search for worthy social causes backed up by large public constituencies.[5] The power of social media as an advocacy tool in pushing marginalized conversations to the center stage can never be overemphasized even in a country deeply entrenched in surveillance culture.

Contemporary China excels in navigating in paradoxes. The internet is seen as an information superhighway and a new pillar industry, on one hand, but is perceived as a threat to the regime and a space closed in by censors on the other hand. Internet-based philanthropy suffers the same contradiction: it will always be held suspicious, but it is nonetheless placed high on the government agenda that prioritizes a policy switch from "social management" to "social governance" and from punitive command to coalition building. During the World Internet Conference held in early 2016, China's Internet Development Foundation, a government affiliated NGO, took the lead in establishing a so-called coalition of IT companies, bringing on board Baidu, Alibaba, Tencent, and more than one hundred Chinese IT companies and media organizations. They co-signed a joint manifesto "Let the Internet Evolve into an Ocean of Compassion: A Proposal for Developing a Web-based Social Good Sector" (China Internet Development Foundation 2016). It is a piece of business-as-usual propaganda meant to impress foreign guests, complete with a call for strengthening public interest networks, promoting positive energy on the internet, building networked platforms for philanthropy activities, and cultivating netizens' participatory consciousness in public service. The ensuing press release highlights the capacity of the internet to build government-led, cross-sector, digital philanthropy platforms without ever grasping what truly defines the digital and social—a mind-set committed to flattening rather than reinforcing hierarchies. A top-down initiative like this official manifesto sings a tune so old that its music falls on deaf ears. Predictably, not a single word in the document refers to the most vibrant player in the social-good sector—grassroots NGOs, or the recently coined substitute name "social organizations" (*shehui zuzhi*).

C-NGOs Are on the Rise: Are We Witnessing the End of the Grassroots Era?

How are NGOs defined in the Chinese nomenclature? Contrary to our common assumption that the "third sector" is one and the same as the nonprofit sector (Qin Hui 2004), the former term incorporates seven sub-categories: social organizations, mass organizations, public institutions, neighborhood and village committees, religious institutions, estate owners' committees, and social enterprises. NGOs fall into the first category— "social organizations"—to which foundations and officially registered online communities also belong. An annual communique released by the Ministry of Civil Affairs indicates that there were 702,000 social organizations in 2016, among them 5,559 foundations and 361,000 formally registered nonprofit organizations (NPOs). The rest were a mixed bag of 336,000 professional associations, youth leagues, and miscellaneous communities (Ministry of Civil Affairs 2017). The official count looks colossal and paints a rather deceptive picture about the actual size of the nonprofit sector, making it difficult for us to distinguish the grassroots organizations from the rest. Those were statistics for 2016. By June 2018, the total number of social organizations jumped to 805,418, a 13 percent increase, reflecting a thriving sector despite tightened political control (Liu 2018).

Since 2009, NGO2.0 has conducted six nationwide surveys of the internet usage patterns of Chinese grassroots NGOs. In our estimation, there are no more than 8,000 stable and viable organizations that define themselves as grassroots with a change agenda and operate like one. However, if you throw into the mix neighborhood hobby communities, street-level administrative organizations, professional associations of all kinds, and GONGOs (government-organized NGOs) nested within tens of millions of governmental units, the number can easily inflate to hundreds of thousands. Furthermore, consider another caveat—that the majority of Chinese foundations such as the Red Cross and the aforementioned Internet Development Foundation are offshoots of the Party-state even though they sit within the larger category of "social" organization. The situation could evolve for the better as more and more businesses are setting up corporate foundations whose "social" attribute may bring positive change to the current configuration of the state-dominated foundation sector.

In my final count, there are about 8,000 stable authentic grassroots NGOs, the majority of which are constantly struggling to survive financially. They are not favored targets for governmental funding, nor are they the usual recipients of foundation support. Of the 7,000 foundations in China now, reputedly less than 1 percent are grant makers. The rest of the 6,900-plus foundations spend their funds on philanthropy projects created by themselves even though they have minimal expertise in hands-on work on the ground. Many well-endowed Chinese foundations also practice what is known as "mandatory philanthropy," sending donations to state-affiliated public service institutions on a regular basis, especially when natural disasters strike. For example, during the Wenchuan earthquake in 2008, over 80 percent of the 76 billion private donations in RMB was either given directly or funneled through foundations to governmental agencies (Li and Zhang 2014).

In the early and mid-2000s, grassroots NGOs turned to foreign foundations for support, a financial avenue gradually closing up due to the state's paranoia about the "threat" those allegedly radical foreign foundations may pose to national security. In 2015, the Xi Jinping regime dealt a severe blow to foreign NGOs in China with the publication of the "The Overseas NGO Management Law." Surviving foreign foundations are now required to work closely with municipal and national public security bureaus. At the same time, widely circulated online rumors constantly created panic among NGOs working under the financial auspices of Oxfam Foundation, Asia Foundation, and several other allegedly "problematic" foreign counterparts.[6]

Luckily, by 2015 a new public fundraising model—online crowdfunding via social media platforms—was firmly established. A new page was turned in the annals of Chinese philanthropy as early as 2011 when noted journalist Deng Fei, a "free agent" in my definition, started the "Free Lunch for Children" crowdfunding campaign on his microblog. The program aimed to provide nutritious lunches to nearly 22,000 school children spread across the poverty-stricken areas of some fourteen provinces in China (Wang 2012). With this campaign, "microcharity" became a household term, and online campaigns using social media to mobilize individual donors became a new normal. In a country where citizen philanthropy is still in its infancy, the success of Deng Fei's campaign is deemed as nothing short of a miracle. His success is due to the always on, real-time Web 2.0 technologies that connect millions of social networks of compassionate strangers. What Deng unleashed was the viral effect triggered by microblogs.

That said, only the most naïve advocates of digital philanthropy would assume that Chinese citizens have all of a sudden warmed up to the notion of personal philanthropy, a tradition relatively foreign to non-Christian cultures. Despite the annual sensational report on the positive outcome of Tencent.com's 9.9 Giving Day, the most successful crowdfunding projects in China are initiated not by nonprofits but by start-ups and business ventures. It is not that NGOs could not raise money on those platforms, but that it's an unreliable and unsustainable source of income. Even the most social media savvy NGOs are not likely to launch crowdfunding on a regular basis, not least because the peer-to-peer networks such campaigns aim at mobilizing are largely confined within the nonprofit sector itself, where the average salary of a staff member is around 3500 RMB (approximately US$500) monthly. Predictably, their donations rarely exceed ten yuan during the Giving Day bonanza. What about the general public? Although it is difficult to make generalizations, most are spectators rather than donors. And very few of those who donated have deep pockets. It is once again the big foundations that garner the most benefit from the Giving Day.

All those auspicious forces and constraining undercurrents yield conflicting viewpoints about the health of the nonprofit sector in China today. It is true that Web 2.0 technologies made it easier for networks of people and charity organizations to exchange resources directly without mediation. In sector guru Xu Yongguang's words, the internet got rid of the middlemen, circumvented interference from rent-seeking government organs, and enabled the "fair redistribution of public donations to NGOs" (Xu Yongguang 2016). Citing the example of Tencent's 9.9 Giving Day that raised over 100 million yuan of public funds, Xu predicts with optimism that digital crowdfunding boosts the exposure of grassroots projects and will eventually place NGOs at the helm of a rejuvenating nonprofit sector. Sitting on the other side of the opinion spectrum is Xu's erstwhile colleague Liu Zhouhong, the now secretary-general of Lin Wenjing Foundation, who shows reluctance to stake high hopes on the power of crowdfunding to solve the problem of NGOs' resource scarcity. "The donations of the Giving Day were mostly circulated between small circles of friends and they really did not spill over into the public domain" (Liu Zhouhong 2016, 2). Even in the US where crowdfunding originated, it is now known that traditional direct paper mail and one-on-one emails remain the bread and butter of fundraising; that is, the payout of crowd-sourcing via social media is complicated. It is "not an easy straight line" (Selyukh 2015).

Despite the official slogan championing the arrival of the era of "everybody a philanthropist," individual donors have also suffered mental fatigue accompanied by overheated crowdfunding drives in recent years. Why did I dwell on the fundraising predicament of grassroots NGOs? Shouldn't I be talking about the capacity building and professionalization of those organizations, a favorite topic for both foreign and domestic Chinese NGO experts? The financial health of Chinese NGOs holds the key to the future of the social sector and yet very few, including the NGOs themselves, are ready to make a full-frontal examination of a crisis that is quietly descending upon the NGO sector. I am referring not only to the government's calculated move to squeeze funding sources grassroots organizations can tap into—making sure that domestic mothers yield little milk and foreign stepmothers face hurdles of getting their licenses renewed[7]—but also a blanket campaign bankrolled by the state to create the so-called "community originated social organizations" (*shequ NGOs*), henceforth C-NGOs. This new development is fanning up like wild fire in metropolitan China and in second- and third-tier cities, giving birth to millions of Party-endorsed and state-funded "grassroots" organizations embedded in neighborhood communities of all sizes, which provide politics-free social services to the elderly, the handicapped, and other state-sanctioned disadvantaged groups. Shanghai and Shenzhen are well-known testing grounds for two different models of Public Service Procurement programs. The capital in Sichuan Province, Chengdu alone, had bred more than 7,000 C-NGOs as early as 2013 (E Fan 2014, 44). Those young community organizations have snowballed since then and are competing with authentic NGOs in service provision and public donation. Perhaps five or ten years from now, real NGOs will wither away noiselessly. That is a bleak scenario prompting discerning sector veterans to foretell, ominously, the beginning of the end of grassroots NGOs in China. Those familiar anxieties, coupled with a sense of foreboding and intensified by the rumored resurgent difficulties of NGO registration, are bound to turn many optimists into skeptics about the future of the NGO sector. And yet paradoxically, all the crisis sentiments did not stop the tens of thousands of new, unregistered grassroots organizations from sprouting up at locales near and far from Beijing. Meanwhile, social media has given birth to new change agents outside the NGO sector that are gradually usurping the once-privileged role nongovernmental organizations have played since 1995.[8] All the active players in China's social sector—NGOs and their new fellow-travelers—share a common recognition at this historical juncture, to wit, social harmony has to be maintained at all cost. We are witnessing the resurgence and reaffirmation of Chinese collectivist values at full play. A consensus is at the same time a constraint. How to push social change without disrupting harmony is a default operating principle activists in China abide by. The question in everybody's mind today can be summed up as follows: How can we combat the dark forces without waging a war?

"The Ultimate Victory Is to Win without Conflict"

That's the question frequently raised by activists of a nonconfrontational kind, a vibrant species thriving in China and other autocratic countries. Even in the face of extreme adversity, swordless sparring is preferred over holding torches and marching on the streets. The NGO sector, however, is not swimming alone in treacherous waters. Other fellow travelers have emerged in the universities, foundations, the corporate sector, the IT sector, and sometimes even in city halls where enlightened individual CCP officials are carrying out what the Party is preaching at the moment—seeking innovative models of social governance that demand flexible collaboration with clear-eyed, strategically minded nonconfrontational activists. Another underrated demographic of Chinese activism is the hundreds of millions of millennials that form the largest donor groups in nonprofit crowdfunding campaigns (Tencent Foundation 2014), many of whom are also techies interested in utilizing technology to solve social problems. Some change-makers are less low keyed than the others, but invariably, none resort to light sabers. Didn't Sun Tzu proclaim thousands of years ago, "The ultimate victory is to win without conflict"?

Chapter 1 zeroes in on the theory and practice of nonconfrontational activism and lays bare the tactics underlying noncontentious social action. Each subsequent chapter incorporates more examples of nonconfrontational strategies. However, lest we look at today's China as a nation full of passive-defensive people enervated by the "can't-do" consensus, I will go beyond the maneuverings of Chinese activists to unveil the equally strong "can-do" ethos that runs parallel to the constraining forces that keep activists at bay. Those are constructive variables, each of its own accord is chipping away the edges of protruding obstacles and making it possible for nonconfrontational activists to accomplish their tasks. To the positive forces we now turn.

University Interventionists

Of all the big trends in the 2010s, the most eye-catching is the emergence of university-based research centers charged with the task of building a wholesome infrastructure for Chinese philanthropy through educational programs and policy research. Beijing Normal University established the Chinese Philanthropy Research Institute in 2012, Sun Yat-sen University launched a similar research center, which was followed in 2014 by Peking University's new master's program in "philanthropy administration," which was later merged into the MBA degree. Shanghai Jiaotong University's Center for Philanthropy Development was inaugurated in 2016. Tsinghua University is relatively a latecomer. But by positioning itself as a policy think tank commissioned by the Ministry of Civil Affairs in 2015, the Tsinghua Philanthropy Center sets itself apart from all the other centers that are primarily devoted to building a nonprofit talent pool. Finally, all those nascent quests for strengthening the philanthropy sector were trumped in late 2015 by the founding of the China Global Philanthropy Institute, an international joint venture set up in Shenzhen by Bill Gates and a team of leading Chinese philanthropists headed by the institute principal Wang Zhenyao (Zhu 2015). The Shenzhen Institute is supposed to evolve, in the coming years, into a full-fledged degree-granting philanthropy university. In an era in which the Chinese nation branding is extended into the social realm, it surprises no one that the Party-state's dabbling in internationalizing the philanthropy sector should involve Bill Gates, an American celebrity capable of bringing an instant spotlight to China.

In what way is the university's involvement in the philanthropy sectoral build-up manifesting the sunny side of things? First of all, those involved in running the research centers—Wang Ming, Deng Guosheng at Tsinghua University, and Zhu Jiangang at Sun Yat-sen University—are well-respected scholars with keen social consciences. Zhu Jiangang is a cultural anthropologist turned activist and a member of the editorial collective of the outlawed grassroots magazine *Unofficial China (Minjian)*; Deng, a professor directing the Center for Innovation and Social Responsibility

(CISR), has long been promoting "equal dialogue, broad participation and in-depth collaboration among academia, industry, government, social organizations and citizens" (CISR 2010). Wang Ming, the inaugural director of the Tsinghua Philanthropy Research Center, is a long-term advocate of governance reform and an unswerving champion of the policy of "separation of government from society" (Wang, Ming 2014).

University intellectuals in contemporary China are in a unique position to be collaborative with the Party-state while remaining autonomous at the same time. At critical junctures they know better than anyone else how to take advantage of policy preferences to move their own agenda forward. Let us not forget many of those sharp academic critics of the CCP are also Party members. The challenge this time around is the degree to which those reform-minded university professors can stretch the definition of *society* in the new policy discourse of *zhengshe fenkai* (separation of government from society). When Party leaders vowed to devolve the *zhiquan* (function and power) of government to society, what did they mean by *society*? Is the "social" pointing to the C-NGOs or grassroots NGOs with change agendas? A carefully manicured garden filled with pruned bonsais, or the deep woods where wild grasses are flourishing among tamer vegetation? As the destiny of the grass roots is hanging in the air, Tsinghua's philanthropy think tank and its director Wang Ming's counsel will be crucial in helping the government define the boundary of its power. How far can the few pristine, unadulterated spaces be extended in the "social"—a habitus of spaces impregnated with the possibilities of change? How much breathing room can be carved out for authentic social spaces?

Government Mandate on the Making of Social Partnerships

For policy watchers of an optimistic bent, the discourse of *zhengshe fenkai* is less about who wins or loses than a signal sent by a government thinking about innovating social governance and planning for a "social reform" no less grand than the economic reform spanning the first thirty years of post-Mao China. The increasing social unrest in the last few decades must have taught the CCP a lesson that sustainable maintenance of a "harmonious society" can only be built on genuine social partnerships. Although it's anybody's guess whether equal partnership with a hegemonic state can ever materialize, I can provide an anecdote that attests to an unlikely alliance in the making.

In 2014, I traveled to Guiyang, the capital of Guizhou Province, to conduct a Web 2.0 workshop and met Mao Gangqiang, a university professor and a veteran activist well known in the province. He wasted no time in bringing to my attention the policy of the "separation of government from society." In a manner typical of grassroots-to-grassroots communication, we dived right into an earnest, confessional exchange, with him sharing stories about his long journey as an activist, past experiences, and present-day engagements. There was a certain desperate excitement in his demeanor. It was as if after being monitored by the local government for so long, a sense of danger was branded deep into his psyche. I had heard that he faded from the day-to-day operations of several NGOs he helped establish in Guiyang. So, when I asked if he had given up NGO work and retreated back into the academy, I was hardly prepared for what he would reveal. "I am working with the Guiyang government to help them implement *shequ zizhi* (community self-governance)." A quick train of thoughts flitted through my mind: Goodness gracious! Was he co-opted by his old nemesis? What did the government do to bring a legendary activist to his knees?

Professor Mao took his time to tell me the turning point in his NGO career. For years, he lived under the surveillance of the state, losing his funding from one donor after another, struggling to sustain his NGOs and barely making ends meet. Although he was by no means a fugitive, it was a tough living for him and his family. Worst of all, this man has a vision for civil society and participatory governance that requires unfettered, scalable experimentation. Not being able to implement that vision was a punishment worse than being hunted down by local security police. On the eve of his metamorphosis, he felt like a bird flying into a brick wall, over and again.

Then came a knock on his door from a Party official in the city government, someone sharing a similar vision and obviously a man with a conviction about making social change in Guiyang. The policy directive of the separation of government from society was already hotly debated in the city government then. A talent hunt was under way to help expedite the vision. The Party middleman engaged Professor Mao in rounds of discussions and negotiations. Mutual trust was built, and the professor agreed to join the government team and work with them to create a blueprint for Guiyang to implement the Separation Project. I imagine their collaboration is not without frictions. But Professor Mao retained his autonomy and his right to critique. Regardless of conflicts here and there, he assured the NGO representation in social governance programs in Gui-yang. In a speech given at the Fifth Forum on "Community Public Interests in West China," he sounded as critically crisp as ever:

> When we overemphasize (harmony) and peace, the government's coercive power will only be further strengthened. This line of thinking is making a negative impact on the growth of society itself. So, today's talk about innovating social management could turn into reinforcing the management of society in many places. This is a serious problem we are now facing. (Mao 2014)

A good foundation for social governance, according to Mao, rests on three major principles: "clearly delineating the boundary of governmental action; activating and releasing the vital energy of the social, and igniting the life force of social organizations" (Mao 2014). To drive home his last point, he asks: Where can we find the right channel for participatory politics? Where is the pivot for collaborative governance? That strategic locale, he responds, can only be sought in "nonprofit organizations."

This is a remarkable example of an unlikely alliance made between two very different categories of change agents, and it depicts the best scenario of a future China where benign forces in the governmental and the nongovernmental come together to practice *xieshang minzhu* (consociational democracy), a new slogan unveiled in a keynote speech given by President Xi to mark the sixty-fifth anniversary of the Chinese People's Political Consultative Conference (Xi 2014). The Philanthropy Law passed in 2016, itself an excellent example of open legislature that involved rounds of negotiations among representatives of different social sectors (including grassroots spokespeople),[9] has given the optimists new hopes that instead of taking its always fraught relationship with NGOs to a new level of hostility, the state is capable of reining in its aggressive impulse and practicing its own nonconfrontational politics.

For those doubting Xi's sincerity and taking the Party credo of incrementalism with a grain of salt, three other policies, part of a social reform packet, may temper our impressions for the better. In 2008, a new policy regarding corporate income tax was published, which incentivizes corporate giving to eligible social organizations by raising the tax deduction from 3 percent to 12 percent of a company's total annual profit. NGO2.0 has directly benefited from such a policy. Earlier on, all state-owned enterprises were required to submit an annual corporate social responsibility (CSR) report, a policy directive satisfactorily completed by the end of 2008. In May 2015, yet another directive was issued to encourage corporations to assimilate underprivileged groups into the work force, formalize CSR units (which previously worked in a haphazard fashion), and institute company-based volunteer service (Ministry of Civil Affairs 2015). Many might see those policies as cost-sharing measures taken to arm-twist businesses into a partnership from which the state emerges as the biggest winner. Seen in a similarly unfavorable light, a globally competitive China is compelled to ensure that a first-rate Chinese corporation be an exceptional corporate citizen. Once again, these policies could be nothing more than an expedient means taken by the Party-state to hone the national brand, not exactly a lofty mandate to protect public interests and divert cross-sector resources to rejuvenate the social sector. Indeed, the notoriety of an authoritarian state is hard to rehabilitate even when it acts in sincerity.

The skeptical take on China's reformist vision notwithstanding, the public interest litigation laws published in 2014 and 2015 provide additional evidence that perhaps we have underrated this government's zest for self-redemption. Following a landmark amendment to the Environmental Protection Law in 2014, environmental NGOs in China registered with city-level or higher administrative tiers are now given the right to bring public interest litigation against polluting corporate enterprises. Given that local governments are often partners in crime with local businesses, this amendment is radical in its potential to challenge and upend the existing power structure at the municipal level at least. Then in 2015, another pilot project was unveiled to enforce the rights of the procuratorate in the Supreme Court to initiate public interest litigation, which had been tested in thirteen provincial-level jurisdictions for two years, covering administrative (litigation against government organs or units authorized by them that act wrongfully or incompetently), civil (litigation against citizens, legal persons, and other organizations), and public interest litigations. The civil-law subject areas addressed include pollution, food safety, and other areas harmful to public interest (The State Council Information Office 2015). In early 2016, the Supreme People's Procuratorate summoned a news conference announcing the outcome of the pilot projects conducted in several provinces. To date, 501 litigation cases were amassed, among them, 383 fell into the "administrative" category and 118 belonged to the "civil and public interest" category. Approximately 313 cases were related to environmental issues, 118 cases were concerned with the rights-transfers of state-owned land use, 59 cases were linked to state-owned asset protection issues, and 11 were tied to food and drug safety cases (The State Council Information Office 2016). In parallel, an environmental law passed in January 2015 led to nine NGO-initiated lawsuits with one groundbreaking victory won by Beijing-based Friends of Nature and Fujian-based Green Homeland (Cui 2015). Progress is being made, albeit gingerly. My point is we risk losing sight of the total picture if we exclude the government altogether from the converging constructive forces in contemporary China. Even within an evil empire, there are as many Jedis as there are Darth Vaders.

At the theoretical level, there could be other possibilities of conceptualizing the relationship between agency and structure if we were to withhold Cold War politics from constraining our perception and if we could bring ourselves to imagine, and tolerate, the likelihood of a great individualistic culture co-existing with a great collectivist culture. Does one ideology have to subjugate and convert the other? If Anthony Giddens saw (individual) action and structure not as opposite terms of analysis but part of a theoretical ecosystem governed by what he calls the law of "duality" (Giddens 1984), why can't social theorists forgo the temptation of opposing agency to determining structures and try to comprehend the Chinese consensus on harmonious society as a choice made collectively by the majority of Chinese people? Is it possible at all for us to conceptualize those two categories—agency and structure—as interdependent and co-evolving? Following this hypothesis, can we also dream about a dual construct defined in terms of the co-evolution of social agents and a potentially negotiable government that may one day feel confident enough to let down its hair, one lock at a time?

A softening Communist Party? This image indeed poses a daunting challenge to our imagination for it hardly squares with American liberals' depiction of a regime that is said to be "regressing into a period of neo-Maoism" (Schell 2016). And yet, there are scenarios pointing to that possibility. Let us turn to a case in which confrontational labor activists met a noninterfering state. I am referring to the organized labor strikes against Walmart that broke out across China in 2016. Given the political sensitivity revolving around labor unrests, the reluctance of Chinese authorities to subdue the agitators has evoked a range of interpretations both at home and abroad. Foreign watchers saw the official reticence as a predictable patriotic posture—that is, under no circumstance would a government acutely conscious of its nationalist propaganda side with a foreign company to squash Chinese protestors (Hernández 2016). Some

Chinese interpreters, on the other hand, detected a hitherto unforeseen development of labor activism in China, which is said to have undergone a subtle reconfiguration in which emerging conflicts of interest between factory workers and radical labor NGOs have given rise to a burgeoning trend of organized labor that is distancing itself from foreign influence on one hand and from labor activists with an explicit anti-state agenda, on the other hand (Ren 2018). The fact that the Chinese authorities largely stood aside during the Walmart turmoil was seen as a positive sign that helped facilitate the subtle change in the relationship between the state and labor rights advocates. In Yongnian Zheng's words, the state and society in China cannot but be "mutually transformative" (*xianghu gaizao*) even while they are locked in an ongoing contentious relationship (Zheng 2008, 28).

Foundation Spokespeople

In developed countries, foundations form an integral part of the nonprofit sector, and they are natural advocates for NGO welfare protection. The situation is quite different in China, where a great majority of foundations are state owned or state affiliated, cumbersome in their bureaucratic operations, and oblivious to the welfare of grassroots organizations. In recent years, an increasing number of corporate foundations came into being, whose mandate is serving corporate interest. Only less than 0.4 percent of 6,000 foundations in China are genuine grant makers. Among them, a small handful of private foundations has sharpened their advocacy role, and their clarion call for the reform of the social sector has gathered traction.

Those foundation spokespeople are propagating two missions simultaneously—nurturing civil society on the one hand and magnifying the representational power of the sector on the other. Three well-endowed private foundations, Fujian-based Zhengrong, Beijing-based Narada, and Hangzhou-based Dunhe, built a collaboration platform named "Togetherness" in 2015. Working with provincially based support-type NGOs to identify viable but small start-up grassroots organizations in second- and third-tier cities, the platform provides much needed seed funding and local resources to the grant targets (Narada Foundation 2016). As an open platform, Togetherness seeks other foundations and corporations to join the effort of empowering grassroots NGOs and strengthening the ecological chain of nonprofits. Its ultimate goal is to nourish regional NGO development and build an ecosystem in which the weak co-exist with the strong—tadpoles with big fish. Although the investment is modest to say the least, building a multilayered ecosystem of grassroots NGOs requires a tiered and incremental approach, a strategy previously neglected by most foundations that are only committed to supporting bigger and well-established NGOs. Inasmuch as this joint effort is symptomatic of the sector's burgeoning awareness that a diversified NGO sector can go a long way, the Togetherness platform has earned its place in the history of modern Chinese philanthropy. As the policy of "separation of government from society" takes deeper roots and as state-owned foundations become the next target for reform, it is likely we will witness the rise of a variety of pluralistic approaches initiated by forward-looking foundations to revive the grassroots NGO sector.

The second mission taken on by foundation leaders is pioneering in a different way—magnifying the representational power of the sector, an effort that occurred in the realm of discourse and relates directly to the representational rights of the nonprofit sector. One of the most interesting news stories in 2015 was a debate over the GDP contribution of China's nonprofit sector. Xu Yongguang, the chairman of the board of Narada Foundation and an influential sector spokesman, took issue with the official data, according to which the nonprofit sector in 2014 made up only 0.22 percent of the GDP of the third sector, a reputed drop of 21 percent from the 2007 statistics (Xu 2915), a fall-off challenged by Xu. In his view, philanthropy in China has been thriving since 2007, and its economic value is on a dramatic rise thanks partly to the impact of the internet on the output of the sector. The alleged low GDP is nothing short of a grievance case that needs to be redressed. The official data was challenged and the debate raged on. A research center based at Shanghai Jiaotong University joined the fray and issued its own statistics that showed the GDP contribution of China's philanthropy sector as seven times larger than the official count. The new data points to a GDP amount of 406.8 billion yuan in contrast to the officially reported 57.1 billion (Shanghai Jiaotong University 2015).

This, of course, was not simply a tempest in a teacup or a battle over the numbers. At issue was not only the absence of a scientific, standardized statistical model tailored to the data infrastructure of the nonprofit sector. More seriously, the statistical gap was accounted for by the improper but habitual transfer of the GDP of GONGO units (government-affiliated NGOs), which is categorically embedded in the nonprofit sector, to that of the governmental sector, an unfair practice intrinsic to the problem incurred by the blurred boundary between government and society. This revelation hit the nail on the head, propelling outspoken foundation advocates to emphasize the urgency of devolving the power of government to society.

The GDP dispute was but one of the many symptoms indicative of the marginalized status of the nonprofit sector. The public image of social organizations adds to the problem. Negative press about bad apples travels far, damaging the reputation of the sector as a whole. The 2015 serial rape scandal involving the founder of a Guangxi rural education NGO dealt a severe blow to the public confidence in the sector. More devastating news came in July 2018 with the landing of the Me Too movement in China. In less than two weeks, young women volunteers reported, one after another, sexual assaults involving high-profile leaders Deng Fei—the founder of Free Lunch for Children Campaign—and Lei Chuang—a legendary rights protection advocate for hepatitis-B patients (Dangpu 2018; Xiao Xi 2018). Anonymous accusations of sex offenses that had occurred a decade ago in the nonprofit sector were now exposed and exploded on WeChat, shattering the moral authority of philanthropists. Meanwhile, sporadic positive reports featured in the mainstream press about nonprofit work are not sensational enough to attract attention, and if they do make an impression, the positive impact is easily compromised by the propaganda overtone the press evokes in the public's mind. It is fair to say that in China, those engaged in nonprofit work carry a stigma. If they are not seen as driven by ulterior motives, they are looked down upon for not being able to find employment elsewhere. The funding difficulties, low salary, and the sector's need for professionalization are problems that cannot be solved overnight. How could such a weak social sector uphold the mission of safeguarding public interest while countervailing the hegemonic state and powerful private interests? At this juncture of the reform of the sector, the most that foundation leaders can accomplish is to propose partnership models. Youcheng Foundation's founder Wang Ping has been a vocal promoter of a social-public-private-partnership model built on a three-way joint consultation platform that brings NGOs, foundations, and other social groups into a dialogue with governmental and corporate agencies (Wang, Ping 2015),[10] a position also held and practiced by Professor Mao in Guiyang. Theoretical models of similar nature were a dime a dozen at the turn of 2014, 2015, and 2016. All those trends reinforce my argument that foundations are stepping up their leadership roles by advocating for the rights of the social sector to fully participate in the now sloganized campaign of Chinese "social reform." With every advocacy speech given, the representational power of marginalized social organizations gets a boost, which is a positive development previously unseen.

I have enumerated the forces behind the upswing of the Chinese social sphere in which the universities, government, and foundations are working together to strengthen grassroots and other social organizations, each playing a significant role in crafting the vision for "strong society and strong government." What about the public? If we designate 2008, the year when a magnitude 7.9 earthquake struck Sichuan, as the beginning of the boom of volunteerism in China, then 2011 saw the public's intensifying participation in charity work via social media. "Free Lunch for Children" and a crack-down campaign on child abduction, both launched on Weibo, have been extremely successful in galvanizing public support. The list of grassroots actions that took place on social media platforms during the 2010s (see Chapter 3) was indeed very long, most of which involved public donation—which means giving the needy a fish rather than teaching them how to fish.

Academics and foundation leaders often dwell on the difference between philanthropy (*cishan*)—giving fish to the poor—and the delivery of public good (*gongyi*), identifying the former as a spur-of-the-moment act of personal compassion and the latter as planned, systemic social change. The mid 2010s witnessed many public critiques of the prevalence of short-term philanthropic actions over sustainable transformation on the ground. Perhaps no trigger for the needed conceptual change from *cishan* to *gongyi* was more poignant than the tragedy that took place in a small village in Bijie, Guizhou province. On June 9, 2015, four "left-behind" children, a brother and his sisters, committed suicide by drinking pesticide together. Their death ignited a belated discussion about the futility and crisis of donation-driven philanthropy. Is money the ultimate problem solver? "What can we do to help every parent of left-behind children to go home and visit their kids?" "Can we save all our donations and use them to build sustainable livelihoods in poor villages so that parents don't have to leave home to make a living in the first place?" Those public reflections marked the intensifying exploration for a new social-good sector guided by reason rather than emotion, professionalism rather than instant compassion (Yongshi 2015).

28

Amidst the somber mood of self-examination, expectations are built up for the social sector to modernize itself. Learning how to leverage the power of the internet to carry out day-to-day work and organize advocacy missions is seen by many as an integral part of the sector's initiative to professionalize itself. True, the trend toward "internet plus public good" sounds more urgent than ever as the entire country is pursuing a digital China dream.

Behind the Rosy Picture

All this may sound breezy and sunny to skeptics who are used to conceptualizing China as a unitary, static entity. Surely there are other shadows lurking in the rosy picture apart from the well-known nemesis of Chinese activism—the authoritarian state? Some critics wonder if digital and social media are the only means of energizing the Chinese social. Obviously not. Critiques of this proposition are spread here and there throughout the book. Even those most enamored with the social function of new media would have to reckon with its limitations. Weibo, for instance, has outlived its heyday and bidden farewell to the contentious politics of virtual spectatorship. Gone are the glorious days when the network effect of microblogging could trigger outbursts of netizen protests against unjust and corrupt officials. The decline of Weibo's political impact was no doubt sped up as a result of tightened political control in Xi Jinping's era, and its deterioration was most poignantly felt in October 2017 when the twenty-seven-year-old actor-singer Luhan, known as China's Justin Bieber, introduced in a Weibo post his new girlfriend, fellow actress Guan Xiaotong. Luhan's surprise revelation caused the Weibo server to crash minutes later, as millions of his female fans, now heartbroken, rushed frantically to the microblogging site to attack Guan and vent their frustration (Shi Can 2017). This incident is a loud and clear indication that Weibo has completed its descent from the altar of social conscience to a mere entertainment platform. It was also a sad reminder that *bagua* (tabloid news), not political stories, is what attracts the eyes of young Chinese netizens. WeChat, too, has slowly evolved into hundreds of millions of echo chambers where like-minded people with strong bonds congregate and chat about things of no particular significance. Surely, there are WeChat public accounts that attempt to address serious issues. But as a closed space, those sundry cocoons or niche communities are too decentralized to function as a public sphere, not to mention the rapidly declining incentives of all WeChat users, including me, to click open articles sent by friends and proliferating public accounts. Call it a symptom of mental fatigue that social media users all over the world are now experiencing.

Caveats about censorship and social media aside, readers may also wonder if nonconfrontational activism always works so well. What kind of limitations or challenges might each involved sector encounter in carrying out noncontentious social-good experiments?

To begin, while it's easy to define successful or failed confrontational action, it's difficult to distinguish successful from failed nonconfrontational action. Whether a success or failure, nonconfrontational action generally does not attract media attention, which makes identifying it difficult in the first place. Qualitative change can only be triggered by quantitative accumulation, but one can never truly tell where the tipping point is. Generally speaking, scalable nonconfrontational action is more successful than a mere local execution. Success in those cases depends on the sustainability or replicability of a project, which is in turn contingent upon the duration or scale of funding. Whereas a failed confrontational activism leads to arrests and martyrdom, failed nonconfrontational action dies a quiet death, its sustainability being cut short by factors such as budgetary drain, staff turnover, or dwindling capacity of the organization to continue a project. For instance, NGO2.0 would fail with our philanthropy map project if we could no longer raise enough funds to pay our software developer, or if the corporate sector all of a sudden turned against the idea of matching their CSR interest with grassroots projects, or if our executive director in charge of overseeing the project finds a better paid job elsewhere, and so on. One may also claim, as Chapter 5 demonstrates, that corporate social responsibility initiatives are especially vulnerable to changing corporate interests that ultimately dictate the social-good agenda of CSR and corporate foundations. Cinnovate, an NGO set up by Intel China, folded its operation entirely as a result of Intel USA's redefinition of its CSR mission. Tencent's Giving Day, a pet project of Tencent Foundation, was rolled out in large part to popularize the IT company's mobile payment solution, WeChat Pay, which is locked in dead heat with its rival AliPay. The corporate sector, in short, operates under certain constraints in producing social good even though it is a state policy they are compelled to follow.

Likewise, socially concerned software coders and makers could one day stop attending our civic hackathons because they could no longer afford the time to participate in those activities; foundations might stop funding an ongoing project simply because their funding categories are changed as a result of a mission repositioning; and university professors like Wang Ming might stumble in their advocacy effort of promoting a "strong society." Consider the most extreme case of failure—what is considered nonconfrontational to activists themselves or to the upper echelon in Beijing may look utterly confrontational to local governments or local public security officers. NGO2.0's social media literacy workshops are a case in point. We held Web 2.0 trainings with impunity in Beijing but were kept under surveillance in Yunnan in the early years of our operation. Different NGO issue areas may also predetermine whether nonconfrontationalism is implementable at all. Predictably, it is nearly impossible for human rights activists to act noncontentiously. Labor activists and LGBTQ rights communities are also susceptible to the government's misconceptions, although we should not forget they are also the most tactically savvy groups in camouflaging their missions.

There is furthermore a constraint all activists encounter sooner or later, that is, the instability intrinsic to volunteer culture—the cornerstone of activism—where discipline and commitment are hard to enforce, a reality that NGOs and all other do-good sectors have to endure. Nonconfrontational activism has an added disadvantage in attracting volunteers. Less dramatic than its confrontational brethren, it holds less appeal to young volunteers drawn to quick action and quick results.

That said, it is virtually impossible that nonconfrontational activists emerging from multiple quarters documented in this book would fail all at once, which is the beauty of incremental change mobilized by multiple agents of diverse professional profiles. What *The Other Digital China* unravels is the coming together of do-gooders from multiple sectors. They are forming quiet, unobtrusive alliances and making cross-sectoral collaborations to create change in China. What emerges is a *networked activism* whose sustainability does not depend on any single node in the ecosystem. With so many change makers converging from different sectors, each according to his or her ability, even the most backward society has to inch forward steadily.

The 2010s China is marked by crossovers of all kinds. There is no better terrain than activism 2.0 to demonstrate the multiple sectoral forces at work to create the agenda for social change, with or without the government's blessing. Social media tears down boundaries and is a generator of converging energy. A book capturing the criss-crossing paths of social collaboration is a tribute to those unknown agents of change that are toiling day in and day out to make a more just and equal society.

Overview of the Book

Chapter 1 examines nonconfrontational activism in China from the NGO, state policy, and social media trajectories, respectively. Starting with a literature review of existing scholarship that challenges the binary paradigm of "state versus society," this chapter conceptualizes the massive middle ground in which NGOs and a host of other actors make their mark. Mapping the fuzzy gray zone also entails the acknowledgment of the Party-state as a historical actor invested in legitimizing the concept of "society" and redefining the boundary of the social. The ensuing analysis of the policy of "social governance"—a discourse emphasizing consensus building and multi-stakeholdership—drives home the crucial role that the CCP is playing in Chinese nonconfrontational politics. This chapter also looks into staple nonconfrontational strategies adopted by NGOs and ponders what happens after the decline of Weibo and the erosion of the once much celebrated politics of *weiguan* (virtual spectatorship).

Chapter 2 features the NGO as change maker and tracks the emergence of a particular brand of ICT activism that promotes the use of social media as a means of helping Chinese NGOs break out of their communication bottleneck. I start with an introduction of NGO2.0, using it as an entry point to examine the practice of "social media for social good" and shed light on the ecosystem of social media usage by Chinese NGOs. The methodological implications of undertaking "social media enabled action research" will be explored, and I discuss what it means to engage in the hybrid practice of "activist as scholar" in the specific context of cultural studies.

Chapter 3 features IT corporations as change agents. This chapter starts with the Guo Meimei scandal in 2011, which gave impetus to the birth of philanthropy 2.0 commercial platforms. The scandal ignited a crisis of public trust in the philanthropy sector and set off a series of chain reactions crucial to the shaping of the culture of activism 2.0. Nonprofit organizations started using microblogs to publicize and make transparent their financial and operational details; individual donors and corporate donors abandoned state-own foundations as the only venue for social giving; IT conglomerates intensified their exploration of Web 2.0 technology as a means of enabling both free agents and grassroots organizations to raise funds on their platforms. The convergence of all those factors led to the bloom of free agent projects and hashtag activism and expedited the march of the philanthropy sector into the era of online crowdfunding. The competition between Weibo and WeChat is unfolded within a critical discussion of the complex relationship between the state, (civil) society, and the (IT) market. Citing incrementalism as an essential ingredient of nonconfrontational activism, this chapter ends with a double critique of the ideology of revolution and the neoliberal paradigm of agency, and in so doing, it carves out a theoretical space for change makers who have perfected the practice of winning without conflict.

Chapter 4 builds a dual framework of change makers—the millennials and the corporate sector, each in its own fashion experimenting with innovative ways of practicing nonconfrontational activism. The chapter opens with the portrayal of millennials as change agents and examines their demographic profile step by step through an analysis of their multiple identities as volunteers, internet incident initiators, virtual spectators, and online donors, respectively. This chapter then moves on to capture another role played by the millennials—target consumers for cause marketing 2.0 campaigns. I argue that the best of global millennials—the Chinese post-1980s and post-1990s included—are not only transforming how civic engagement is fashioned but how corporate social responsibility initiatives are programmed. As the best specimen of "Generation 2.0," those creative youths are acting as conduits between two previously irreconcilable worlds—markets and civic habitats. As new media are reshaping our social relationships and slowly eroding the cognitive mapping of elites, critical categories emphasizing the principle of play are on the rise again. Concepts like *the crowd* (as in "crowdsourcing") are discussed, and exemplary advertising 2.0 and social media civic campaigns in the US and China are sampled.

Chapter 5 features hardware techies as change agents, situates the Maker Movement in contemporary China in the complex ecosystem of national innovation policy, and explores "change maker" as an alternative proposal to China's ruling paradigm of "maker as digital entrepreneur." Through the discussion of a popular TV soap opera "Tiger Mom," this chapter ponders the changing ethos of Chinese educators and the implications of the spread of makerspaces to those dreaming about the arrival of "Creative China." By realigning the Maker policy discourse with "maker as social-change engineer," I highlight a Future Village project that

NGO2.0 is sponsoring in collaboration with a grassroots environmental NGO and the Shenzhen Open Innovation Lab.

Chapter 6 is a method chapter that investigates the relationship between social action and action research in the larger context of participatory action research (PAR). I examine the methodological traditions of Western PAR before looking into the Chinese experiment with it. Contrary to the androcentric drift of PAR in the English-speaking world, the Chinese pioneers evoke Western feminism—black feminism in particular—as a crucial source of inspiration. I ask how we can begin to understand PAR practices in authoritarian regimes where the default equation between resistance and action is an exception rather than the rule. This chapter discusses the short history of Chinese action research, detailing the convergence of influences that include the Taiwanese PAR school, Mao Zedong's revolutionary tradition of practice, and the black feminists' emancipatory vision. The Chinese PAR scholars' exposure to feminism is particularly noteworthy. It drives home a lesson that mainstream male PAR mentors cannot teach: that action researchers sit at the edge between public knowledge and private lived experiences and that the emotional agenda of the researcher is an overpowering motivator of action. I conclude the chapter with a discussion of two specific strategies of nonconfrontational activism and argue that there is infinite space for action and activism in countries where the liberal tradition is weak.

The Conclusion wraps up the book with a debate on and critique of ICT for development and other issues related to technological determinism. The chapter lays bare why "social media for social good" and "tech4good" are more appropriate conceptual frameworks than ICT4D (information and communication technology for development) and ponders the pros and cons of technology-driven pubic good deliverables. My overall message is technology is enabling, but it has limits. But while critiquing technological utopianism, we cannot deny that in the twenty-first century, the internet is a powerful platform on which social movements of underrepresented minorities can bypass corporate and government gatekeepers to speak for themselves. I conclude in the activist voice, asking whether NGO2.0's social media training workshops benefited the NGOs we have worked with and recalling the pains and joys of engaging in ICT-powered activism in China.

1

Nonconfrontational Activism
and the Chinese "Social"

During my ten years' journey of running NGO2.0 in China, I encountered a variety of puzzled responses from home. Sympathizers worried that an NGO founded by an American academic would be doomed because of its foreign origin; skeptics wondered about the likelihood of doing activism in modern China where authoritarianism and censorship has defined its brand for more than a hundred years. In fact, internet control has been tightened more stringently than ever after President Xi Jinping took the helm of the Communist Party. How could a "foreign" grassroots NGO specializing in ICT-powered (information and communication technology) activism survive at all in such an adverse environment?

That question is a false one. NGO2.0 was set up not as a foreign organization by design, but as a local Chinese NGO operated by a largely indigenous Chinese team from the very start. The challenges at the core of our operation were not much different from those faced by other grassroots NGOs in China. Our attention should then be focused on a different question: How have Chinese NGOs fared through the successive reigns of the oppressive regime? How do we name the kind of activism grown out of an ecosystem that runs counter to the Western ecology of nonprofits for whom activism has no other manifestation than a decisive act of resistance to the oppressor? To fare well in China requires a different mind-set and strategy—learning the art of restraint and following the centuries-old cultural logic of finding the middle ground whereby missions, however difficult, will get accomplished eventually. For Chinese activists, it means producing social good without inciting a revolution in the streets.

This chapter centers on the concept of nonconfrontational activism, and I begin with a review of its conceptual variations in the critical literature of China studies, especially works written with an analytical pivot to the changing relationship between the Chinese state and society. The literature review is undertaken for two purposes. First, all the case studies and interpretations—some implicitly and others expressly—dovetail each other around the theme of nonconfrontational activism even though they do not name it as such; second, the literature lays bare the hidden and camouflaged spaces that are germinating the "social," understood in its most constructive sense—a habitus of spaces impregnated with the possibilities of change and traversed by change makers of multiple identities.

Next, this chapter argues, making the "social" in contemporary China is not the sole prerogative of grassroots agents. The other historical actor is surprisingly the Party-state. An in-depth analysis of the changing configuration of the Chinese "social" needs to reckon with two policy discourses—"the separation of government from society" (*zhengshe fenkai*) and the shift of the state's governing strategy allegedly from social management to "social governance" (*shehui zhili*). The benefits and limits of this set of policies will be discussed in the rest of this chapter. In theory, Beijing's new policy directive has laid the foundation for the onset of a social reform unleashed by the government to roll back the administrative state and devolve its power to "society." However small, nonexistent, or hidden the Chinese social appears to be, there is little doubt that the CCP's (Chinese Communist Party's) current policy architecture is designed to legitimate the conceptual category of "society" while delimiting its boundary. Bearing in mind the discrepancy and incompatibility between what the Party is and what it claims to be (Xie 2014), we should ask if this is just another authoritarian ploy adopted by the Communist state to define the boundary of the social so as to better control it. Or, could this set of social policies entail the emergence of a bigger playing field for nonconfrontational activists to navigate? This chapter raises a number of questions that link policy making to the practice of nonconfrontationalism, shares staple nonconfrontational strategies adopted by NGOs, and ends with a discussion of the impact of social media on redrawing the boundary of the social. Many wonder what will happen after the decline of the utopian politics of *weiguan*—the myth that "crowd spectatorship" of contentious Weibo incidents could challenge the status quo? This book unravels the birth of a quiet, decentralized ecosystem in which do-gooders from multiple sectors are recognizing each other, converging spontaneously, and making alliances, whereby rhizome-like cross-sectoral collaborations are forming and sprouting up everywhere. Gone is the *wei-guan* era. What is emerging is networked spectatorship on a grand scale. Is this outcome anticipated by the policymakers of social governance? I cannot tell. But the trend is here to stay.

Nonconfrontational Activism and Its Conceptual Variations: A Literature Review

Practitioners of nonconfrontational activism are anonymous as their actions purposefully attract little attention. They stay on the margin of history, if their presence is reckoned with at all. Conceptually, nonconfrontationalism is equated with nonresistance, and it remains peripheral to academic discussions of social action even though it prevails in all autocratic regimes, where activists resort to other means of serving social good rather than openly critiquing and rebelling.

It was not until 1985 when James C. Scott published *Weapons of the Weak: Everyday Forms of Peasant Resistance* that the concept of invisible agents and their quiet and piecemeal tactics were given due recognition and the practice of "calculated conformity" was given credit. Scott's peasants typically avoided direct or dramatic confrontation with authority or with elite norms. Instead of condemning such silence as "complicitous" and devoid of politics, he locates the sites of peasant action in micro, inconspicuous everyday forms of "foot dragging, dissimulations, false compliance, pilfering, feigned ignorance and so forth" (Scott 1985, 29, 36). Scott's book represents a significant milestone in valorizing the powerless and subjugated as political agents. And yet the ideology of resistance has taken such a tenacious hold over those schooled in the intellectual tradition of liberal democracy that despite the author's avowal that "revolt" as a political option was precluded for those exploited groups (297), he recategorizes, with a Foucauldian stroke, the peasants' nonconfrontational tactics into acts of "resistance" (as the subtitle of his book signifies). Such renaming reveals a contradiction: Scott's peasants and slaves cannot be nonconfrontational and resistant to the status quo at the same time. Once again, the author seems compelled to fold nonconfrontationalism into the old conceptual frame of resistance in order to justify his argument for the "agency" of those peasants. His ultimate discomfort with the idea of passive, nonconfrontational peasant "actors" is revealing. It revalidates "resistance" as an absolute qualifier for human agency even in a framework intended to transcend it.

James Scott's dilemma is understandable. In Western democratic societies, it is possible to rebel with impunity, and the rights culture embedded in the ideology of individualism takes contentious expression for granted. Citizens and scholars who are natives traversing in such a relatively unrestricted universe are deeply convinced of the validity of dichotomy as a universal mode of knowing the world (domination versus resistance, collective versus individual, structure versus agency, state versus society, passivity versus activity, absence versus presence, and so on). Such habitual subscription to binary epistemology renders Western liberal scholars less ready to reckon, *unapologetically,* with analytical tools underlying nonconfrontational ethos.

When we turn to a country like modern China or other illiberal societies where open resistance is not the norm but an exception, researchers are called upon to conceptualize beyond the dichotomous mode of thinking to solve the puzzle—why do the exploited in those countries accept their situation as a normal, or even a justifiable, part of social order? Are they fatalistic, actively complicitous, or perhaps paralyzed by fear and cowardice? Surely, if the Chinese government can hire "as many as 2,000,000 people to surreptitiously insert huge numbers of pseudonymous and other deceptive writings into the stream of real social media posts" (King, Pan et al. 2017), shouldn't we have good reasons to believe that the Chinese censorship program has penetrated every corner of society and that the censors have sent truthful reporting to the wind and manipulated public opinions effortlessly? That is the conventional reading of the muted consensus of the Chinese people on maintaining the status quo. This neat formulation relegates the entire population of China into the category of the brainwashed, which hardly squares with the fact that NGO activists, academic and public intellectuals, the millennials, and other commoners are not only busy debating policies and politics with each other at dinner table and other social gatherings, but they take opportunities and risks here and there to post biting political commentaries on social media platforms. Truly, as James Scott argues, what's missing in scholarly research is the "massive middle ground in which conformity is often a self-conscious strategy" and that "it might be possible to think of *a continuum of situations* ranging from the free dialogue between equals that is close to what Habermas has called the 'ideal speech situation' all the way to the concentration camp" (Scott 1985, 285–287, italics mine). *The Other Digital China* documents this massive middle ground—China's gray zone.

Mapping the Gray Zone

The "massive middle ground" scholarship, which is reportedly missing in Western academic writings, found a home in China studies, not surprisingly. That is because the majority of Chinese people are living in a gray zone that spans across two binary poles of existence—being brainwashed dummies or becoming Spartan warriors. In real life, the average Wang's and Zhang's have more choices than becoming puppets or rebel-martyrs; neither are desirable options for these clear-eyed people with strong survival instincts. The majority of Chinese citizens are camping in the fuzzy middle ground, which I argue is where the "Chinese social"—the utopian space of change—can be located. Social action unfolded in that gray terrain is by default nonconfrontational, and the change occurring there is by definition incremental. Coming to grips with that gray reality dictates that scholars explore a state-society model unrestricted by the dichotomous mode of thinking deeply embedded in the normative Western civil society paradigm.

Not surprisingly, mainland China–based researchers are quite active in challenging that paradigm. That said, it is the scholars outside of China who enjoy the natural advantage of undermining the Western paradigm without having to worry that their critique might be mistaken for CCP propaganda. But first, they have to overcome the methodological limits embedded in binary epistemology. The scholars cited below have all skirted that analytical pitfall. Together, their observations and interpretations conjure up a social ecology where nonconfrontational practices carry sociopolitical value in unforeseen terms.

The late 2000s and 2010s saw the emergence of a rapidly growing literature on the forms of social contention that routinely receive blessings or even support from the state because they occur "within the official discourse of deference." Kevin J. O'Brien and Lianjiang Li proposed the term "rightful resistance" (O'Brien and Li 2006); Peter Ho and Richard L. Edmonds named it "embedded activism" (Ho and Edmonds 2007); Jessica Teets called it "consultative authoritarianism" (Teets 2014); and Cole Carnesecca introduced a similar concept of "responsive authoritarianism" to characterize regimes that "alternatively use repressive and conciliatory tactics" to manage social discontent (Carnesecca 2015, 118).

What those arguments share in common is the urgent call for scholars to reevaluate Chinese nonconfrontational politics from both ends of the spectrum.

Sitting on one end of the spectrum are NGOs, whose noncontentious and piecemeal measures, previously belittled as guilt-ridden collusion with power elites, are seen, under this critical lens, as constructive strategies that lead to incremental change on the ground. Sitting on the other side of the spectrum is the authoritarian state. Formerly stereotyped as a "forbidding monolith" (Herbst 1989, 199), the state is now reconceptualized as an entity with multiple identities, conflicting interests, and contradictory ruling tactics, a riven entity, which grassroots actors can exploit to their advantage. However oppressive an authoritarian regime appears, it affords resisters opportunities to build fruitful alliances and "make authorities work for them rather than against them" (Klandermans 1997, 194). Operating within the official framing of "harmonious society," bottom-up pressure and top-down openings are in fact working together to produce change in China. Implicitly, all those scholars contend, in one way or another, that nonconfrontational activism can be productive.

In O'Brien and Li's definition, "rightful resisters" game the system by appealing to receptive Party or government officials who champion policies of social justice that have been abused elsewhere in the hierarchy. Such resistance is "a form of popular contention that operates near the boundary of authorized channels" and utilizes the regime's own "policies and legitimating myths to justify their challenge" (O'Brien and Li 2006, 3). In the name of serving the people, those unlikely alliances between political elites and grassroots actors often break down "simple dominant-subordinate distinctions" (1) (see my story about Mao Gangqiang in the Introduction), prompting the two authors to consider it analytically unwise to disentangle the state and social actors. In fact, I would argue that activists operating by utilizing *guanxi*—pulling the strings of influential relationships within the system to facilitate a deal—are already practicing nonconfrontational action. It is an act taken for granted by those navigating in a society that is ruled by relationships rather than by law.

Published a year apart, Ho and Edmonds' edited volume *Embedded Activism* treads a similar narrative path to *Rightful Resistance*. Rather than devalue Chinese NGOs as passive codependents of the authoritarian state, they make a case for asserting the impact of the NGOs' advocacy work on social and policy change in China. In their view, the operational success of grassroots organizations belies the conventional point of view that state and society in China are antagonistically positioned against each other. Like O'Brien and Li, these two authors highlight the complex ties and symbiotic relationship between NGO workers and state agencies/personnel, a liaison that constitutes what they call "embedded activism." The concept redeems not only the NGOs, who are now seen as agents of change, but also the Chinese state, which is seen to play out not just a restrictive role but an enabling one in producing social good (Ho and Edmonds 2007). Since it takes a working partnership of the state and the NGOs to perform "embedded activism," it entails that the state, like the NGOs themselves, contains within itself the motivation and capability for nonconfrontationalism—an implication that I will flesh out later in my analysis of the twin policy discourse of "social governance" and the "separation of government from society."

Succeeding years saw fewer groundbreaking works pursuing this line of argument until 2014 when Jessica Teets proposed the conceptual model of "consultative authoritarianism." Challenging the "victim narratives" predominant in the Western scholarship on civil society in authoritarian polities, Teets characterizes the relationship between social organizations and the state as a potentially productive one. In her view, even the weak can produce value for the powerful, and she defines that value in terms of policy feedback sent by civil society actors to the state so that the latter can learn how to govern better and more effectively (i.e., meeting goals, reflecting on poor policy implementations, and learning about public-private partnerships that work in other locales). The implicit sender-receiver and teacher-student analytical framing provides a much-needed communication angle to scholarship on state and society. Reframing the oppressor-oppressed relationship in terms of meaningful policy feedback on the one hand and mutual learning as a form of cooperation on the other, Teets equalizes the lopsided power relationship between the two and in so doing, she finds that "civil society needs less autonomy from the state to accomplish goals of advocacy" than one might expect and that "[NGOs'] increasing channels of interaction with the state might help these groups have more impact on policy making" (Teets 2014, 4). In short, civil society plays a crucial "role in good governance especially under authoritarianism" (5). Most significant, Teets' conclusion is built on a latent assumption that the authoritarian state is an eager learner capable of making self-improvement and "'endogenous' institutional change," a perspective that paves the way for my following analysis of the rise of "social governance" (*shehui zhili*) and its underlying logic—"consultative politics" (*xieshang zhengzhi*) as a ruling theoretical paradigm of governance in China today.

Teets and her fellow travelers have come a long way from the earlier generation of China scholars who felt the need to challenge Western civil society theories but stopped short of cutting to the chase. Timothy Hildebrandt's early statements that "making changes at the margins is not only possible but important" and that the "agency of social organizations does matter" (Hildebrandt 2013, 163) have now been vindicated and fleshed out in a rich variety of case studies. Later variations of the revisionist take on the state-society relationship in China, such as Cole Carnesecca's "responsive authoritarianism," continue to trickle in as more fieldwork on the nuanced relationships between the two is undertaken. A 2018 opinion piece on China's social credit system in *The Washington Post* is one of the latest examples that describes such relationships as "more complex and less sinister in its intent than the West's neat dystopian vision suggests," a piece that acknowledges the mixed reality of China, which is neither white nor black (Song 2018).

My quick literature review demonstrates a variety of conceptual models of activism prevalent in an authoritarian country like China. My proposal for using "*non*confrontational activism" as an umbrella term carries two implications: the term explicitly questions the universal validity of the liberal definition of "activism," and accordingly, it drives home the urgency of examining the agency of activists operating in authoritarian regimes.

Three Strategies of Nonconfrontational Activism: Incrementalism, Strategic Positioning, and the Camouflage Reflex

As is evident from the literature review, Chinese social organizations adopt diverse strategies to evade censorship and leave their footprints in the social realm. Many of them create state-sanctioned nonprofit programs such as poverty alleviation, social welfare provision to the elderly and other disfranchised groups, and educational assistance to children in poverty-stricken urban and rural households, for example. Those pursuing politically sensitive NGO issue areas have to maneuver more laboriously to avoid tension with the authorities. Successful nonconfrontational activists resort to basic rules of thumb: taking an incremental approach to social change, staking out a politically correct position, or resorting to tactics of camouflage.

O'Brien and Li's "rightful resistance" provides ample lessons about how smart resisters can resort to the rhetoric of the powerful to curb the exercise of power (O'Brien and Li, 2), such as framing and legitimizing their contention by employing state laws, official policy discourse, government commitments, and state propaganda to hamstring concerned Party elites for support and collaboration. Hildebrandt discussed how HIV-AIDS activists resort to a public health approach in framing their work rather than dwell on the issue of human rights (Hildebrandt 2013, 14, 77). I will cite one more category of strategic positioning—grassroots organizations run by Muslims and Tibetans typically identify their mission as "cultural preservation" rather than promotion of religious diversity. My own strategy during the early years of the founding of NGO2.0 was to position our expertise not in terms of (new) media—a loaded keyword—but in the politically neutral term "nonprofit technology." This positioning benefited us especially after 2015—the year Premier Li Keqiang turned the slogan "Internet Plus" into a mainstream policy discourse.[1]

However diverse those framing strategies are, the core skill of nonconfrontational activists consists of their sensitivity to the policy wind of the moment and their mindfulness of the fluctuating list of terms and concepts that are falling in and out of the regime's favor at a given moment, a task that tiptoes the fine line between compliance and self-empowerment, which is not an intuitive exercise at all. The following chapters are strewn with framing exercises that illustrate the rich repertoire of nonconfrontational practices.

Apart from careful framing strategies, Chinese activists' steadfast adherence to incrementalism is another important formula for successful nonconfrontational activism. Hildebrandt has put the case succinctly. In a political climate that prioritizes harmony over contention, NGOs are compelled to make deliberate efforts to ensure that their activities do not appear to be effecting social change too quickly (Hildebrandt 2013, 75–76). A measured, step-by-step change agenda alleviates the anxieties of the state and stands a better chance of being implemented without too much governmental intervention. Incrementalism is in fact taken for granted by Chinese activists as a whole. In the NGO sector, this approach is brought into full relief when we compare "capacity training," a legitimate pursuit of many support-type NGOs, with the mission of building civil society, which raises red flags immediately. The former represents an incremental, technical approach to strengthen the philanthropy sector, while the latter evokes the specter of regime change and ideological disruption.

Indeed, since the state accelerated its propaganda on "social governance," the task of professionalizing social organizations and preparing them for the "participatory mode of communication" has appeared more urgent than ever. It looks like my strategy, made in 2009, of positioning NGO2.0 as a support-type organization specializing in communication capacity training and social media literacy training, is both forward looking and politically correct.

Whether incrementalism is political wisdom or a nemesis to progressive politics is hard to tell. However, those remembering the aftermath of the Cultural Revolution and that of the failed students' revolt in 1989 can appreciate why the Chinese now have a weak stomach for disruptions of a violent order. There is a general acceptance that this is how change works, by inches, and that this is how Chinese activism should manifest itself—by taking a long view and biding time rather than making short-lived convulsive movements.

Yet, nothing seems as safe and peaceful as it looks. Those who harbor an agenda for social change in authoritarian countries will always be conscious of the potential risks their action entails. What is considered nonconfrontational by activists themselves or by the upper echelon in Beijing may look utterly offensive to local governments or local public security officers. The danger compounds as the boundary between what's allowable and what isn't shifts, from time to time, locale to locale, and regime to regime. Jiang Zemin was missed because under his rule, the gray areas expanded noticeably, an opening that subesequently suffered a significant contraction under President Xi Jinping's watch. We could thus find in all Chinese nonconfrontational activists an omnipresent anxiety about risks of confrontation and with it, a reflex I shall call "camouflage consciousness."

Hanna Rose Shell defines camouflage as strategic concealment, a "systematic mimicry" aimed at effacing "the traces of one's own presence from photographic media of surveillance" (Shell 2012, 23). Camouflage should not be conceived of as an absence or a lack. Instead, the visual evanescence of camoufleurs needs to be understood as *productive* engagement and calculated performance of the weak and the powerless. Seen as such, strategic hiding is nothing less than "a form of cultivated subjectivity" (19) and itself denotes an acute consciousness. Shell's excellent analysis of this particular form of self-preservation captures as well the vulnerable condition of nonconfrontationalists working in the fields of danger. I can detect in the positioning strategies of nonconfrontationalists the play of the same adaptive logic, which allows them to escape from photographic representation and blend into inhospitable environments. Savvy activists in China are more often than not smart camoufleurs hiding in plain sight. This mode of cultivated and calculated subjectivity constitutes the core of the agency of nonconfrontational activists.

Sometimes, camouflage consciousness can evolve into material practices. Diana Fu's example of "disguised collective action" is a case in point. She discovered that underground labor organizations in China resort to a tactic of "atomized actions" that can lower the political cost of organizing strikes against the regime. How is this done? Aggrieved individuals are coached by those subversive labor organizations to deploy strategies of performative protests to claim their rights. She argues that those individual instances are in fact *organized contention* in disguise. What we are witnessing is an innovative "form of organized activism in which civil society groups play a vital but under-the-radar role in coaching citizens to advance rights claims" (Fu 2017, 501). This pedagogical process, which is largely invisible to the authorities, serves as an instance of camouflaging, whose strategic value is obvious.

As I point out at the beginning of this chapter, the literature review of the different strategies of nonconfrontational activism serves an important purpose. It maps out the expansive gray zone where Chinese activists make their mark. Those sites are germinating the "social" understood in its most constructive sense—a habitus of spaces, camouflaged or not, that is impregnated with the possibilities of change and traversed by change makers of multiple identities. Behind each nonconfrontational act and advocacy lies an avenue of change that cannot be dismissed simply because it produces quiet action and is invisible by design. "As long as such advocacy is effective," said Elizabeth Knup, Director of Ford Foundation in China, "it is legitimate, regardless of whether it fits the prevailing Western norm."[2] And just as You-Tien Hsing and Ching Kwan Lee argue in *Reclaiming Chinese Society,* there is "far more to 'the [Chinese] social' realm than overt 'mass disturbances'" and that small change may "result in more *sustainable* progress than mass protest" (Hsing and Lee 2010, 2, italics mine). Rather than making an apology for nonconfrontational activists, we can do better by reckoning with their existence and reevaluating the one-dimensional frame in which China is represented by Western mainstream media.

Too often, academics and journalists concerned about the future of China are only watching the top. What they see is an implacable regime that arrested a Nobel Peace Prize winner; banned Google, Facebook,

Instagram, Dropbox, What's App, Winnie the Pooh, you name it; persecuted contentious writers and artists and imprisoned human rights lawyers and activists; subjugated foreign NGOs under state supervision and control; forced Apple Stores to remove all VPN software; encroached on Hong Kong's autonomy and free speech; doubled down on socialist ideological campaigns on campuses and at work places; and censored the reasoned call to loosen online censorship (Spencer 2017). The list goes on and on. Nothing seems to have changed since Mao's era if we turn our gaze exclusively toward the top. Some would say that under Xi Jinping's rule, China's political system appears to have "shifted from what experts have called 'fragmented authoritarianism' to just plain authoritarianism" (Johnson and Kennedy 2015). But as a Beijing-based journalist once discovered, "There is another, contrasting trend that is much more promising" (Ash 2017). The answer to the question he rightfully posed—has China gone forward or backward?—hinges on whether you are looking up or looking down. The social bottom portrayed by Ash appears to be "steadily more progressive" because of the generational shift in population. The millennials' outlook on life and politics is certainly making an impact on the Chinese social. The majority of NGO workers I met in the last ten years, the post-1980s and post-1990s youths, bear further testimony to Ash's insightful observation. Although the young in China are no less a bundle of contradictions than their older counterparts, looking downward does yield a more balanced view of China's social transformation, however incremental and invisible it may appear to outsiders.

After examining nonconfrontational actors from the bottom up, I now move on to the second focus of this chapter—the state as a historical actor in drawing the boundary of the social, a mission often mistakenly conceived to be the sole prerogative of grassroots agents. Hsing and Lee have highlighted the shift of the Chinese official rhetoric toward the "social" since 2005 as a "telltale sign" of the Party-state's gradual but versatile response to escalating social ferment and unrest. They cite examples of piecemeal social policies (i.e., rural tax reform, educational subsidies to poor households, labor contract law reform, and so on) created by the versatile state to treat the symptoms of social instability. But if the previous decades brought in the government's ad hoc measures of crisis management, the mid-2010s saw the crystallization of such versatility into a comprehensive, long-term social policy directive. My analysis of the changing configuration of the Chinese social will thus be incomplete without taking into account two complementary policy discourses on the social—"social governance" and the "separation of government from society."

Drawing and Governing the Social:
The Party-State in Action

One of the most authoritative insider-interpreters of the changing Chinese policy culture is Yu Keping, director of the Center for Chinese Government Innovations at Peking University. He portrays the changing technology of governance in China in terms of a clear movement "from the rule of man to the rule of law and from regulatory governance to service-oriented governance" (Yu 2014). He attributes such a reorientation to the state's pressing priority to release social pressure and tackle discontent before it erupts. None of Yu's reasoning is new except for this statement: "Although the government has never made reference to the term 'civil society' in official documents, it now recognizes its importance" (Yu 2011). Yu is not reading the tea leaves. The shift from "social management" to "social governance" is seen by policy analysts as a formal invitation made by the Party-state to NGOs and other grassroots actors to come to the negotiating table and partake in community decision-making processes so as to facilitate the "politics of accommodation" (Chinese People's Political Consultative Committee in Chongqing 2017, 4). This new round of social reform prompts an NGO worker to characterize the process as "a fascinating collaboration between political elites and grassroots leaders" (Liu Tao 2014, 9). Is this new form of "civil society" even a theoretical possibility in an authoritarian country?

Law scholar Simona Novaretti traces, in chronological order, the emergence of "social governance" as a new regulatory paradigm for Chinese social organizations. Although it seems that the emphatic shift of government policy from "management" to "governance" was a slogan rolled out under Xi Jinping's tutelage and originated in the third plenum of the Eighteenth Party Congress in November 2012, she tracks down the first appearance of this official discourse to a speech given by Hu Jintao in July 2012 shortly before the country's stewardship changed hands (Novaretti 2014, 6–7). Other researchers trace back to 2006 the genesis of the notion of "social collaboration" and "public participation" (Zhou 2013, 3). This indicates that the aspiration of the Party leadership to modernize social control has been in the making across two regimes, a previously more moderate government and the now ultraconservative one. The idea of social governance itself suggests a more liberal outlook on politics than we would associate with Xi Jinping's regime.

What is the difference between social management and social governance?

I can pinpoint the difference in two key phrases—top-down control versus multiple social stakeholder cooperation, and government-centric logic versus consensus-building rationale. This shift of governing methods implies that the Chinese government would encourage and support the participation of multiple stakeholders in initiating a virtuous cycle of societal self-adjustment and community self-rule (Leng 2014; Novaretti 2014; Yu 2011). Theoretically, this new model promotes the concept of a "limited government" that voluntarily yields to citizens and civil society *some* control over how public policies are shaped. It also means the devolution of governmental power and the recognition of the importance of public participation and social coordination. Pursuing this line of logic would theoretically propel a state to build a mechanism of co-governance with multiple social stakeholders including the NGOs.

The new model led to a series of measures implemented with the purpose of catalyzing the separation of government from society. Under the "guidance" of the state, public service procurement is professionalized and has proliferated at a fast pace all over the country. Residential subdistricts in Beijing alone invested 1 million yuan in government-purchased social projects between 2016 and 2017 (China Financial and Economic News 2017). Outsourcing social services has benefited qualified NGOs and is now evolving into a standardized flagship program of the new social policy. The other agenda of the "separation" imperative, that is, banning government personnel from running social organizations, yielded mixed results. Provinces and municipalities championed the cause by publishing regulations aimed to decouple GONGOs and government units. Five major GONGO categories were targeted in the Beijing regulation (industry associations, chambers of commerce, charity organizations, urban and rural community services, and science and technology) (Zhu 2016, 96). Thus began the nationwide process initiated by the Party to eject public officials from running those GONGOs. In the final analysis, the state's mandate of separating government from society has more to do with disciplining boundary-crossing officials than empowering social organizations. The political and financial prowess of GONGOs is so lopsided in comparison to the grassroots NGOs that a superficial disentangling of their affiliation with civil servants and government agencies does little to level the playing field of the nonprofit sector. Many even suspect the governmental connection of GONGOs has gone underground in the wake of the separation.

Another compelling question to raise is whether a service-oriented administrative state necessarily leads to a "limited government." Can the devolution of state power genuinely happen in a regime that rejects the separation of the Party from the government and which is undergoing a radical recentralization of power at the moment? And how do we interpret the contradiction that with each passing month, news about more stringent online regulations comes to light? It seems that the government's power is expanding rather than waning. At the moment when I am penning this chapter, friends in China are complaining bitterly about the blocking of major VPNs that previously allowed netizens to climb over the Great Firewall to access foreign news and research content. Complaints about tightened rules for NGO registration also resurfaced. And the Party's meddling in affairs big and small is surely squeezing the gray zone, prompting intellectuals to feel nostalgic about Deng Xiaoping, Jiang Zeming, and even Hu Jintao.

Having reflected on the limits of the new social policies, I return to Novaretti's question "Is there any evidence that the new focus on 'social governance' is *currently* opening a novel space for (acceptable) social organizations' involvement in public choice?" (Novaretti 2014, 22). Her answer is yes, citing the example of Friends of Nature, a Beijing-based environmental NGO that won a public interest litigation. The anecdote in the Introduction about Mao Gangqiang, the veteran grassroots activist in Guiyang and his participation in co-governance at the invitation of the city officials, is also an example. There is also the possibility that progressive Party officials—whose number is growing as a result of the generational shift—may undergo self-education while practicing social governance and transform themselves into genuine servants of the people, *little by little*. Their collaboration with NGOs and other community-based constructive forces could in the long run open up spaces here and there that may erode "the distinction between service provision and advocacy" (29).

Such optimism, however, can hardly explain away the deep contradiction of a political power obsessed with autocratic control but enthusiastic about adopting the liberal discourse of modern governance. What are the driving forces behind the making of the CCP's new policy discourses? The familiar argument is that social governance policy aims to prevent social disharmony by nipping it in the bud. The second push factor is said to be pragmatism—the idea that co-opting the NGOs seems easier than suppressing them. This latter proposition is questionable because the majority of social actors called on to participate in the so-called co-governance are largely GONGOs and community-NGOs (the C-NGOs unveiled in the Introduction), not grassroots NGOs, a point most Chinese analysts missed. C-NGOs are extremely small entities grown out of residential communities with the primary purpose of serving the elderly and retirees and providing lightweight educational assistance to mothers and children. Calling them NGOs is a big stretch. Completely depoliticized and devoid of a change agenda, they are loosely strung together as community leisure centers, definitely not prone to advocacy tasks.

Likewise, the prime targets for the policy of "separation of government from society" are not NGOs but public servants. It is a policy less about the empowerment of social actors than the disciplining of Party officials entangled in GONGOs, making it appear nothing more than an extension of the ongoing anticorruption campaign. Indeed, the gain of grassroots organizations from the new policy has not been obvious thus far, and it is largely confined to the government procurement program. The dialogic relationship implicit in the policy of social governance is therefore more rhetorical than substantive. To save the policies from descending into mere slogans, the Party-state needs to do more to develop genuine partnerships with social actors and change the public perception that the separation policy is nothing more than an effort of improving the system's capability of forecasting and preventing social risks.

Analyzing new social policies in a critical light is one sure way of delivering responsible scholarship. Another equally pressing imperative for scholars outside China is to familiarize themselves with the interpretations of mainland researchers, learn about their perspectives, and read between the lines. Generally speaking, articles and books published in China after 2012 are prone to reiterating the well-trodden ground of the Chinese mainstream interpretation of "social governance." A few quotations are sufficient to capture the main thrust of such arguments. For example, the socialization of governance is said to be "no longer a unidirectional domination and control of society by government" (Zhou 2013, 35); social governance "points to the organic merging of the top-down social management and bottom up social governance, a process of co-governing that guarantees the maximization of public interest" (Xu Ming 2016, 13); "consultation has emerged as an important form of political participation. . . . It has emerged to bridge the gap between a still unitary political leadership system and an increasingly pluralistic society" (Lin 2014); "this change [toward social governance] reflects the inability of government acting alone to recognize and to address comprehensively the type of social problems that require co-ordination of social forces" (Liu Jinfa 2014, 1). Occasionally, I came across formulas such as "building a strong government and a *strong society* through social governance" (1, italics mine) that apparently toe the party line. However, nearly all recent publications on the subject have named the "social" in "social governance" in precise terms of "civil society" (*gongmin shehui*). Obviously, the censors have given a belated nod to the previously tabooed expression, which is a sure sign of incremental change occurring in China!

Zhou Hongyun, a sociologist working at the Central Compilation and Translation Bureau, goes a step further by claiming that the very concept of "civil society" requires the transition of governance from government-centric to society-centric models (Zhou 2013, 32). There is no shortage of examples of social consultation at work in his volume. However, closer scrutiny of the case studies he discussed in Shanghai, Cixi, Ningbo, and Shenzhen belies our perception of what "society" denotes. Those examples are based exclusively on the interactions between GONGOs, street- or district-level Party-affiliated offices, and the government. However productive those "social" collaborations may appear, they put into question the definition of the social in "social governance." If the social is interchangeable with GONGOs and C-NGOs, then our expectations about the empowerment of grassroots NGOs under the new policy regime may be greatly exaggerated. Consultative governance may be deemed a new reality by the Party-state, but it is built, in the words of two mainland scholars, on the old logic of "authoritarian populism" (Wang and Guo 2016). The utopian vision, articulated by optimistic Chinese scholars, that the new social policies could entail "a greater role for NGOs at all levels of governance" seems farfetched, at least for the time being (Lin 2014, 160).

Defendants of the regime's good intentions want to give more credit to the CCP for launching the social policy reform. After all, the state is shifting its ruling tactics from the strategy of conflict to that of connection, which is a significant step forward and seen by scholars like Yu Keping as the state's embrace of "good governance" (*shanzhi*), a term that co-evolves with other dictums of social reform (Yu 2016). Meanwhile, the resurrection of "civil society" as a popular discourse in Chinese academic circles and the nonprofit sector can be seen as hard-won progress, prompting political scientist Mary Gallagher to observe, "Ironically,

Chinese civil society was expanding and gaining strength at the very time Western scholars were neglecting it" (101). Although it is difficult to reconcile the pessimistic and the optimistic predictions about the development of civil society in China, a myriad of social groups and change makers have nonetheless emerged in diverse sectors of Chinese society, to which this book bears witness. Inasmuch as governing models are concerned, we can be certain that all three models—social control, social management, and social governance—will co-exist in contemporary China in the short run, just as open-minded reformists, militarists, ultraconservatives, and other factions of divergent ideological persuasions are running the Communist Party as a collective behind closed doors—regardless of who the Party's poster child of the moment is. Xi Jinping's regime is no doubt making such political maneuverings more strenuously than ever, but the Party remains a heterogeneous entity regardless of the appearance of ideological unity.

A Voluntary Retreat of the State?

Equally important, policies such as "separation of state from society" and "social governance" are reminders of the difference of the political processes that drive the birth of civil society in an illiberal regime vis-à-vis modern Western democracies. While Western civil society came into existence as the result of the agitating growth of the social, the Chinese civil society could only be born as a consequence of the *voluntary retreat* of the state from society. For optimists, the twin policies on the social have signaled the beginning of such a retreat, no matter how gradual and how measured it appears. The pessimists, on the other hand, see in Xi Jinping's iron rule a permanent setback to the process of the said retreat. In their view, the progress toward the opening of the social is being thwarted indefinitely, and "social governance" is nothing more than an empty slogan. Those stationed in the middle ground (including myself in my activist persona) have remained hopeful for a gradual retreat of the Party-state. Not only do they argue that such a retreat would take a zigzag course, but that it would only occur after the leadership feels completely assured that the social is reined in on their terms.

It is eventually a game about waiting and biding one's time. The very fact that the Chinese government and even the CCP are *not* homogenous entities works to the advantage of social actors. Over time, as political scientist Yongnian Zheng anticipates, "an implicit, invisible coalition" (*yinxing* lianmeng) between the reformist leadership and progressive social groups is taking shape. Internet-mediated interaction between state actors and social forces are playing an effective role in facilitating a "gradual political liberalization" because such interactions are bound to be "mutually transformative," with the reformist leaders actively leveraging online discussions as a catalyst for policy reform. For example, netizens' furor over the death of Sun Zhigang and the outbreak of other contentious Web incidents gave the liberal wing of the Party an opportunity to push for much-desired policy adjustments (Zheng 2007, 184–185, 179). Indeed, those involved in Chinese activism and other hands-on practices like China's "rural reconstruction movement" could enumerate the "thousands of subtle links and interactions" that are operating between the "alternative" and the "mainstream," rendering the pseudo-propositions about "monolithic binaries" invalid (Pan, Luo, and Wen 2017, 126). Eventually, like any systemic change, top-down openings and bottom-up pressure will act together to make it happen.

The last thirty years have borne testimony that Chinese policies are more than just state propaganda. For those doubtful if state policies of a communist country can be transformative at all, my earlier study of the "Double Leisure Day" policy in the mid-1990s and its impact on the rise of popular culture provides a good case in point (Wang 2001). A few other authors have also remarked on the built-in capacity of Chinese policies to trigger social change. Joshua Cooper Ramo puts it most succinctly in *The Beijing Consensus,* "Here the traditional metrics for looking at power in China need adjustment. The often-expressed sentiment or hope in Washington that China's Communist Party is on the verge of collapse because of all the change in China is an example. In fact, the CCP *is* the source of most change in China in the last 20 years" (Ramo 2004, 13, italics mine). In subtler terms, Elaine Yuan reminds us that "while the Chinese state and its censorship regime are an important context in which we understand the parameter of online activism, this should not overshadow our efforts to arrive at a historical understanding of the complicated role of the state in the Chinese media system" (Yuan 2015, 217)—a role media scholar Zhao Yuezhi neatly captures in her observation that the authoritarian state is playing a performative role as the designer of Chinese modernity in general (Zhao 2012). This is a view echoing my earlier study of the enabling effect of the CCP policies in the late 1990s on China's media market reform. (Wang 2008b, 247–287). All those trajectories are presented here not to suggest that China's social policies under discussion in this chapter will definitely bear the fruit we all wish to see, but that we try to resist the temptation of rejecting China's social policies categorically and prematurely.

Social Media and Nonconfrontational Activism

There is a large corpus of world literature on the new forms of grassroots political contentions enabled by digital and social media. Popular expectations about the potential of the internet to challenge and even overthrow autocratic regimes reached a climax in the mid-2000s as the Jasmin Revolution in Tunisia brought the utopian fantasy of civil society dreamers to a fever pitch. But the myth about the internet's liberatory potential suffered a quick reversal when it became obvious that authoritarian states and other reactionary groups are equally adept at mobilizing online and using networked strategies to serve pernicious purposes. Once the bubble of techno democracy is burst, the pendulum is swung to the other side of internet scholarship. We began to see the rise of what Elaine Yuan calls a dominant "state-centric perspective" that shifted academic discussion from grassroots change agents to the overpowering state, from the "liberating power of 'open network' technology" to the ways that "'closed regimes' employed the Internet for policing and censoring purposes" (Yuan 2015, 216). This polarizing trend of scholarship has also dominated Chinese communication studies and media scholarship for at least a decade. No matter how indispensable the state-centered focus is to our analysis of the constraints of Chinese online activism, the normalization of such an analytical angle carries its own limits. Not only is the authoritarian state flattened out into an entity devoid of complexities and contradictions, also absent are the unsung agents of change that use social and digital media to produce social good and, together with it, the critical perspectives of studying them as actors rather than victims.

Nonconfrontational activism carves out a middle ground between those two competing frames of interpreting the social effect of the internet in China. Digital communication has empowered netizens and activists on the one hand, and the censoring state, on the other hand. The former scenario needs little elaboration. Networked communication helps create civic engagement from the bottom-up and gives voice to disfranchised communities. In China especially, digital media "have become the conduits and the locus where millions of Chinese engage in self-representation, creative expressions, and civic participation" (Chen and Reese 2015, 5). How is the authoritarian state enabled by the internet and social media? It resorts to confrontational measures to shut down online protests and erase traces of popular discontent. Common tactics include tightening the Great Firewall, blocking VPNs, filtering tabooed keywords, closing down influential Weibo accounts, arresting the so-called online rumor mongers, and other means of micro–social management. In the last decade, the state also employed less confrontational strategies to control internet speech, which included hiring trolls, nicknamed the "50-cent-ers" to post progovernment propaganda and steer online interactions from tabooed subjects to safe topics. A lesser-known and understudied trend is the recruitment of university research centers based in communication and journalism departments all over the country to build elaborate "public opinion monitoring systems" (*yuqing jiance*) that allow the government to study the drift of public opinion on a regular basis and to contain it, if necessary (Hu and Chen 2017).

As the Chinese state experiments with different nonconfrontational strategies of social control via new technologies, it is slowly evolving into what Cole Carnesecca calls "responsive authoritarianism," a form of governance that thrives on the instant detection and timely treatment of viral grievances found online. In this view, the internet provides a set of "tools for creating the feedback necessary for a system of responsive authoritarianism to function effectively" (Carnesecca 2015, 120). Given that such feedback often elicits nonconfrontational responses from the state, we are witnessing the regime's social policy transformation from violent and idiotic measures to a smarter game plan. All this validates the observation that the internet is "a critical force affecting policy making in China" (Ngok 2016, 27).

The Transformation of "Crowd Spectatorship"

Previous sections of this chapter take a double-pronged approach to mapping the Chinese social—on the one hand are social actors' strategies of making incremental social change, and on the other hand is the state's effort of redefining the social via the participatory policy of "social governance." Neither approach is confrontational. It seems both—social actors and the authoritarian state are capable of cultivating the "middle ground" stretched between two poles brought about by the internet—digital contention (of confrontational activists) and digital censorship (of a confrontational state). A conceptual middle ground is thrust open to legitimize noncontentious politics from both ends of the spectrum.

This book provides many examples of nonconfrontational activism, the majority of which are enabled by social media technologies. What happens, then, when we throw into the mix a third factor—social media? If we are to take seriously the emergence of the gray zone embraced by both grassroots and state actors, we will need to flesh out the brand of nonconfrontational activism staged on platforms like Sina Weibo and ask: What is the relationship between social media and noncontentious politics? At first sight, this inquiry seems runs counter to our conventional perception of what social media usually do—wreak havoc and stir up revolution.

The early part of this chapter already validates the existence of this strategic middle ground. Linking it to social media poses an immediate conceptual challenge. The internet and social media are normally associated with contentious action and theatrical change. Nonconfrontational activism is all about incrementalism and piecemeal changes that do not trigger quick structural transformation. In fact, despite the popularity of Weibo (the Chinese Twitter) in the 2010s, law professor and public intellectual Yu Jianrong's clarion call for action—"everybody has a microphone [in hand] now" (Yu 2010)—is reducible to a ritualistic slogan because under the gaze of censors, the mic in hand is often self-muted. Even in its heyday, contentious Weibo posts were less about movement making than making room for "crowd spectatorship" (*weiguan*), an act perched on the cusp between action and nonaction. *Weiguan* embodies an ambiguous form of politics that is only potentially antagonistic. For most participants, it is a form of noncontentious action.

Weiguan, "to surround an event and watch it as an anonymous crowd," refers to large-scale virtual incidents on Weibo, blogs, and other interactive forums which are triggered by (micro) bloggers, network editors, forum moderators, muckraking informants, journalists, or backstage word-of-mouth marketers. Who counts as a "surrounding crowd"? Those who read the original post, comment on it, or retweet it to his or her own circle of friends, including those who gather virtually to like, annotate, or debate initial or subsequent comments during the time between when an online incident broke out and when it came to fruition. Given that the synonym of *weiguan* is "onlooker" and its antonym "participant," Chinese crowd-gazing activities denote a wide range of nonconfrontational actions, which occupy the gray zone between the legitimate and the illegitimate. Decentralized and hard to contain once it is triggered, *weiguan* wields the power of igniting the "nuclear explosion" of public opinion (He 2011, 141).

Recent scholarship on the virtual gazing crowd is prone to emphasize its positive influence on Chinese internet politics. Xu Jian, for example, depicts *weiguan* optimistically as an avenue of "unofficial democracy," for it allows "Chinese people to exercise the critical practices of 'active spectatorship' through which the ordinary people can discipline abusive officials (Xu 2016, 105). The term *weiguan,* however, has traveled a long shadowy path since the early twentieth century, and it has not shed all of the negative connotations packed into the word *crowd.* Those well acquainted with modern Chinese history will recall the faceless, random crowd congregated around public spectacles, like the soulless Chinese spectators watching the public beheading of a Russian spy of Chinese nationality by Japanese soldiers, an event well chronicled in Lu Xun's 1906 Lantern Slide Incident and cited by him as an illustration of the moral apathy of Chinese commoners. From the twentieth century all the way to the late 2000s, the *weiguan* crowd has served as a familiar metaphor for the morbid Chinese national character condemned by Lu Xun and successive generations of writers and intellectuals. The national penchant for "surrounding to watch" was taken as a shameful and "sickening" attribute of Chinese people who live by natural instincts. Like Ah Q, an antihero in Lu Xun's novella on the backward and wretched national character, such people are devoid of an interior, reflective self. Fast forward to the mid-2010s, thanks to the rise of social media, a different kind of crowd emerged and the public spectacle was no longer public executions but controversial online incidents.

What kind of the crowd is involved in a *weiguan* activity? Are they the same kind of crowd critiqued by Lu Xun? Or are we talking about a crowd mobilized subconsciously to serve a political end? It is difficult to make a choice since both types of crowds were present in incidents that set off the phenomenon of *weiguan.* Offline, we continued to encounter nonchalant and repulsive spectatorship throughout modern and contemporary Chinese history—at public executions, during scuffles at market places, and on the streets where injured pedestrians lay unconscious and unattended. This blank and indifferent crowd, in Winne Wong's analysis, is utterly "useless for the formation of a body politic" (Wong 2015, 95). But the mid-2010s witnessed the emergence of a spectator crowd whose virtual gaze was imbued with political meaning. *Weiguan* reappeared as an online phenomenon defined sometimes as the "weapon of the weak" and "an entry of the public into politics" (Hu 2010a; 2010b, 98), a form of "networked power" (Xu Jian 2016, 77), and as a mechanism where "collective intelligence meets mobilized people power and public opinion" (Zhang 2014). Those various attempts of revalorizing the previously questionable ethos of crowd spectatorship has given birth to a romanticized catchphrase *"weiguan gaibian Zhongguo"* (virtual crowd spectatorship is changing China) (Xiao Shu 2010). My analysis of the Guo Meimei weblog incident in Chapter 3 is a case in point. Online spectatorship in her case led to the bankruptcy of the public trust in state-owned foundations, which facilitated the emergence of commercial crowdfunding platforms that benefited grassroots NGOs. Many early internet incidents featured in Guobin Yang's *Power of the Internet in China* (i.e., the South Tiger incident,[3] the Sun Zhigang incident,[4] the nailhouse incident,[5] the Xiamen PX incident,[6] etc.) can all be interpreted as examples of the transformative power of crowdsourced justice delivered through the collective act of *weiguan.*

There were other popular *weiguan* occasions that did not revolve around physical incidents. I am referring to the meme culture grown out of *egao,* a Chinese neologism for making mischievous mockery. We can track the origin of this subculture to January 2006 when a netizen named Hu Ge released his 20-minute video "A Murder Caused by a Steamed Bun" to parody director Chen Kaige's 2005 blockbuster film "The Promise."[7] Hu's personal prank went viral, which kicked off a national trend, however short-lived it was, of audacious netizens going online and making fun of all things serious and pompous, with relative impunity. Before long, *egao* became wedded to political puns and took its shape as a nonviolent form of virtual protest while instigating numerous "crowd gazing" occasions. We can indeed trace one of the remarkable beginnings of nonconfrontational practices in contemporary China to a series of memes such as "Grass Mud Horse," "the River Crab," "Three Representatives," "Green Dam Girl," and "10 Baidu Mythical Creatures." Those politically motivated *egao* examples, like other *weiguan* incidents named above, has fanned the imagination of liberal critics who are eager to draw an equation between satirical internet culture and the political valence of "cyber-assembly" (Link and Xiao 2013).

What Comes after Weiguan?

But has the crowd politics of Chinese netizens led to momentous political reform? Obviously not, if we are speaking of a regime change. Since 2013, Weibo regulations have allowed the prosecution and arrest of netizens for defamation and rumor mongering if their posts are viewed by more than 5,000 internet users or retweeted more than 500 times (The Supreme People's Procuratorate 2013). This punitive measure practically put an end to *weiguan* and doomed Weibo to an early decline, resulting in the quick waning of contentious online incidents (Yang Guobin 2017). Political memes have also suffered a rapid decline since then.

Weiguan, lest it should escape our attention, is actually neither a form of action nor that of confrontation even though it could add fuel to contentious politics. It triggered a crowd phenomenon precisely because spectatorship, free and anonymous, is the least risky and relatively effortless, and in short, a token form of participation. Therefore, treating it as a unambiguous synonym for political mobilization and political action is to turn a blind eye to the uneven make-up of w*eiguan* participants—some were motivated by progressive politics, some were indifferent onlookers reminiscent of Lu Xun's depoliticized mob, while others participated as a response to peer pressure. The majority of virtual "gazers" were drawn in, just like in the old days, by the entertainment value of carnivalesque spectacles (He 2011). Let us not forget that *weiguan* also lurked behind China's cyber vigilantism, particularly its offline consequences, set in motion by in-the-flesh search engines,[8] a variation of cyberbullying largely driven by righteous online spectators. Whether we consider *weiguan* a form of the "tyranny of the majority" (Zhao Dingxin 2012), it is certain that "crowd spectatorship does not represent democracy" (Wang Ruohan 2011).

In the face of the rapid decline of online crowd gazing, what then is left in the digital gray zone of nonconfrontational activism? The answer, I suggest, resides in what *weiguan* was never meant to achieve—a nonepisodic and nonsensational presence around what is considered safe networking. That is exactly what the tens of thousands of grassroots NGOs are doing online day in and day out—promoting social causes, learning how to create captivating digital content, and building communities to serve their respective constituents whether they are engaged in HIV/AIDS rights protection, preservation of minority cultures, advocacy of feminism and LGBTQ rights, food safety, poverty alleviation, welfare for left-behind children in rural China, or environmental activism. The deradicalization of *weiguan* after 2013 does not mean that Weibo should be cast aside—a cautionary message NGO2.0 continued to emphasize through our Web 2.0 training workshops. We urged grassroots actors to invest more time and energy on Weibo even after WeChat rose to dominate the Chinese social media ecology. The former is media, therefore open to the public, while the latter constitutes a closed ecosystem of private communications that is inimical to the building of open communities.

What new shape can a *weiguan* habitus take in the post-contention era? We can find some clues in the policy of social governance. A shift in the official rhetoric toward the "social" carries several implications. First, multiple stakeholder partnership is said to be the key to the transition of Chinese governance from strict top-down control to collaborative consultation. Second, this new form of governance suggests that the CCP is ready, at least in theory, for a state-led social pluralism, seen by some commentators as "networked governance" (*zhili jiegou wangluo hua*) (Chen Shihua 2016, 135; Liu Jinfa 2014, 9). Third, by promoting the separation of state from society and emphasizing the state's reliance on NGOs as providers of quality social services, the CCP is committed to professionalizing the nonprofit sector, with the implication that the capacity building of NGOs, GONGOs and C-NGOs has become a legitimate pursuit. This last task is especially urgent because statistics demonstrate that the public trust in nongovernmental organizations is as low as 33.46 percent (as compared with 88.45 percent in the central government, and 56 percent in village Party committees and neighborhood committees) (Wang and Guo 2016, 104).

The Center has carved out small openings to social actors and activists. Multisocial stakeholdership and cross-sectoral networking, two complementary facets of the same policy, are greatly encouraged. NGO capacity building understood in the context of professionalization now sits high on the government agenda, which leaves ample space for NGO2.0 and provincially based support-type NGOs to navigate. Since 2009, we and our provincial partners have been providing digital communication and social media capacity training to small and mid-size grassroots NGOs. To date, we have trained over 1,600 organizations in different provinces. Chapter 2 tracks the emergence of this new brand of ICT activism that promotes the use of social media as a means of helping Chinese NGOs to break out of their communication bottleneck. Chapter 2 also provides details about the program of our training workshops and illustrates how we teach NGOs to create spreadable content, use social media to identify like-minded supporters, and sustain the public gaze beyond a single activity. It is worth noting that NGOs' social media capacity building has become crucial to the cultivation and growth of the gray zone or the middle ground traversed by nonconfrontational activists.

After 2013, *weiguan* was bound to evolve beyond the reactive, episodic blast of public attention and transform itself into a durable, quiet commitment of socially concerned spectators to following the day-to-day, undramatic activities posted by grassroots organizations and other change agents on social media sites. This kind of spectatorship is a mutual companionship that's unfolding in multiple sectors simultaneously—the NGO sector (Chapter 2); the universities where students play the role of volunteer-donor-spectators of nonprofit work (Chapters 4 and 5); the IT sector where corporate social responsibility programs are engaged in "social media for social good" practices (Chapters 3 and 4); and software and hardware developers' communities where young makers and programmers participate in hackathon-like events to produce prototypes of tech4good solutions (Chapter 5). I shall call all those social actors "change makers," and in the context of *weiguan,* they are loosely configured multisectoral crowd-spectators bearing witness to their own participation in the making of the new social.

Such decentralized, multisectoral collaboration has also involved the public in generating benevolent interactions that cross the hurdles of state censorship. After all, it is too late for the government to turn back the clock and condemn the harmless semiofficial catchphrases such as "everybody a philanthropist" that have given justification to the involvement of players from multiple sectors to invigorate the ecology of the social sector. This is exactly the ideal kind of social mobilization—enduring but peaceful and dependable—that the government has hoped to achieve with its multiheaded policy of the separation of government from society.

Finally, this new form of spectatorship is a kind of collective witnessing that is purposeful but noncontentious, driven by a powerful unspoken consensus of all parties involved in building a strong, healthy society. Gone are the days of flash mobs. The next ten years will witness the steady development of cross-sectoral collaborations among diverse social good producers—a momentum hard to stop.

Conclusion: The Cultural Politics of
Silent Endurance (*Yinren*)

This chapter examined nonconfrontational activism in China from the NGO, state policy, and social media trajectories. As this brand of incremental activism is slowly evolving, the "Chinese social" defined in terms of the utopian space for change is also quietly growing. Starting with a literature review of scholarship that challenges the binary paradigm of "state versus society," the chapter conceptualized the massive middle ground in which NGOs and a host of other actors make their social mark. Mapping the fuzzy gray zone also entails the acknowledgment of the Party-state as a historical actor invested in legitimizing the concept of "society" and defining the boundary of the social. The ensuing analysis unfolds the policy of "social governance"—an official discourse emphasizing consensus building and multistakeholdership—and drives home the crucial role that the CCP is playing in Chinese nonconfrontational politics.

Incrementalism, positioning, and camouflage, strategies of nonconfrontational activists, are explored side by side with the impact of social media, "virtual crowd spectatorship" so to speak, on the future of activism in China. Do the state's new social policies entail the emergence of a bigger playground for nonconfrontational activists? Thus far, the answer is equivocal. While the dialogic relationship implied in "social governance" sounds more rhetorical than substantive, a multilayered collaborative network that links free agents, NGOs, the corporate sector, university volunteers, and programmers and maker communities has already emerged. If we expand our definition of "social actors" beyond NGOs, we will be able to appreciate the optimism felt by change makers in multiple sectors of the Chinese social. Given time, perhaps the proposition about "strong society" may not be a completely improbable vision.

In the remainder of the conclusion, I would like to probe nonconfrontational politics from a slightly different vantage point. "Social harmony" as a concept, as we know, is not just embraced by the censorious state but also by the Chinese middle class, whose unwillingness to rock the boat accounts for the relatively stable relationship between the people and the CCP. Why do the majority of Chinese people, activists included, choose to behave differently from rebels like Ai Weiwei and Falun Gong followers? Is censorship the only viable frame of explanation for the prevalence of a nonconfrontational ethos in China? Are there other interpretive possibilities?

Those aware of the pitfalls of fundamentalism would caution against taking a culturalist perspective on the Chinese penchant for "striving for the middle." Discussions of the Confucian Doctrine of the Mean have graced writings from Imperial China to the present. Ming Ding and Jie Xu, authors of *The Chinese Way*, turn to a familiar Chinese saying to illustrate the doctrine, "A pig is afraid to be strong and a man is afraid to be known" out of which grew the popular wisdom that "just as the strong pig will be slaughtered first, someone who is well known is an easy target" (Ding and Xu 2015, 1). The two authors continue to argue that "most members of Chinese society do not like to express radical ideas. However, once someone starts something, others will readily follow" (1). This analysis is useful not only for our examination of nonconfrontational politics Chinese style, it also provides us a refreshing analytical frame for interpreting *weiguan,* crowd gazing online. The other relevant folk practice worth noting is the "face saving" practice that requires little explanation. Anyone who can help others save or gain face will be greatly valued (13). Needless to say, confrontational actions are socially unacceptable in China. Helping the powerful not to lose face is considered especially an unspoken obligation for all. Since concession seeking is a required skill for members living in extended families, it is fair to assume that the Doctrine of the Mean has evolved from the day-to-day practice of communalism in imperial times and the modern-day engagement in collectivism for thousands of years. Translated into social behavior, the communalistic and collectivist principles generate a variety of what Western individualists consider "submissive actions."

I can go on and dig myself deeper into the trap of cultural determinism. I was, however, tempted to bring up the topic of collectivism and its alleged impact on Chinese nonconfrontational activism for a different reason. I was motivated by the recent turn of the Chinese foundation sector to publicize "research on traditional Chinese culture and philosophy" as a legitimate funding category for NGOs.

I can find no better explanation for this rising trend than to interpret it as the foundation sector's timely response to the state's emphasis on cultural renaissance (*wenhua fuxing*) via research on traditional Chinese philosophies. As the secretary-general and major fundraiser of NGO2.0, I started an interesting, albeit frustrating, exercise of trying to identify the common ground, if any, between Web 2.0 culture and Confucian and Taoist ethics to justify a funding application. This is not the place to share my findings. What is relevant to this chapter is my rediscovery of passages in ancient texts about a behavioral characteristic that bears resemblance to the practice of nonconfrontationalism, namely, *yinren,* literally, to "hide and forbear."

The word *yin* ("to hide [emotions]") points indirectly to camouflage discussed earlier as a strategy for nonconfrontational activists. Not putting one's emotion on full display and not speaking one's mind is a survival tactic for commoners (not just the underdogs) in Chinese society. Combined with *ren* ("to endure), the term *yinren* is translated into the practice of "silent forbearance." We can find numerous references throughout Chinese history to well-known heroes such as Gou Jian and Wu Zixu (political figures during the Spring Autumn Period) and Wen Tianxiang (a scholar-general in the last years of the Southern Song Dynasty) who left behind anecdotes of silent endurance at times of crisis to return to power, avenged and triumphant. Deng Xiaoping himself famously declared in 1992 that China's foreign policy was one of "hiding (strength) and biding (time)," a strategic response to the economic sanctions the world imposed on China after the 1989 Tiananmen Square crackdown (Communist Party Central Documentation Research Center 2004, 1346). All those anecdotes echo the same message—one endures in adversity in order to return with redoubled conviction and fulfillment.

I would further note that *yinren* is so deeply ingrained in Chinese culture that most people are not even conscious of the practice. Indeed, we can trace the construct of *yinren* back to old times when the extended family formed the basic social unit in China. "Hide and bide" can be understood as a material practice and *a survival tactic* for individuals obliged to living with three, four, or even five generations of immediate and extended family members under one roof. Traditional Chinese literature was littered with portrayals of the repressive practice of *yinren.*

Remember the frail Lin Daiyu and her tragic exit from a life doomed for quiet sufferance in the walled garden of the Jia clan in *Dream of the Red Chamber?* Liu Bei's and Cao Cao's hushed and camouflaged existence before their rise to power in *Romance of the Three Kingdoms?* Even the legendary rebel in *Journey to the West,* the monkey king, had to endure Master Xuan Zhuang's righteous rules and regulations, an inviolable existential condition that spurred many later-day subversive writers and filmmakers to create remakes of the parent story.[9] Fast forward to contemporary China, it is very likely that censorship—the political—and *yinren,* an epiphenomenon of collectivist culture, reinforce each other to consolidate the present-day ethos of nonconfrontationalism.[10]

Over the course of long centuries, the Chinese ethos of silent endurance was occasionally disrupted by outbursts of peasant revolts and radicalism (Mao's revolution springs to mind) and failed movements such as the Tiananmen Square protests in June 1989. Can we read the practice of nonconfrontational activism as a contemporary variation of *yinren,* a kind of endurance that will eventually reward those who persevered? If so, could this partly explain why the "hide and bide" change makers in China are indefatigable optimists? To those bright-eyed utopian dreamers and their social media practices I devote the following chapters.

2

NGO2.0 and Social Media Activism

Activist as Researcher

This chapter features NGOs as the most visible but vulnerable change agents in contemporary China. I track the emergence of a particular brand of ICT (information and communication technology) activism that promotes the use of social media as a means of helping Chinese NGOs break out of their communication bottleneck. I start with an introduction of NGO2.0, using it as an entry point to examine the practice of social media for social good and shed light on the ecosystem of social media usage by Chinese NGOs. The methodological implications of undertaking "social media enabled action research" will be explored, and I discuss what it means to engage in the hybrid practice of activist as scholar in the specific context of cultural studies.

Web 2.0 has revolutionized how people communicate and how content is created and distributed. The rise in the popularity of social media is particularly important to those living in authoritarian countries where state-controlled media pay little attention to lone activists, not to mention politically sensitive nongovernmental organizations dedicated to serving the underprivileged in systematic ways. This chapter examines the emergence of ICT-powered activism that promotes the use of information and communication technology to help NGOs claim their rights to communicate and provide them with possibilities of producing social good through technological means.

NGOs in China have developed rapidly since 1995 across diverse fields.[1] However, small, mid-sized, and emerging NGOs have encountered a bottleneck of growth for a number of reasons. First, nurturing nongovernmental civic participation is hardly a priority for the Chinese government. Second, a significant number of NGOs are semilegal and highly constrained in acquiring resources and regularizing program activities. Third, they cannot compete with GONGOs (governmental-organized NGOs) for media coverage. This lack of media exposure makes NGOs invisible to each other and to the general public. We do not get to hear their stories, learn about the causes they are promoting, and respond to their needs. Many NGOs toil quietly until their thin workforce burns out. Social media arrived in China around 2009, providing NGOs an alternative means of communication to break this vicious cycle.

Tencent QQ, an instant messaging platform, has been popular among NGO users since 1999, but it was not until 2009 when Sina.com's Weibo became a mainstream microblogging platform that the interactive, open, and "writerly" web began to flourish in China. Here I wish to make a distinction between the media experience of individual users and that of organizations. While individuals are autonomous media users free to try anything new, organizations are risk averse, and hence conservative, in new media adoption. Before Weibo had gone mainstream, it was often the case that individual staffers in an organization were active microbloggers, but the NGO itself could be mired in debates about whether to set up a microblog account in the name of the organization.[2] In fact, the primary ICT experiences of most NGOs are still confined to building traditional websites. The caveat: there is little traffic to those sites. And to make the situation more challenging, Web 2.0 tools and services have proliferated quickly, making it even more demanding for NGO staffers to navigate the digital landscape, which has created another bottleneck of growth for Chinese NGOs.

Enter NGO2.0 (www.ngo20.org), an organization I launched in China in 2009. Together with the University of Science and Technology of China,[3] we established a flagship program—Web 2.0 workshops—that provide digital and social media literacy training to grassroots NGOs in the western and central provinces of China. Guided by an instructor team, participants learn how to use social media to increase the transparency of their operations, engage in participatory thinking, launch interactive advocacy campaigns, and gain hands-on experiences in creating digital content while examining successful worldwide NGO2.0 case studies. As of July 2019, we have completed over fifty-five workshops, trained approximately 1,600 organizations, compiled an online toolbox (http://tools.ngo20.org), and built a Web 2.0 philanthropy map (www.ngo20 map.com) on which over 24,797 NGOs have registered their organizational and project data.[4] Literacy training is only one part of our program. In recent years, NGO2.0 has developed a larger mission—advocating a new brand of public interest sector that utilizes digital and mobile nonprofit technologies to build a better society. Toward that goal, we collaborate with philanthropy actors from multiple sectors such as foundations, NGOs, IT corporations, universities, communities of software developers, digital DIY makers, and interaction designers.

This latter vision—an open, multisectoral collaboration—is true to the spirit of network society and crucial to my attempt of mapping the changing ecosystem of Chinese change makers in the era of Web 2.0, which this book is mainly about. That NGOs should partake in such an eco-system was unthinkable ten years ago. Nonprofits are not natural adopters of digital trends. More importantly, promoting social media to NGOs entails joint investments by multiple sectors, and the condition for such cross-sector collaboration did not mature until 2011.[5]

At the turn of the 2010s, forward-looking enthusiasts began asking whether NGOs have a role to play in China's rush to a rosy ICT future. This was not just fortuitous futurism. The transition of the Chinese Communist Party (CCP) to Xi Jinping's regime led to new slogans, among them the familiar "Chinese dream" and a lesser-known depoliticized discourse of *zheng nengliang* (positive energy)—a call to old and new media for stories celebrating good deeds and glorifying the brighter side of society that incorporate fantasies about the elimination of all inequalities, the digital divide included. In the ascendance of this ideology of "positive energy," I saw the consummation of a mutual consent, or a sturdy pact, made between the leaders and the led—be upbeat about the status quo. Stability trumps all other needs. As for ICTs, the politics is consistent: if one cannot rattle the government through a systemic overhaul of the status quo, one can at least trumpet the transformative possibility of digital technologies in bringing about social good *piecemeal*.

To minimize governmental scrutiny, I positioned NGO2.0 as a technology project (rather than a media initiative) imbued with a utopian roadmap of redressing the digital divide, a discourse well accepted by the authorities. It was a journey filled with obstacles at the beginning. Yet four years after NGO2.0 was founded, "social media for social good" has become a popular concept embraced not only by the nonprofit sector but also by IT industries, and tacitly supported by the central government.[6] Collaborators flowed in from multiple sectors to propagate the benefits of social media in effecting social change. It all suggests a deeper shift in social consciousness than a fleeting cultural fad.

This happens at a poignant moment when anything aspirational that can be brought to serve the discourse of "positive energy" is considered legitimate. In China's precariously balanced political climate, actions aligned with the production of social good have potential to reduce distrust and withstand censorship. The fact that NGO2.0 has navigated the terrain with relative impunity suggests that technologically motivated social transformation is a "change" category tolerable to the authorities.[7]

Moreover, the state's agenda of developing China's IT industries has undeniably played a significant role in alleviating political concerns over social media practices. Meanwhile, major Chinese internet portals (such as Sina.com and Tencent.com) have a vested interest in promoting a new brand of philanthropy driven by social media. Under the sway of the popular slogan "microcharity" (*wei gongyi*), compassionate citizens in first- and second-tier cities are called upon to perform good deeds. All of a sudden, protecting public interest and contributing to the common good via social media seem well "within the reach of everyone" (*renren ke gongyi*). Crowdfunding 2.0 generated many successful platforms, among them Tencent's Micro-Compassion Program and Sina's Micro-Philanthropy platform.[8] (See Chapter 3 for a detailed account of the making of social-media powered corporate philanthropy.)

It is within this ideological context that my subsequent inquiries into Chinese NGOs' social media usage are conducted. Given NGO2.0 itself serves as a prime example of how ICT and social media can be leveraged to produce social good, this chapter starts with the introduction of NGO2.0, using it as an entry point to examine the ecosystem of social media usage by Chinese NGOs.

Methodological Considerations

The study of ICT and activism in China is a fairly young field. Jack Qiu and Wei Bu have mapped the terrain while making a clarion call for research that highlights the ways disenfranchised groups use ICTs to facilitate social transformation (Qiu and Bu 2013). Several scholars have paved the way for the evolution of this field, among them Guobin Yang who set a milestone in investigating citizen activism in cyberspace (Yang 2009b). Jack Qiu's seminal work on mobile phone usage by migrant workers and his proposition of "working-class ICTs" embody another landmark of ICT scholarship (Qiu 2008). The excellent book published by Ding Wei—*Mobile Homelands* (Ding 2014)—investigates the communication practices of taxicab drivers in Shenzhen. Both Qiu and Ding make inquiries into the mutual constitutiveness of new communication technologies and the making of new spatial and social relationships in China. Although their ethnographic scholarship is focused on specific urban communities (migrant workers and taxicab drivers) rather than on NGOs per se, their insights on visual participatory research and community communication are highly relevant to what I study here. Research on the relationship between media making and activism will continue to evolve. This book joins those critical efforts. And I believe that a predominant media trajectory, when complemented by the vision of tech4good (a theme treated at length in Chapter 5 and the Conclusion), will enrich the critical literature on Chinese civic associations.

Action research driven by social media is leading to research opportunities opened up by the convergence of social action and social media. Much work has been published on the impact of Web 2.0 on corporate strategies and social media users as consumers. However, not enough scholarship has focused on the ways with which Chinese grassroots NGOs are leveraging those free tools and platforms to produce social good. NGO2.0 possesses by far the most up-to-date datasets of social media usage and internet communication patterns of Chinese NGOs. With those data in hand, we can begin to take a structural look at the ecosystem in question.

Since NGO2.0 went into operation, the method question has loomed large. I continue to contemplate how to articulate my hybrid practice of scholar as activist in the context of cultural studies, my home discipline. Furthermore, the foundational discourses underlying communication studies and cultural studies are so divergent that the definitions of *change making* have to be negotiated differently. Chapter 1 already registered my thinking on our necessity of redefining *social change* and *change making* in illiberal societies. Some of those method questions can also be addressed through my reconstruction of what motivated me, a cultural studies critic, to launch NGO2.0.

NGO2.0: How Did It All Start?

There are multiple story lines with which NGO2.0 can be narrated. Apart from enhancing NGOs' social media literacy, the project is designed to mobilize indigenous Chinese resources and build grassroots leadership by identifying and training media and tech-conscious NGO change makers. We are not the first to leverage ICTs as a means of empowering Chinese NGOs. Green Web, New Philanthropy Partners, Microsoft China, and Google China have all sporadically held IT training workshops, serving Beijing-based NGOs and elite foundations. But NGO2.0 pioneered the effort of targeting grassroots NGOs in China's hinterland—organizations based in western and central provinces of which more than 30 percent were not registered with the Ministry of Civil Affairs when we started NGO2.0 in 2009.[9]

What is NGO2.0? Are we a project or an organization? We have successfully transformed ourselves from an international academic project to a localized nonprofit organization formally registered in Shenzhen in 2014. We started off with six institutional partners—MIT New Media Action Lab (of which I am the founder-director), the Institute of Knowledge Management at the University of Science and Technology of China,[10] NGOCN (China's largest grassroots NGO portal), Friends of Nature (an environmental NGO), the Institute for Civil Society at Sun Yat-sen University, and last but not least, a corporate partner, Ogilvy & Mather Public Relations with which I have nurtured a decade-long research relationship.[11] To be honest, not all of them are active collaborators.[12] The real work is done by three staff members and fifteen volunteers who live in different Chinese provinces and, in my case, abroad. I run NGO2.0 long-distance through social media platforms (QQ, WeChat, Skype, JoinMe, Tower, and so on). For ten years, I have presided over weekly Skype meetings with my core team, which take place *every* Sunday, Beijing time from 8:30 PM to midnight. Program ideas are brainstormed, strategies discussed and debated, and work assigned and completed during those meetings. Highly dependent on digital and social media, NGO2.0 has also grown several additional virtual volunteer teams including two interaction design teams[13] and civic hackathon teams[14] based in first- and second-tier cities.

What does NGO2.0 do for grassroots NGOs? During the first three years, we focused on communication capacity building for grassroots NGOs. Web 2.0 is known as the poor man's communication tools.

With those tools in hand, NGOs stand a better chance of finding and collaborating with each other, branding themselves at little cost to attract volunteers and other resources. Theoretically, all NGOs are change agents. If they are familiar with social media, they can be better equipped to push creativity to the next level. Thus, NGO2.0 is not only a project about ICTs but one built on the belief that social innovation, enabled by new media, can be triggered at the grassroots level. This phenomenon—the coming together of the NGO sector and social media—is a transnational phenomenon with the US leading the way[15] and China a decade behind, at the time when I created NGO2.0.

A Critique of Creative Commons via Cultural Studies Imperatives

How did we come into existence? NGO2.0 has international roots that began in 2006 when I started a research project on the "public domain" and discovered Creative Commons (henceforth CC), a global open-content movement built on a Web 2.0 legal protocol that promotes a set of open digital licenses. CC became popular all over the world. Once internet users began to create, post, and freely distribute content digitally, new copyright questions popped up. How do we go about distributing our own work online while making personal decisions about how others can reuse and redistribute our work? CC provides an excellent solution.

Creative Commons was founded in 2001 and China joined in 2006. After working as a CC volunteer for two years, I later chaired the International Advisory Board of CC China Mainland and began envisioning a model that could benefit the underprivileged in China's less developed regions. At CC-China's launch ceremony in Beijing in March 2006, Lawrence Lessig, the mastermind behind CC, made the auspicious remark that "CC's global user community exploded instantaneously with the addition of 1.3 billion Chinese users overnight." Lessig's upbeat sentiment notwithstanding, I felt a bit dubious not least because China's several hundred million peasants and the disenfranchised were not able to create digital content. They had no use for CC licenses.

As Creative Commons spread across the globe, I also wondered whether one concept would fit all. I continued to ask how we could feed the indigenous needs encountered in developing countries back to the license-centric approach of global CC. And how could we meet the enormous challenges of propagating CC in places where digital elites are a minority? My answer was later translated into a vision for NGO2.0. Around 2008, I conceptualized a project that put less emphasis on CC licenses than on the spirit of Web 2.0 culture that gives life to open-content movements like CC. In my view, the blind spot of CC's global model resides not only in its assumption about universal digital literacy but also in its lack of attention to the needs of the underprivileged.

NGO2.0 quickly gained a life of its own. In hindsight, my critique of Creative Commons had come from a trained intuition with which all serious cultural studies critics are equipped. More aware of the blind spots of CC than its founders—cyberlaw scholars—I am concerned with the center/periphery power relationship. Meanwhile, more than a critique of CC, NGO2.0 represents the return of my critical practice to the empirical and the experiential, and a radical response I made to the ongoing crisis of cultural studies as a discipline.

Many critics have deplored the ominous shift of cultural studies from its early substantive social, political, and material roots to metatheories on the one hand, and a postmodern indulgence in textualism, on the other. Indeed, entire books such as *Cultural Studies in Question* (Ferguson and Golding 1997) were devoted to the subject, laying bare and mourning the depoliticization of the original project of cultural studies—its retreat from "class" as a prism of social analysis and the growing indifference of critics to the fundamental questions of structured inequality. More than two decades have passed since such a collective soul searching was undertaken. NGO2.0 is, in effect, my own answer to those critiques and a mirror of my desire to move back to the discipline's intellectual "roots once firmly planted in the social and material" (xxvi). I am once again drawn to the notion of praxis, be it Marxian or Deweyian. It preaches something that Stuart Hall would have endorsed: the missing link of academic practice is not to reflect society in discourses but to change it in practice.

This critical ethos guides every step we took in building NGO2.0 into a practice conscious of its own promise and limits. As a scholar, I saw clearly the boundary of what new media and technology can achieve. But as an activist, I am by nature an incorrigible optimist. The complex pull between social action and action research deserves a chapter of its own, and I save the discussion for Chapter 6, "Participatory Action Research and the Chinese Challenge." Right now, the visionary speaks. The story of the practice continues.

Internet Infrastructure in West China

When I started NGO2.0, there were many questions my team had to deal with: First, do our target areas of west and central China—provinces like Yunnan, Sichuan, Qinghai, Gansu, Ningxia, Shaanxi, Chongqing, Guizhou, Guangxi, Henan, Shanxi, Shandong, and Anhui—have adequate digital infrastructure? Second, are Chinese grassroots NGOs *ready* to leapfrog into Web 2.0? Could we have overestimated the sector's readiness in both regards?

To address the first question, I turned to China's Village-to-Village (*cuncun tong*) Project. Launched in the early 2000s with the goal of alleviating the digital divide between rural and urban China, the governmental project had already enabled 98 percent of townships to gain internet access by 2008. In twenty-seven provinces, people living at the county level could log in either at an office, information kiosk, or internet café. By 2013, 87.9 percent of administrative villages had broadband access,[16] which indicates that the lack of infrastructure was no longer the main issue for western and central provinces. The dividing line was knowledge about how to navigate the Web, a real obstacle for grassroots NGOs.

The Ecosystem of Social Media Use by Grassroots NGOs: A Bird's-Eye View

If infrastructure was no longer a worry, were our target NGOs ready for Web 2.0? Had the digital generation of NGOs emerged in China? Statistics from NGOCN (China's biggest grassroots NGO internet portal) and our own survey results both look positive. Traffic volume on NGOCN .org is telling: between June 2007 and June 2009, the website had 723,941 single absolute visitors. The total volume of visits in June 2009 alone amounted to an astounding 1,401,383. On average, a single visit lasted four minutes and the number of page view was 3.30.[17] This is not bad for a civic media channel with little entertainment value. One can imagine how the traffic must have multiplied ten years later, although the page views, due to the proliferation of digital platforms, must have declined. Nonetheless, we can be certain that a critical mass of NGO-relevant internet users already existed around 2009. The digital ecosystem of grassroots NGOs in China was taking shape.

But what about social media? Since 2009, NGO2.0's effort of promoting social media has created a trickle-down effect. To capture the usage data, we have conducted eight online surveys, including six nationwide NGO Internet Usage Surveys (henceforth NGO-IU Survey), and two follow-up surveys to track the social media use of organizations trained by us (henceforth NGO-SM Survey). Survey participants came from western-central provinces and eastern provinces evenly. Unexpectedly, even in 2009, 79.67 percent of the organizations sampled already accessed the web through broadband (see Figure 2.1). This trend continued to dominate our next survey. Of the 401 organizations surveyed, 72.57 percent used broadband (NGO-IU Survey 2, 2010). NGOs with regular web access identified the following barriers: "insufficient skills of navigating online," "internet access fees," and "no appropriate hardware device." Successive surveys confirmed that "insufficient skills of navigating online"

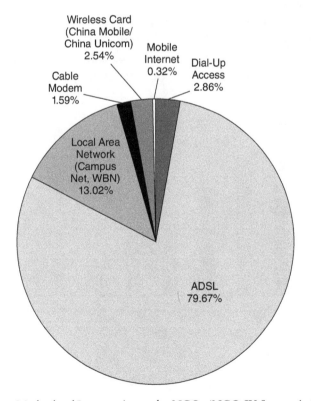

Figure 2.1. Methods of Internet Access by NGOs (NGO-IU Survey 1, 2009)

stood out as the most serious problem to solve. Despite those barriers, an overwhelming majority—86.24 percent of those in Survey 1 and 85.54 percent in Survey 2—considered the internet extremely important to their operation.

Approximately 93.52 percent of NGOs in Survey 2 had used QQ or MSN for internal and external communication. More than 50 percent of organizations used either QQ, MSN, or Skype to conduct online meetings (NGO-IU Survey 1 2009), which climbed to 63.59 percent in 2010 (NGO-IU Survey 2 2010). In the latter study, 84.04 percent of NGOs not only produced organizational videos with software tools or smartphones, but they also uploaded them to video-sharing websites like Youku and Tudou. In all, a variety of social media content was produced and published (see Figure 2.2). Noticeably, microblogging had not developed into a trend in 2010, when photo-sharing, blogs, and video platforms were the most popular. The least adopted were wikis, which stayed that way in the following years.

Chinese Wikipedia is unfriendly to grassroots NGOs for political reasons. Even NGO2.0 failed to gain a footing there. Even without that entry barrier, however, collaborative writing online is not an easy task for NGOs to sustain. Equally surprising was the high percentage of NGOs

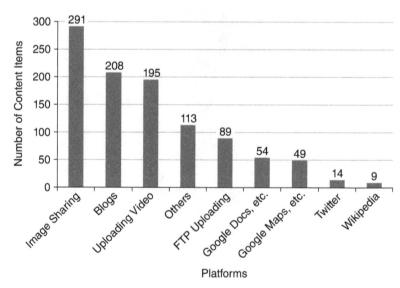

Figure 2.2. NGO Content Published by Platforms (NGO-IU Survey 2, 2010)

owning organization blogs—45.71 percent in 2009, which increased to 56.11 percent in 2010 but dropped to 53.58 percent two years later—with Weibo usage surging to an overwhelming 68.94 percent (See NGO-IU Survey 3, 2012 Figure 2.3). Soon, however, with the popularization of We-Chat, blogs sank into oblivion. Weibo lost its footing as well, with its usage declining to 25.96 percent in 2015 (NGO-IU Survey 4, 2015a) and a deplorable 9.98 percent in 2016 (see Survey 5, Figure 2.4).

Mobile media picked up its momentum around 2012 and foretold the rise of mobile applications like WeChat. By the time we conducted the third NGO-IU survey during that year, 46 percent of NGOs already factored "wireless service in the office" as a "means of internet access." The internet now ranked as NGOs' favorite medium of communication with volunteers and the communities they served, with "face-to-face meeting" trailing in as second, and "telephone" the third (NGO-IU Survey 3, 2012). This was no small change for grassroots organizations who used to rely heavily on in-person meetings and telephone calls. These statistics may also indicate the expansion of their activities geographically.

The meteoric rise of WeChat was the biggest news for our fifth survey. Comparing the most frequently used media in this survey with the four major digital platforms listed by NGOs for Survey 3 (Figure 2.4)—QQ, Weibo, organization website, and blog, in that order—we found a few

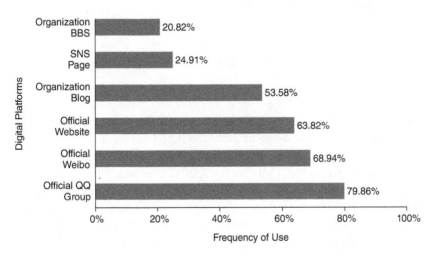

Figure 2.3.   Most Frequently Used Digital Platforms by NGOs (NGO-IU Survey 3, 2012)

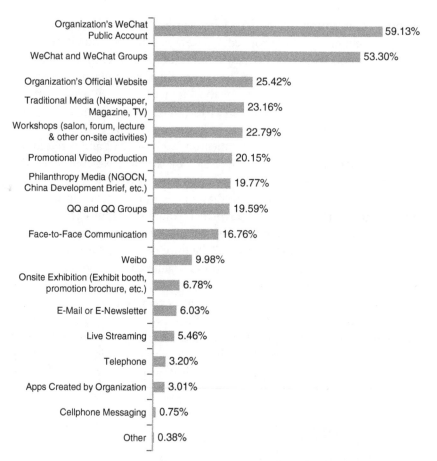

Figure 2.4. Most Frequently Used Media in 2016 (NGO-IU Survey 5, 2017)

disturbing trends on the rise. First, we noticed the sliding importance of BBS, whose 58 percent usage in 2009 (NGO-IU Survey 1, 2009) had declined dramatically to 20.82 percent, losing NGO users to more nimble and interactive platforms (NGO-IU Survey 3, 2012). Second, NGOs now relied disproportionately on WeChat as their most frequented communication channel—59.13 percent of surveyed organizations had created WeChat public accounts (known as *gongzhong hao*) and 53.30 percent used private WeChats and group WeChats to publicize their work—a phenomenon not at all conducive to community building, which is a vital mission for all NGOs. True, the kind of social networks NGOs need to weave are built primarily on weak relationships (which an open, public platform like Weibo provides), not segregated enclaves of strong relationships, on which WeChat is constructed. The statistics showed not just the jousting between those two frenemies in China's social media space and who had won the latest round, but more seriously, the new communication bottleneck grassroots NGOs began to suffer as a result of their mass exodus from Weibo. Setting aside the theoretical debate over network dynamics for activism, by mid-2016, WeChat users already felt the mental fatigue. Few users were motivated to click open the regular newscast sent by WeChat's proliferating "official accounts." In fact, 80 percent of WeChat public accounts now enjoyed less than a 5 percent open rate (laoyu201703 2017), which means most mobile content created on that platform never saw the daylight.

Apart from the worrisome decrease of Weibo usage, the fifth survey conducted in 2016 yielded some encouraging trends, which demonstrated that Chinese NGOs had become exploratory in their experiment with new media. For example, 21.85 percent of those surveyed had started deploying Constituent Management Systems, and 38.23 percent organizations had the experience of using an online management system for volunteers (NGO-IU Survey 5, 2017), doubling the statistics received for the same category in survey 4 (NGO-IU Survey 4, 2015a).

To sum up, the overall picture of NGOs' media practice conjures up an interesting vista where spreadable content is actively produced and distributed across social media platforms. But in a country pervaded by censorship, does the politics of NGOs influence the role of ICTs? Will they attract government attention and get into trouble by disseminating sensitive content over social media? By enhancing their capability in using social media, is NGO2.0 putting our trainees at risk?

Grassroots NGOs: The Logic of Semi-Autonomy and Nonconfrontationalism

The above questions presume the oppositional impetus of grassroots NGOs in China, a premise that needs to be demystified. The concept of NGO caught on in China via the World Conference on Women held in 1995. Since then, Chinese grassroots NGOs have grown rapidly, but their total number fluctuates a great deal. Some experts have assumed there are 82,000 (China Development Brief 2011). My estimate is much more modest. There are approximately 8,000 institutionally stable entities.[18] Although not all grassroots NGOs are registered, they fill in the big service gaps neither the government nor the market can mitigate. In the wake of the 2008 Sichuan earthquake during which NGOs contributed tremendously to postdisaster relief efforts, the government's perception of those *semi-autonomous* organizations softened. Prior to the consolidation of President Xi's power, the reform of the NGO registration system had paved the way for relaxing control. More grassroots organizations in progressive provinces like Guangdong had gained legal status. The thawing trend had also spread from the coast to hinterland. Our fifth survey of 2016 reveals that 95 percent of the 531 participating organizations were established after 2000, and the largest number of registered grassroots organizations occurred in 2014 (NGO-IU Survey 5, 2017), statistics that indirectly validate the impact of policy change on the Chinese nonprofit sector. That said, 2018 was a bleak year that witnessed the tightening of NGO registration for many grassroots organizations working on agendas deemed sensitive. The recent meteoric rise of neighborhood NGOs endorsed by the state muddled the picture even further. Although categorized as "grassroots, " the latter are community service organizations (C-NGOs) without a social change agenda.

Regardless of how hard-won progress was held back from time to time, China passed its first Philanthropy Law, one significant step taken by the state toward normalizing nonconfrontational politics.[19] Although it's too early to assess its full impact, there has been a consensus in China among NGO workers and scholars that the benefits brought on by the new law are many (Zhu 2016). It broadens the definition of philanthropy beyond antipoverty and postdisaster relief, clears many obstacles for nonprofits to register, makes it legal for nonregistered citizen groups to exist and carry on activities, and lifts the ban on public fundraising by allowing special status to big social organizations with proven credentials. These open measures prompted the *Wall Street Journal* to make a rare endorsement that "the law could be a rare ray of light for a Chinese civil society" (Chin 2016), balancing an opposite, darker forecast that new regulations were set to create "a less free civil society" (Hasmath 2016). Regardless, NGO2.0's sixth online survey of NGOs reflects the upswing of the total number of grassroots organizations after 2016 (see Figure 2.5) (NGO2.0 2018).

The negative impact of the law? While there is little dispute that the new Philanthropy Law allows for greater accountability and profession-

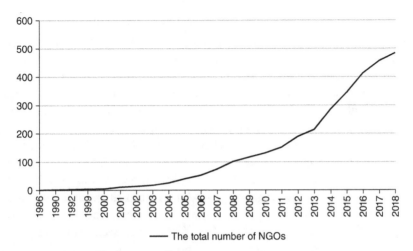

Figure 2.5. The Total Number of NGOs from 1986 to 2018 (NGO2.0 2018)

alization of the sector, it is associated, in the Western press, with an un-friendly law, published in the same year, that governs foreign NGOs in China: the "Law of the People's Republic of China on the Administration of Activities of Overseas Nongovernmental Organizations in the Main-land of China."[20] The government seems to be replicating what it has done in the commercial sector—clearing the way for domestic Chinese entities to take center stage by relegating foreign entities, whether Google or the Open Society Foundation, to the dust bin. When the good news came that credible foundations like the Asia Foundation and Ford Foundation passed the reregistration hurdle, Chinese grassroots organizations joined the cheer heartily. But most domestic NGOs mired in the day-to-day struggle with bread and butter issues do not consider the "stifling [of] the proliferation of foreign NGOs in China" a serious threat (NGO2.0 2018). If we have to find fault with the new Philanthropy Law, it is that a theoretically sound law may be poorly executed by local governments. Let us also not forget that the actual number of nonprofits allowed thus far to do public fund-raising is a pitiful 916 (Xinhua Net 2017). There are still many hurdles to cross for grassroots entities like NGO2.0 and other comparable organ-izations to acquire the official permit to raise funds in public.

Back to the semi-autonomous status with which I characterize Chinese grassroots NGOs. All of them, registered or not, maintain a decent and sometimes cordial relationship with the state. As I argue in Chapter 1,

NGOs in illiberal societies practice nonconfrontational activism by default, and it's imperative that they make change *within* the system. Former Ford Foundation Beijing chief Anthony Saich teases out this paradox most succinctly: Chinese NGOs' voluntary subordination to the existing state structure should be viewed not as a measure of expediency but a strategic move to enhance their ability to "manipulate the official and semi-official institutions for their own advantage," which means making more impact on society and gaining a louder voice in policy-making discussions than if they were to remain completely autonomous (Saich 2000, 139). Herein lies the fundamental difference between Western NGOs and their Chinese counterparts. There is no shortage of American, British, and Australian advocates who believe that by transplanting to China the universal standard of operation, often in the name of "NGO capacity training," they could professionalize Chinese NGOs, normalize the sector, and build a civil society that would eventually challenge the autocratic regime. The zest for such cross-pollination is missionary and has borne fruits here and there, but the primary political agenda remains unrealizable. Western NGOs act like pressure groups whose raison d'être is to contest government policies. In contrast, with the exception of a small handful of rights advocacy nonprofits, the majority of Chinese NGOs serve as informal social service or welfare relief organizations that are compelled to work and make incremental change within the system. Those wishing to see them move toward "an antagonist model" have insufficient understanding of the social ethos of Chinese people, activists or not (Hasmath 2016).

There is already a scholarly consensus characterizing the Chinese NGO-state relationship as nonconflictual (Howell 1994; Perry 1994; Shue 1994; Lu 2009; Spires, Tao, and Chan 2014). Whereas such scholarship calls into question the application of the American paradigm of civil society to the Chinese case, there is something implicitly and intrinsically condemning about this paradox: the potential incorporation of NGOs into the state agenda. Apologies, or lengthy explanations at least, have to be made for and by social service–oriented NGOs whose work has little to do with the notion of "social change" valorized in Western epistemology. I emphasize that the Chinese practice of nonconfrontational activism should be seen as less ideologically rooted than strategically driven, as Anthony Saich has pointed out. Paradoxically, although Chinese NGOs are heavily dependent on the state, they enjoy "a remarkable degree of *de facto* autonomy" (Lu 2009, 9). Sometimes, speaking from my own experience of running NGO2.0, the closer a grassroots NGO is to the government, the less suspicion it arouses, and the more autonomy it gains.

Regardless of their legal status, NGOs in China have to learn how to navigate within the state apparatus. More precisely, they should be conceptualized as "semi-official" and "semi-popular" entities (Wang, Zhe, and Sun 1993). I have written elsewhere about the pitfall of treating all organized spaces in contemporary China as devoid of transformative potential (Wang 2005, 2015). This is not just a theoretical issue. The Chinese have a saying, "The most *invisible* place is the spot right underneath the light," meaning no place is safer than the place of danger. In other words, under Party-state surveillance, it is easier to carve out "breathing spaces" within the planned space than create them outside it (28). This supple mind-set compels Chinese activists to imagine creative ways of evading censors and walking around obstacles. Chapter 1 brings to light the repertoire of nonconfrontational strategies that lone activists and NGOs resort to in contesting the status quo silently.

Suffice it to say, those habitually clinging onto dichotomous paradigms will have difficulties grasping how Chinese NGOs navigate in the seamless web of political control. Do they ever criticize the government openly? Of course they do. They complain to sympathetic officials in private or present themselves as contentious, anonymous individuals rather than as members of NGOs. That said, NGOs in China tend not to use social media to stir up revolution like the cantankerous architects of the Arab Spring, although in recent years we have witnessed more and more NGOs identifying "policy advocacy" as an arena of their work.[21] Let us also not forget that the once popular Weibo was the battleground where many public controversies were staged and ignited. Chapter 3, "WeChat versus Weibo: Microblogging and Peer-to-Peer Philanthropy," provides many such examples. Most NGOs, however, are using interactive media for less risky tasks, such as building social networks to mobilize resources to bring relief to the underprivileged in impoverished rural and urban communities. How to improve an organization's communication capability is therefore a major concern. The mobile apps and other ICT tools that interest Chinese NGOs naturally gear more toward service provision than contentious lobbying.

This reality, which many consider crippling to the operation of Chinese NGOs, gives rise to a potential point of contention—is social service not as valuable as social change? I mentioned earlier that the meaning of change making is interpreted differently from discipline to discipline. Cultural studies scholars are acutely aware of the traps of subscribing to dichotomous analytical frames. Quoting myself—"Domination is not total, resistance is never complete" (Wang 2001, 99)—I cannot stress strongly enough the importance of delivering ourselves from "the conceptual deadlock of power versus subjugation versus resistance" (99) when it comes to our understanding of mainland Chinese society. Chinese grassroots NGOs understand this antibinary thinking intuitively because consciousness raising and triggering small change, which often means bringing relief to the disadvantaged in the communities they serve, is what they can do and what they do best. Using social media to engage in oppositional politics is not on their agenda. I wonder if this is something that scholars in communication studies whose disciplinary premise is built on freedom of expression and oppositional activism would find problematic. Is social service to the poor and disenfranchised leading to social change? The answer ultimately rests on whether reform or revolution is deemed the most sustainable motor of social transformation in contemporary China. And who has the right to respond to that question on behalf of the entire country? These difficult inquiries continue to be debated in Chapter 3.

NGO2.0 in a Snapshot: Addressing NGOs' Communication and Technology Needs

Sorting through the issues above cleared the way for our understanding of what Chinese NGOs can do and what NGO2.0 is capable of achieving. We now turn to the programmatic design of NGO2.0 (see Figure 2.6) and the ICT needs of grassroots NGOs in China.

First, a discussion of the basic communication needs of Chinese NGOs is in quick order. I will showcase two grassroots organizations—one rural and another based in a third-tier city—that attended our Web 2.0 training workshop in 2009. Rescue Minqin in Gansu Province, an environmental NGO located in a county town undergoing drastic desertification, has a traditional website (http://www.minqin.cn/) that attracts few visitors, a dilemma typical of small and mid-sized NGOs. The faster such small websites mushroomed, the more insulated they grew from each other, fragmenting the online NGO landscape in China. Rescue Minqin had to rethink their communication strategies so that they could become more interactive. Hui Ling, a Lanzhou-based NGO helping children with learning disabilities to cope with discrimination, faced a very different problem. They did not have a website due to insufficient resources and were thus unable to reach out to a broader audience beyond the small

Figure 2.6. NGO2.0 Program Infrastructure: Addressing NGOs' Communication, Resource, and Technology Needs

city of Lanzhou. NGO2.0 addresses those needs with a twofold task: *training NGOs that already have websites to start using social media for interactive communication and convincing those without websites to bypass the expensive 1.0 architecture to leapfrog into social media practices.*

Through Web 2.0 workshops, we instruct NGOs in how to develop social media strategies and build their social network across major platforms. Initially held twice a year, these workshops train NGOs spread across seven issue areas (i.e., environment, health, women and children's rights protection, community development, rural education, LGBTQ issues, and support-type NGOs). We bring together representatives from approximately thirty to thirty-five organizations per workshop for a three-day immersive training of 2.0 concepts and tools. A critical mass of our trainees are congregated in the vicinities of Kunming (Yunnan), Xi'an (Shaanxi), Chengdu (Sichuan), Nanning (Guangxi), Hefei (Anhui), Changsha (Hunan), Lanzhou (Gansu), Yinchuan (Ningxia), and Guiyang (Guizhou), and more recently, Shenzhen, Beijing, Chongqing, Hangzhou (Zhejiang), Nanchang (Jiangxi), and Wuhan (Hebei). We anticipated, but were still pleasantly surprised by, the snowball effect triggered by our trainees who, after attending the workshops, voluntarily held local workshops training smaller grassroots in their hometowns. Our teachings have thus trickled down from province to province and from mid-sized to tiny organizations.

The C in ICTs: Communication 2.0

How is Web 2.0 changing the ways NGOs mobilize support and empower themselves and the communities they serve? The best of our trainee NGOs have developed skills in using ICTs to fulfill specific missions. Rural-based Rescue Minqin, for example, resorts to Weibo and WeChat to build an ecologically conscious online community, to which they make open calls for volunteers to travel to Minqin and plant trees in the desert bordering the county. Rescue Minqin's media-savvy not only brought the national spotlight and resources to Minqin, but also helped slow down the exodus of local youngsters fleeing to cities in search of a better livelihood. Just as a greener Minqin is dependent upon the ability of the NGO (and its local government) to impress upon the general public the urgency of "saving the next Lop Nur,"[22] so can we argue that ICTs for communication is a prerequisite for the survival of grassroots NGOs. The C in ICTs can never be overestimated.

Let us examine another example, Greening Han River, a Hubei-based grassroots NGO we trained in 2011. Inspired by our training, the organization live-broadcast the entire journey of water testing the polluted Han River using microblogs. Members of NGO2.0 followed the water testers on Google Buzz and shared the results of their stop-by-stop inspection in real time. The day-long connectedness was remarkable, given we all lived in different parts of China! The benefits of this experiment were numerous: it helped Greening Han River gain more transparency about this annual event. Donors and the NGO's board members could follow the team virtually and participate as active observers in real time. Most interestingly, they attracted a few strangers to virtually follow the water-testing team and spontaneously report polluted spots. A crowdsourced practice like this raises consciousness and mobilizes local residents to care about their own river and not litter.

These two examples led me to postulate that NGOs could play a role *as facilitators of behavioral change,* an insight promoters of ICT for development need to learn by heart. Just as I will propound later in the conclusion of this book, ICT4D (information and communication technology for development) evangelists often fail to understand that tech-driven projects must not begin with, or stop, at technological innovations. Consciousness raising and community building should go in tandem to achieve sustainable collaboration among multiple stakeholders (donors, NGOs, local government and local communities, engineers and other technologists, as well as the private sector). NGOs should be enlisted to do what they do best: advocating their cause (saving water and planting *suosuo* trees in Minqin's case, and keeping their river clean in the Han River example). A better and more just society demands a change of old attitudes, something technology alone cannot achieve. Relegating technological matters to other players such as the engineers and the private sector, NGOs can better concentrate on knowledge transfer and community building—that is, *making their contribution through the C in ICTs by resorting to social media as a means for sustainable and scalable communication.* Indeed, returning to our earlier debate on social service versus social change, I argue that changing consciousness and behavior constitutes the first step toward transformation of any kind.

I should add that such transformations are rarely extreme, for China's advocacy efforts are characteristically nonconfrontational. Even potentially controversial campaigns are staged in calculated restraint to achieve a longer-term impact. A 2013 campaign organized by Chinese LGBTQ communities is a case in point. When news broke that Iceland's prime minister Jóhanna Sigurðardóttir and her lesbian partner were paying China an official visit, a grassroots NGO based in Guangzhou, Supporter4Gay-Love, strategized ways of using new media to promote social acceptance of homosexuality. During and after the Prime Minister's visit, her wife was purposefully removed from all mainstream media reports. The NGO founder A Qiang spread the news through a blog post which the host publisher Sina featured on its front page. The author's second blog also turned out to be an instantaneous eye-grabber. With a click rate of 816,031 times within a few days, it kicked off a tongue-in-cheek campaign slogan "let's search for the Prime Minister's 'harmonized' wife" (A Qiang 2018). This example and other various Weibo case studies showcased in Chapter 3 indicate that the early 2010s witnessed the heyday of creative activism enabled by blogging and microblogging.

The T in ICTs: Designing Nonprofit Technology

As mentioned earlier, NGO2.0 is designed to mobilize indigenous Chinese resources and build grassroots NGO leadership by identifying and training *media* and *tech-conscious NGO change makers*. Although in the beginning our strength lay in meeting the communication demands of NGOs, as early as 2009 we had aspired to build technology cooperatives. As we matured, building local technology expertise became a priority because two missing pieces had fallen into place in the mid-2010s: a technology-ready nonprofit sector and an emerging critical mass of socially concerned techies based in first-tier cities.[23] This new phase of programming enabled NGO2.0 to shift gear to pursue a double-tracked approach of strengthening the C (communication) and T (technology) in ICTs simultaneously.

Greening Han River's 2011 water testing journey on Google Buzz and Twitter via Follow5 was an inspirational experiment. Since then, NGO2.0 has explored ways of motivating more NGOs to create customized social media solutions to the problems they face. Since most NGOs are incapable of conceptualizing or making tools by themselves, they need help from programmers and interaction designers. By 2013, socially concerned techies from IT companies had formed communities in Beijing, Shanghai, and Guangzhou. Mobilizing them is a matter of tapping into the venues they frequent and building activities appealing directly to their faith in the transformative capability of technology to make a more just society.

In 2013, with the help of TechSoup Global, a US-based technology nonprofit, NGO2.0 kicked off a series of civic hackathons or hackfests, where techies and NGOs congregate and design nonprofit tech solutions together. Hackathons were originally events where programmers, interface designers, and product managers got together to create software prototypes in a day or two. Traditional hackathons usually take place in areas where tech companies are thickly populated such as Silicon Valley, but they can easily be repurposed if we throw NGOs into the mix.

What does a typical civic hackathon look like? We create a local cluster in each chosen city made up of three stakeholder groups—local NGOs, local techie communities, and a local university with strong software and interaction design departments. Together, the three groups come together for regular hackathons and tech salons, through which local resources are mobilized to solve local problems, a model we successfully implemented in Guangzhou, which we later replicated in Beijing, Shanghai, and Shenzhen. The overall goal is to spread the concept and practice of collaborative design that integrates the combined expertise of programmers, NGOs, makers, interaction designers, and ideally, product managers. This model emphasizes seamless collaboration of all stakeholders and is structured to trigger mind-set change in all parties involved. It only works if participants opt for horizontal rather than vertical decision making. When the hacker ideal of openness is faithfully observed, hackathons have a lot to teach to leaders of the first-generation ICT4D projects—top-down projects driven entirely by technological determinists and the GDP-focused definition of development—a topic I will treat thoroughly in the conclusion of the book.

Civic Hackathons in Action

Civic hackathons, however, are not silver bullets. They need to overcome many obstacles as well. Besides technological determinism, techies are prone to mistake trending technology for the best technology. On the NGO side, articulating technology needs is not their forte. Easily intimidated by technology, many of them see ICTs as nothing more than website construction or some grand digital system not deliverable through a thirty-six-hour long hackathon.

How does a civic hackathon work on the ground? I attended one held by NGO2.0 in July 2013.[24] We first held a preparatory session where eight NGOs were invited to present user stories that became the basis for defining the functions of software that techies would help design. A user story captures the who, what, and why of an NGO's needs. Programmers and designers are then called upon to provide suggestions to sharpen the user stories. Out of the initial eight organizations, we picked six to attend the hackathon. Each of the six teams included at least one techie, one interaction designer, the NGO who proposed the user story, and other idea generators like myself. The team I joined was tasked with designing a crowdsourced audio book app for the blind, an idea proposed by an NGO serving that particular community.

We first discussed our project goal. Although plenty of similar products exist in the market, most e-readers have a limited inventory of books. Furthermore, they are read by robots, the syntax is broken up, the voice cold, with no interaction between the reciter and the listener. The NGO wanted to break down the boundary between blind and seeing people, reciter and listener, so that the blind would not feel different and insulated from "normal" people. If implemented, this dream app could enable the blind to read for seeing people and for themselves. This is a typical example of service-oriented nonprofit technologies that are in great demand.

Edinburg-based web designer and critic Justin Reynolds provides several critiques of digital solutionism and writes about the limits of civic hacking. One of his criticisms highlights the problem-solving mentality of the engineer (Reynolds 2013). The early experiments of NGO2.0 with hackathons confirmed Reynolds' critique. To further complicate the task, NGOs expect nothing short of a miracle from tools. And their lack of understanding that collaborative design does not end with a thirty-six-hour hackathon often doomed the well-intentioned efforts of techies to failure. Over time, to make them work, NGO2.0 has had to repurpose solution-focused hackathons and turn them into design-thinking (DT) workshops, teaching NGOs how to adopt a user-centric mind-set and helping them identify real needs by pinning down the who (the flesh-and-blood community they serve), what (the service they wish to provide), and why (confirmation of why the community needs the proposed solution). In 2016, we tried this new model by collaborating with the Demoo Team of Tencent.com—the IT company's volunteer techie community—and held a hackathon in the famed Tencent Academy, training Shenzhen-based NGOs to use design thinking to create prototypes of the mobile apps they proposed to create. The output was an assortment of programmed interfaces drawn with a mobile prototyping tool Modao, among them an interface for a family tree project (see Figure 2.7).

The design-thinking model works because its focus has shifted from the engineer-maker to the community of users, and from the stress and hardship required to iron out an end product to having fun in the design process. NGO2.0 continues to hold regular hackathons, such as the Minqin Challenge detailed in Chapter 5. But we are happy to find that design-thinking workshops provide a real alternative to hackathons. They help NGOs to return to the basics—positioning their mission in accurate terms,

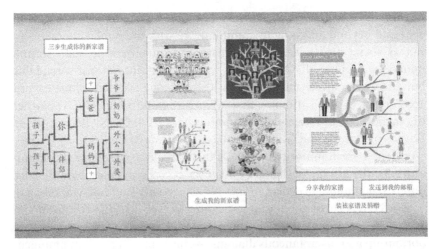

Figure 2.7. A Prototype Output for the 2016 Hackathon Held at the Tencent Academy

finding what differentiates them from competitors, and revalidating the demand for any service, digital or not, they propose to deliver to the communities they serve.

Technology Determinism Revisited

Hackathons and design-thinking training notwithstanding, and in spite of what I presented above, only a minority of China's grassroots NGOs can take full advantage of ICTs. Most of them serve small communities and their services remain local, whether or not they have gone digital. Many NGOs in our workshops are locale-*bound,* facing very locally defined problems. Sometimes, young NGO workers quit their jobs and relocate for better livelihoods. Yet a strong commitment to their rural hometown summons them back, as in the case of Ma Junhe who left a comfortable life in Kunming for his beloved desert town Minqin. Rescue Minqin's clientele is predominantly located in Minqin County and Lanzhou City of Gansu Province. Daba Mountain Environmental and Poverty Research Association helps impoverished townships and villages at the Daba mountainous areas in Sichuan.[25] Both rural NGOs have built Web 1.0 websites, which is a feat in itself already. But simply going digital does not guarantee sustained visibility. Their main challenge lies in learning how to market their conviction and service to a national audience and beyond and how to communicate with the public interactively. But as social media went mainstream and our attention span shrank minute by minute, NGOs have had to make content not just spreadable but also competitively creative, a task technology trainings alone cannot accomplish. I should also note that NGO2.0's three original NGO partner organizations—the erstwhile Kunming-based NGOCN, Beijing-based Friends of Nature, and Guangzhou-based Institute of Civil Society (ICS)—represent a small minority of NGOs that serve *cross-provincial* communities. To the dismay of digital evangelists, ICS accrues national influence purely from holding regular, *offline* NGO capacity-building workshops.

For NGOs currently bound to traditional websites, the constraints of Web 1.0—an essentially top-down broadcaster that cannot generate bottom-up and instantaneous dialogue—constitutes but one communication bottleneck. I often wonder if the acquisition of social media knowledge and skills can help NGOs attract not only eyeballs but also long-term resources as Ma Junhe did for Rescue Minqin. I also ponder other questions beyond NGO operations. Will the translocal networked communication we promote affect our target NGOs' identity formation? Is the theoretical emphasis on translocality, transnationalism, and globalization really relevant? I am acutely aware of these questions as we move forward. The bottom line, I argue, should not be about the validation of academic theories or the celebration of social media for its own sake, but whether these new concepts and tools can make a difference—helping NGOs improve their transparency, sustain growth, and trigger real change on the ground.

Now the inevitable question of scale: To what extent is the concept of the local and the provincial still crucial to the operation of NGOs who are now entering the digital era and functioning in a Web 2.0 environment that is supposedly geography blind? To do justice to that question, I suggest that we undo the conventional association of the local and the provincial with offline reality alone. We also need to readjust our perception that offline is somehow less progressive than online experiences. To do that kind of unbundling necessarily entails another radical conceptualization, that is, untying the inextricable link of the global reach with "bigger" and somehow more "advanced" humanity. What NGO2.0 has taught me is that as far as humanity is concerned, the scale of "big" and "small" doesn't apply. Local, individual lives are worth as much as, if not more than, the abstract formulation of the "global village." Each act of compassion counts. How can we care about the globe if we have little interest in serving our local community?

Researcher or Activist?

Those inquiries signaled just the beginning of my methodological reflection, which I pursue in a full-fledged fashion in Chapter 6, "Participatory Action Research and the Chinese Challenge." Equally pertinent is this question: What is the proper relationship between research and practice? How do I treat NGO2.0 as something accountable in research terms? To be frank, no matter how much I think that the project naturally falls within the domain of participatory action research (PAR), I remain uncomfortable with the positivist tradition ingrained even in this progressive brand of scholarship. Although PAR theorizes "research objects" as full decision-making subjects whose relationship with the scholar is nonhierarchical (Heron 1996; Reason and Bradbury 2001), writing about action as lived experience is in itself an "othering" practice, as Olav Eikeland (2006) puts it.

Regarding the basic tenets of PAR, Paul Atkinson and Martyn Hammersley proposed a fourfold typology: complete observer, observer as participant, participant as observer, and complete participant (Atkinson and Hammersley 2012). I belong to the fourth category. Regrettably, the holistic ontology of "complete participation" is undermined as soon as the reckoning of scholarship emerges to dictate the agenda of writing. Can I write as an activist in a scholarly journal? Do I have to choose in whose voice—an activist or a scholar—I am writing? The insider/outsider question is one I struggle with constantly. The same question can lead to a mind game that turns a living project into a mere representation, crystallized and flattened out.

Although there is a prolific corpus of PAR handbooks, none seem to satisfactorily help resolve those questions. I return to the basics. For instance, Rebecca Hagey saw in PAR a focus on serving the "oppressed groups whose issues include inaccessibility, colonization, marginalization, exploitation, . . . etc." (Hagey 1997, 1). All PAR scholars would agree that the "research problem" originates within the community and that the relationship between researcher and community is characterized by a dialogue between intellectuals and the people they wish to serve (Reason 1994). All these theoretical propositions come very close to the practice of NGO2.0.

That said, I remain wary of a complete subscription to PAR because it can arrest motion and movement, reduce what is amorphous and experimental into *"planned* action," and turn experience into a didactic handbook on empowerment. Eventually, I coined the term *social media enabled action research* in the spirit of cultural studies, using the term to evoke an activist's Geminian imagination of a born-again researcher. To cultural studies I turn in search of an agenda that takes "the whole system of knowledge itself and, in Walter Benjamin's sense, attempt[s] to put it at the service of *some other project*" (Hall 1990, 18, italics mine). That "some other project" is NGO2.0 in my context. Concretely speaking, in my vision, social media enabled action research approximates a scholarly affordance that captures the authenticity of NGOs' practices and my own *modus operandi* as an activist-scholar. The possibility of "knowing in practice"—this entire book being the ultimate testimony—can be as tangible as activism itself.

On the other hand, activism, like knowledge production at large, involves a reflexive process. Critical engagements make me a better advocate for NGOs and get me better prepared for examining the strengths and blind spots of our venture. This includes an honest assessment of the relationship I have established with the NGO community and how much control we give community members to mold the future of NGO2.0. In what ways does such research help strengthen digital activism? I am also intrigued by a question relevant to those living under authoritarian regimes: How are grassroots institutions regulated, and enabled in turn, by policy discourse and how can these discourses be maneuvered by those subject to hegemony? These are staple questions that both cultural studies critics and PAR researchers should ask, to which the framework of nonconfrontationalism, detailed in Chapter 1, provides partial clues. Could a thoughtful blend of PAR and cultural studies, being made self-conscious of their own disciplinary vulnerabilities, serve as an antidote for a full-length academic treatment of NGO2.0?

Conclusion

This chapter highlighted grassroots NGOs as the most taken for granted but the most vulnerable change makers in contemporary China. I examined the ecosystem of social media usage by Chinese NGOs via an introduction of a new brand of ICT-powered activism practiced by NGO2.0, an ongoing nonprofit I founded in China ten years ago. Critical issues contributing to our understanding of the intertwining of social media and social action were laid out, and the context in which NGOs function in a regime known for its censorship vigor was reexamined in terms of non-confrontational activism. The discussion unfolded, layer after layer, methodological questions regarding the relations between "action" and "research" as well as the promise and limits of the tech4good vision.

The next chapter moves from NGO to a less notable change maker—the IT corporation as an enabler of social media activism. I illustrate how Sina .com's and Tencent.com's peer-to-peer platforms serve Chinese activists and socially concerned mass audiences. These two rivals on China's social graph linked social networking with social good, pulling open the curtain of the era of "everybody a donor" and bringing social media enabled mass activism into the spotlight.

3

WeChat versus Weibo

Microblogging and Peer-to-Peer Philanthropy

Scandals travel far everywhere in the world but very rarely have we seen a nation where people react to notoriety on such an epochal scale. Just as in 2003 infamous cyberfeminist Mu Zimei single-handedly popularized blogging in China via her sex diaries,[1] so too in 2011 did Guo Meimei, a second-generation internet celebrity, who identified herself as the "commercial general manager" of the Red Cross, tarnished the reputation of the philanthropy sector, and turned upside down the dynamics of charity donations in China. Thanks to the scandal, enraged netizens on Sina Weibo, the microblogging site on which Guo showed off her luxury handbags and Maserati, made a public parade of her vanity and depravity, drawing hundreds of thousands of fellow netizens to shame the Paris Hilton-like vainglorious woman.

No matter that it turned out that Guo Meimei feigned her identity as a Red Cross manager; the damage to the state-run foundation was done. Red Cross China never fully recovered from the 2011 furor. But what did Guo Meimei have to do with social media activism?

The Scandal of Guo Meimei: The Good, the Bad, and the Super Good

The many and varied consequences of the scandal can be divided into three categories: the good, the bad, and the super good. Conceivably, the public trust in the philanthropy sector went bankrupt—bad news for all employed in the sector—but Guo Meimei also inadvertently kicked off a rigorous national discussion about philanthropy, a topic previously not considered sexy enough to attract media attention. Furthermore, by dragging the reputation of the philanthropy sector through the mud, the incident did a huge favor to nonprofits by alerting them to the importance of building credibility online. It seems as if overnight, Chinese philanthropy in its entirety underwent a transformation, with grassroots organizations and foundations alike flocking in unison to Weibo and other digital platforms to post their missions and activities, thus providing easy access for the public to check the details of their operations and financial accountability. Since then, transparency has become a key ingredient of the digital content created by NGOs. In the wake of the Guo Meimei scandal, restoring public trust was an urgent matter felt acutely by the nonprofit sector. Although mastering the nuts and bolts of social media took time, by 2016, when NGO2.0 conducted our fifth survey on Chinese NGOs' internet usage patterns, 60.45 percent of the 531 participating grassroots had posted their financial report regularly on digital and social media platforms (NGO2.0, NGO-IU Survey 5, 2017).

Triggering an entire sector's pursuit of accountability was one of the many good repercussions the scandal set off. China's most despised woman made an even bigger impact on the social ethos—she unwittingly gave impetus to the rise of the discourse and practice of "everybody a donor"—a tale to be told later—and expedited the march of the Chinese philanthropy sector into the era of crowdfunding.

This chapter tracks the rise of commercial players as crucial enablers of activism 2.0 through the spinning of the slogan "everybody a donor" and ends with a theoretical discussion of the "agency versus structure" problem seen in the larger context of nonconfrontational activism, Chinese style.

Before we turn to social media enabled activism, a quick critique of the phenomenon is called for, not because starting with a disclaimer is an efficient way of clearing the path for the main task at hand, but just as I was critical in the previous chapter of the limits of tech4good activities, I deem it important that we stay alert to the pitfalls of celebrating a medium conceived as open to all and therefore taking for granted its "liberatory" potential.

Social Networking and Social Action

Many founding architects of the internet have deplored the falling from grace of the open web. The first question is "Does cyberspace offer a new forum for emancipatory politics?"[2] The answer to that question is no longer as crystal clear as Howard Rheingold and other internet enthusiasts envisioned a decade ago (Rheingold 2005). It doesn't help that the 2018 Facebook data breach scandal continues to generate negative press about Facebook and big tech. The misuse of user data for covert political purposes by Cambridge Analytica, an erstwhile collaborator of Facebook, dealt a severe blow to the fairy tale that social media is a panacea for activism and global connectedness. The past decade also witnessed the internet falling into use as an instrument of surveillance manned by authoritarian as well as democratic regimes (Assange and Appelbaum 2016; Chase and Mulvenon 2002; Corera 2016; Fuchs, Boersma et al. 2012; Lovink 2016; Nayar 2010; Stanley and Steinhardt 2003). Internet trolling committed by heinous provocateurs had evolved into "an alt-right's version of political activism" long before Donald Trump took white supremacists mainstream (Stein 2016). The hyperinterconnectedness brought on by social media further escalated the tyranny of the smart mob. Cyberspace, once a haven for counterculture ideologists, is now subject to as many reactionary forces as progressive ones. By the time the *MIT Technology Review* published a long overdue reflection on the road digital technologies traveled from Tahrir Square to Trump, it was already a well-known fact that the same instruments for spreading democracy can also become weapons for attacking it (Tufekci 2018). This validates once again the truism that no medium is inherently liberatory.

Taking the beneficial potential of cybercultures—in which social media dominate—with a grain of salt, let us now turn to the brighter half of the story: new media utilized as alternative media in progressive politics. Movement researchers, communication scholars, and network analysts have reached a consensus that mobilization today has evolved into "mediated mobilization" through which activists resort to blogging, tweeting, social friending, and other software tools to cultivate participatory networks for sporadic or sustained political action (Castells 1996, 2009; Shirky 2008; Downing 2008; Lievrouw 2011; Milan 2013; Carty 2015). Previously marginalized and disadvantaged groups can now gain visibility, upload their stories for viral dissemination, and in so doing, they can now advocate for alternative views typically shunned by mainstream media.

Numerous cyberactivists have borne witness to the efficacy of social media as a means of building networked communities and find in them infinite possibilities of altering power relations in the material world. Those challenges to the status quo, however, are usually made up of discrete moments of disruption and resistance—nomadic, episodic political acts that often do not add up to sustainable and revolutionary changes on the ground. Tactical in nature in the true de Certeau spirit, those forms of hit-and-run media practice are rightfully dubbed "tactical media" (Garcia and Lovink 1997; Cubbitt 2006). Whether this phenomenon was an inevitable outcome of the radically fragmented subjectivity of postmodernity as David Garcia and Geert Lovink have suggested (Garcia and Lovink 1997), we are surely entering an era where the networked, sporadic form of social action is becoming the norm of contemporary activism.

This raises the question: What impact have the disruptions of Web 2.0 technology wrought on the pillar of civil society—the NGOs? Is the new networking practice, the politics of connection so to speak, breaking down their long-established patterns of doing organized work? Have the fundamentals changed? Chapter 2 picked up those questions in the context of social media literacy training and found that Chinese NGOs' adoption of Web 2.0 tools is confined to the tactical rather than the strategic. In fact, when the term *activism 2.0* is invoked in China, what usually comes to mind are not NGO-driven activities but a commercial campaign of "social media for social good" associated closely with two Chinese IT conglomerates, Sina.com and Tencent.com. Why aren't NGOs the major players of social media activism?

Web 1.0-Style Communication Dies Hard

In 2009 when I founded NGO2.0, a China-based nonprofit organization specializing in ICT-powered activism, I made an assumption that Chinese NGOs were more than a decade behind in their adoption of social media practices compared to their US counterparts. At workshop after workshop for grassroots NGOs, I emphasized to our trainees that microblogging is used to create interactive communities instead of broadcasting original content top-down around the clock. "Don't perform 1.0 tasks on Web 2.0 platforms" is the clarion call I made to all workshop participants. Listening not uploading, conversing not broadcasting—are the golden tenets I impart to all my students. I was tireless in my propaganda, but the students who ended up following the prescribed 60/30 principle (listening and conversing versus uploading and broadcasting) were rare. The great majority did exactly the opposite—60 percent of their microblog posts were self-promotional, a miniscule 15 percent were retweets and conversational posts.

Years later, I came across studies that explored how US-based NGOs fared in the social media environment. To my surprise, the statistics showed that their social media behaviors are no different than the Chinese grassroots NGOs. Most American nonprofits still use Twitter as an extension of their information-heavy official websites. The tweets are informational rather than dialogic and action-oriented (Lovejoy and Saxton 2012). That is, American organizations are also missing the bigger picture of social media as a community-building and mobilization tool. A second study on advocacy organizations yields similar findings—NGOs in the sample used Twitter "mainly for information dissemination and public education purposes . . . Tweets that carry an explicit call to action are proportionally small" (Zhao and Saxton 2014, 69, 72). A third article offered a content analysis of one hundred organizations and found that most of them adhered to one-way messaging strategies and that they "overwhelmingly prefer" to use their traditional 1.0 website to cultivate relationships with their stakeholders (Waters and Feneley 2013). A fourth study on US human service NGOs conducted in 2015 reached a similar conclusion; to wit, the use of social media as a major communications outlet is not as pervasive as one might expect (Goldkind 2015, 393). Those four reports strike the same note, that NGOs in the most technologically advanced country have yet to truly embrace genuine social media communication. Regardless of location—North America or China—a paradigm change in the nonprofit sector will be slow because the gap between the purported use and actual use of interactive tools is not closing any time soon.

The reasons for NGOs' timidity in adopting social media strategies vary from organization to organization, but include, to name a few, the absence of a communication officer for small organizations, inadequate social media literacy for legacy organizations, and no less important, the lack of plans for evaluating the success of social media campaigns for all NGOs, big or small. For those grassroots NGOs located in places with slow processors and limited bandwidth, such as Africa or the backwaters of China, text messaging remains the dominant technology of the future, not Web 2.0 tools (Singel 2008). With a small handful of exceptions, NGOs are not the earliest and most creative practitioners of activism 2.0, wherever they are located.[3] Other players—IT companies with increasingly heavy investments in corporate social responsibility—have stepped up as the pioneers of social media enabled, peer-to-peer activism.

This is especially true in China where censorship and totalitarian politics made digital mobilization—mediated or not—by NGOs a forbidden terrain. So, what else is left for social media powered activism in the Middle Kingdom? Just as most American NGOs treat social networks as a fundraising instrument rather than a mobilization venue (Luege 2015), so do their Chinese counterparts. *Social media use by Chinese NGOs is pared down to online fundraising and an instrument for validating accountability.* Crowdfunding and accountability are, in fact, two sides of the same coin, and they should be seen as the dual symptoms of the Chinese public's anxiety about a philanthropy sector that lacks transparency partly because of its structural embeddedness in the Party-state. Perceivably, the nerves of the nation are excessively fragile and supersensitive to scandals pointing to the alleged corrupt system.

Enter Guo Meimei whose notoriety brought many benefits to Chinese philanthropy, as mentioned at the beginning of the chapter. Savvy Chinese netizens thanked Guo for shattering their faith in the Red Cross and even more important, for triggering the question that matters to all: "Where should my next donation go?" (Derogatory Scholar 2014). Nonprofits and private foundations in China don't have the license to raise funds publicly. If corrupt state-affiliated foundations like Red Cross China are the only legitimate recipients of public donations, what other venues can Chinese charity donors turn to in the wake of the Guo Meimei scandal? Inevitably, online controversies of this order bring up parallel concerns about China's fundraising law that forbids grassroots NGOs from engaging in public fundraising. Where on earth can those organizations go to raise funds?

Those queries did not have to wait long for an answer. In a timely fashion, Sina.com rolled out its MicroCharity Program (*wei gongyi*) in 2012 and Tencent.com's Monthly Donation Project (*yue juan*) broke the threshold of one million donors in February of the same year (Tencent 2012). Those alternative paths for charity donation allowed the public to bypass the traditional model of donating to state-run foundations like Red Cross China. From then on, the two IT conglomerates brought on a new trend of "everybody (becoming) a donor." Peer-to-peer philanthropy for grassroots projects on those two commercial platforms took off on a scale bigger than anyone might have expected. Sina and Tencent designed a mechanism to enlist credible foundations and turned them into stand-in recipients of public funds raised in the name of targeted NGOs. Salute to Guo Meimei!—this is the "super good" consequence of the scandal.

"Everybody a Donor": The Rise of Peer-to-Peer Philanthropy

Although both Sina and Tencent would want to take the credit for initiating the discourse of *renren ke gongyi* (everybody a philanthropist), a slogan deeply ingrained in their respective social good offerings, the scale is slightly tilted toward Tencent as a supreme practitioner of philanthropy 2.0, not least because unlike Tencent, Sina did not succeed in establishing its own charity foundation. Without a nonprofit arm, Sina is crippled in its competition with Tencent whose corporate foundation serves as the primary platform on which the IT company rolls out its various experiments with social giving initiatives. The ultimate goal for both internet companies is to find ways of unlocking the philanthropic capital of Chinese society via microcharity *(wei gongyi)*.

I am giving Guo Meimei credit for initiating that trend because she sowed the seeds of public doubt about social giving sent in lump sums to big charity organizations; she ignited the public debate over the direction of philanthropy in a well-to-do society; and finally, she helped to diversify corporate thinking about donations, possibly nudging both Sina and Tencent to quicken their pace in finding creative ways of galvanizing the average Joes and Janes of China to join "social media for social good" campaigns. In short, I would designate 2011, the year of the Guo Meimei scandal, as a milestone in the history of Chinese philanthropy. Throughout that year, the Chinese public was under the sway of proliferating discourses generative of the social imaginary about a kinder China—whether we are talking about *wei gongyi, renren ke gongyi,* or *quanmin gongyi* (people's charity). The circulation of those public narratives delivered an optimistic scenario that the internet, and social media in particular, was a harbinger of digital commons in which the people could voluntarily support grassroots causes and make social donations on a massive scale.

For those understanding the inner workings of China, that was no small progress for the nonprofit sector. As I discussed in the Introduction, scarce resources and lack of stable funding are the Achilles' heels of Chinese grassroots NGOs. Unlike American nonprofits, they do not possess the legal status to raise funds in public. Now for the first time in the history of the PRC, the state gave the green light to commercial platforms—internet platforms no less—to divert the cash flow of the populace from state-owned foundations to grassroots projects. If the entire nation can be mobilized to support worthy grassroots projects on Sina's MicroCharity platform and through Tencent's P2P channels, wouldn't that be a real blessing for Chinese civil society? This suspiciously innocent rhetorical question calls for an analysis that may not be entirely optimistic, a topic I return to in the next section. For now, suffice it to say that *renren ke gongyi* has continued to dominate online and offline speeches and commentaries to this day.

On the brighter side of things, the discourse has already helped the Chinese public to formulate new societal values, challenging Fredric Wakeman's erstwhile argument that "Chinese citizens appear to conceive of social existence mainly in terms of obligation and interdependence rather than rights and responsibilities" (Wakeman 1993, 134). In a word, the year 2011 gave birth to a burgeoning consciousness, however symbolic it might appear to pessimists, that the populace can take social responsibilities into their own hands by recognizing that doing good deeds for strangers in need starts with the self and with microaction. Arguably, this discursive practice has signaled the arrival of an unofficial and a diversified philanthropy that is evolving into a mainstream activity (Center on Philanthropy 2011, 1). Although this is nothing more than making donations on open platforms rather than taking radical social actions on the streets, it seems that the experimental project of post-1989 Chinese socialism has finally found its discursive footing in linking the intrinsically interconnected ideas of common people, common good, open platforms, and digital commons.[4]

Microcharity and the Weibo Revolution: A Technical Solution for "Harmonious Society"

As shown above, it was the IT corporations rather than NGOs that were early Chinese adopters of the creed of "social media for social good." This section opens with an introduction to the scaled interventions of commercial players—Sina's MicroCharity platform, Tencent's MicroCompassion Project, and their variants. Each platform gives impetus to the emergence of a large number of 2.0 campaigns, grassroots style.

I asked earlier in the Introduction whether interventions by commercial actors and their newfound role in shaping social ethos and citizen responsibility can be seen as a boon in disguise for Chinese society. Truly, if we argue that the social is constructed discursively, what does it mean that the Communist state has given a free rein to the IT sector in shaping public discourse?

My first analytical order is to decipher the politics underlying the corporate discourse of "everybody a donor" by situating it in the larger picture of the Chinese social. The popularization of a discourse in an authoritarian country riven by acute class divisions cannot merely be seen as symptomatic of awakened social conscience long overdue. Nor should the state's blessing of the corporate-engineered discourse be seen solely as the result of the Communist Party's sanctioning of the profit-making impulse of internet conglomerates. Yes, there is the old premise that the internet is seen by Party leaders primarily as a sector of informationalization whose prosperity benefits China's economy. I argue there is something else at work here, which is mediated by technology.

If we define the social as the meeting place of collective relationships and contending values, then the social media sector—the spinner of networked relationships—participates actively in constituting a new sociopolitical order. I will go a step further by attributing the political legitimacy of *renren ke gongyi* to its perfect alignment with the Communist state's governing strategy that prioritizes the making of "harmonious society."

China scholars of right and left ideologies have shown us how various inequitable forces crisscross a society fractured along class, rural/urban, labor/capital, and regional conflicts. What role does media communication play in a country besieged by both real and imaginary threats of collapse? Foregrounding the central role of communication in the process of China's social transformation, media scholar Zhao Yuezhi treats communication not only as a key phenomenon of politics, but as an increasingly important site of capital accumulation and a crucial means of *social organization* (Zhao 2008, 11, italics mine). I will push her viewpoint a bit further by arguing that media platforms like MicroCharity and MicroCompassion serve as effective tools of *social management* as well, by which urgent social problems like the gap between the rich and the poor are harmonized through a 2.0-style philanthropy that creates open networks of compassion by connecting the haves and the have-nots, enabling the former to lend a helping hand to the latter. Come show your compassion to the needy! Donate 10 yuan every month to grassroots projects and bring relief to the marginalized! *Through Web 2.0 technology, Sina and Tencent offer the Chinese state a dream solution of mobilizing the middle class to give to the poor and the underprivileged.* Technologies utilized for the purpose of nurturing rather than disrupting harmony are the real reason that the longevity of the discourse of "everybody a donor" is guaranteed in China.

The corporate sector, furthermore, occupies a privileged position in China. It is not bogged down by responsibilities that plague the state nor is it tied to the politically sensitive civil society. A freer entity in the triangle, it has nonetheless maintained a natural synergy with activism, as communication scholar Guobin Yang attests. The synergy exists because "Internet businesses make profit from promoting online contention" (Yang 2009b, 15). In a similar fashion, Tencent and Sina's philanthropy 2.0 portals benefit from their provision of technical solutions to sustain a "harmonious society." I hesitate to use the term "complicity" to characterize the relationship between corporate 2.0 players and the government not least because as Zhao Yuezhi points out, the Chinese state is a multiheaded contradictory entity and morally ambiguous. It is too easy, and intellectually irresponsible, to dump it summarily into the category of "evil empire." Nor can we talk about consumerism and the market today in the same critical idiom endorsed by critical theorists trained in the tradition of the Frankfurt School. The tech class is a different brand of business elite. Sina.com and Tencent.com are internet companies priding themselves in promoting the value of the open web. And the digitally adept, post-90s generation of young donors, which contributed 79 percent of total donations on Sina's MicroCharity platform, is a new demographic that calls for careful scrutiny (Meng 2014)—a topic treated at length in Chapter 4, "Millennials as Change Agents on the Social Web."

In police states, walking around political landmines while concocting a liberatory vision is a delicate matter to say the least. Human agency in those places is exercised on the interstitial scale in between the legitimate and the prohibited. Passing a clear-cut moral judgment on the technological elites at Sina and Tencent is difficult. Web 2.0 technology has disrupted hierarchical mechanisms and top-down mandates. Open platforms like Weibo have opened up a space for socially concerned Chinese netizens to create a new brand of bottom-up, peer-to-peer philanthropy. But if there is any cautionary tale I want to deliver to cyberutopianists, it is that technopower is also a form of power that can be used either in its full constructive capacity or abused. Right now, it looks like under Charles Chao's guard, Weibo is undergoing depoliticization by doubling down on frivolous celebrity charities, and Pony Ma is equating philanthropy with the extravaganza of the Tencent Giving Day, an annual event discussed in detail later. The two CEO-presidents of Sina and Tencent need to dream *bigger* and leverage the power of the internet to create a philanthropy whose impact would exceed corporate branding.

MicroCharity and Grassroots Advocacy

Once upon a time, Sina had a dream. It launched in 2012 a new social platform named MicroCharity *(wei gongyi)*, which allowed its millions of verified users to initiate charity activities through microblogs. Platform users were divided into two basic categories—those in need of help and those answering those calls. By 2013 when the Ya'an earthquake hit Sichuan Province, 60,000 users donated approximately 80.4 million yuan (US$13.01 million) through the open platform (Chen 2013), and on MicroCharity's third anniversary, a cumulative total of 240 million yuan were raised (Sina.com 2015). The competitive advantage of the Sina model resided in its tireless experiment with grassroots formulas that lowered the threshold of public charity. In a matter of three years, the offerings on MicroCharity multiplied into numerous subbrands, the better known among them are "individual call-for-help initiator" *(geren qiuzhu)*, "branded cause" *(pinpai juan)*, and "micro hotspots" *(wei huati)* which initiated China's hashtag activism.

How does one set up "individual call for help" on Weibo? Lu Ruoqing, a twenty-three-year-old woman diagnosed with leukemia, was in desperate need of a stem cell transplant. She kept a microblog diary detailing her daily condition and finally, thanks to the retweeting effort by Weibo celebrities, she attracted the attention of Charles Xue, an angel investor who initiated a fundraising Weibo campaign on Lu's behalf and raised enough funds in just three days to pay for her transplant. In the typical fashion of microcharity, the donations were all small but they added up quickly. Not all individual help seekers on MicroCharity are credible. However, despite the occasional negative press revolving around false information fabricated by dishonest individual initiators, calling for help from strangers online has turned into a popular practice. And for compassionate bystanders, answering those calls has become a new form of citizen action.

Lest one should question the broader social impact of such action, famed journalist Deng Fei's influential 2011 Weibo campaign—which fed 80,000 children per day in more than 300 schools spread over central and western China—forced the government's hand to respond in kind. In 2012, China's State Council rolled out "The Project to Improve the Nutrition of Rural Students Schooled under Compulsory Education" with a pledged investment amounting to 16 billion yuan per year. By early 2015, 32 million children in 1,315 counties have benefited from the governmental subsidy program that parcels out 4 yuan per student per day to improve their school meals (The State Council Information Office 2015). This exemplary case shows how microcharity can actually lead to successful advocacy. I call it "shadow advocacy," as Deng Fei and his Weibo supporters were not consciously engaged in policy advocacy. We can also label it a savvy "human-sea military tactic" *(renhai zhanshu),* Chinese style. What is the underlying message? Beware, the crowd has spoken, can the government please pay close attention?! This case study goes beyond simple philanthropy, and I will enter it into the chronicle of Chinese nonconfrontational activism.

The second well-known offering on MicroCharity is called "branded cause," whose signature specimen was the Ice Bucket Challenge, a campaign formula designed to raise money for both research and NGO work focused on ALS, a chronic disease better known as Lou Gehrig's disease.[5] The Ice Bucket Challenge was actually a copycat practice borrowed directly from the US where the challenge raised nearly $100 million (Kanter 2014). In China, the online sightings of billionaires and movie stars dumping a bucket of ice water over their heads was less about consciousness raising for ALS than watching a replicable, networked carnival. Notwithstanding, the video live-streaming of the challengers raised 8 million yuan on Weibo (Zhang Ruwei 2016, 68).

The Ice Bucket Challenge has other implications for philanthropists in China. It taught the public that charitable giving can be highly experiential and therefore fun. From then on, the promotion of social causes rich with the personal-experiential became a popular Weibo formula. For example, Hunger24 is an activity Sina launches every October on World Food Day. Actors and actresses are invited to participate in a twenty-four-hour fasting campaign, which has in turn mobilized netizens to post their customized plan for the one-day fast online. A Weibo community of 160 million people was formed overnight, with many conscientious members donating money saved from the day's meal to poverty alleviation NGOs.

Hashtag Activism: When Hotspots Are Linked to Public Good

The online appeal for Lu Ruoqing and viral activities like Hunger24, Free Lunch for Children, and the Ice Bucket Challenge spread far and fast partly because they utilized hashtags (for example, #Lu Ruoqing, #experiencehunger, #freelunch, #icebucketchallenge) to good effect. Unique hashtags can generate quick online following, boost engagement, and help pin down what makes a cause unique. Hashtags have the potential of turning topics into "micro hotspots" *(re huati)*—a value proposition initiated by Sina even though it is prevalent on all social media platforms today. But Sina's MicroCharity, because of its conscientious effort in cultivating hotspots, pioneered the trend in China.

The trend of hashtag activism has been a point of contention in the US cause circles. From #StopKony, a viral campaign of 2012 that turned into a fiasco, to the powerful #MeToo movement in 2017, hashtags have been endorsed as a manifestation of "narrative agency" (Yang 2016) on the one hand, and critiqued as "oversimplification of complex problems" (Keating 2014), or "vanity activism" in which narcissistic slogans replace actual engagement (Berlatsky 2015), or "vigilante justice" in Margaret Atwood's take on the MeToo movement (Atwood 2018), on the other hand. Regardless of which camp we affiliate ourselves with, the debate can be seen as a reactivated controversy over the merits or perils of social media activism vis-à-vis traditional activism with its emphasis on systemic social change on the ground. The conclusion, likewise, will not raise many eyebrows: hashtag activism is an effective way to get the public involved in social causes, but it should not be seen as an endpoint to activism (Aalai 2018).

Oftentimes, cultural elites are reluctant to accept what marketers know: that our minds are crowded and our attention short, the simpler a message is, the better chance it gets of being heard and recalled. Consider the research findings of three experimental psychologists who studied the audience reception of the Kony2012 viral video and its more nuanced sequel (Sullivan, Landau, and Kay 2016). Their empirical findings substantiate the hypothesis that it was the simplicity of the Kony-as-enemy narrative that triggered the network effect—more than 100 million viewers watched the original Kony video within six days—which escalated the moral outrage and generated 3.7 million citizen pledges calling for the arrest of Joseph Kony (Invisible Children 2012). Disappointingly, the same group of viewers lost their interest in acting on behalf of the cause when they were shown a more contextualized picture about Uganda's problems in the video's sequel, which made clear that quick solutions weren't at hand because there were larger historical issues at play that went beyond the monstrous warlord and the guerrilla rebels under his command. Indeed, social mobilization is never about subtle intellectual argumentation. It is understandable that critics of hashtag activism target the oversimplification of the messaging encapsulated in a short hashtag.

Such criticism, however, contains within itself an implicit critique of the gullible internet crowd—a typical elitist condescension that has been reactivated in the twenty-first century toward the "masses." I saw in this ongoing controversy over hashtags a contemporary reiteration of the perpetual joust between elite culture and popular culture, between the riotous mob and smart mob, and between old-styled activists and activists coming of age in the era of Web 2.0. Returning to the Chinese context, hashtags bring us two very different problems—the degradation of hashtags into mindless hotspots in cyberspace and the lack of hashtag literacy among grassroots NGOs.

Today, if we surf on Weibo and look for the most frequently searched hotspots, we will be greeted with hashtags of the day initiated by PR agents who are promoting the trivial pursuits of the movie stars they work for, for example, #JingBoranandNiNiKissingGoodbye, #ShorthairedGaoYuanyuan, or "#Revealed:XueZhiqian'sWifeIsPregnant,"—hot topics no different from tabloid feeds. This is not surprising as Weibo positioned itself, from the very beginning, as a brand of celebrity fandom (Zhang Yi 2015), a value proposition that seems to run counter to the cultivation of citizen culture. This symptom, however, is hard to treat as the Chinese internet is ruled by the principle "entertain or die." The other problem, the "hashtag literacy" of grassroots NGOs, is not entirely intractable. NGO2.0, for example, holds regular social media literacy trainings for Chinese grassroots NGOs. We begin our instruction at every workshop with "social media communication strategy," a staple offering that contains a unit of how to use hashtags to build virtual communities and mobilize like-minded comrades (Wang 2016b, 15–17). More specifically, we teach NGOs to learn how to utilize hashtags to position themselves, gain content exposure, recruit like-minded supporters and volunteers, and identify opinion leaders within and outside the philanthropy sector. There are many rules of thumb for hashtag usage. Once they understand hashtags in terms of user-generated keywords, even the least social media savvy organization can accomplish the exercise with modest success.

Back to Sina's MicroCharity platform, regardless of my critique of its celebrity content focus, many noteworthy nonprofit projects, with or without hashtags, have thrived on the Weibo platform. Success stories include not only Deng Fei's Free Lunch for Children and the Ice Bucket Challenge but also a host of lesser-known grassroots projects. Relying on the network effect afforded by microblogging, those various examples illustrate how social networking mobilizes netizens and engages them in peer-to-peer social actions, big and small.

Activism 2.0: Case Studies

Case #1 The Bare-Head Brother.   On May 27, 2011, Guangzhou activist Peng Yanhui wrote a blog calling for 1,000 fellow citizens to shave their heads as a symbolic gesture to stop the city's Night Illumination Project on the Pearl River banks, which would cost tax payers 150 million yuan with little justification.[6] Peng posted photos of himself before and after the head-shaving on Weibo, and in twenty some hours attracted 4,000 retweets and recruited more than twenty people to follow his example and shave their heads bald—including a young woman and several children whose environmentally conscious parents encouraged them to participate (Brainbrighter 2011). What does shaving your head have to do with energy conservation? Peng argued mockingly that a thousand shaved heads could generate enough brightness to light up the Pearl River and render the expensive city project unnecessary (Figures 3.1a and 3.1b). "Every joke is a tiny revolution," says George Orwell (Orwell 1945/1998, 119), because it upsets the established order. The cheeky Weibo post went viral precisely because protests stirred up by humor—a potent form of nonconfrontationalism—camouflaged the agitators while dumbfounding the censors. Under the pressure of media exposure and public outcry, the city government trimmed down the original budget of Night Illumination by four-fifths. The joyful tempest revolving around this project continued to inspire like-minded fun-seeking activists.

Case #2 Thumbs-Up Sister.   When Peng Yanhui posted his photos and held up the protest sign subtitled "Let's Knock Off Guangzhou City's 150 Million Night Illumination Project," a young woman who dubbed herself "Thumbs-Up Sister" did a simultaneous protest against the city government for its lack of transparency about the decision-making process that led to the creation of such a wasteful project. In the name of safeguarding public interest and in pursuit of governmental accountability, she

Figure 3.1a. Peng Yanhui Before the Shave

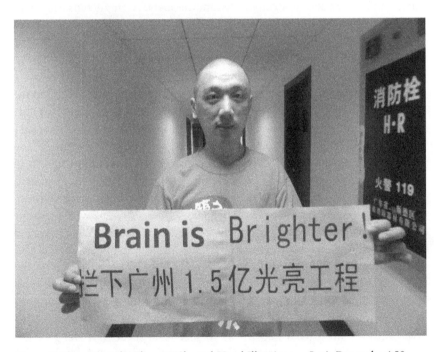

Figure 3.1b. After the Shave ("Shaved Head Illuminates: Let's Deter the 150 Million Yuan Project")

demanded that city administrators make available one of the crucial documents that underwrote the Night Illumination project. Predictably, her petition for a copy of that report hit a stone wall. The buck was passed from one office to the next with no response. A frustrated Thumbs-Up Sister eventually turned to Weibo to recruit 1,000 netizens willing to post their thumbs-up photographs, a satirical play signifying the opposite: thumbs down. While waiting for responding posts to trickle in, the daring young woman raised the stakes by bringing to the city hall two gifts meant to embarrass the authorities—a jumbo white pear (the fruit's name *yali* is homophonous to the word *pressure*) and a plastic ball shaped like a porcupine, alluding to the government's antics of passing citizen petitions from court to court like a hot potato (Figures 3.2a and 3.2b). Hundreds of thumbs-up photos turned up under the hashtag #ThumbsUpSister, delivering the facetious message to targeted officials. Damning by "fake praising" *(mingbao anbian)*—a form of indirect censure—is a tactic of nonconfrontational activism familiar to the Chinese schooled in the politics of sarcasm for thousands of years. Playful Weibo fans grasped Thumbs-Up Sister's meandering strategy instantaneously. A small sensation was created online, and not surprisingly, the feisty young woman got a belated face-to-face interview with city officials after waging war for forty-nine days (Liang 2011; Hai 2011).

Case #3 Digital Snapshot Campaigns.   2011 and 2013 also witnessed the appearance of two highly publicized grassroots Weibo campaigns made possible by the popularization of smart phones that enabled ordinary people to take digital snapshots anytime and anywhere they wanted. Sociologist Yu Jianrong launched a viral campaign "Take a Photograph to Rescue Child Beggars" in 2011, which quickly assembled an online network of more than 220,000 people retweeting on a regular basis thousands of uploaded photos of child beggars sent by netizens with the hope of identifying trafficked children (Li 2011). Inspired by Yu's project, in 2013 Deng Fei initiated an equally famous micro hotspot campaign, this time, a campaign urging ordinary people to take snapshots of polluted rivers in their hometown and upload them onto Weibo. Deng posted on his Weibo a question and a request: "How is your hometown river faring? When you are back home for the New Year, please take a photo of the river and upload it to Weibo for us to see." The success of Deng's campaign generated many sensational headlines that touted the efficacy of social media in problem solving. Reports like "China's Netizens Tackle

Figure 3.2a. Thumbs-Up Sister

Figure 3.2b. Thumbs-up Sister Brought a Pear ("Pressure") to the City Government

Water Pollution Through Weibo" and "Chinese Take Fight Against Water Pollution to Social Media" made many wonder about the actual impact of crowdsourced visual documentation of social ills. The answer was rather mixed.

Scholars in China and North America have been debating the vices and virtues of slacktivism, or "fingertip philanthropy" *(zhijian gongyi)* rendered in Chinese (Svensson 2016; Du-jitang 2017; Morozov 2009; Christensen 2011). Both are derogatory descriptions of casual and random philanthropic acts such as taking a snapshot of polluted air or rivers, as opposed to engaging in sustained environmental activism and longer-term systemic action on the ground. As an activist myself and a believer and practitioner of *both* online and offline activism, I support the argument that Twitter and other social networking platforms have enabled activists to create new communities and spread social causes to a wider public. I also believe that small acts add up and can trigger qualitative change over time. Why do activists have to choose between online and offline action? And why do researchers feel compelled to arbitrate which form is superior? Shouldn't we be happy that the internet opens up more channels for social action and that previous nonactors are now pulled in to do good at their convenience? The Chinese have a saying that runs parallel to "all roads lead to Rome"—"all rivers find their way to the ocean." The ocean of compassion does not discriminate against small streams or drops of dew.

Case #4 Environmental Testing, Public Campaign Style. "PM2.5 Monitoring"(particulate matter with a diameter of less than 2.5 micrometers) and "Measuring My City's Temperature" are good examples in this category of activism 2.0. Bare-Head Brother, Thumbs-Up Sister, Yu Jianrong, and Deng Fei are all free agents on the social web. But collective action through microblogs was as frequently invoked by grassroots NGOs as by free agents, especially organizations specializing in environmental protection. In 2003, Friends of Nature and Global Village (two environmental NGOs headquartered in Beijing) started the "26-degree campaign," which advocated for energy conservation by setting room temperatures no lower than 26 degrees Celsius in air-conditioned buildings and other public venues during the hot summer months. But it took four more years for the State Council to legitimate the grassroots effort and turn it into a policy decree (Huo 2014). Did the arrival of 2.0 platforms like Weibo make environmental advocacy easier and faster? The answer is a definite yes in view of the proliferating number of air, soil, metal, and water-testing campaigns galvanizing citizen participation that has taken root on Weibo. I will cite two more examples for illustration.

Green Beagle, an environmental NGO, launched a PM2.5 air monitoring campaign, whereby it loaned out portable air monitors to local residents who then reported the testing results online. Consciousness raising was not the only goal for Green Beagle. Its spokesman Feng Yongfeng integrated a fundraising initiative into their multicity advocacy campaign. Simply put, his objective was to mobilize 1,000 donors per city, requesting a minimum of 25 yuan per person to purchase air monitoring equipment for each city. Beijing, Shanghai, Guangzhou, and Wenzhou have all reached the goal (Wang, Jin et al. 2012). True to the Web 2.0 spirit, the original Beijing-initiated movement was soon decentralized into multiple local campaigns with netizens all over the country responding to the call by setting up their own city-named Weibo hashtags #PM2.5AirMonitoring (Han and Xu 2011).

My second example is "Measuring My City's Temperature," a microaction organized by Friends of Nature. As mentioned earlier, the city temperature monitoring campaign began as early as 2003. Although in 2007, China's State Council legalized 26 degrees as the highest temperature allowed for all public buildings in summer time, the implementation of the decree was slow and very spotty. In 2012, Friends of Nature stepped in to hold annual Weibo activities, recruiting volunteers from all over the country to measure temperatures in malls, city libraries, banks, exhibition halls, theaters, restaurants, government offices, hospitals, and on vehicles of public transportation (Friends of Nature 2014). Participating citizens were given detailed instructions about how to use different kinds of thermometers to carry out the task, complete with tips about how to post their findings on Weibo using the hashtag #measuringmycitytemperature. Thanks to the networking power of Weibo that made the campaign replicable and scalable, the annual summer activity snowballed into a multicity activity both online and offline and accrued into a valuable environmental brand in itself. Its hashtag has generated 1,799 entries and 1.71 million browsing volume (Friends of Nature 2017). Compared to other environmental campaigns nested on Weibo, Friends of Nature's 26-degree microaction fared better probably because the mission was endorsed by the state. A double win tactic is undoubtedly a popular strategy widely adopted by nonconfrontational activists in China. Can we call it activism? Of course, we can. Did an NGO necessarily compromise its integrity by engaging in what the Chinese government considers a legitimate pursuit?

No, especially if we recall that Friends of Nature has a long history of taking on offensive initiatives that touched the nerves of the state.

Case #5 Nail Biter Rescue Rhinos Campaign. This trendy campaign, jointly produced by the transnational NGO WildAid and OgilvyOne (the digital arm of a transnational advertising company), exudes the typical charm of celebrity philanthropy with an added experiential angle. The campaign opens with the striking visuals of celebrities like Richard Branson, Jing Boran, Li Bingbing, and Chen Kun biting their nails and staring into the camera. Embedded in their cute photos was the core message: "Rhino horns have nothing your own nails don't have" (WildAid 2015). Linking nail biting with WildAid's mission of ending rhino poaching was a smart marketing ploy. Young netizens loved it. They swarmed to Weibo and uploaded their own nail-biting photos. The hashtag #BiteNails-NotRhinoHorns hit the top of the micro hotspots bulletin swiftly (see Figure 3.3). A WeChat campaign was launched simultaneously, where visitors could create their own "Nail Biter" posters and share their nail-biting selfies in WeChat Moments.

Case #6 One Foundation's Winter Solstice Campaign. Can you help poor children survive the winter by wearing only a T-shirt and engaging in a fun activity on December 22, the winter solstice? One Foundation, the brain child of China's martial arts champion and kung fu movie star Jet Li, launched this experiential campaign to help children living in provinces struck by natural disasters to survive the coldest days of the year (see Figure 3.4). Each participant was asked to submit their own "cold experience" plan, share it through social media, and answer One Foundation's call for wearing a T-shirt to work on December 22 and uploading the photos of that action to Weibo. Each time a user shared his or her winter solstice experience, a business would donate one yuan to One Foundation that sent a packet of gifts to individual children (One Foundation 2015).

I am citing the example of One Foundation for comparative purposes. A Weibo search for #Cold-ExperienceVolunteers yielded only two entries and a paltry browsing volume of 411 times (Hanleng tiyan guan 2015), which pales pitifully in comparison to 23,000 entries and the 12 million browsing frequencies for the hashtag #BiteNailsToRescueRhinos (Ken zhijia jiu xiniu 2015). This comparison sent a troubling message especially because the two campaigns were rolled out a day apart from

Figure 3.3. #BiteNailsToRescueRhinos (The nutrients in your nails are the same as those in a rhino horn. Don't murder rhinos ignorantly. No rhino horn transactions, no killings!)

Figure 3.4. "I am Jet Li. I want to do Tai Chi boxing in a T-shirt at the South Pole."

each other in December 2015. What does the comparison tell us? The most obvious is that nonprofit organizations like the One Foundation were clueless about using hashtag marketing to drive online traffic. Second, trending on Weibo depends a great deal on celebrity engagement. Jet Li, alas, is a celebrity for older generations. The millennial fans, I am afraid, are pursuing younger, flashier, and often soulless idols. Third, the idea of "biting nails to save rhinos" is a cooler concept than taking off your clothes to experience what a poor kid felt on a cold winter night. Just as a Sina survey says that 62.75 percent of people interviewed expressed their reluctance to join hardship projects like the Bare-Head Brother (Wang Yiming 2015), we can assume an equal lack of enthusiasm for the winter solstice experience. I am willing to bet that the rhino campaign mobilized more slacktivists, understood in its worst connotation, than the One Foundation campaign.

As shown above, successful activism 2.0 campaigns relied on viral communications set off on Weibo. They shared one thing in common: campaigners who were well equipped with the skill of leveraging hashtags to generate online hotspots, enhance engagement, and build spectatorship. The formula of success varies, but the winning campaigns were all crowdsourced activities infused with a heavy dose of the experiential and an emphasis on the visual documentation of playful experiences. Those shared features aside, the six case studies undermine a common assumption that quantity decides impact. Take the Bare-Head and Thumbs-Up actions in Guangzhou, for example. The two free agents had a very modest proposal that called for the participation of no more than a thousand netizens apiece. In the end, neither accomplished the said quota, but both succeeded in breeding public concern about the issue and forcing the hand of the city government to modify its plan. What lesson do the two case studies deliver? While quantity often translates into social influence, there is no shortage of counterexamples that decouple the two and validate the opposite, that social impact can be brought about by microaction. Although not all microactions are clickable, I agree with Marina Svensson's analysis that we should not be too quick to dismiss slacktivist activities in China (Svensson 2016). Two formulae can be derived from this discussion:

Microaction ≠ microimpact
Slacktivism ≠ small impact

Tencent Philanthropy 2.0: The 9.9 Giving Day Sensation

As mentioned earlier, hashtags are an extremely powerful tool for maximizing content exposure, identifying people and organizations that share similar concerns, and most importantly, building civic communities online. Shaping the publics via Weibo is especially important for grassroots organizations because they have no presence in mainstream media and no better means of mobilization. In our social media literacy training workshops, NGOs are taught specific methods to create winning hashtags of their own, with which they can expedite the friending of like-minded netizens and create as well as sustain microcommunities with few management headaches. Above all, advocacy programs need to galvanize the public on a large scale, a task only an open media platform like Weibo can make happen. However, since 2014, NGOs have been fleeing in droves from Weibo to WeChat (a free mobile instant messaging app created by Tencent.com), totally oblivious to the fact that WeChat messages don't carry the same viral potential as Weibo posts because the former are circulated on a closed platform made up of atomized, private chatrooms. By the end of 2016 when NGO2.0 conducted the fifth online survey of Chinese NGOs' online communication behavior, the use of Weibo by the grassroots had decreased to 9.98 percent in comparison to WeChat's 53.3 percent upswing (NGO2.0 2017). And the hashtags? Given that most conversations on WeChat are fragmentary and visible only to highly select circles of friends, there is no use for topic hashtags. The only known tags on WeChat are used as static markers of community circles, which are not the same as Weibo's content hashtags that can mobilize and leverage person-to-person and group-to-group interactions.

What about the numerous official accounts set up by NGOs on WeChat? Aren't they "open" to a certain extent? Not exactly. Unlike Weibo, there is no option for registered official accounts on WeChat to friend each other. As a result, it is much more difficult to gain a following on WeChat than Weibo. Take myself for example; although I routinely receive invitations from known and unknown NGOs to friend them, I rarely accept those offers for fear of getting swamped by instant WeChat messages sent by hundreds of members in each group. Yes, I can block them, but then why sign up for it in the first place? Furthermore, even after I join a group, rarely have I clicked open messages sent through those official accounts, and over time, those messages have deteriorated into seasonal greetings and dull NGO propaganda materials, which further discourages recipients to click open. The vicious cycle continues. Since 2015, we have begun to witness the proliferation of dead relationships on WeChat now that the charm of the new toy is wearing out. I am not alone in using WeChat to communicate *only* with close friends, relatives, team members, and collaborators of NGO2.0.

Data speaks out loud. NGO2.0 has gained, to date, 29,361 fans on Weibo and only 3,208 on WeChat, a result hardly surprising as the size and growth rate of an online community depends a great deal on the degree of the openness of the platform. The more open it is, the bigger the crowd, and the faster community building is. Armed with similar data in hand, we consider the current trend of NGOs' exodus from Weibo to WeChat a losing communication strategy. Most NGOs forget that community building constitutes the core mission of all nonprofit organizations, a goal crippled by closed platforms that render viral communication much more difficult to achieve, which is a desirable result for the Chinese state.

WeChat versus Weibo

The rapid rise of WeChat had indeed much to do with a 2013 governmental offensive targeting VIP microbloggers—verified Weibo accounts owned by the most influential users of the platform that consist of popular writers, journalists, and other opinion leaders who attracted millions of followers. Weibo lists 347 users with "more than five million registered fans each; each of the top five has more than 50 million" (Buckley 2013). In the name of safeguarding national security and eradicating online rumor mongering, the government lashed out against a number of highly visible VIPs and issued a bylaw that would throw into prison, with a minimum of three-year sentence, any Weibo user authoring a controversial post that is viewed more than 5,000 times or retweeted more than 500 times (The Supreme People's Procuratorate 2013). The intimidation tactics silenced both vocal critics of the state and its regular users, dealing a killer blow to the platform and driving netizens to WeChat where conversations are private and thus trouble free. By cleaning the raucous platform of influential voices, the state has also brought to a halt the era of controversial viral campaign, at least for the time being. From then on, microactions like the Thumbs-Up Sister and Bare-Head Brother would have a harder time spreading, and increasingly, harmless campaigns like the Nail Biter Rescues Rhinos will take the center stage of Weibo. Some big VIPs stayed, but their posts are now tamer and feature Hollywood movie reviews and promotions for online businesses (Hatton 2015).

The sparring between WeChat and Weibo does not end there, of course. Pony Ma, the CEO of Tencent.com, has a bigger vision than simply attracting commercial brands to WeChat's 960 million-plus active users. In 2007, five years before Sina.com launched its MicroCharity platform, Ma established the first Chinese corporate foundation run by an internet company. *Renren ke gongyi* (Everybody a philanthropist) became a rallying cry for Tencent to consolidate its various philanthropy offerings. One of its staple offerings—Happy Donation—brought in a steady stream of contributions from supporters to bankroll grassroots projects that range from "one child one desk," "rescuing a migrant worker undergoing chemotherapy," "making book donations for a village school in a poverty stricken county," "sending orphans a happy spring festival," "clean water project," "preserving Tibetan culture through video production," and many other microtasks initiated either by individuals or organizations including NGOs and foundations (Tencent Foundation 2016–2017).

At first sight, Happy Donation seems like a lackluster counterpart of MicroCharity's "individual help initiator," which has utilized the celebrity effect with tremendous success. It looks like Tencent lagged behind its rival during this first round of competition. But if Sino kicked off a trend of celebrity philanthropy and cool philanthropy, Tencent Foundation delivered a gimmick-free populist philanthropy that would eventually overtake its rival in social significance. At the beginning, Tencent took a more conservative approach by posing itself as an educator introducing its huge user base to the mind-set of "everybody [can become] a philanthropist," while Sina pursues the flashier path of turning philanthropy into mass entertainment (Liu Changchun 2015). We can go a step further by congratulating Tencent for its contribution to the growth of the culture of personal philanthropy in China, a practice that Tencent started with its Monthly and Happy donation programs and reached a small breakthrough with MicroCompassion (a sub brand of Tencent Foundation), before it peaked with the 9.9 Tencent Giving Day.

The Bang of Microcompassion: The 9.9 Tencent Giving Day

Tencent Foundation's MicroCompassion Program (2011–15), also dubbed NPO+, has a clearly delineated beneficiary—grassroots nonprofit organizations—and a programmatic focus on training them to do fundraising via social media. Although it was short-lived, the program generated almost 7 million yuan in 2012 and 2013 alone (Tencent Foundation 2015)—all of which was donated by parent company Tencent itself but executed with a Web 2.0 twist. Three steps were stipulated for each nonprofit participant to follow:

Step 1. The NGO proposes a MicroCompassion project to the foundation, and upon approval, the organization releases the project information and a budget on Tencent's own microblogging platform;

Step 2. The NGO mobilizes users to retweet its posted message or share it with friends in the QQ space (another Tencent product). Each retweet or QQ share earns a 0.6 yuan donation from Tencent for the NGO. However, each user ID can only retweet the message once a day per project.

Step 3. The maximum level of support for each participating NGO is respectively 50,000 yuan (for beginner entrant), 200,000 yuan (for mid-level entrant), and 500,000 yuan (for the highest-level entrant). In a period of three months, if the organization raises more than 50 percent of its proposed budget, Tencent Foundation will pay the exact amount of the funds raised. But if the NGO fails to reach the 50 percent threshold, the project is considered aborted and Tencent pays nothing to the fundraiser.

I want to explain the rules at length so as to demonstrate the educational purpose of the program. A nonprofit organization reaching out to the lowest hanging fruit—50,000-yuan—has to flex its communication muscle to trigger 83,333 retweets of its project message in a span of three months. That's a lot to ask for organizations whose knowledge and practice of social networking is limited to say the least. To get funding from Tencent, they have no other options but to throw themselves into viral communication practices and take a crash course on Web 2.0—an act no different from plunging oneself into the ocean to learn how to swim. Tencent's move with MicoCompassion was multipronged. It boosted the volume of Tencent's microblog users overnight, outshone Sina in its savvy use of social media thinking, and paved the way for the launch of the groundbreaking 9.9 Giving Day in 2015 (Tencent Philanthropy 2015).

MicroCompassion taught Tencent Foundation a few valuable lessons. First, a three-month long viral campaign burned everybody out. Secondly, one can rely on enthusiastic public support if the funds to be raised come not from individual donors directly but from Tencent the company itself. MicroCompassion can thus be taken as a warm-up exercise for a bigger scheme of P2P philanthropy. In September 2015, Tencent Foundation replicated the idea of Giving Tuesday in the US and rolled out China's first online giving day extravaganza.

A three-day event held annually from September 7 to 9, Giving Day is short enough to sustain the (com)passion of donor-supporters but long enough to grab national attention and turn itself into a monumental brand. Although Giving Day was bankrolled by Tencent's generous matching commitment of 99 million yuan ($14,418,585) in 2015 and 199 million yuan ($28,838,612) in 2016, in 2017, the total sum donated by the public amounted to 829 million yuan ($125,000,000), which surpassed Tencent's own matching fund of 299.9 million yuan ($45,190,000) (Tencent's Report on the Result of 9.9 Giving Day 2017), a development that seems to indicate that personal philanthropy has landed in China, a false proposition I critique in the Introduction and later in this chapter.

During the first year of the campaign, if an organization raised a million yuan, the foundation would reciprocate a million yuan. The 1:1 matching scheme turned many NGOs into a frenzied crowd. Just after midnight on September 6, 2015, millions of Tencent's charity funds evaporated like mists on a sunny day, with a hefty 5 million matched away in the first five minutes and 10 million grabbed in the next fifteen minutes. Thrown into a crisis mode, the foundation staff had to step on the emergency brake and change the rules of the game at the last minute to prevent those resorting to dishonorable measures from cleaning up Tencent's pledged funds (Han 2015).

Many loopholes aside, the 2015 Giving Day was a watershed event as it unwittingly lifted the eligibility restrictions the government imposed on NGOs and other charity entities for public fundraising. Although the rules of the game have tightened in succeeding years, participation in the activity affords NGOs a precious opportunity for public exposure and a short-term increase in donor base. Sure enough, Tencent Foundation came back with a cheat-proof Giving Day program in 2016. To better motivate netizens to transform themselves from charity ambassadors into charity donors, Tencent introduced an element of play into the matching formula, a method also meant to prevent fraud. The exact amount of the match was no longer 1:1, but determined by a random algorithm. Just like playing a dice game, luck rules. By a fortunate stroke of serendipity, I earned for

NGO2.0 the maximum match for each of my three consecutive throws. Years later, I may forget how much I "robbed" Tencent of, but I will always remember the gambling thrill while awaiting the unknown matching reward I would receive during the 2016 Giving Day. Surprise is an addictive element that can turn a donor into a silly competitor with herself. In three days, I made donations ten different times with the hope of outdoing myself in getting Pony Ma's matching funds. How large was the volume of public donations processed through the event? 305 million yuan given by 6.77 million participants (Tencent Philanthropy 2016). In 2017, the amount of public donations more than doubled, and the number of donations reached an astounding 12,684,038 (Tencent's Report on the Result of 9.9 Giving Day 2017).

A record breaking 12,684,038 donors giving money in three days?! Not exactly. Lest the number lead us into assuming that China has entered the era of "everyone a donor," I need to do some statistical digging to prove it otherwise. First of all, the statistics above only indicates the total number of *times* a donation was sent rather than the number of people making a donation. The difference is huge. Take NGO2.0, for example, each of us and those we mobilized in our network donated as frequently as possible in order to grab Tencent's matching funds. That is, each of us made no less than five separate donations between September 7 and 9, a general practice for other participating NGOs. Divide 12,684,038 by 5, we derive approximately 2.5 million donors for the entire event, which amounts to only 0.27 percent of the 9 hundred million active WeChat users (Tencent Foundation 2017). The other 73 percent of them, who are unconnected to the NGO sector, paid no attention to Giving Day, a fact prompting many NGO workers to complain, legitimately, that the annual Giving Day burned them out and risked overwhelming their capacity to give. Regardless of the critiques, however, Tencent's Giving Day set a milestone for unlocking social capital by turning a minority of Chinese netizens into aggressive donors for three contiguous days.

At closer scrutiny, the significance of Giving Day goes beyond sheer numbers. The fact that those donations were made via mobile devices demonstrates that "Chinese donors are leap-frogging traditional forms of donation" (Chao 2017) and that mobile pay and social cash may be the real prey of the game. Behind charity lies the goal of beating business competition. Just like Tencent's MicroCompassion platform redirected the traffic of NGOs from rival Weibo to its own, so did Giving Day in 2015 and 2016 give WeChat Pay a leading edge over AliPay (launched by rival Alibaba). The parasitic relationship between Tencent Philanthropy and Tencent.com overdetermined the master-servant relationship between those two entities, a weakness inherited by all corporate foundations in China.

The critique of Chinese Giving Day did not stop at the criticism of the lack of Tencent Charity's autonomy from its parent company. After the fanfare ebbed a little, many thoughtful reflections emerged to question the social efficacy of the 9.9 donor festival. I mentioned earlier in the Introduction that so-called personal donations of Giving Day were mostly circulated between small circles of friends and did not spill over into the public domain. There was also a general sentiment that the outcome of Giving Day might have been be overstated by mainstream media. After all, less than 0.2 percent of charity donations in a country with 1.3 billion people came from individual donors, compared to a high 60–70 percent of donor-initiated contributions in Western developed countries (Liu Zhouhong 2015). Compared with the United States, where giving amounts to more than 2 percent of the GDP, China's giving was about a fifth of 1 percent of the GDP in 2015 (Nelson, Gao, and Li 2015). Despite the catchphrase "everyone a donor," a utopian society as such is nothing more than an ideological state of mind (Liu Zhouhong 2015; Li Xiaoyun 2016). Lastly, when IT companies encounter Web 2.0, they compete to out-maneuver each other for profit even though they innovated decentralized ways of mobilizing citizen-consumers for microactions. Can we assume that, given time, those corporate led, bottom-up mobilization models may strengthen citizen consciousness and evolve into something beyond mere donations? Many may wonder: When the power of social media is fully released, can the relationship between the state, (civil) society, and the (IT) market remain depoliticized for long?

I am afraid the answer may disappoint those wishing to witness the collapse of the Party-state. The three-way interaction is going to be fraught with nuanced maneuvering on all sides, but corporate philanthropists harken to the creed of nonconfrontational activism as vigilantly as NGOs and foundations. Whether such a scenario is seen as beneficial or detrimental to the welfare of the Chinese people may depend on where you reside, within or outside China. Meanwhile, the state seems to be willing to make some compromises, at least rhetorically, by propagating the new politics of "consultation" *(xieshang),* which spells out the Party's acknowledgment that it alone cannot maintain a harmonious society.

Grassroots NGOs and Activism 2.0

As described earlier in this chapter, NGOs are usually not the earliest and the most impactful practitioners of activism 2.0; innovative IT companies are—especially those invested in charity branding. Sina and Tencent have pioneered the emergence of peer-to-peer philanthropy in China through their building of microblogging platforms that enable change agents to post participatory projects and deliver their messaging at a grand scale. However, activism 2.0 has many faces. It is by no means contingent on the financial prowess of conglomerates and monopolized by corporate players, no matter how far-reaching their influence. A history of this new brand of activism would need to incorporate projects that did not originate in MicroCharity and MicroCompassion platforms. The following are three innovative examples of activism 2.0—an offline experiment, an online project, and a mobile app.

1KG More (2004–) is China's earliest 2.0 experiment initiated by blogger Andrew Yu, a Guangdong native. His activism is built on a simple concept: connecting backpack travel with social responsibility. Travelers who go sightseeing in rural places are asked to carry one kilogram worth of gifts (such as books, pencils, notebooks, or toys) which they donate to kids in village schools. 1KG More backpackers are also encouraged to spend fun time with those children and post their shared fun activities on social media sites. Numerous researchers have written about 1KG More in the context of cyberactivism (Yang 2009a; Yang 2009b, 32, 37; Jiang 2010; Luo 2012), but few caught the fact that although Yu's project was launched on his blog, the core experience of 1KG More takes place *offline*. In fact, the ingenuity of Yu's backpack project rests less on the digital means of mobilization and P2P sharing than on his progressive idea that activism can be decentralized and recomposed into self-generated and self-organized activities freed from the control of traditional top-down organizational form. What ensued is a free-style philanthropy, which is idiosyncratic, burden-free, happy, "ready anytime" *(suishou),* and completely rooted in personal and personalized experience *on the ground.* The basics of 2.0 thinking is well materialized in decentralized, user (traveler)-generated activities offline, and in the forming of a virtual community of strangers made up of like-minded 1KG More travelers. Andrew Yu drives home the message that what truly defines a genuine activism 2.0 experience is the value of decentralized thinking and its scalable potential rather than technology itself.

NGO2.0 Philanthropy Map (2010–). At its core, 1KG More is an off-line activity with scaled online user-generated content as added value. My next example is a digital project in which I have been personally involved from the very start. Shortly after NGO2.0 was established in 2009, Endy Xie (our CTO), teammates, and I began to explore technological means that would allow NGOs to make themselves visible to each other and to potential corporate donors. Why do we the focus on corporate partnership? Although sporadic crowdfunding opportunities are available, even the most optimistic NGOs have to come to terms with the fact that the practice of "everybody a donor" benefits big foundations and large NGOs, not grassroots organizations. I mentioned earlier that the typical contribution for a typical grassroots project during 9.9 Giving Day is between 1 fen ($0.001) and 10 yuan ($1.44) per donor (Han Qing 2015), which earned for itself an apt epithet—"small change philanthropy." Public fundraising is an unreliable source of income for resource-hungry NGOs. With foundation and government funding equally difficult to secure, grassroots must learn how to build partnerships with the corporate sector. Playing matchmaker is easier said than done as creating partnerships at scale involves savvy social media solutions and offline networking.

NGO2.0 took a first step in 2010 to create a decentralized infrastructure to connect NGOs to corporations. We turned to crowdsourcing technology as the starting point of our endeavor and found the Ushahidi Crowdmap which allows the public to aggregate data / information and visualize it on a map or timeline. Ushahidi, which translates to "testimony" in Swahili, was first developed to crowdsource reports of violent incidents occurring in Kenya after its calamitous election in 2008. Soon, many global users repurposed Ushahidi's original function (crisis mapping) and set up their own deployments of the Crowdmap without having to install it on a web server. One of the most famous deployments since its release in 2010 was the global Occupy Movement (Ushahidi 2017). Regardless of how Crowdmap is utilized, users are drawn to it because it can crowdsource large volumes of data in a bottom-up, decentralized fashion.

What kind of data does NGO2.0 crowdsource on our own map? Data about NGOs and their projects on the one hand, corporate social responsibility (CSR) projects on the other hand. In order to better explain how crowdsourcing works on our map, I need to backpedal to the era prior to the existence of this map and ask: Where could one go to obtain a reliable list of NGOs operating in China? Previously existing NGO data platforms kept a simple record of the most visible organizations in a time-consuming,

Web 1.0 manner by which platform managers entered the data about each organization manually. Once entered, the information became instantly outdated. Not only are updates labor intensive and unaffordable for those platforms but more importantly, only the organization itself would know when its data needed to be altered, not the platform personnel. We solved this logistical issue by resorting to crowdsourcing that made scaled projects like Wikipedia a huge success.

In a similar fashion as Wikipedia, NGO2.0 outsources to grassroots organizations the microtask of filling in their own data on our map, which has evolved cumulatively into a digital common. The mechanism for voluntary updates is baked into crowdsourcing. Any organization self-registered on the map can come back any time to edit their own content by themselves. A project manager was hired to run the map and verify all content entries. Today, our map features 4,799 voluntarily entered NGOs and more than 3,100 CSR philanthropy projects. There are another 20,000 NGOs on the map, data acquired through web crawling and awaiting to be claimed and updated by their owners (see Map 3.1).

It is important to note that our current map is no longer Ushahidi's Crowdmap. We scrapped it and built a new structure complete with a user system which Ushahidi lacked.[7] Through simple search functions, NGOs all over China can now use this map to look for potential corporate partners as well as NGO partners. They can search for each other by geographical locations and by specific NGO issue areas. CSR managers can now identify NGOs whose mission is well aligned with its corporate brand.

My third activism 2.0 example is an online app called Pedestrian (2015) launched by Han Jing, deputy secretary-general of the Youcheng Foundation. Behind each activist project is an inspiring story about the founder's discovery of his own philanthropic self. For Han Jing, a motorcycling hobbyist, his epiphany arrived while he was watching a documentary showcasing tattooed members of the American Motorcycle Club visiting an orphanage on Thanksgiving Day. Struck by the tender sight of those rough guys showering gifts on the orphans, Han was committed to looking for ways of motivating ordinary people to become "compassionate pedestrians" (Han Jing 2015). Given enough incentives to do good, Hang believes, ordinary people would transform themselves from indifferent passersby to responsible citizens. Built on the notion of reciprocation, the app is a fixed-donation platform (10 yuan each time) on which donors are rewarded, after each donation made to a cause, with ten-yuan worth of coupons paid by corporate sponsors. The app has other features that

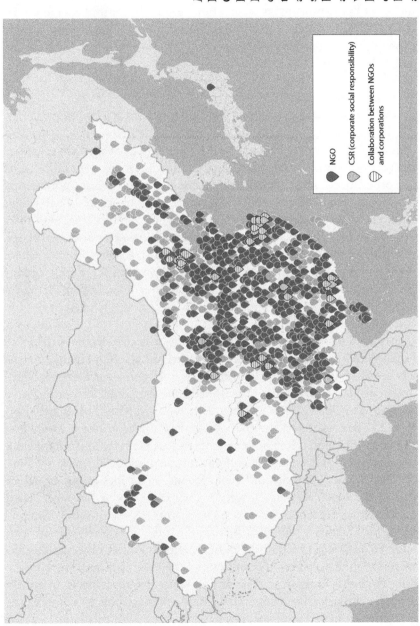

Map 3.1. NGO2.0 Crowdsourced Philanthropy Map. The black dots are NGOs, the gray dots are corporate social responsibility projects, and the dots with horizontal lines are collaborative projects between NGOs and corporations.

NGO

CSR (corporate social responsibility)

Collaboration between NGOs and corporations

encourage the donors to participate in a sustainable way. Although it is still too early to tell if this app will be successful, the practice of offering material rewards to the giver is an innovative idea, although this new model of "philanthropy as transaction" arguably contradicts the fundamental idea of altruism embedded in the concept of philanthropy. It could probably speed up the phenomenon of "everyone a donor," but can we still call it charity?

The Tyranny of Revolution and Nonconfrontational Activism

This chapter showcased a wide variety of examples of activism staged on the two dominant social networking platforms. Some were initiated by IT corporations, some by free agents, and others by NGOs. While many projects are intended as short-term disruptions—almost all the campaigns featured on Weibo discussed in this chapter fall into this category—there are also projects, especially the three grassroots examples discussed above, that aim at achieving longer-term change and transformation. I cannot speak for Andrew Yu and Han Jing, but I can vouch for myself and my NGO2.0 teammates that we are in it for the long haul. In fact, incrementalism is seen as the most important characteristics of Chinese-style nonconfrontational activism.

My idea of framing Chinese activism as a nonconfrontational ethos began with a media studies thesis I directed at MIT. Sun Huan, a former advisee in comparative media studies, was shopping for a thesis topic. I questioned her initial choice of censorship and suggested the topic of "nonresistant activism," a term she eventually replaced with "hidden activism" (Sun 2013). I had reservations about her first topic because it would lead her to the conceptual trap of domination versus resistance—a binary mode of thinking that falls short of capturing the nuanced social reality of China.

This chapter identified different specimens of nonconfrontational activism, 2.0 style. Some stood out for their creativity, for instance, Deng Fei's "human sea tactics," the Bare Head Brother's use of satire, Thumbs-Up Sister's tactic of "damning by praising," and the double-win strategy adopted by Friends of Nature. Those examples and the other case studies discussed in this chapter and throughout the book demonstrate that winning the battle without conflict and in spite of censorship is an apt description capturing the existential condition of grassroots NGOs in China. Oftentimes, incrementalism goes hand in hand with this nonaggressive mode of activism. Walking around, rather than walking through the obstacles characterizes the routine strategy to which all savvy grassroots NGOs are subscribing. Paradoxically, incrementalism works not just because it is the safest route but because it is the *fastest* way to fulfill social goals in China. Lest some critics out there want to label this kind of action "nonaction," a cop out, or even a compromise made to the authoritarian regime, I would like to quote at length from Nobel Peace Prize winner Liu Xiaobo's poignant reflection on the failure of June 4, 1989, which was published three years after the Tiananmen Square crackdown and long before his arrest.

> Each and every one of us is both victim and carrier of that word, revolution. . . . "Revolution" implies unyielding, uncompromising, intolerant, uncooperative qualities—a radical justice that shows no forgiveness; the more radical, the more extreme; the more absolute, the more revolutionary . . . an obsession with "revolution" caused us to lose our humanity and rationality, to lose our social conscience and tolerance, to lose the most basic standards of right and wrong . . . We have been driven mad by "revolution." We have been suffocated by "revolution." (Liu Xiaobo 1992, 311)

Those stumbling through each successive revolution in modern Chinese history would understand Liu's impassioned plea and his hesitation of welcoming another earthshaking upheaval, whether it takes the shape of a top-down directive like the Cultural Revolution or a bottom-up movement like the students' demonstrations in 1989. It is not because Chinese people lack revolutionary consciousness, it is because they discovered, like Liu Xiaobo, that a worship of the radical means of political change, once ignited, would only give ammunition to the ultraconservatives in the Party, sabotage reformers' progressive agenda, and push the country into a frenzied confrontation with an indomitable power that nonetheless has a "widespread and deep popular support and a solid, practical legitimacy" (Liu Xiaobo 1992, 313).

> The despotism of the Party, gunning down people, dictatorship—all of those are evils that must be rectified, but when we face the realities of China, we recognize that this rectification must be *gradual, peaceful, and long term.* We must not only rely on political pressures from the people but also rely even more on *the self-reform of the Communist Party.* (313, italics mine)

Liu Xiaobo's daring but profoundly sad speculations of a once-fervent revolutionary remind us that the history of modern China is a bloody history of revolutions. Indeed, which country has generated more revolutionaries than China between 1911 and 1989? I am not quoting Liu Xiaobo for the sake of legitimizing the notion of "nonconfrontational activism" but to provide an interpretive possibility to contest the popular neoliberal myth that Chinese people are either brainwashed dummies, paralyzed weaklings, or intrinsically impaired by the culture of collectivism.

"Gradual, peaceful, and long term" changes are now the mandate picked up by Chinese change makers of all persuasions, a lesson learned the hard way. Finally, are incrementalism and nonconfrontationalism—two characteristics defining the practice of Chinese change agents—a social ethos unique to that country? Absolutely not. Western critical literature is filled with discussions about "agency" and "structure" that challenge the liberal-democratic model of civil society construed as a space populated by resistance-driven "autonomous individuals. " Gramsci has long undermined the popular conception that civil society is separate from and oppositional to the state (and the market). His theory of hegemony dismantles the illusory concept of autonomy and views civil society as an entity fundamentally shaped by existing power structures emanating from the bourgeois state and capitalist economy (Gramsci in Forgas and Nowell-Smith 1985). In her analysis of alternative artistic strategies against the museum establishment, Chantal Mouffe states that "it is a mistake to believe that artists who choose to work with museums cannot play a critical role and that they are automatically recuperated by the system" (Mouffe 2013). She counts "engagement with institutions" as a form of counter-hegemonic politics much in the same way as I argue that nonconfrontational tactics are a better way of engaging with the current power structure than withdrawing from it. Even Herbert Marcuse, known for his absolute faith in individual autonomy, finds in iconoclastic American hippies a "nonaggressive form of life," which amounts to nothing less than giving a nod to the social value underlying in-betweenness (Marcuse 2005). Equally surprising are Marcuse's musings on "revolution" and his observation that too many revolutions were waged to sustain, rather than destroy, the continuum of repression and exploitation. Anthony Giddens declines to see determining structure and action as separate, oppositional terms of analysis but emphasizes the idea of duality in which agency and structure are best thought of as interdependent theoretical categories (Giddens 1984). Finally, poststructuralism is populated by Western theorists who are eager to explore more complex views of the dyad of domination versus resistance, and by extension, the subject versus agent. Here I also want to draw from Lawrence Grossberg's acknowledgment that cultural studies critics too readily celebrate resistance "which rested upon a taken-for-granted analysis of domination and subordination" (Grossberg 1993, 26). Citing Stewart Hall's nonessentialist concept of agency, Grossberg writes about a fragmented and decentered human agent "who is both subject-ed by power and capable of acting against those powers" (Grossberg 1996, 157). This formula of a split agency and political humanism returns us to the question of the complex identity of change agents practicing non-confrontational activism in China.

Should I theorize such a change agent in terms of her instinct to spot danger and avoid it? That's too simple a characterization. A more precise way of defining such agency is to recognize its doubled-edgedness. That is to say, change agents in China would in theory have a less unified identity than his or her counterpart living in a society where free expression prevails. This is not about poststructuralism, although living under a prohibitive, oppressive system yields exactly the same result—that is, contradictory identities that are highly performative, therefore, *purposefully* inconsistent. Navigating the shifting space between the private self (that always harbors a forbidden thought or two) and its public persona (that plays the predictable role of a submissive subject) is in fact a cultivated skill in which citizens of authoritarian regimes excel. This is not only true for activists who need to master the art of camouflaging to survive (as Chapter 1 illustrates) but also for communist officers whose job is to police activists. An anecdote will serve to explain the paradox.

In the early 2010s, NGO2.0 encountered several attempts made by provincially based public security bureaus to shut down our social media training workshops. During one particular workshop, a policeman dressed in plain clothes was dispatched to sit in on my class. Before I started teaching, I walked up to him in a doubly ambiguous gesture to welcome him and shame him at the same time, a mocking tactic which is simultaneously nonconfrontational. Fairly soon, the guy became so enchanted by what I taught that he started engaging himself in the Web 2.0 exercises I assigned to student trainees. He seemed a fast learner and quickly took on the role of mentoring those who were slower in picking up my instructions. At the end of the class, he walked up to me just like any normal student, addressing me politely as "Teacher Wang" and telling me subtly not to worry about the report he would submit to his boss about our workshop. Too often, we forget that a watchdog has a split identity too. At critical moments, his public persona—the police / censor in this case—gives way to the private self that makes a moral choice in favor of the activist. Stories like this abound in China, among them a *Newsweek* mention of a rescue mission that involved the relatives of Chinese high-ranking cadres who helped smuggle activists out of the country (M. Liu 2014). Perry Link and Xiao Qiang also observed that many Chinese reporters work as journalists toeing the Party line during the day and as unofficial, subversive bloggers in the evenings (Link and Xiao 2013, 84). Let us by no means count out change agents embedded in the system itself.

The dual character of the agency of Chinese activists, ordinary citizens, and censors with conscience gives birth to infinite possibilities that work in favor of nonconfrontational activism. In authoritarian countries where censors also have double identities and move among various subject positions to negotiate their momentary allegiance, nonconfrontational activists stand a good chance of functioning as change agents. This scenario is akin to what John Fiske calls "nomadic subjectivity" although he is quite ambivalent about how autonomous it can be (Fiske 1989, 181). In the Chinese case, the role play of the dual agency of nonconfrontational activists is a fascinating thing to watch, more so because unlike the Western counterparts, their primary goal is not to create agonistic spaces, but to package those spaces with exquisite care so that they appear nonagonistic to authorities. The process of packaging is where research is most needed. Luckily, China is so big and so decentered that there is plenty of room for activists to plough through with success, which renders confrontation an unsavory tactic. Indeed, power operates microphysically even in a country known to be a top-down, seamlessly controlled entity. Every local city, county, or province has its own yardstick for defining what is permissible and what is not, which turns China into a gigantic playing field for those aiming at winning without shedding blood.

Conclusion

This chapter started with the critical year of 2011 that gave impetus to the birth of philanthropy 2.0 commercial platforms. That year, a scandal involving Red Cross China triggered a crisis of public trust in the philanthropy sector, setting off a series of chain reactions crucial to the shaping of the Chinese culture of activism 2.0—nonprofit organizations started using microblogs to publicize and make transparent their financial and operational details; individual donors and corporate donors ditched state-owned foundations as the only venue for social giving; IT conglomerates intensified their exploration of Web 2.0 technology as a means of enabling free agents and grassroots organizations to raise funds on their social networking platforms. The convergence of all those factors led to the bloom of free agent projects and hashtag activism. The first half of the chapter zeroed in on the aftermath of the Red Cross scandal and detailed how it helped popularize the ideology and practice of "everybody a donor," which in turn expedited the march of the philanthropy sector into the era of crowdfunding.

The contestation between Weibo and WeChat was examined within a discussion of the complex relationship between the state, (civil) society, and the (IT) market. Almost all of the case studies sampled in this chapter are nonconfrontational. Citing incrementalism as an essential ingredient of nonconfrontational activism, this chapter ends with a double critique of the ideology of revolution and the neoliberal paradigm of agency. In so doing, I carve out a theoretical space for Chinese change makers who have perfected the practice of winning without conflicts.

Young practitioners of activism 2.0 are versatile social media influencers, craving fun and cool stuff, meaning and impact, all at once. The next chapter zeros in on millennials as change makers and their twin personae as citizen and consumer. They seem to be everything and everywhere—as volunteers participating in philanthropic microactions and as donors giving to online crowdfunding initiatives. The post-1980 and the post-1990 millennials also make up the largest segment of virtual spectators behind contentious internet incidents, and they are at the same time target consumers for social cause marketing 2.0 campaigns. To the most giving and multifaceted demographic we now turn.

4

Millennials as Change Agents
on the Social Web

In spring 2011, a new digital speak called the "howling style" (*paoxiao ti*) became an internet sensation in China. It was a digital speak with no fixed form or content. What made it stand out was a long string of exclamation marks attached to the end of every sentence, a fad originated by a niche group on Douban—China's influential social networking platform where users post content related to favorite books, films, TV drama, and urban cultural trends. This group had set up a Douban entry devoted to Ma Jingtao in 2008, attracting a modest cult following. Enamored with the Taiwanese actor's exaggerated performance style, Ma's fans anointed him jokingly as *paoxiao di,* the "howling god." But it was not until March 2011 that this randomly coined epithet *paoxiao* evolved into a discursive style and turned into a craze on the web. Since then, the howling style has been fetishized by netizens of all professional stripes.

To get a feel of this digital style, let's travel back to March 2011 and take a look at the *lianghui* (Two Meetings), a term for the annual plenary sessions of the National People's Congress and the Committee of the Chinese People's Political Consultative Conference (CPPCC)—which provide policy consultation and make national-level political decisions. During the 2011 sessions, a CPPCC committee member Wang Ping made an astonishing remark:

> We should not encourage children from rural areas to attend college. That's because once those rural children attend college, they will be unable to return to their hometowns. Furthermore, there is

severe employment shortage in the city. There is no way that rural kids cramped into cities can be happy. (CPPCC 2011)

In response to Wang Ping's comment, an online comedy production group, "Longyan Dayue" (The Dragon Show, literally, "the emperor looks greatly pleased"), created a biting mashup video in animation form, spoofing Wang and the entire CPPCC. In the episode called "The Dragon's Take on Two Meetings," the cute animated anchor-woman retorts in extreme agitation:

> What the f*** does it have to do with you if I decide to go to college!!! What the f*** does attending college have to do with finding jobs!!! I'm sure your whole family are pure-bred city-dwellers dated at least eight generations back!!! I bet your family have lived in cities from the very time they evolved from monkeys, isn't this the case!!! Are you saying that rural people should stay cramped in their villages forever!!! So, are the nation's leaders suggesting we should go back to feudal times when political power was hereditary and people stayed put!!! Don't you understand the old saying, don't throw the baby out with the bathwater!!! Don't you get it, don't you get it !!!. . . . What kind of crappy ass logic is this!!! (Longyan Dayue 2011)

Listening to the oral delivery of the howling style is quite an experience. Its theatrical impact doubles and the seething exasperation can turn your guts inside out. On the surface though, this brand of simulated verbal violence seems harmless because it celebrates mock fury and nothing more. Many authors and performers of the howling style have indeed proclaimed that this is nothing more than a new version of the old trend of *zhaole* (seeking fun) and a quick way of decompressing oneself in an urban life fraught with bottled-up stresses. The *paoxiao* genre is thus said to be yet another variation of contemporary spoof culture, not to be taken seriously.

But is that so? The ranting style had lain dormant for three years before it spread like wildfire in China's blog sphere, especially on microblogging platforms. The fad only lasted for the months of March and April 2011 when censors tightened their grip in response to two politically sensitive events, that is, the "Two Meetings" on one hand, and the 2011 prodemocracy protests, also known as the "Chinese Jasmine Revolution," on the other.[1]

Indeed, every year during the Two Meetings period, the Chinese public knowingly exercise utmost restraint. Netizens across digital platforms are under the gag rule, and the web is pared down to a dull space for at least two whole months. Was it a mere coincidence that the howling style caught on with such speed in no other time than March and April that year? I think not. March is always associated with the state ritual of the Two Meetings. What made March 2011 more maddening than ever were the mass revolts popping up in Tunisia and Egypt and the spillover impact of the Arab Spring on China. The multiple arrests in April 2011 marked another wave of the regime's repressive measure against dissidents, among them were international celebrity Ai Weiwei and several rights protection lawyers.

I interpret the howling style as a symptom of mediated disobedience, simultaneously loud and muffled. It is a descendant to a lineage of internet parodies in China, the most famous are the Grass Mud Horse[2] and the River Crabs.[3] You want us to be quiet? We're going to deafen you with our howls and have fun at the same time! That's the underlying message. Style itself became a form of transgression. And of course, social media played a crucial role here. The outburst of such dramatic expression and its contagious spread online would be quite difficult without the ascending popularity of Chinese microblogs and the network effect triggered by this new medium.

I picked this example as an opener to this chapter for two purposes. First, the howling style has become hugely successful in China because of its appeal to a specific target audience known as the "digital natives"—the post-1980s and the post-1990s generations in China, otherwise known as the millennials—the demographic focus of this chapter. Second, my argument above pinpoints a specific style of nonconfrontational politics prevalent among the Chinese millennials—self-entertainment as a form of political participation. This chapter explores the twin personae of millennials as citizens and consumers. They are volunteers participating in philanthropic movements; they are also the most giving demographic for online crowdfunding initiatives; they make up the largest segment of virtual spectators behind contentious internet incidents; and they are at the same time the target consumers for social cause marketing 2.0 campaigns. I argue that as movers and shakers of the twenty-first century, millennials are transforming not only how goods are consumed but how civic engagement is fashioned. Web 2.0 technology is the enabler, tearing down silos and bringing together unthinkable partners. As the best specimen of "Generation 2.0," a growing number of creative youths are acting as conduits between these two previously irreconcilable worlds—markets and civic habitats. This chapter is built on a dual framework of change makers: millennials play out their social agency in the triple capacity of volunteers, virtual spectators, and crowdfunding donors, while the corporate sector appeals to civic-minded millennial consumers with memorable cause marketing 2.0 campaigns. Both the millennials and the corporate sector are experimenting with innovative practices of nonconfrontational activism, Chinese style.

Global Millennials: Are They Narcissistic or Altruistic?

It is difficult to pin down the precise dates for the start or the end of the Millennial Generation. In the global context, millennials follow the cohort of Generation X and consist of individuals born between the early 1980s and late 1990s. The Chinese have a different naming system. The term *millennials* is replaced by references to the post-1980s and post-1990s generations. Generally speaking, Chinese millennials share many characteristics of their Western counterparts; for example, they are socially liberal, digitally savvy, and more tolerant of gender and sexual experimentation than their predecessors. Western critical literature on millennials revolves around a debate: Are they self-absorbed narcissists or civic-minded citizens (Twenge 2006; Arnett 2010; Palser 2010; Kanter and Fine 2010; Paulin and Ferguson 2014; Ertas 2016; Hubbard 2016; Ng, Gossett, and Winter 2016)? The jury is still out, obviously. Although we need to caution ourselves against a blanket generalization, this ascending demographic possess certain cultural practices and lifestyles that seem to transcend geographical borders. Urban digital youths all over the world share their love for making and posting funny videos online; they befriend strangers on social networking sites; zoom in and out of multiple identities through avatars in game worlds; and most important, they are viral agents frittering away their time spotting and spreading cool trends like the howling style. It's not an exaggeration to say that their hobbies, creative work, social interactions, consumption habits, and learning activities are all mediated by digital and mobile technologies (Palfrey and Gasser 2008).

The lingering debate about their true identity—are they Generation Me or Generation We—is a strawman question especially for those acutely aware of the pitfalls of binary thinking. There is no shortage of anecdotal evidence that points to millennials being both. On the one hand, they are "brand" children and trendsetters of consumerism across all sectors from fashion to food. Statistics also reveal that 78 percent describe themselves as "not politically active" (Lawless and Fox 2015). But we also knew that Bernie Sanders won an overwhelming share of millennial voters during the 2016 Democratic presidential primaries, with an astounding 84 percent of such votes in Iowa and 83 percent in New Hampshire (Taylor 2016, 2), which speaks volumes about the millennials' penchant for political engagement. "Meaningful work" is valued the most by members of this generation, as opposed to "freedom" by Gen X, or "money, title, and recognition" by Boomers (Ertas 2016, 524). The longing for meaningful jobs, coupled with an equally fervent desire to create a positive impact in the world, has made millennials highly susceptible to cause marketing campaigns themed in poverty alleviation, environmental protection, and other change related social causes. Thanks to social media, the digitally savvy millennials are also globally connected and are highly conscious of their role in effecting change beyond local neighborhoods. Community for them is "not defined by location, but by mind-set" (Cone Communications 2006, 7). It is no wonder that the "2006 Cone Millennial Cause Study" considers millennials the "most socially conscious consumers to date" and "one of the most civic-minded generations since World War II" (4), an observation valid to this day.

A similar scenario greets us when we turn to China. I crossed paths with numerous youths in both urban and rural China during my ten years of social engagement through NGO2.0. The 1,600-plus grassroots organizations that we trained are all staffed with idealistic members of the post-1980s and post-1990s generations. Through NGO2.0's tech4good hackathon program, I also worked with millennial techies as well as university volunteers majoring in computer science/software design, and media/communication studies whose social mores mirrors closely those of the college students I teach at MIT—they are confident in their ability to effect social change and eager to take on weighty responsibilities of the world.

A word of caution here: urban millennials in China as well as those in other affluent societies belong to the privileged class. Their rural brothers and sisters don't share the same luck in developing the two-headed value system characteristic of global millennials in general: the self-conscious pursuit of personal growth and an altruistic involvement in serving the greater good. We should also take note that urban youths are by no means a homogenous entity. Lu Xun's famous teasing of the May Fourth youths[4] is a reminder of the historical diversity of this demographic:

> Some of our youths are fully awake, others are asleep, some are caught in a daze, others are lying there motionless. Still, there are youths that are playing hard . . . and naturally, there are youths that are charging forward." (Lu Xun 1926, 52, translation mine)

The heroes and heroines of this chapter are the fully awake and progressive millennials. Yet little did Lu Xun know that today, progressive youths can be playful at the same time, especially on the internet. Politics and entertainment are not mutually exclusive, especially in the context of non-confrontational activism!

Chinese Millennials in Action

What are the specific social capacities that Chinese millennials take on that enable us to conceptualize them as change agents? We can picture them as volunteers, philanthropy donors, internet agents, and virtual spectators respectively. 2008 was a pivotal year for the Chinese youth volunteer movement. Parallel to the government's mobilization of college students for the Beijing Olympics, self-organized young volunteers from all over China flew in to Wenchuan to provide postdisaster relief in the immediate wake of the Sichuan earthquake that took place a little over two months before the Olympics. Some grassroots NGOs set up by the post-1980s volunteers in 2008 survive to this day. NGO2.0 trained many of them between 2009 and the early 2010s, teaching them how to use social media to engage in their work. It is well noted that no matter how radical Chinese millennials may sound in speech, action-oriented youths in China know very well that their "choices are to work within the government's terms or not at all" and that "achieving meaningful change demands more from them than joining a one-time protest" (Fish 2015, 180–181). For Chinese millennials, the most popular avenue for sustained, nonconfrontational action is volunteer work.

Millennials as Volunteers

This section examines two major types of millennial volunteers in action—those who join the ubiquitous campus volunteer clubs organized by the Communist Youth League and those who participate in Enactus, an international nonprofit organization committed to using the power of entrepreneurial action to make the world a better place for the underprivileged.

Since the early 1990s, the Communist Youth League of China has served as the most important impetus for propelling formal volunteering of college students. The best-known program established under its auspicious is the Young Volunteers Operation. Since its start in 1993, approximately 1.7 million young volunteers have delivered voluntary services for the 2018 Beijing Olympics and 2.18 million for the 2010 Shanghai World Fair (Ye 2017, 48). According to the 2009 statistics released by the All-China Youth Federation, the operation provided more than 150 million person-hours in the service areas of community development, poverty alleviation, assistance for the elderly and the handicapped, environmental protection, postdisaster rescue and relief, and overseas programs. (All-China Youth Federation 2009). Young volunteers also participated in the Go West program, rendering their services to people living in poverty-stricken areas of West China. Following the new fad of "exporting Chinese philanthropy overseas," the Communist Youth League also completed a pledge of sending 300 young volunteers to Africa (Ye 2017, 48).

Campus-based official volunteer programs constitute a popular avenue for university students notwithstanding, those government overseen programs often appear too tame for those aspiring for more adventurous roles in carrying out civic duties. Enter Enactus China, the national chapter of an international NGO that promotes sustainable growth of communities through smart strategies designed collaboratively by college students, academic mentors, and business elites.

Enactus, previously known as Students in Free Enterprise (SIFE), arrived in China around 2002 and worked its way quietly through universities to help student-entrepreneurs create community empowerment projects. It was not until 2012 when the CEO of SIFE changed its name to Enactus (*En*trepreneurial: *Actio*n: *Us*) that a cross-sector alliance of college students, academic advisors, and business leaders finally gained momentum. Working with a large number of leading corporate partners and more than 286 membership universities in China (Enactus China 2018), Enactus propagates the idea of leveraging entrepreneurial action to transform the lives of the disadvantaged and to achieve sustainable social progress. Local Enactus chapters hold regular competitions to identify talented students and train them as socially responsible, future business leaders. The goal is simple but powerful: Enactus student ambassadors make a pledge to leverage viable business concepts to help every person and community in need to "live up to their fullest potential (s)" (Enactus 2015). Considering its enormous reach—16,042 student participants created 1,126 community development projects between 2016 and 2017 *alone*—Enactus has made a significant impact on mobilizing Chinese youth to get socially engaged (Enactus 2017). Moreover, regional Enactus champions enter national competitions, and after rounds of tournaments, the winning teams advance to the prestigious Enactus World Cup and are given opportunities to be recruited by sponsoring companies. The three-stage value proposition of the platform—community programs, leadership connection, and career linkage—forms a virtuous cycle. No wonder Enactus has grown at a lightning speed in China.

Lest you think short-term student outreach projects may be small in scale and their effectiveness not visible, Project Golden Pond will help make a different impression. The project was the brainchild of an Enactus team at Sun Yat-sen University that assisted tilapia fish farmers in a Guangdong village in solving a pollution problem that had plagued the village for years. Chemical overuse in the ponds, isolated fish farming, and low winter harvests had taken a toll on the 750 fishing families in the region. After conducting rounds of research, the student team discovered that planting ryegrass could bring villagers multiple benefits: it could improve the ecosystem of the ponds, and enable the farmers not only to earn extra income by selling the grasses but also create a new sideline business that supplies grass feed to local rabbit and cattle operations. Since the implementation of Golden Pond Project, previously arid land is now utilized to plant ryegrasses, and the "average summer fish yield has risen from 18 tons to 23 tons" (Enactus 2015).

Another Enactus project, Trash to Treasure, reaped similar benefits for a seaside village where 20 percent of its residents rely on oyster harvesting as the main source of livelihood. Due to the lack of a shell disposal mechanism, the whole village was overrun with discarded shells that polluted its water source. Students in the Xiamen University's Enactus team discovered that oyster shells can be treated and turned into fertilizers and construction materials. The research findings led the team to work with the local government to set up an oyster shell processing facility in the village. More than

4,000 tons of shucked shells are now processed each year, yielding 82.8 million yuan for the villagers thus far (Enactus 2013). It is also reported that the oyster meat tastes better as a result of the cleaner water habitat!

Enactus projects that improve the livelihood of poor communities while treating environmental problems are plentiful. The 2017 Chinese national champion team, led by students at the Guangdong Pharmaceutical University, developed technologies that utilize the residue of medical herbs to plant straw mushrooms and turn mushroom waste into organic fertilizers simultaneously. A whole recycling ecosystem was created, helping pharmaceutical companies and the mushroom sector solve the problems of medicine residue and mushroom waste accumulation (Huanqiu 2017).

The Golden Pond project, Trash to Treasure, and the Mushroom Project are case studies that drive home the core message of Enactus—socially concerned entrepreneurial spirit can transform people's lives. The success of Enactus also demonstrates that Chinese youths are drawn to innovative social practices and committed to making change.

Very often, when we speak of urban youths, we think of them not as social change agents but as consumers of cool fashion, hip-hop, animation, and online games. Marketers have churned out one study after another pondering how Chinese youths view luxury, drawing a very partial picture of China's millennials. The reality is always more complex and less visible. Truly, if I had not created NGO2.0, I would never have imagined the existence of the *other* China where idealistic urban and rural youths are busy weaving their dreams as social engineers. Having trained more than sixteen hundred post-1980s and post-1990s NGO workers and getting to know them at our digital literacy camps (see Chapter 2), I now have a growing faith in a kinder China to come. Just like NGO2.0's training camps that bring together like-minded youth activists, Enactus provides a space for young activists to meet, collaborate, and form communities. We all know that maker-entrepreneurs follow the law of the jungle, but change makers thrive on collaboration, a point I will return to in Chapter 5, "Makers and Tech4Good Culture."

I am not alone in taking an optimistic view on the future of the world in which utopian millennials are passionately engaged in innovative, grounded social action. Whether such actions need to be confrontational to the status quo is beside the point. An elderly and well-established literary scholar at Peking University, Qian Liqun, argues in a similar spirit that we need to be open-minded about millennial politics by examining them in a different light from how we viewed the student activists of the May Fourth Movement:

> Different from those participating in the political movements of the past, [youths in China today] don't share our sublime and tragic sentimentality. On the contrary, they are engaged in an entertaining, singing, dancing, and playing flash mob action. It is a kind of performance art . . . Politics engaged by those youths is bound to be different, they are playing by a different set of rules. (Feng and Zhang 2016)

Professor Qian was interviewed on May 4, 2016, significantly. He saw something "constructive" arising out of contemporary youth volunteer action and youth reading clubs that are now proliferating all over university campuses, something that must have brought him nostalgically back to 1919 and prompted him to utter: "I saw something very 'May Fourth' emerging from college students today."

Millennials as Agents and Spectators: The Politics of Self-Entertainment

What Qian Liqun meant is not entirely contradictory. By acknowledging the difference of contemporary youth from his generation of activists in 1919, he rejects the pessimistic view that the post-1980s and post-1990s youth are politically apathetic. What are their politics? Chapter 3, "WeChat versus Weibo," discusses a number of activism 2.0 examples on Weibo, in which millennials loomed large both as political agents and as virtual spectators who played a key role in demanding greater accountability from the government to uproot injustice and corruption. The heroes and heroines featured in the previous chapter include the Bare-Head Brother and the Thumbs-Up Sister, prime embodiments of the post-1980s youth in action. Their verbal taunting of the city government of Guangzhou was a performance act per se, hugely entertaining but politically subversive. Both examples highlight the phenomenon of the millennials assuming the role of political agents and operating "near the boundary of authorized channels."[5] If we draw a distinction between the initiators of such action—risk takers—and the spectators (the anonymous followers), then certainly both the Bare-Head Brother and the Thumbs-Up Sister fall into the category of agent-initiators. Peng Yanhui went on Weibo to recruit a thousand shaved heads, which he jokingly argued could "generate enough brightness" to light up the Pearl River banks and render Guangzhou's costly Night Illumination project unnecessary. Likewise, the Thumbs-Up Sister turned to Weibo to recruit a thousand netizens willing to post thumbs-up selfies, a satirical wordplay signifying the exact opposite: "thumbs down," to protest against the city officials' lack of transparency in creating the wasteful Pearl River project. Those cheeky Weibo posts went viral, accumulating potency with every share. And just like the howling style, they were appealing to fun-loving millennials on the social web.

Ziyu (self-entertainment) is a form of nonconfrontational activism widely practiced by Chinese millennials. Numerous instances can be found on social media platforms where humor and satire serve to camouflage netizens' censure of the regime. In those examples, self-entertainment is indistinguishable from political commentaries. A similar case in point is the hilarious sentence-composition contest on the internet meme "My Dad is Li Gang!"

The Li Gang incident took place in Hebei Province in 2010. A young intoxicated driver sped a black Volkswagen through a college campus and killed two students. It was a hit and run. When the culprit was finally chased down by angry bystanders, convinced that his father's position would give him impunity, he shouted out to the crowd: "Go ahead, sue me if you dare. My dad is Li Gang!" The phrase became an instant sensation on the web. Within days, posts containing the meme appeared on all social media platforms: 35,000 threads appeared on the Tianya Forum, 86,000 entries on the Renren Net, and 3,300,000 posts on Weibo (Li Miao 2015, 148). On the Renren Net, a once-popular destination for the post-1990s youth, a spontaneous sentence-making contest caught on quickly. The meme was spoofed in diverse genres—Tang poetry, Song Dynasty lyrics, ancient prose, kung fu novels, modern poetry, film scripts, pop songs, commercials, you name it.

> The luminous moon shines above my bed,
> It looks like frost fallen on the ground.
> Looking up at the security guards,
> My dad is Li Gang! (Tang poetry style) (Lam 2010)

> Not every glass of milk is deluxe milk,
> Not every father is Li Gang. (commercial jingle) (Li Miao 2015, 148)

Click-Clack! Click-Clack! went the loom,
Mulan is weaving by herself,
If my dad were Li Gang,
Would I have to go join the army? ("Ode to Mulan") (148)

Life is like a journey, I don't need to care about my destination. But
one thing I do care about is that my Dad is not Li Gang! (proverb)
(148)

I could have used the emergency brake to stop the car so that I
wouldn't run over the girl. But I wouldn't entertain that idea, it's
really too much trouble! If Good Old Heaven gave me another
chance, I would whisper to her: "Please stay away from me, my
Dad is Li Gang!" (film script) (148)

In this contest of silly wit, the entry that amused me the most is the one
that contains a meme within a meme: "Li Qiming [Li Gang's son], your
Dad is calling you back home for dinner!" (Ogreenworld 2011). "Coming
home for dinner" makes reference to a nonsensical catchphrase posted on
China's WoW Forum, in which a fictional mother is calling her son, an
addicted player, to come back home for dinner, a meme that had seen its
own heyday in 2009.

But a good laugh at those tongue-in-cheek exercises is not what this
virtual contest was all about. What kicked off the memic festival was the
millennials' pointed critique of the *guan erdai* phenomenon, a term referring to the second generation of corrupt officials that is seen to have inherited the double-dealing of their fathers. The extravaganza around "My
dad is Li Gang" was captivating precisely because entertainment and politics were seamlessly intertwined.

There are, of course, less entertaining and riskier incidents initiated by
the millennials. The high school students participating in the 2012 Shifang protest in Sichuan province made a heroic call to fight against the
construction of a copper refinery that could pose environmental and public
health risks to the city. In a city without a single university, all student
protesters came from Shifang High School, but their defiance was no less
loud and clear: "We are ready to sacrifice our lives for Shifang. We are
members of the post-1990s generation!" (Zhang 2012). Other post-1990s
political agents that are active on social media include those who initiated the Guo Meimei Incident (which I elaborated on in Chapter 3), the

Wukan Incident,[6] the Foxconn suicide scandals,[7] the Watch Brother Incident,[8] the Yihuang self-immolation,[9] the 7.23 Wenzhou high speed train wreck, and the anti-Japanese Diaoyu Island protests. In recent years, we also witnessed an increasing number of requests made by post-1990s millennials to local officials for open data with the clear purpose of pushing for greater governmental accountability. More intriguingly, the National People's Congress began to incorporate post-1990s representatives into their rank and file (Guo, Liu et al. 2017). The future will probably see more political engagement, both formally and informally, of the twenty-somethings.

I should take note, however, that with a handful of exceptions, statistics show the majority of the post-1990s generation are spectators rather than opinion leaders (Center for Psychology of the Chinese Academy of Sciences et al. 2013, 19; Li Miao 2015, 139, 141). On microblogging platforms, most millennials are the faceless crowd retweeting or simply quietly reading the posts sent by daredevils like the Bare-Head Brother, Thumbs-Up Sister, "Asshole wetman" who allegedly started the Li Gang meme contest on MOP.com (Lam 2010), Chen Weixiang who infiltrated Foxconn as an undercover factory temp (Li Miao 2015, 154), or "WK Chicken Bouillon" and "Super-HeroX," online pseudonyms of post-1990s activists who orchestrated the media warfare in support of Wukan villagers (157–159). Spectators on Weibo, in contrast, are twice removed from the eye of the storm and can be seen as a much tamer version of agitator-initiators.

I started my discussion of crowd spectatorship (*weiguan*) in Chapter 1 and explored the relationship between crowd gazing and crowdsourced justice within the larger context of social media politics. Neither a form of purposeful action nor that of confrontation, *weiguan* can add fuel to sparks of controversy, however. It can trigger a domino effect precisely because virtual spectatorship, free and anonymous, can scale up the stakes for the government even though it is often seen as nothing more than token political participation.

As we know, the twenty- and thirty-somethings are spirited followers of internet incidents. The post-1990s generation is particularly vulnerable to peer pressure and the bandwagon effect. Impulsive, extroverted, and prone to moral nonconformity and political radicalism (Peng 2008), they are easily driven into the attack mode (Wang 2007). Other scholars emphasize the copycat psychology of millennials and characterize their fa-

148

vorite online behavior, *weiguan,* in terms of the "collective unconscious" (Li Miao 2015, 143). The duality of the post-1990s generation often makes them flip between the rational and irrational, and for them, carnivalesque protests and boisterous fun-making are ultimately indistinguishable from each other. But just as you think they are on the brink of total anarchy, they are quick to return to the mean. Pessimists wondering about the potential of cyberspace to transform the Chinese public sphere often see this generation as a hybrid species that "vents on the Web, compromises in real life" (168).

The Fanke Style

The pendulum can swing the other way, of course. Millennials are capable of evolving themselves into mature social agents, and an additional footnote to the demographic profile of the post-1990s generation can be found in another popular crowdsourcing practice—the *fanke* style.

> I love "A Call to Arms," I also love bringing up the old. I love *Hometown;* I also love Xu Guangping. I love keeping a diary; I also love exploding in silence. I don't eat steamed buns because it's bloody murder.[10] I've hesitated in my life before. I dread spondylitis. However, I've traveled many different roads. My spine is no longer hurting. I'm willing to bow my head, my back will be the straighter for it. My pen name is Lu Xun. Don't even think about erasing my name from textbooks, I am still alive. Actually, I am no writer, I'm just a doctor, I specialize in spinal treatment for citizens. (Bian 2010)

This was one of the thousands of creative name cards written in the *fanke* style which parodied the billboard advertising by VANCL in 2010—an online apparel retailer relatively unknown when it launched its business in 2007 (Lin 2010). One of the original VANCL billboards was especially inspirational to China's digital natives because it featured their idol Han Han wearing a VANCL T-shirt and posed against a backdrop of teasing statements written in a stream of simple, fragmentary syntax—"I am . . . I am not . . . I like . . . I am still . . ." As reported by *LEAP* magazine, this copywriting style became an instant viral hit, its popularity exacerbated by a July contest "Come Make Fun of VANCL" launched by Douban. The mock contest generated more than 3,000 Photoshopped, user-generated spoofs (Bian 2010).

The closest Chinese transliteration of VANCL is *fanke* (since there is no "v" sound in Mandarin Chinese) which translates into "a commoner," neatly capturing the brand appeal of a simple, commonplace fashion sense. Netizens who played with the *fanke* style by creating mock name cards targeted everything from political and pop culture celebrities to national symbols like the panda and foreign icons like Steve Jobs, Homer Simpson, and even Captain Jack the Pirate of the Caribbean!

What's intriguing about the style is that it wasn't a viral marketing campaign. VANCL and ad agency Ogilvy Beijing denied that they were behind the trending of this hilarious cloning phenomenon (Baidu Baike 2010; Xie 2010). It was a marketing accident and a craze spontaneously triggered by Chinese millennials' love for parody and copycatting. The *fanke* style continued to generate buzzes, drawing millions of millennial netizens to dive in to the online carnival and co-create what is seen as a collective lampoon. It is obvious that they found in the style an inspirational vehicle for making jibes at the political and cultural mainstream. Needless to say, online incidents like "My Dad is Li Gang" and other breaking news are favorite topics for *fankers* as well (Figure 4.1).

Fankers stood out as trendsetters not least because those creative name cards are miniature social commentaries, and in some cases, tactful critiques. The *fankers* certainly do not represent the majority of young Chinese consumers, but their presence is symptomatic of the emergence of a mixed breed of digital natives, who, like those who breathed life into the howling style and the *fanke* style, are devoted to blending pleasure with

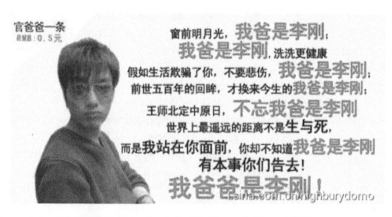

Figure 4.1. My Dad Li Gang for Sale (Nanfang de Feng 2014)

politics and are earnest in their pursuit of social conscience. They are citizens as well as consumers.

Cause Marketing 2.0: Millennial-Citizens as Target Consumers

The VANCL case drives home the duality of this generation—brand-conscious consumers and socially concerned netizens merged in one. This mixed-breed of millennials, a new class of hybrid trendsetter so to speak, is *simultaneously* a pleasure-seeking brand child and a playful networked citizen. Many marketers have exploited the double personae to the full through cause marketing 2.0 campaigns. Academic researchers are less ready to follow suit. There are books written about millennials as brand children, and there are philanthropy reports on digital natives acting as social citizens. But rarely do we mix those two personae, for it is hard to imagine that the same consumer-actor can cross the boundary and play in both worlds simultaneously. In our usual perception, a gulf separates the for-profit and the nonprofit worlds. We assume they do not converge and that the millennials swimming in both ponds must have conflicting identities. I argue the opposite: a growing number of millennial consumers is already acting as a conduit between those two previously irreconcilable worlds. Social media is key that enables this new demographic to bridge the market and the civic habitat. Needless to say, forward-looking marketers took note of it, and advertisers today are compelled to re-imagine the ways commercial brands interact with socially concerned millennials.

There is no question that millennials are brand experts. But few of us knew that millennial citizens opened up a new marketing opportunity for companies that were farsighted enough to give traditional cause-related marketing a facelift. What emerged are CSR (corporate social responsibility) campaigns that pulled in millennial fans en masse to Web 2.0 platforms that promote various social causes.

Before I provide examples of CSR 2.0 campaigns, it is important to bear in mind that the birth of this phenomenon is a complex matter. The rise of the socially concerned twenty- and thirty-somethings is an important factor driving the popularity of cause marketing, but it alone cannot propel the marketing landscape in that direction. What is equally significant is the conceptual evolution of corporate social responsibility in North America and Asia.

Corporate Social Responsibility (CSR) in Flux and Cause Marketing 2.0

From India and Singapore to China and the US, a seismic change in CSR practices has occurred in recent years. Multinational corporations started to see the economic benefits of integrating sustainability and social cause into their businesses. For example, the corporate sector in India has witnessed a conceptual transformation "from the charity-oriented approach to the stakeholder-oriented approach," where the consumer target group is now seen as a stakeholder in the community whose well-being is integral to the long-term success of a company (Mahapatra and Visalaksh 2012). Researchers based in Singapore made a similar observation that corporate responsibility is increasingly a driving factor in brand preference and purchase behavior. It was said that "79 percent of consumers would rather buy from companies who are doing their best to reduce their impact on the environment" (Arnold 2011). A similar trend is surging in China—a Baidu search on *green marketing* yields 1,520,000 entries in July 2018. In the US, the 2017 Cone Communications CSR Study yielded statistics validating that 87 percent of Americans will purchase a product from a company because it advocated for an issue they cared about, and a whopping 76 percent of millennials are likely to conduct online research to verify whether a corporate's claimed social cause is authentic (Cone Communications 2017). All those statistics, old and new, propel a *Forbes* journalist to postulate, "Want to engage millennials? Try corporate social responsibility" (Peretz 2017). While the same high percentage may not apply to consumer action in all developing countries, corporate social responsibility is surely gaining importance in brand strategy all over the world. Various cause marketing 2.0 campaigns came into being to capitalize on millennials' desire to work as change agents to transform local and global communities. A CSR initiative will resonate best with young consumers if it not only allows them to build networks with each other but also succeeds in evoking their deep-seated urge to make a difference in the world.

My favorite cause marketing campaign is Ecotonoha, an aesthetically appealing CSR initiative rolled out in 2003 by NEC, a Japanese company specializing in broadband network and IT business solutions. With each click, netizens could create a leaf on the bare branches of a virtual tree, generate a personalized message, and send a digital postcard to friends who then brought in more fans to plant more leaves ("Ecotonoha Tree" 2008). At the end of each day, a virtual tree grew into full foliage on the miniplatform while real trees—7,423 trees total by the end of the campaign—were planted by NEC on Kangaroo Island, south of Australia (NEC 2003). I was enchanted by the ethereal Ecotonoha tree and followed its virtual growth for several years. When the initiative was finally concluded in 2010, many fans, including myself, felt they had lost an old friend.

Then an even more tech savvy campaign appeared. The Talking Tree was another crowdsourced, user interactive CSR project designed by Belgium magazine *EOS* in 2010. It is an ongoing initiative that gives voice and emotion to a one-hundred-year-old tree living in Boi de la Cambre on the edge of Brussels. The tree was hooked up to an ozone meter, light meter, weather station, fine dust meter, webcam, and microphone, delivering regular sound bites, images, and other updates to fans and followers on an assortment of social networking sites such as Twitter, Facebook, Flickr, YouTube, and SoundCloud. On muggy days, we found the tree sunken in a forlorn mood: "Ouch! Lots of pollutants in the air right now." Occasionally, it struck an upbeat note, "On my-to-do list for today: clean up the air" (Talking Tree 2012). All those mutterings and asides were assembled on the tree's main website (and control center),[11] gathering as many as 16,964 fun-loving worshippers on that site alone as of May 7, 2011.[12] The campaign ended in 2012.

The success of the Talking Tree campaign, like Ecotonoha, depends entirely upon the empathy and participatory fervor of a young audience. What types of digital youths congregate on those two platforms? Young men and women who may or may not be at the forefront of street movements but who are enthralled enough with the creative participation afforded by those platforms to be drawn in, in a surprisingly sustained manner. Ecotonoha and the Talking Tree share one thing in common besides evoking interactive user experiences: their success is built on the formula that *something fun and cool can generate social good*. Precisely because having fun for digital natives means engaging in participatory, creative experiences together, more and more cause marketers offer them entertaining, networked DIY involvement. Millennials planting leaves on Ecotonoha year in and year out, Twitter and Facebook fans busy dialoguing about the daily mood of the Talking Tree are all, in one form or another, producing and consuming a Web 2.0-styled micro civic engagement.

Clicktivism: Networking for Fun and Networking for a Cause

There are numerous skeptics, of course. Opponents charged that millennials' obsession with prompting and tracking clicks turned digital activism into clicktivism. In fact, even before the debate over clicktivism broke out, controversies already engulfed digital activism. Online petitioning led by the political group MoveOn.org was seen as competing unfairly with legitimate offline local organizations. If reducing activism to online petitions is considered bad, how about inducing clicks on a marketing campaign to produce social benefits? Quite predictably, click-through CSR campaigns irked social change proponents of older generations even more, bringing forth heated disputes among old-school NGO workers, cause marketers, and digital activists. Many questions were raised: Is cause marketing 2.0 simply a new trend of online entertainment and a symptom of the marketization of activism? Are virtual communities only skin-deep and as inauthentic as critics assume? Can surfing the web effect real changes on the ground? In short, is clicktivism to activism "as McDonalds is to a slow-cooked meal" (White 2010)? One could argue, eventually, that internet-based civic organizations like Generation Engage and TakeIT-Global have successfully reached out to politically apathetic youth but that calling the Talking Tree's Facebook fan groups an activist community is indeed a bit far-fetched.

Those questions and debates will probably not be resolved just as the controversy over millennials has raged on since the 1990s. For this chapter, my focus is on the actualization of the millennials' double influence on commercial and civic communication. Regardless of which analytical camp we place ourselves in—whether we perceive such an influence to be auspicious or pernicious—there is no denying that a paradigm shift has already taken place, with repercussions reaching both the commercial and civic communities. For brand strategists, the critical task is to leverage the digital natives' consumption habits and turn them into catalysts for producing social good. I am reluctant to support the hypothesis that millennials are "used by" social cause marketers. The incentive to make the world a better place is not something marketers can manufacture. What cause marketers have done is to tap into the hybrid energy field of millennials—their lust for fun and their equally strong desire for making a difference—and find the means to unleash both instincts.

If Ecotonoha and the Talking Tree played out that double strategy well, my next example, GamesThatGive, a guilt-free gaming platform founded by two American techies in 2008, drives home even more rigorously how it works. GamesThatGive combines gaming with charitable giving to create a digital platform for socially engaged gamer millennials (GamesThatGive 2011). You log on to the website, pick a charity you wish to play for, choose your favorite casual game (Solitaire, Sudoku, Blackjack, or Crazy Taxi, among others), and start playing. Advertisers deliver messages throughout the games, but a large chunk of the advertising revenue goes to the cause of your choice. In addition, the longer you play and the better you are at the game, the more funds you raise for your favorite charity.

Social games for social good open up a new market many brands are eager to tap into. An important takeaway is that digital natives are a generation defined by the faith that they can change the world by small steps—one timely donation, one voluntary click, or one leaf at a time. They are less adept at shaping public policy than performing microvolunteerism at their own convenience. The easier, the better. Cause marketers who figure out a quick and easy way for millennials to serve the social good will be big winners. Theirs is a cause culture built on instant gratification, which blurs the line between playing and volunteering, between networking for fun and networking for a cause. If it is possible to be a gamer and a citizen at the same time, the more fun there is for millennials! Of course, social media is key. If you can't share it and make your friends jump on board too, it's not fun (McDonald 2014).

The Crowd and the Networked Publics

Thus far I have assembled a psychographic profile of the *networking* millennials. Whether our focus is on the howling style and the fanke style, Ecotonoha or the Talking Tree, we are witnessing not only the creative power of millennials but also a remarkable *aggregate* effect of their action on the social web. In a nutshell, we are witnessing the rise of a spectacular trend of *online* crowdsourcing, which can be best understood as a viral phenomenon made possible by the voluntary mobilization, through social networks, of netizens to create open content for a common cause. A wide range of players—social cause advocates as well as advertisers and marketers—have exploited this trend with varying degrees of success. The cases we discussed earlier—the *fanke* style, Ecotonoha, the Talking Tree, and GamesThatGive—are all crowdsourced projects.

Academic critics would probably agree that one of the difficulties of grappling with precipitous social and cultural changes triggered by network technology has been the lack of critical vocabularies we can lean on to describe those changes. As new media are reshaping our social relationships and eroding the cognitive mapping of cultural elites, critical categories emphasizing the concepts of *false consciousness* and *complicity* are no longer sufficient for us to understand the dynamics of mass collaboration that turned crowdsourcing into a favorite pastime for millennials, in whose minds the practice is not really about exploitation of unpaid labor. Digital natives engaged in crowdsourcing don't seem to care very much about the intellectual property rights of the open content they create, either.

What is crowdsourcing? A crowdsourced project can achieve noncommercial as well as commercial goals. The most familiar example of the former is Wikipedia. Its commercial counterparts are DIY advertising campaigns that solicit user-generated content (UGC) for making actual commercials, copywriting, co-designing a product, or co-developing brand strategies.[13] Give millennials a template and a few digital tools, and they will create, share, and distribute their personalized content on the customized platforms of advertisers. Situated between Wikipedia and those UGC ad campaigns is cause marketing 2.0, which spans the civic and market domains.

Evaluating the social value of crowdsourced projects is bound to be a controversial task. It requires, at the very least, revisiting the concept of the *crowd*, which I treated in Chapter 1 in the context of nonconfrontational *weiguan* (crowd gazing) and where I laid out the conceptual transformation of the *crowd* in the Chinese context since Lu Xun's time. How has the concept fared in the Western history of ideas? How much has the emergent crowd on the social web changed since French social psychologist Gustave Le Bon published his *La psychologie des foules* (1895)?

Just like its counterpart in China (the swarming Red Guards cheering Chairman Mao come to mind), Le Bon's crowd did not enjoy a good historical reputation. A crowd event conjures up the haunting images of a riotous mob storming the Bastille, faceless crowds gathered at the guillotine, looting crowds set loose at the breakdown of law and order, and the list goes on and on in different periods of history. Crowd theorists of the nineteenth and twentieth centuries all agreed that the category stood for a uniform collective mind, unconscious and undisciplined, but powerful enough to destroy everything in its path when primed for action. For "what happened in the crowd, like what happened in the mind of the born criminal, was the antithesis of what was supposed to happen in the mind of the rational, self-conscious, individual" (McClelland 2010). In modern times, the easy elision of terms like *crowd, masses,* and *mob* is continually symptomatic of the negativity endemic to the term.

Le Bon's work on crowd psychology demands our special attention because the book's lasting popularity can be read to look backward at the nineteenth-century fear of mobs, but also to look forward to the twentieth-century denunciation of mass audience. "In crowds it is stupidity and not mother-wit that is accumulated" (Le Bon 1897, 8). I doubt if any of us who have participated in organized mass demonstrations today would ever agree with Le Bon on his observation about the incapacity of the crowd to reason. And if we keep in mind the example of Wikipedia and our nascent faith in the notion of "collective intelligence," we may find his next statement equally anachronistic and perhaps even a tad insolent. "This very fact that crowds possess, in common, ordinary qualities explains why they can never accomplish acts demanding a high degree of intelligence" (9). I am dwelling on the stark contrast between the timeworn European social theory and the modern-day progressive belief in what Howard Rheingold calls "swarm intelligence" (Rheingold 2002) because it takes such a dramatic contrast to bring us to the realization that the twenty-first century marks the turning point in the history of the idea of *the crowd.* Just like in the mid-nineteenth century when the crowd became central to social and political theorizing, so is the millennial crowd and the network effect it triggered indispensable to the making of contemporary theories of communication and culture. As I have shown, the crowds immersed in the new media environment appear in different guises: the DIY crowd, virtual howling crowds, smart mobs, mass petition crowds, the clicking crowd, voting crowds in social media campaigns, the gamers-that-give crowd, fan communities on Facebook, Twitter, Weibo, and so on. It is in sum a Generation 2.0 crowd with diverse value propositions and mental profiles.

Whether those are "good" or "bad" crowds isn't the point. Nor is it my intention to go to the other end of the spectrum by romanticizing the "crowd" and "collective intelligence" uncritically. There is, however, explanatory value in summarily juxtaposing Le Bon's landmark contribution to the theorization of the crowd and the contemporary tributes paid to millennial netizens in crowdsourcing activities. Jeff Howe's 2009 book *Crowdsourcing* may just be the beginning of a trend to revalorize the meaning of *crowd* in glowingly positive terms.

Two central themes stood out in Howe's celebratory literature about the digital crowd. He considers the erosion of the boundary between producer and consumer a major driving force behind all crowdsourcing culture. Second, he puts his finger on the difference that separates this proactive crowd from any other crowds. A proactive crowd, he says succinctly, demonstrates a marvelous "tendency to work well not only with others, but *for the sake of others*" (Howe 2009, 273, italics mine). This reference to altruism harks back to my earlier point about the desire of digital natives to make a difference in the world, however incremental and small the steps are each time. It is in light of that hearty belief that they can make the world a better place that makes crowdsourcing so inviting and appealing. Socially concerned millennials find in crowdsourcing a vehicle for engineering social change. The crowds that listen in to the Talking Tree are not clicking mindlessly. By checking in on the tree and networking with each other as its default care group, they expressed concern for global warming and joined the lobbying force for the environmental cause. Similarly, the Ecotonoha crowd created virtual leaves with the understanding that the more clicks they made, the more real trees the corporate sponsor would plant on Kangaru Island. The throngs of the howling style and fanke style emulators were venting and playing while pushing the envelope of censorship. And it is the same kind of self-perception that "we are change agents" that underlies the success of GamesThatGive and accounts for the huge success of the United Nation's FreeRice game.[14]

Not all crowdsourcing projects are equally purposeful, you might say. But the fundamentally unselfish spirit underlying those projects is indisputable. In Howe's terms, "crowdsourcing paints [an] all flattering portrait of the human race. We are more intelligent, more creative, and more talented than we tend to give ourselves credit for" (Howe 2009, 16). As if to contradict Le Bon even further, he considers crowdsourcing adding "to our culture's general store of intellectual capital" (16), a view that has come a long way from the Marxist critique of culture industry which is now seen as the exploiter of "affective labor" via crowdsourcing. Arguably, young innovators may look naïve to give up their own intellectual property rights to commercial crowdsourced projects, but more likely than not, millennials rank money and intellectual property much lower on their list of incentives than play-to-give, reputation capital, the pleasure to participate in making change, and the opportunity to share their DIY content with fans and friends. For this generation at least, the drive and reward for taking part in crowdsourcing can certainly not be measured in monetary terms alone.

The descriptors we have used to characterize the creative and socially responsible netizens and their online activities evoke the image of a crowd that undermines Le Bon's dichotomous scheme. His crowd was identified as lowbrow rather than highbrow, reactive rather than reflective, illiterate rather than literate, and susceptible to thinking in images rather than thinking in ideas. Instant gratification and sensual indulgence were tightly attached to his crowd as negative qualities. Indeed, Le Bon and many later theorists of the crowd treaded a similar theoretical path, charting the boundary that separates pleasure from restraint, irrationality from reason, immoral from ethical, image from idea, barbaric from civil, consumer from citizen, sensual from the cerebral, and consequently, a division sharply drawn between the "crowd" and the "public."

A theoretical dilemma arises when that division is crossed over by millennials whose double identity of consumer-as-citizen comes with a mixed bag of attributes. I have already shown why this new demographic is *not* the old crowd. What I would like to examine next is the degree of the commensurability of this demographic with the other term in the binary—the public.

Certainly, not all millennial communities are exemplary. There are some crowds that appear more like an irrational and barbarous crowd than a responsible public. Cyberbullying and doxing, for instance, are found in all cultures. They are thriving in China in the guise of the "human flesh search engine" mentioned earlier in Chapter 1 (see also note 8 for that chapter). Although not all victims ground piecemeal into the flesh engine deserve our sympathy, it seems justifiable to say that cyberspace is a chaotic communication space that has evolved far from the modernist conceptualization of the public sphere. This said, a comparison of the internet and the public sphere is fair game. Numerous critics already theorized that the "digital habitat" is the new public. As that argument goes, social technology has reinvigorated popular participation and given rise to a transformed public sphere (Macnamara 2010, 157–208). Just how transformed the public sphere is becoming has been widely debated among cyberutopians and critics of technological determinism. While utopianists play up the leveling potential of the social web in eliminating the hierarchy of political communication, pessimists complain that the sphere has been fractured into innumerable echo chambers where like-minded netizens attract each other, recycle, and reinforce each other's partial views (McPherson and Smith-Lovin 2001). Such an inbred culture, also known as *homophily* in network studies, makes us less open, as Ethan Zuckerman argues cogently in *Rewire,* to "serendipitous" encounters that may foster cosmopolitan learnings and genuine cross-cultural understanding. The internet, as he sees it, is failing the test of generating real global connectivity (Zuckerman 2013). I am less interested in taking sides in that debate than in exploring what we can learn from Yochai Benkler's middle-road formulation of "the networked public."

The Wealth of Networks factors in a discussion of information technology and the internet in ways that can help us break out of the insular discourse of political philosophy. By substantiating the analysis of the public sphere in terms of network topology and architecture, Benkler turns our attention from the metatheory of the public sphere to empirical methods such as a study of the link structure on the web. Instead of repeating the truism that "the public sphere is always a product of representation" (Coleman and Ross 2010, 3)[15] and lamenting the impossibility of filling in the utopian void, Benkler shows us what the networked public does, how it works, and why this digital public has more liberatory potential than the mass-media–dominated public sphere (Benkler 2007, 212–272).

Those insights notwithstanding, Benkler's renamed "networked public sphere" has its own theoretical limits. The main problem is rooted in his liberal democratic thinking that habitually associates the market with moral corruption and the nonmarket with agency and freedom. Although the medium has changed and the boundaries of the nonprofit and for-profit are breaking down, we find ourselves stuck in the same dichotomous universe that is split between nonmarket and market actors and actions, which leaves the hybrid millennials straddling both worlds, conceptually homeless. In several chapters, Benkler elaborates on how the "nonmarket form" of networked communication enables "anyone with an outlet to speak, to inquire, to investigate, without need to access the resources of a major [commercial] media organization." (11). He constantly pits the nonmarket habitat against the market ecosystem and perceives the "networked public sphere" as a universe existing parallel to, rather than intersecting or even interwoven with, the commercial, mass-media markets. In his framework, the shift toward decentralized production in the network information economy is seen as a movement away from proprietary, market-oriented action "to a world in which nonproprietary, nonmarket transactional frameworks play a large role" (18). While Benkler is right in suggesting that that this emergent sphere is not easily corruptible by market logic since many social productions are indeed labors of love, his theoretical framework does not leave much room for hybrid productions that take place within the market but which nonetheless produce social value and public good. In reality, network communication has produced *mixed productions and mixed agents*. The traffic is merging from both directions. As shown earlier, Ecotonoha, the Talking Tree, and outputs from GamesThatGive, like other double-headed projects, have thrown into question theoretical claims based on the strict dichotomy that keeps social production separate from market production.

If we apply Benkler's binary paradigm to China, we find ourselves stuck in a similar conceptual dilemma. The Chinese corporate sector has launched various social responsibility initiatives and maintained a natural synergy with grassroots activism, as is argued in Chapter 3. Big Tech entrepreneurs, Bill Gates and Mark Zuckerberg in the US, Jack Ma and Pony Ma in China, and their numerous counterparts all over the world are business elites who are keen to change the world for the better. Sina.com and Tencent.com, for example, are companies priding themselves in promoting the value of the open web. Thanks to their social media experimentation with corporate philanthropy, Chinese grassroots NGOs, formerly forbidden to raise funds in public, can now participate in crowdfunding activities. We are at a crossroads. New media and technology have changed the concept of space, time, and work, but where is the theoretical language that we can rely on to capture and assess this transformative reality?

Corporate Change Agents and Generation 2.0: The China Example

A new critical language has been missing probably because Generation 2.0 appears alien to critics and theorists of our generation whose impulse is to tame and judge.

> In October 2007, Thomas Friedman wrote in the *New York Times* that young people are members of Generation Q. He meant "Q" for quiet, and inactive, on the important social questions of the day. The celebrated American globalist could not have been more wrong. This generation is making noise, whether adults can hear it or not. (Fine 2008, 5)

This passage is taken from a report on the culture of social citizens commissioned by the Case Foundation. Many insights from Fine's study are culled from interviews of digital natives, and they provide numerous clues to the activist persona of millennials. Those young people are seen as hands-on seekers, eager to experience social change, "to touch and feel it, and they want a menu of options for acting *now*" (12, italics mine). The most entrepreneurial among them are merging for-profit and nonprofit structures and concepts, and they are turning social activism into a new marketplace, where online business models emerge in diverse sectors, providing public goods and services while generating excellent revenue. Well-known success stories like Kiva, Magnatune, and Change.org inspired a slew of emulators who are passionate about doing social good and making money at the same time. Thanks to them, a new subsector of nonprofit technology has also emerged in the US.[16]

Instead of dismissing the social influence of click-through campaigns, it may be more productive to ask why digital natives gravitate toward crowdsourced online activism. Unlike their parents, this is a generation that grew up with digital tools at their fingertips. Their motto is to take swift action and see immediate results. In part due to short attention spans and in part due to their irreverence toward the hierarchical structure of organizations, digital natives are drawn to the concept and practice of microvolunteering wherever they can help out in small, convenient ways that do not require a long-term commitment to an organization or a cause. As long as quick funds are raised, awareness of critical issues built, and mobilization through the social web trickles down fast, they consider those actions "social" and themselves "change agents." How much agency do those agents really command? The answer to that question depends upon how change is defined in the twenty-first century, or more precisely, how *they* define it.

Whether we like it or not, the very concept of change is changing although our theoretical language hasn't caught up. Lance Bennett entertains the idea of a paradigm shift of citizenship in postindustrial democracies where networked young citizens are veering away from "dutiful citizenship" that serves formal ideological programs toward seeking "*personally* meaningful, life-style-related political issues" (Bennett 2008, 14, 20–21, italics mine). His perception captures well the cause style of millennials. Indeed, as online and mobile activism and networked organizing are creating new ways for young people to fulfill their service goals, notions of citizenship, civic engagement, and social change will be transformed and redefined accordingly. Theories that are falling out of sync with the changing reality are bound to lose their explanatory potency.

Do I have a solution to this theoretical impasse? No. But as always, I emphasize the importance of doing on-site fieldwork, collecting and investigating case studies, and above all, allowing data to lead us to new critical questions rather than reversing the process by starting with a set theoretical agenda. Furthermore, the process of remaking theoretical paradigms can only be triggered after the scholarly community acknowledges, collectively, the urgency of reinventing old categories. We haven't reached that tipping point yet. But we are already witnessing the rise of a new brand of scholarship that questions the artificial boundary between knowledge and practice, academic research and lived experiences. I have little doubt that the millennial-scholar generation can do better than we have in collapsing the boundary between academic and popular discourse, market and nonmarket activities, work and play, writing and practicing what they write. The hybrid lives in both worlds because it is intuited to do so.

Since the hybrid millennial culture is near universal today, has the mixed-breed that straddles both the for-profit and nonprofit worlds also appeared in China? In a country where both consumer activism and citizen entitlement are weak, can cause marketing 2.0 programs take root and be effective?

Just as Chinese millennials share many characteristics of their global peers, corporate social responsibility as a concept and practice has caught on with mainstream Chinese corporations. Even five years ago, the idea of the consumer as social citizen and brand scion seamlessly blended in one would sound outlandish to marketers in China. Corporate buy-ins took time. Today, the sector is committed to catching up with the global standard of CSR. Efforts appealing to millennials through social cause branding have begun to take shape. If during the Sichuan and Qinghai earthquakes in 2008, corporate giving still meant parachuting hundreds of millions of disaster-relief funds to China's Red Cross, Chinese corporations today have realized that giving is a form of social investment that requires a long-term strategy. As Chapter 3 demonstrates, the Guo Meimei/Red Cross scandal on Weibo marked a turning point in the history of Chinese philanthropy: It motivated corporations to think about diversifying social giving and accounting for every dime of their contributions; it also provided unstoppable momentum for internet companies like Tencent.com and Sina.com to popularize their peer-to-peer crowd-funding platforms. Apart from developing cause marketing campaigns dovetailed with corporate branding, Chinese companies are also eagerly seeking worthy grassroots NGO projects to fund. Some corporations have created their own CSR projects. For example, China Mobile launched a series of funding activities for orphans of AIDS patients (NGO2omap 2009); the China-UK joint venture Aviva-COFCO Life Insurance Company launched a "Compassion for Left-Behind Children" project that helped township and village schools in ten provinces to renovate classrooms and equip them with modern facilities (NGO2omap 2010); Guangdong-based Apollo Group has persistently built libraries in elementary schools located in poverty-stricken areas all over China (Apollo Group 2015); Shunfeng Express initiated various projects supporting village education (Shunfeng Foundation 2017); live-streaming companies like NOW Live, QQ Live, and Tencent Live enabled netizens to tour the Palace Museum from the vantage point of the wandering cats in the palace and donated cat food and cat toys to the Stray Cat Foundation (Maker Sustainability Consulting 2017); Foshan-based corporations participated in the Choose Your NGO Project Contest between 2011 and 2013 and funded more than fifty grassroots NGO projects (NGO2omap 2017); Beijing Weixi Agriculture Company, itself a social enterprise, is committed to saving the last oasis in West China by planting ecofriendly water-saving millet in the Alashan area (Zhang Weisheng 2015). The list goes on and on.

Those were top-down, traditional corporate social responsibility programs. However important, they are not directly relevant to a book focusing on social media activism. I will now turn to three Chinese CSR 2.0 campaigns that gripped the attention of millennials and triggered a networked snowball effect.

In 2009, Sohu.com rolled out a brilliant social cause 2.0 platform called Green Forest. You log on to the miniplatform and take a lifestyle quiz that calibrates your annual carbon footprint. Like most quiz takers, I was declared guilty and compelled to redeem my ecological sin by donating twenty-four virtual trees online. Better still, every virtual tree I clicked to donate yielded a real tree offline, all paid for by corporate sponsors and planted in chosen county towns battling severe desertification. The network effect kicked in fully when I recruited friends to visit the platform and take the quiz as well. Sponsors paid double per tree when an invited friend donated trees. Altogether, as many as four million trees were planted during the campaign period. Green Forest successfully enacts a triple formula—you play, we donate, and causes win.

Similar corporate CSR 2.0 projects followed suit. In 2016, Alibaba launched an ambitious "Ant Forest" Program. Linking finance service and social good, the program motivates Alipay users to undertake low-carbon activities so that they can earn virtual green energy out of which virtual trees are generated in each user account. These are then convertible into real trees offline (Ant Forest 2016). Baidu.com is a latecomer in creating innovative CSR visions. In 2018, a program nicknamed the Little Du Eco-Farm connected a water-conservation and millet planting project in the desert with travelers who follow green travel routes recommended by Baidu map ("Xiaodu nongzhuang" 2018). All those CSR 2.0 programs bear the hallmark of crowdsourcing and emphasize fun making and the experiential.

Not all Chinese co-creation campaigns have a soul, however. Sometimes, even those that are potentially promising fall short of completing the cycle from the recreational to the social. One such example is a once-popular game "A Nail Household Combating the Demolition Team." A *nail house* is a Chinese neologism for households that refuse to relocate when the land they sit on is requisitioned for development projects. News about illegal land seizure and residents' defiance against court orders to evacuate have turned nail household combatants like Wu Ping into a national cause célèbre. It is no surprise that the flash game made by savvy game company Miragine won the title of the hottest online game in 2010. The game unfolds with round after round of guerrilla warfare waged between the besieged Ding family—residents in a nail house—and the demolition team that is closing in to tear down the house by force. Each player is given the option to pick a role in the resistance at each threshold of the game. One could choose to play Grandpa Ding, who guns down the enemy, or Mother Ding, who tosses flip-flops at her targets, or Pop Ding, who wreaks havoc with Molotov cocktails, or Ding Junior, who drops dumbbells onto the opponents, or the Grandson, who shoots slingshots with glee and precision, or the Granddaughter, who hurls firecrackers at the approaching foes, and so on. It is exhilarating to try different roles and use different weapons while elevating oneself to the next level of the game. But the question is: How many players actually associated the game with property rights protection? Although Miragine's edge-ball tactic—cashing in on a political hotspot without truly engaging in activism—has created a marketing practice that seems half entertainment driven and half social critique oriented, the little social value the players bring to the game isn't fully realized because it is not convertible to cause value. The triple link between the player, the corporate donor, and the social cause that underlies the success of Green Forest and GamesThatGive is eclipsed by the familiar corporate norm—you play, we (the company) benefit.

My next example is a financial product developed by a paragon of Chinese corporate citizenship, CreditEase, a company specializing in small-business and P2P lending. CreditEase has recently evolved into a leading wealth management institution aspiring to become the Chinese Merrill Lynch. Few people would associate it with poverty alleviation, and yet that was exactly what its daring CEO Tang Ning strove to do. In 2009, inspired by Muhammad Yunus, the founder of Grameen Bank and pioneer of the idea of microfinance, Tang rolled out YiNongDai, a philanthropic P2P microcredit platform that matches charitable lenders with impoverished, albeit credible rural borrowers. Lenders log into the website, choose their favorite projects created by poor farmers, invest the required minimum 100 RMB for each project, and get a 2 percent interest return annually. The funds provide the rural underclass who do not qualify for bank loans with the means to lift themselves out of poverty. Tang believes that credit loans are more sustainable than donations because they go beyond helping the underprivileged by "empowering them to determine the direction of their lives" (CreditEase 2016). By December 2018, YiNongDai had collected over 325 million RMB ($47 million) from 178,200 lenders and helped more than 27,000 needy entrepreneurial farmers to pursue livelihoods of their choice.[17] In 2010, YiNongDai won China Merchants Group's first "Innovative Action Award for Poverty Alleviation" (China Merchants Group 2010).

Millennials as Donors

Although no statistics have been published about the demographics of lender-supporters on YiNongDai, I would not be surprised if a large number of them are millennials. I made that assumption partly because a 2017 research report on digital donations in China showed that the post-1980s and post-1990s generations form the "backbone of individual donors online" (Ma 2017). More specifically, the make-up of online donors was broken down as follows—41 percent of donors were between the ages of 24 and 30, 24 percent between 18 and 23, and 26 percent between 31 and 40. The numbers are strong indicators that millennials live out their compassion not just as occasional volunteers and virtual spectators, but their pocket speaks out loud too!

My last example of a CSR 2.0 action brings us back to Tencent.com and its extremely popular WeRun, a social walking program embedded in WeChat, roughly defined as a mobile practice of *xingwei gongyi*—

(healthy) behavior as a social good. Similar to Charity Miles, which logs exercise distance and allows users to donate their miles to the charity of their choice, WeRun can track your daily step count and motivate you to become a competitive fitness walker and contribute to social good at the same time. If you stack up more than 10,000 steps on a given day, you are eligible to making a donation to a charity featured on the platform. If by the end of the day, your total mileage tops your friends', your photo will be featured on your group's leaderboard. No matter how you rank though, you'll be able to like your friends' steps, share your results to Chats, and even post them on Moments (WeRun 2017). The app also allows you to set daily targets and sends you notification with details of the number of steps remaining for you to achieve your set target (Neurogadget Staff 2015).

Most industry reports about WeRun focus on the fitness aspect of the application rather than its value as a philanthropic motivator. My own experience with the step tracker brings out another competitive raison d'être of WeRun. And it changed my daily routine in a significant way. First of all, I make sure that I always carry my cell phone in hand so that WeRun can record very single step I take. More importantly, I now take longer walks in the morning and early afternoon, which increases my odds of winning the day's competition early enough so that I can gain the opportunity to donate to the charity of my choice before midnight. That is, you cannot be a donor until you reach 10,000 steps during the day. If you accomplish that goal late in the evening, chances are the slots for charity donation are used up already. You are driven not only to challenge your friends on mileage but compete with them for the opportunity to give on a daily basis. Those small twists make WeRun an effective CSR 2.0 tool.

State Policies on Corporate Social Responsibility

Sohu, Baidu, Alibaba, CreditEase, and Tencent share one thing in common—they utilize Web 2.0 technology to create crowdsourced CSR programs. Is this all about the corporate drive to innovate? Are we witnessing voluntary social action spearheaded by the corporate sector? The answer is no. The Chinese state has played a crucial role in kicking off and sustaining the trend of corporate citizenship. Public discussions surrounding the concept of CSR began with China's accession to the WTO in 2001. But it was not until the government tackled sustainable development in the Eleventh Five-Year Plan (2006–2010), which created the strategy of developing a "harmonious society," that all stakeholders of Chinese society, including the private sector, were called upon to carry out their social responsibility. The recognition that corporations need to play a vital role in this process was written in law. From then on, corporate management was compelled to incorporate social and environmental responsibility. Subsequently, the 2006 "Company Law of the PRC" and the 2008 "Guidance on Social Responsibility of State Enterprises" serve as two prime examples of how the government regulates CSR activities. Two mandatory measures in the latter document caught my attention especially: all state enterprises are required to publish an annual CSR report, actively participate in community development, and encourage their employees to do volunteer work (State-Owned Assets Supervision and Administration Commission [SASAC] of the PRC's State Council 2008). By the time when the Twelfth Five-Year Plan (2011–2015) was published, the state had set up a committee on CSR within SASAC to work on an evaluation system assessing the results of CSR implemented by state-run enterprises. The emphasis on the necessity of importing CSR theories and practices from abroad appeared in the same document (SASAC 2011). Those various state policies spell out one message we are often reluctant to reckon with: the role of policies in enabling a constructive trend. Just as the Double Leisure Day policy in the 1990s ignited the rise of popular culture in post-Mao China (Wang 2001) and the policies dictating the separation of station and network breathed new life into China's radio and TV sector (Wang 2008b, 253–256), so have the officially sanctioned CSR directives pushed the corporate sector to contribute to the making of the new "social."

While the government was busy publishing regulations for state enterprises, private corporations have also undergone a process of self-education and voluntary self-regulation. The influence of international standards and the United Nations Global Compact provided further incentives for them to implement CSR strategies. Equally important, the toy and pet food scandals in 2007 and the melamine milk incident of 2008 have renewed the debate on public trust of enterprises, "the loss of which may tarnish the 'Made in China' brand" (GTZ et al. 2008, 8). Consumer demands for corporate accountability are thus another push factor for the emergence of CSR culture in China. All those factors, combined with the coming of age of socially concerned millennial consumers, have converged to nurture in Chinese companies a collective awareness that they too can strive to become change makers. As seen in Chapter 3 and all the CSR 2.0 examples cited in this chapter, forward-looking tech conglomerates like Sina and Tencent enjoy an added advantage: they can scale up their change agenda on the Web 2.0 platforms they created, on which millennials are surfing as volunteers, players, spectators, and donors.

Conclusion

This chapter built a dual framework of change makers—the millennials and the corporate sector, each in its own way experimenting with innovative ways of practicing nonconfrontational activism. The chapter opened with the portrayal of millennials as change makers and examined their demographic profile step by step through an analysis of their multiple identities as volunteers, initiators of internet incidents, virtual spectators, and donors, respectively. The chapter moved on to capture another role played by the millennials—target consumers for cause marketing 2.0 campaigns. I argued that the best of the global millennials—the Chinese post-1980s and post-1990s generations included—are not only transforming how civic engagement is fashioned but how corporate social responsibility initiatives are programmed. As the best specimen of Generation 2.0, those creative youths are acting as conduits between two previously irreconcilable worlds—markets and civic habitats.

The life of millennials is a busy and creative one. They follow the DIY ethos heartily and produce not only user-generated content en masse but algorithms and smart gadgets in response to Premier Li Keqiang's call to launch a Chinese maker movement. To 2015 and the emergence of (change) maker communities we now turn.

5

Makers and Tech4Good Culture

This chapter highlights techies as social actors and investigates grassroots tech4good projects as well as the implications of maker culture to the national, official pursuit of cultivating a creative China. Since the mid-2010s, socially concerned makers in cities like Beijing, Shanghai, Shenzhen, and Hangzhou have been quietly challenging the official paradigm of "maker as entrepreneur." Creativity and the urge for change are the twin faces of transformative social imagination. This chapter situates the outbreak of the Maker Movement around 2015 in the context of national innovation policy, examines a variety of maker output, and probes community driven tech4good models.

In February 2014, the US-based *Tea Leaf Nation,* a news site dedicated to Chinese citizens and social media, published an editorial titled "It's Official: China Is Becoming a New Innovation Powerhouse." The title should surprise no one well informed of the scale and strategy of China's national innovation policies. Vacillating between an alarmist message that "the world's factory is turning into an R&D machine" and a consolation sentiment that China will not out-innovate the US anytime soon, the article ponders statistics that seem to work in China's favor. Data reveal a spike in Chinese college graduates, from less than a million in 1999 to almost 7 million in 2013; more revealing however is the fact that 31 percent of these graduates received engineering degrees, in stark contrast to the 5 percent receiving engineering degrees in the US. In addition, other data show the US share of global R&D dropping from 37 percent in 2001 to 30 percent in 2011 while China's share jumped from a low 2.2 percent in 2000 to 14.5 percent in 2011 (Wertime 2014). By way of downplaying these startling numbers, the editorial draws attention to the weakness inherent in Chinese-style education whereby rote learning is prioritized over creative thinking.

Not all is as it seems, however, and change is a constant in China. While contemplating these issues, I indulged myself in binge viewing a popular 2015 Chinese TV serial *Tiger Mom* (*huma maoba*) and stumbled upon a rising trend of "creative education." *Tiger Mom,* produced by Tianjin Satellite TV, is China's first serialized drama to pick up on the debates about schooling practices. In a country as heavily populated as China, passing the fiercely competitive college entrance exams has become the overriding goal, if not the only purpose, of education. Should China's generation of singleton children be put through the ordeal year after year, foregoing their happy childhoods? The ratings of the TV serial were surprisingly high and so it is worth asking: why was this kind of drama so popular? Why now?

The story revolves around a city couple—a disciplinarian mom and a low-key dad, their young daughter Qian Qian, and her four grandparents. The family is torn apart on a daily basis by the warring education doctrines of Qian Qian's caretakers. The audience is led into a battlefield split between exam-score obsessed Confucianists and overseas-trained experts committed to a modern, creative pedagogy. While this was a well-crafted story, I couldn't wait for the full forty-six episodes to unfold to find out the outcome of the competition. So I fast-forwarded to the finale where surprisingly, the militant mainstream ideologists were defeated by the new school of creative thinking; better still, it was an ending accompanied by the conversion of the diehard Confucian grandpa to the camp that trumpets the freedom of the mind and body and the new educational philosophy that emphasizes the necessity of giving children ample space to play and explore, getting their hands dirty, and creating what their heart desires. The ratings success made me wonder if Chinese education is ready to undergo some theatrical changes. Indeed, one of the climactic moments in the drama occurs in a conflict between the conservative and modern pedagogues: the daughter's handmade paper fish mobile is suddenly smashed by her incensed grandfather who deems *making things* instead of studying a total waste of time. The reaction of national audience was revealing: their sympathy went to Qian Qian predominantly.[1]

To put this into context, it's worth examining the political winds blowing across Chinese national innovation culture. Since January 2015, news reporters have been propagating a new culture movement initiated by Premier Li Keqiang. In September 2014 and January 2015, in two consecutive meetings of the World Economic Forum in Davos, Li promulgated his now well-known slogan *dazhong chuangye wanzhong chuangxin* (mass entrepreneurship and mass innovation), seamlessly linking grassroots maker-innovators with national wealth. According to the premier, "every cell in society" will be activated to innovate; moreover, the "twin engine" of China's economic growth will rest on a scaled mobilization of individual makers and mass entrepreneurs (Li Keqiang 2015).

Prior to his Davos speeches, a well-orchestrated domestic media blitz accompanied the premier on his visit to Chaihuo Makerspace in Shenzhen, China's high-tech manufacturing hub and a frontier of the maker revolution. A subsequent series of statements and high-profile events propelled *chuangke* (makers) onto the agenda of China's national innovation system. In March, during the annual Two Sessions held by the PRC's top legislative and advisory bodies, the term *maker* formally entered national policy discourse. Then on May 4, a historical milestone marking the anniversary of the 1919 student-led New Culture Movement, Premier Li delivered another poignant message, this time to the young makers studying at Tsinghua University, the Chinese MIT. Promising to clear up policy obstacles for small-to-medium enterprises (SMEs), Li said, "Making and creating is no longer a privilege reserved for the elites but an opportunity afforded to the greater majority of people" ("Li Keqiang zongli" 2015). This measured statement implies nothing less than the shift of the government's pet policy project from creative industries (Wang 2004; Keane 2011)—a top-down, closed, elitist line-up—to "mass entrepreneurship" which is anchored on open innovation and made available to grassroots actors.

Makerspaces have popped up all over China—not only in first-tier cities but also in Zhengzhou (Henan Province), Guiyang (Guizhou Province), and Ürümqi (Xinjiang Province). The term *maker* (*chuangke*) has entered the lexicon of new fashionable phrases. The fact that *Tiger Mom* implicitly endorses the ethos of maker culture made me wonder whether the show would still be such a crowd pleaser if Premier Li had not championed the maker's cause. Regardless of the excellent timing of the broadcast though, winning the hearts of Chinese television audiences is no small victory. Children, the subject of this drama, watch the narrative unfold together with their parents and aging grandparents who are often the most stubborn gatekeepers of traditional pedagogy.

Although the real focus of this chapter is maker as change maker, I want to first investigate the status of creativity in China by offering my reflections on the Chinese maker culture. I begin by defining the maker concept and then situating Premier Li's Maker Initiative in the complex ecosystem of China's national innovation policy. Against that larger context, I will examine several maker projects which have emerged at the grass roots. After scrutinizing the maker-driven start-up culture, I argue that the official discourse of "maker as entrepreneur" offers limited value proposition. Only a small handful of young makers turn into real entrepreneurs, and an even smaller number of entrepreneurs create businesses that actually hire paid staff.[2] The coupling of makers and entrepreneurs produces at best "hope value." It is a bubble that can burst any time.

The second half of this chapter realigns this policy discourse with an alternative term *change* maker, a maker as social-change engineer. This does not have to be an either-or proposition. Makers can be both entrepreneurial and socially concerned, and this hybrid is already in existence in China. Chapter 4 provided a few innovative samples of poverty-alleviation projects created by youths participating in Enactus China (an offshoot of an international NGO). This chapter addresses two other models of maker as social innovator—innovation challenge contests spearheaded by Intel China and the Future Village Initiative that sits squarely on tech4good practices. This chapter then ends with an account of NGO2.0's ongoing collaboration with maker pioneer David Li in transforming the Minqin County of Gansu Province into a future village.

Makers and Makerspaces

At the outset, it's important to establish a definition of *makerspace* and the Maker Movement. Often associated with democratized innovation, the Maker Movement is inseparable from web culture: think of DIY garage culture moved to the internet. Chris Anderson identifies four major factors for this flourishing digital DIY movement: the new default of sharing and collaborating online; the appearance of digital desktop tools for hobbyists to design and prototype new products; the birth of a web-based manufacturing model that functions like an on-demand cloud service, enabling the emergence of a maker-driven market for one-off products; and the popularity of crowdfunding platforms that are creating a new class of mass investors willing to provide seed money for daring start-ups (Anderson 2012, 13, 21, 66, 77, 168).

This is not just about amateur content creation, but also the "long tail" of user-generated innovation, a twenty-first century mode of production anyone can access from web browsers and scale up and down at will. The "spaces" where these wide varieties of niche products are designed, pro-totyped, and manufactured are called makerspaces—workstations usually equipped with 3D printers, 3D scanners, laser cutters, and other metal-working and woodworking tools, and in the case of Shenzhen's Chaihuo Makerspace, open-source computer hardware like Arduino circuit boards. Central to the US concept of maker culture is the quadruple idea of make, create, hack, and learn. The Maker Movement envisages a renewed interest in learning through tinkering and engineering (Martinez and Stager 2013).

The Chinese official definition of *maker* is merely functional. *The People's Daily (renmin ribao)* provides an official interpretation:

> Makers are devoted to innovation passionately. They control the production tools themselves. Taking "user-innovation" as a core concept, they excel in discovering problems, unearthing (customer) needs, and providing solutions. Through creativity, design, and manufacturing, they offer a variety of products and services. (Yu and Deng 2015)

The emphasis is placed on a dry industrialist take on innovation. Con-spicuously missing from the definition above are the spirit of collabora-tive engineering, the pleasure principle of hobbyists, and the educational perspectives of inventing to learn. Significantly, three of the leading mak-erspaces in China—Chaihuo Makerspace (Shenzhen), Maxpace (Beijing), and XinCheJian (Shanghai, literally, the "New Workshop")—have all de-fined themselves as *dream factories;* they view makerspaces as venues for hackers to build dream machines,[3] places where "makers from diverse backgrounds gather to brainstorm in teams and create visions,"[4] labs where they can "experiment with new technology" and "seek pleasure from making things collaboratively,"[5] and last but not least, open plat-forms for knowledge sharing and learning.

Indeed, Chinese maker communities existed long before Li Keqiang discovered the economic value of makers. Two open-source hardware pro-viders were founded as early as 2008—Seeed Studio in Shenzhen and DFRobot in Shanghai. In 2010, David Li built the first Chinese maker-space—the New Workshop—in Shanghai, and since then, a large community catering to future innovators has emerged in first-tier cities. The flurry of activities revolving around tinkering and DIY hardware culture flourished quietly without the government's notice or blessing. In fact, by the end of 2014, approximately 1,000 hardware start-ups had already sprung up in China, among them, 200 succeeded in finding investors. Then came the official promotion and the media blitz on the Maker Movement. By December 2015, China was populated by over 2,300 makerspaces and 2,500 tech start-up incubators. About 80,000 young enterprises were being "hatched" and approximately 60,000 of them were set up by college graduates (Li, Luo, and Zhang 2016). By the end of 2017, the Ministry of Science and Technology unveiled new statistics: the total number of makerspaces escalated to 5,500 and that of the incubators jumped to 4,000 (Lu 2018).

What did Li Keqiang find in the makerspace that ignited his embrace of this movement? Many analysts attribute it to the government's attempt of tackling the unemployment crisis of college graduates; others consider it a reasonable way of boosting the GDP. Whatever the catalyst, the movement signals a watershed moment in state innovation policy that has embodied, over the past three decades, a well-focused national pursuit of rebranding China as a creative nation. This triple shift—from "made in China" to "created in China" and now to "making in China"—is perhaps a sign that innovation is now a societal concern: every maker is called upon to participate in this long tail revolution, not just state designated IT and creative industry clusters (Wang 2016a).

Major Milestones of Chinese Innovation Policy

In order to understand the context of Premier Li's Maker Initiative, it's worth briefly noting China's catch-up game in innovation policy. Since 1988, a Chinese national innovation system has gradually taken shape. In that year the Ministry of Science and Technology (MOST) rolled out the Torch Program with the aim of establishing Science and Technology Industrial Parks, Software Parks, Science-Tech Business Incubators, and Productivity Promotion Centers.[6] A decade later in the wake of China's WTO accession, the Tenth Five-Year Plan (2001–2005) raised the R&D funding to over 1.5 percent of the GDP (CPC Central Committee 2001). Then in 2006, innovation came center stage. The State Council unveiled a mid- to long-term plan (2006–2020) to strengthen science and technology (S&T) development. Under this plan, China would become an innovation-oriented nation (*chuangxing xing guojia*) by 2020 with the new leadership of Hu Jintao and Wen Jiabao enthusiastically endorsing the slogan of *zizhu chuangxin* (independent or indigenous innovation). Also eye-catching was the new investment target set for science and technology R&D, which rose from the 1.5 percent of GDP benchmarked in 2001 to 2.5 percent (State Council 2006).

Around the same time, in the cultural sphere the mood was buoyant and policy was being formulated at a rapid pace. A national cultural development plan for the Eleventh Five-Year Plan (2006–2010) was published, formally putting the compromise term "Cultural and Creative Industry" (CCI) on the state agenda and kicking off a series of CCI initiatives in cities rich with resources and creative talents. Local Blue Books[7] catalogued the excitement of cities racing against each other to reach output targets; animation industry parks and creative clusters mushroomed all over the country (Keane 2016).

In 2008, on the twentieth anniversary of the launch of the Torch Program, Minister of Science and Technology Fang Gang announced that the program would undergo major changes, one of which was a strategic shift from S&T-centered initiatives to entrepreneurship-centric innovation projects (Fang 2008). Torch would continue to evolve in 2015 with makerspace becoming a subcategory of S&T intermediary organizations.

All those varying initiatives notwithstanding, China's national innovation system (henceforth NIS) is not well integrated. As its critics point out, it's a system made up of a large number of innovative islands with "many linkages between actors and sub-systems (e.g., regional versus national) remaining weak" and disconnected (OECD 2007, 22). To remedy the problem, throughout the 2010s, Chinese NIS took a new turn by emphasizing collaborative innovation. In this new vision, universities would be designated the primary drivers of multisector collaborative networks, a move that later also paved the way for the emergence of campus-based maker incubators.

In 2010, the Ministry of Education published a new directive that allowed university science parks to take on the major responsibility of setting up incubators and internship bases to house and train students. Preferential policy treatments for student entrepreneurs included seed funding, tax reductions, and free office rentals for the first twelve months of the launch of a new business (Ministry of Education 2010). To ensure outputs and raise public awareness about this new initiative, college student innovation contests were broadcast nationwide by CCTV.[8]

An equally significant milestone occurred on April 24, 2011. On that day, Hu Jintao attended the 100th anniversary of the founding of Tsinghua University and gave a speech sanctioning the concept of *xietong chuangxin* (cooperative collaboration). Less than a month later, the Ministry of Education and the Ministry of Finance jointly launched Plan 2011[9] that laid the infrastructure for strategic networked alliances, under which universities would cooperate with peer institutions, the corporate sector, local governments, and international research organizations to engage in national competitions revolving around four innovation categories: advanced science and technology, preservation and reinvention of cultural heritage, sector-specific innovations, and creative design of regional development plan (Ministry of Education 2011).[10]

The impact of the 2010 and 2011 policy decrees changed the innovation landscape of universities at an accelerating pace and laid down a solid foundation for maker policies, which target college students by incentivizing their entrepreneurial engagement. Since that time, new academic programs on innovation and entrepreneurship have sprung up in colleges all over the country. Many new Schools of Innovation and Entrepreneurship (SIEs) were established in April and May of 2015, following the media feeding frenzy about Premier Li Keqiang's Shenzhen trip. Guangdong Province, for example, released policies bidding all provincially based colleges to set up SIEs, and in an effort to double and triple the number of student-entrepreneurs, it allowed youngsters interested in establishing start-ups to take legitimate academic leaves (Lei 2015)! All this has been crucial to the quickened transformation of college students into makers.

Then came the policies well calculated to unleash the long tail effect of China's grassroots creativity. In June 2015, in response to the premier's Maker Initiative, Shenzhen took the national lead in publishing a set of experimental policies with the ambitious goal of creating fifty new makerspaces per year to reach a designated number of 200 by the end of 2017 (Shenzhen City Committee 2015). This was an unprecedented open call for proposals targeting the entire city. Newly built or existing makerspaces with an expansion plan can receive up to $833,333 per recipient; an additional $500,000 is up for grabs for maker labs that wish to make hardware upgrades. Predictably, other cities are following Shenzhen's footsteps and preparing similar policy statements. The most eye-catching prize category is the $166,666 per recipient to qualified primary and middle schools, higher education institutions, and technical and apprentice schools that demonstrate a sound plan for integrating maker education into the curriculum and installing school-based maker labs (Shenzhen City Committee 2015). Chinese authorities are apparently mindful of the role creative education plays in moving China up the ladder as an innovation nation. Given time, tiger moms may lose their raison d'être as the whole society is mobilized to think and make things creatively.

Copycat or Bottom-Up Innovation?

Meanwhile, complaints about the lack of creative impetus behind Chinese education, echoed in the TV serial *Tiger Mom,* are often accompanied by equally harsh criticisms of the *shanzhai* (copycatting) phenomenon. A nation of rote learners is seen as a parallel to a nation of imitators producing counterfeit products, which is surely a blot, critics say, on China's aspirations to be a creative nation.

Since the 2010s, however, the ideology of open innovation has paved the way for a revisionist interpretation of *shanzhai* to surface. A report in *Wired UK* describe *shanzhai* practitioners as "guerrilla innovators" who apply "as much innovation and ingenuity as their legitimate counterparts." (Johnson 2010). David Li, founder of China's first makerspace, the New Workshop, compares *shanzhai* with "the Robin Hood spirit" that inspires "legitimate and often quite innovative products" (*The Economist* 2013). Among *shanzhai*'s celebrity endorsers is Chris Anderson, author of *The Long Tail.* Calling the bootleg business practice "lightweight innovation," he echoes David Li's assessment and equates the phenomenon with the "ultimate openness we in the open-source world are looking for" (Anderson 2012, 212). Proclaiming that "a copy can be better than the original," Rainer Wessler, creative director of Frog Design, asks whether *shanzhai* has proved that the Western approach to innovation is outdated (Wessler 2013).

Eventually, the philosophical debate over *shanzhai* may not be as crucial as it used to be as the world witnesses the outburst of China's entrepreneurial dynamism—by 2017 more than 10,000 new businesses were born in China per day—that's seven Chinese start-ups born every minute. Consider also that one in three of the world's 262 unicorns[11] is Chinese (Woetzel, Seong et al. 2017). Those statistics prompted *Wired Magazine* to declare that China is no longer a nation of copycats. The Chinese, as the magazine proclaims, are leading in key technology sectors such as mobile payments and catching up with the US in advanced microchips and artificial intelligence (Kline 2017).

What is worth noting, however, is the intangible connection between *shanzhai* and open-source hardware. Claiming that they are "twins separated at birth," David Li evokes a scenario in which the world of *shanzhai* converges with that of makers (Li 2014). Exactly how that happens however is left for speculation. Silvia Lindtner, cofounder of the Hacked Matter blog, argues that those two phenomena are complementary in essence. In her view, what we are witnessing is a natural partnership built between the founders of Chinese hardware start-ups (the makers' businesses) and the erstwhile *shanzhai* factories (Lindtner 2014). If we follow this logic, it appears Shenzhen's thriving maker culture owes a great deal to the bottom-up infrastructure and network ecosystem put in place by a myriad of *shanzhai* plants over the past decade.

Even if we cannot be conclusive about the tangible link between makers and *shanzhai* pirates, we can dig deeper into what distinguishes homegrown innovation from *shanzhai* by turning our attention to the changing profile of the new generation of innovators themselves. China's policy preferential treatments for indigenous innovation and university incubators, as detailed earlier in this chapter, have triggered a new round of start-up fever embraced by the post-1980s and post-1990s generation, many of whom are college students or new graduates, the twenty- and thirty-somethings. It is important to note, however, that not all makers are hardware tinkerers since software developers and digital platform builders are also included in the Chinese maker family.[12] The following section illustrates examples of young maker-entrepreneurs.

Young Makers at a Glance and Homegrown Start-Ups

Long before Premier Li promoted makerspaces, embryonic communities of makers had already sprung up here and there, joined by younger and younger participating members. One of the winning teams in a 2014 China-US maker contest that created Night Edge—a laser and ultrasonic musical instrument—was spearheaded by fifteen- and sixteen-year-old high school kids;[13] and a Wuxi-based makerspace presented a "crazy crab" invented by a third grader who utilized what he learned from BIT@DIY to engineer the talking and crawling functions of the crab.[14] Underage hobbyists aside, China is witnessing the rise of adult makers who are keen to turn themselves into full-fledged entrepreneurs. For example, Jason Wang made his name by raising funds on Kickstarter for his Makeblock, a private tech company that develops Arduino-based hardware, robotics hardware, and Scratch-based software to create educational tools for engineering and programming activities. They sell a set of flexible components—including slots, wheels, sensors, drivers and controllers, timing belts, and motors—for building robotics, machines, toys, or even art-ware. When interviewed by *Wired,* Wang called this combo kit a "lego for adults" (Finley 2012).[15]

Not all twenty-something makers are capable of replicating Jason Wang's success. Although an increasing number of his followers are creating robots, some are dull inventions like ticket-selling bots in movie theaters. More newsworthy examples are actually platform and software creators like Sun Yan. The founder of SmellMe, Sun is in his thirties. Like typical young entrepreneurs, he is a magnet attracting kindred spirits from the same age group. Sun rounded up an investment of US\$7.8 million to roll out China's first pet social network *wenwen wo,*[16] a funny name that sounds like "smell me" (Yan 2015).[17] SmellMe can be accessed via mobile apps. It boasts of having a user membership over 5 million.

SmellMe is but one of the thousands of emerging software start-ups in cities all over China. Where there is a gap in demand, there are competing start-ups. Venture capital investors are busy signing up carpooling apps, test-prep start-ups, various internet-of-things start-ups, efficiency apartment finders like Mofang and MogoRoom, services like Wifi Skeleton that unlock free connections to hotspots, on-demand valet parking services, fresh produce e-tailers, even a medical tourism app that connects Chinese tourists to overseas clinics for cosmetic surgery! With the boom of interest in online citizen entrepreneurship, new business categories like the training schools for start-up pioneers have also emerged. Chinaccelerator, a Shanghai based company founded in 2009, has already graduated seven batches of promising start-up founders.[18]

Side by side with those platform and app start-ups are diverse hardware start-ups: home robot companions; smart toasters that show today's weather on a piece of toast; smart cushions like HealthButt that tell you when you need to rest or fix your posture; smart food makers automatically mixing ingredients in, making the dish, and cleaning itself; smart bottles for infants that keep track of a baby's milk consumption, weight, and other relevant statistics; smart travel mugs that remind you to drink water and stay hydrated; smart devices you can place inside the refrigerator to purge fruits and vegetables of pesticide residue and bacteria; umbrellas that emit beautiful colors on rainy days; phones that reveal the temperature of the surrounding area when plugged into an outlet; robots acting as tutors for children and completing projects and homework with them; and planters that ensure a plant's growth with minimal human attention. The smart list goes on and on. Those products came and went with only a small chance of survival. Easily cloned by competitors, they carry little commercial value, and worst of all, they are socially meaningless. By 2017, it became obvious that Premier Li's vision of "maker as entrepreneur" had run into serious bottlenecks. College makers are amateurs after all, whose understanding of the market is superficial and whose ideas about invention may not go beyond trivial needs.

Maker as Change Agent

That said, where are the civic-minded creator-citizens capable of building a genuinely creative society that would presumably occur at the third stage of China's "creative century plan," a futurist blueprint spun by Liu Shifa's and Li Wuwei's futurist blueprints? (Liu 2006; Li Wuwei 2011)? Where can we spot creative change makers in twenty-first century China? How do we characterize their activities? They are not quite the cocreative drivers of a "user-led, demand-side" knowledge economy as John Hartley has speculated (Hartley 2010, xvii). Nor are they amateur content creators like Hu Ge (the maker of the sensational spoof, A Murder Caused by a Steamed Bun[19]) emerging from the sphere of "grassroots recreation" in Michael Keane's terms (Keane 2011, 177–178). The problem is we don't know much about change makers with a civic twist because they are completely left out of the vision of Chinese policy makers and mainstream Western media reports about social change in China.

And yet, idealistic creators with the maker mind-set are emerging all over the Chinese internet and technology sectors. These are mature, older makers, many of whom are comfortably employed in China-based multinationals and domestic Chinese IT companies. Since 2013, NGO2.0 has been collaborating with techies seeking opportunities to channel their social energy into tech4good outlets. We regularly recruit volunteers for NGO2.0's hackathon program who include employees from SAP, Thought-Works, Frog, Tencent.com, and Oracle, as well as students and faculty from the now defunct School of Software of Sun Yat-sen University and the iCenter of Tsinghua University. These makers and programmers have all made contributions to the bridge-building activities NGO2.0 designed to link grassroots NGOs with socially concerned techies.

Why hackathons? NGOs have technological needs to meet, and techies, as believers of the can-do hacker ethic, have a missionary passion for using technology to make the world a better place. But neither understand what the other is doing. Civic hackathons came into existence as a bridge that connects these two groups and brings them together to practice collaborative design. By complementing each other's strengths, they stand a better chance of finding solutions to the social problems put on the table. Since 2013, the number of civic hackathons has grown in Beijing, Shanghai, and Shenzhen where techies are forming communities with a social goal. Chapter 2 treats the hackathon logic and output in detail. Suffice it to say that only a small number of problems can be treated technologically (the Minqin Hackathon I will describe later comes to mind). It did not take us long to discover that customizing solutions for participating NGOs is not cost effective and not a goal that a single hackathon can achieve. However, our hackathons continued, and the focus gradually shifted to training NGOs to master design thinking rather than creating one-off prototyped solutions for them. Meanwhile, it is worth noting that the civic hackathon is but one venue for Chinese techies to fulfill their urge to serve society.

Parallel to those hackathon activities, a small cluster of start-ups emerged on the horizon, making one-size-fits-all blanket tech solutions to serve NGOs and the public good. Those tools are community-driven technologies revolving around constituent relationship management, financial transparency, project and donor management tools, and so on. For example, Tower.im and Lingxi360.com have become indispensable platforms for grassroots organizations looking to operate office work efficiently. Our own crowdsourced philanthropy map—ngo20map.com—is a modest social tech experiment, launched with the goal of connecting NGOs with the corporate sector. The Web 2.0 toolbox, also created by NGO2.0, is filled with gadgets that are made up of existing for-profit software and tools that we repurposed for NGOs, which drives home the message emphasized by civic-tech tinkerer Laurenellen McCann: "Some of our best civic tools are the ones we already have in hand, their 'civic' utility is unlocked just by wielding them differently" (McCann 2015).

Meanwhile, a palpable generational shift is taking place in the nonprofit sector. In earlier times, the middle-aged pioneers of Chinese philanthropy have taken pride in constructing a purist's vision of social innovation, one that is in essence anti-entrepreneurial and oblivious to new technology. The younger generation, especially those nurtured under state innovation policies, takes a different approach to producing social good. Generally speaking, this new generation is social media savvy and entrepreneurial, and some of them are good at creating IT solutions to pressing social problems. The latter are a rare breed indeed because it's hard to be both a thinker and a doer successful in blending the visionary and the practical.

In fact, if I had not run NGO2.0 and worked for over ten years in China's nonprofit sector, I would not have had access to the rich literature and sporadically emerging events involving social entrepreneurs of all ages, the most innovative of whom are twenty-somethings. They have largely escaped mainstream media attention both at home and abroad and have received no endorsements from Premier Li.

There have been three notable incubators of social entrepreneurs in urban China—Cinnovate, Enactus (which I described in Chapter 4), and Shenzhen Open Innovation Lab. All three share a vision for cross-sector collaboration. Like other grassroots movements, they see the primary source of creativity originating in individuals. The starting point to identify talented citizen-individuals for all three incubators is making an open call for creative social strategies.

Cinnovate

In the summer of 2010 I met Joyce Zhou, a passionate, socially concerned manager at Intel Beijing, who subsequently spearheaded a series of "social innovation challenge" contests, sponsored by Intel and supported by a few foundations and the Ministry of Civil Affairs. Those were China's earliest social innovation tournaments, and I was lucky to be involved as a judge for the initial two rounds of contests. The open competitions were part of an impressive corporate social responsibility (CSR) campaign that promoted an Intel-style tech-fetishist view that "information technology can advance and expedite social innovation." The 2010 call for proposals reads, "Do you know what ICT means to nonprofit organizations? Metaphorically, it gives wings to compassion and enables it to fly far" (Cinnovate 2010). Initially, the contest was made up of three categories—Best Tech Development, Best Tech Avant-Guard, and Best Tech Application. In 2011, other prize entries were added, including Best Collaborative Innovation, a category I recommended. Intel China scored big in the public eye with those annual tournaments, but they were discontinued in 2013 because of mixed results.

Many prizewinners failed to implement their proposed action, and some plans, although materialized, were not sustainable. Qifang Net, a 2010 contest winner, closed down its P2P lending platform for college students without notice. In 2013, the founder was hunted down and forced to reckon with angry lenders. The scandal about his delinquency cast a shadow over newly established online philanthropy initiatives. Another 2010 winner, Rescue Minqin, an environmental NGO of which I am strongly supportive, failed to mobilize enough technology resources to deliver their proposed Plant Virtual Trees platform. IT-driven solutions are easier said than done. In the early 2010s, e-commerce was just taking off, techies had not yet formed communities, and cross-sector resources in technology were scarce to say the least. But a few successful pioneers also made their names, bringing public attention to the then raw concept of social enterprise.

One of the most celebrated cases of technology as problem solver was a 2010 Cinnovate winner, the Qiang Embroidery Help Center. The Qiang Center is an NGO specializing in minority cultural protection funded by Jet Li's One Foundation. Its earlier incarnation, an occupational service center for Qiang women, was established in the immediate wake of the devastating Wenchuan earthquake. Since 2008, the NGO has established embroidery stations in small Sichuan villages with the goal of providing impoverished minority women with a sustainable means of livelihood. The number of Qiang embroidery trainees went up to 168,000 in a few years (Wang Shuang 2012). Later, the founder of this organization opened up specialty embroidery retail shops from Chengdu to Suzhou, Beijing, Shanghai, and Taipei, successfully turning the NGO into a social enterprise. They also built a business-to-consumer e-commerce store through Taobao.com and a business-to-business platform on Alibaba.com to reach multiple markets outside the remote county town. By modernizing a craft on the brink of distinction, ICT technology solved the problems of unemployment among rural Qiang women (Qiangxiu bangfu zhongxin 2013).

More importantly, the Qiang Center overcame the difficulty of transporting embroidery instructors to mountainous areas by providing online video trainings (Abei zhou funu Qiang xiu 2010). Without leaving their home or quitting farm work, diligent Qiang women now have access to online instruction. This model of flexible employment was replicated by embroidery centers in other southwestern provinces—in Guizhou, Xinjiang, and Sichuan, where minority women are enlisted to reinvent the Miao, Kesai, Shu, and Tibetan embroidery traditions.[20] Digital communication not only popularized skill training at low cost, it also opened a door to the outside world and enriched the information flow in remote minority villages, benefiting not just the embroiderers themselves but other villagers as well.

Sporadic successes notwithstanding, founders of the Cinnovate tournaments soon found themselves caught in a dilemma. Initially set up as a mechanism encouraging grassroots NGOs to use IT means to solve social problems, the Cinnovate Award attracted a large number of government-affiliated and well-endowed players in following years. The integrity of the awards could not but be compromised by the entry of those rich and powerful official organizations that were picked and rewarded for half-baked ideas. Luckily, Cinnovate gained a second life in 2013 by bidding farewell to the contest formula. In its place, a new tradition of Innovation Week was launched. Through an assemblage of fun and inspiring workshops, speeches, activities, and offline interactive games, the new platform was designed to step up "efforts to ignite public interest in emerging models of social innovation" (Cinnovate Center 2013).

"Be the change" was the new motto. Harnessing individuals' creative power appeared high on the agenda, as was Cinnovate's desire of building "a vibrant ecosystem for social innovation" (Cinnovate Center 2013). The 2013 Innovation Week was said to have drawn one thousand makers, philanthropists, and members of nonprofit communities (Cinnovate Innovation Week 2013), not to mention talent-spotting venture capitalists that began to appear regularly at those events. It is worth noting that the target demographic for Cinnovate, Enactus, and other social innovation incubators are the post-1990s generation.

The internet is filled with journalists and academic researchers discoursing about the connection between youth organizations, social action, and social movements in democratic societies. Chinese youth activists share the same utopian ideals as their Western counterparts and are deeply involved in a quest for equity and social justice, but they have to navigate carefully to stay clear of political landmines. As I point out in Chapter 1, street demonstrations are certainly off-limits in China, but the state is tolerant of social service initiatives which are often equated with poverty alleviation and other state-endorsed social welfare categories. Mindful of the limits set for youth activism in China, Cinnovate and Enactus, both of which have international origins, decided to put their programmatic emphasis on innovation and entrepreneurship, which has been a state-endorsed policy over the past three decades, as I detailed in the first half of this chapter. Like all "grassroots" activities in China, both platforms function with relative political impunity probably because they have made partnerships with state organizations.[21]

As I discussed in Chapter 4, Enactus is perceivably the most influential platform for mobilizing youth activists in China. Not only does it reach out to young people while they are still in their formative years, it doesn't target affluent regions exclusively. A glance at the list of the 227 membership universities reveals that Enactus casts its net far into western and central provinces, the lesser developed regions of China (Enactus 2014). The scope of Cinnovate, on the other hand, is more confined. All of its activities took place in Beijing.

Cinnovate, however, enjoyed one huge advantage, at least at the beginning—it was an Intel-sponsored NGO. A pioneer of social innovation contest and the originator of the Chinese term *chuang bian ke* (maker-changer), Cinnovate was nonetheless not the only player promoting the agenda of innovators as change makers in the mid-2010s China. It had cruised along more successfully than its competitors because Cinnovate could pull the weight of Intel to build multisector alliances quickly. I recall watching with envy Cinnovate's cordial relationship with elite foundations and the Chinese government, not to mention the extensive press coverage it enjoyed. But to be frank, a CSR-driven social innovation machine has its own vulnerabilities, among them the hubris of a multinational. A powerful company like Intel is sometimes guilty of paying lip service to cross-sector collaboration. For when it came to brainstorming at the table, its own voice dominated, leaving little room for other partners-in-name to play a significant role in shaping the agenda. In the end, building "a vibrant ecosystem" for a new philanthropy model requires real and multiple collaborators, and a networking vision not bound to a domineering mind-set. That's perhaps the hardest lesson change-making incubators in China have yet to learn.

This said, Intel Beijing was one of the pioneers of tech4good culture in China. Sadly, Cinnovate folded its operation in 2017 as a result of the change of Intel's global CSR agenda. Despite its short life, the model of social innovation promoted by Cinnovate was inspirational. Behind it was an expansive vision bolstered by four grand pillars—"supporting change-makers, enabling cross-sector collaboration, catalyzing effective strategies and solutions to tackle social challenges, and creating a vibrant social innovation ecosystem" (British Council China 2014). Such a vision, because of its very expansiveness, rendered it unmeasurable however. Once Innovation Week was over, the energized crowd dispersed. After the curtain fell over its social innovation forum, the enthusiasm of the press died down. Tracking the implementation of Intel-sponsored social challenges was as difficult as evaluating the potency of the cross-sector "ecosystem" Cinnovate claimed to be building. In the end, the more magnificent the vision, the quicker it dissolved into thin air. That's perhaps why profit-conscious Intel stopped the social experiment. Predictably, corporations lack neither the patience for nor interest in letting incremental change run its course. That task is eventually up to the local communities, not elites parachuted in from Silicon Valley.

Shenzhen Open Innovation Lab and the Future Village Initiative

The Intel example tells us that since the mid-2010s, tech4good as a culture and practice has caught up with many IT companies in urban China. Multinationals initiated the culture, but domestic Chinese enterprises were quick to follow suit. Those practices range from mature pro bono programs to spontaneous experiments driven by individual techies. For example, Baidu.com launched a Smart Campus Project in Guangxi's five poverty-stricken villages, leveraging its internet-of-things technology to solve the problems of water and electricity shortage on school campuses.[22] Makeblock, Jason Wang's company that develops Arduino-based hardware and robotics hardware, built a prototype of Braille typewriter for the visually impaired that consisted of an XY plotter, printer, and a MegaPi microcontroller. Combined with conversion software, the typewriter could convert Chinese and English texts into Braille (Makeblock 2015). There are numerous other ad hoc pro-bono projects I can enumerate here. But there is little doubt the paragon of tech4good practice is the China subsidiary of ThoughtWorks, a global software design and consulting company. Well known for its work on social justice and social impact, the parent company works closely with organizations driven by social missions. In China, ThoughtWorks was exemplary in providing design thinking solutions to nonprofit organizations through two different channels—pro bono projects and regular "GeekSeek" training workshops which began in 2014. The latter, in particular, aims to break down the boundary between the technology and philanthropy sector through a persistent effort of designing tech4good products with, not for, nonprofit clients. Their numerous achievements include developing a tracking system for used clothing for the One-Click Philanthropy Alliance, providing a blueprint for a project management system for a foundation serving social enterprises, and constructing an ICT system for Fruticosa Blossom, a Qinghai-based grassroots NGO specializing in educational assistance to children of impoverished households. This company-led, systematic approach to using technology for social good has made ThoughtWorks China the quintessential model for IT companies wishing to fulfill corporate social responsibility with tech expertise.

Other sporadic attempts of tech4good were initiated by enthusiastic employees working in tech companies. For example, programmers at Alibaba unveiled a coding4good volunteer platform in 2017, connecting NGOs with individual techies interested in teaming up with each other to meet the former's tech demands.[23] Only time can tell how far those non-company-initiated tech4good practices will travel. We already know that Cinnovate did not last long once its umbilical cord was cut off from Intel. Frankly speaking, all those attempts, successful or not, share a problem intrinsic to all tech4good projects. The techies, whether they are software developers, interaction designers, or hardware makers—many of whom NGO2.0 has crossed paths with—are preoccupied more with tech output than *process and learning*.

Learning from whom? The marginalized communities they seek to serve. Enter the Future Village Initiative and its twin architects, Shenzhen Open Innovation Lab (SZOIL) and its partner Future+Academy. SZOIL is a social enterprise with four programmatic foci—undertaking Fab Lab 2.0 research and development,[24] creating a maker education program on social innovation and social entrepreneurship, building a global maker platform, and establishing mechanisms for cross-sector collaboration. The Future+Academy promotes itself as the first independent design4good academy whose pedagogy is built around the idea of a sustainable urban ecosystem and public art projects. It brands itself as a "hybrid research institute, think tank, and experimental laboratory" with a commitment to facilitating the learning ambitions of individuals (Future+Academy 2017).

I knew SZOIL well even before David Li, its founder, became a collaborator of NGO2.0 in December 2017. An influential maker, Li founded China's first makerspace in Shanghai as early as 2010. He saw the bubble of "maker as entrepreneur" blown and burst in the short span of two years. Forever action prone, Li is rechanneling his energy into socially engaged maker projects that emphasize the importance of making incremental change in the physical infrastructure of chosen locales. He thus extends the definition of tech output from ad hoc local treatment to the building of a holistic ecosystem, from product-based solutions to open-ended participatory design, privileging the process of design over making smart products as an end. Letting the community drive the whole process became a new motto and new method. This entails that the ideation and design of civic solutions has to start with deep and direct collaboration with the communities in need.

With this new vision in mind, David Li began seeking opportunities of working with nonprofit organizations. In a winter tech camp held in 2017, he collaborated with Public Lab (a communal volunteer group) and Greenovation:Hub (an environmental Think-Do organization), recruiting and training young makers to create autonomous underwater robots and water-testing hardware (Shenzhen Open Innovation Lab 2017c). Li sought out NGO2.0 in 2016 after he found out we are building NGO networks and holding regular hackathons. But the opportunities for collaboration did not materialize until fall 2017 when we kicked off a civic hackathon serving the needs of Rescue Minqin, a grassroots environmental NGO battling desertification in Northwest China.

The Minqin Challenge

Rescue Minqin is a grassroots NGO I introduced at length in Chapter 1. Its founder Ma Junhe, one of the most innovative NGO leaders in environmental activism, is an alumnus of our Web2.0 training workshops. Ma and fellow villagers live in a thinly populated and water-deprived county engulfed by fierce desert storms every spring. Since 2007, he has been leading teams of volunteers, manually planting desert-resistant suosuo seedlings to save Minqin from being swallowed up by the encroaching sand. Meanwhile, capable young people left the village one after another to look for better livelihoods elsewhere, leaving behind children and old people fighting for survival.

With indomitable spirit, Ma Junhe and volunteers have planted 25,000 *mu* (approximately 1667 acres) by hand in the past decade, averaging 2,500 *mu* per year. Thanks to such Herculean effort, coverage of green vegetation in his hometown increased from 11.52 percent to 17.91 percent, temporarily holding back the drastic ecological deterioration of Minqin.

But the desert is boundless. There are 24.14 million *mu* waiting to be greened. Starting in 2017, Ma set up a new but unreachable target for his NGO—planting 20,000 *mu* each year.

NGO2.0 has long harbored the desire of helping Rescue Minqin to find technological solutions to speed up the laborious tree planting process. In 2017, after sealing a collaboration with the iCenter at Tsinghua University and David Li's SZOIL, we launched a crowdfunding campaign during Tencent's annual Giving Day, raising funds to hold a hackathon in December of that year—our first step toward building a Future Village project in collaboration with SZOIL.

Unlike the software-focused hackathons NGO2.0 has held in the past four years, this one required maker expertise. Ma is searching for feasible solutions for machine automation. He envisions the making of a nimble robot that would complete a three-step robotic operation, of digging a pit into the sand, placing the Suosuo seedling into it, and backfilling the pit.

The marathon lasted less than twenty-four hours. Two representatives flew from Minqin to brainstorm with the techie participants we recruited. Together, four solutions were proposed at the end of the day:

Option 1: Implementing a semiautomatic planting method that is based on hole drilling technology and complemented by GPS and sensor devices to gradually achieve automatic planting function;

Option 2: Creating a cone-shaped mechanical device made up of two layers of carbon steel pipes with a built-in eversion device attached to the outer pipe. During the implementation process, the two pipes are thrust down into the sand by a hydraulic press engine, with the outer pipe loosening up the soil while the inner pipe, triggered by the eversion device, automatically depositing the suosuo seedling, releasing water, and covering up the pit, sequentially.

Option 3: Designing and assembling a seed package that contains a mixture of suosuo seeds, slow-release fertilizer, water retaining agents, and nutrient soil and sand. The package would be pressed down into the ground by a hydraulic press engine.

Option 4: Designing a walking mechanical turntable that rotates to perform the four functions of digging a pit, placing the seedling, watering, and backfilling the sand. (Zhang Qiang 2017; iCenter 2017)

These four blueprints were the first steps toward building prototypes. Next, each team leader, SZOIL, and NGO2.0 would work together to build the prototypes, a process to be followed by on-site testing and feedback. Meanwhile, additional funding needed to be raised for the project to come to fruition.

Open Design and Collaborative Design:
Visions and Practices

This said, the December 17, 2017 hackathon was by no means the end of our engagement with Minqin. As mentioned earlier, the hackathon marked the start of a Future Village project David Li invited NGO2.0 to co-design, together with the villagers at Minqin. "Village vision" and "engage by design" are coded terms that embody the trend of utopian intervention staged by socially concerned architect-designers to revive the self-repairing capacity of debilitated villages. It can be understood as a movement of rural renewal empowered by the village community working side by side with social design and public art activists.

The multiheaded origins of this movement can be traced back to a Hong Kong NGO named Future Village and a mountain architecture festival in a Southwest village of Guizhou province. Whether the rural community is located in the deep woods of Katunge, a village 100 km north of Nepal's capital, or shrouded in the mountainous Louna Village in Guizhou, participants share the same goal of transforming the pristine hamlets into sustainable and resilient communities. Founded by an anthropologist in mid-2004, the Hong Kong NGO takes a top-down approach to bring educational, health, and agricultural assistance to Katunge villagers (weilai zhi cun 2004–2015). Although this persistent effort is admirable, it smacks of the old-school thinking of city elites descending to the wilderness to rescue the noble savage. The Guizhou Village Vision Festival, on the other hand, was a 2017 project spearheaded by open-design practitioners, which elevated the idea of a "future village" to a whole new conceptual level. Its manifesto lays open a design4good vision:

"Village Vision and Future Village" is looking to create a future "Peach Blossom Spring"[25] and exploring the living landscape for the ideal mode of productivity for the village. Bearing this goal in mind, the International Architect Commune of Louna Village are making efforts, through art and design, to integrate new culture and new forces of production into the indigenous village infrastructure. Through creativity and cultural protection, we aspire to facilitate the growth of indigenous culture and trigger the outburst of the organic life force of the village from inside out so that Louna will witness its own transformation and development. (Village Vision 2016)

A mix of cultural events unfolded during the four-day festival at Louna, including a folk music festival, a public art and rural architecture exhibit, a village sports showcase, a camping tent design competition, and two capstone summits on "landscript" and "village vision" (Village Vision 2016). All those activities were planned to reconstruct the villagers' self-awareness of the beauty of their own culture so that they can rebuild their confidence in the future.

All this energy is inspiring. But when all is said and done, the coupling of sustainability and design calls for longer-term strategic intervention and community engagements that are difficult to sustain for nonlocals. How frequently can the members of the International Architect Commune travel back to Louna? Would Louna end up becoming another pressed butterfly specimen, beautiful but transient? That is just one of the problems inspirational projects like Village Vision present. Fast forward to NGO2.0 and David Li's Future Village project, which is tied to the maker movement. Can we experiment with a model whose life span can be better guaranteed?

Putting aside the Minqin project for the time being, let's look at what David Li has achieved with Xinguang village near Shenzhen. Mature makers like Li are savvy practitioners of collaborative design. Branding Xinguang an "international Open Source Village," SZOIL and Future+ Academy have started creating deep onsite conversations with villagers and the village committee to explore the possibility of developing Xinguang through internet and maker technology. They have undertaken the project through a succession of winter camps that recruit young makers and other volunteers to work with the village stakeholders, phase by phase, under the guidance of expert mentors. Because Xinguang is within a short distance to Shenzhen, the team is now focused on bridging the city and the village through the Fab Lab model, creating facilities connecting villagers through high-speed links to the world repositories of open knowledge, bringing "the latest innovation in open source living to rural environments" (Shenzhen Open Innovation Lab 2017a). This vision may sound grand at the outset. On closer scrutiny, it becomes obvious that this is an ongoing experiment. Taking into consideration the easy access of the village to

Dongjiang, a tributary of the Pearl River, Phase I of the project evolved around the making of a blueprint for a water-tech village. That is, Li and his team of young makers are planning to rejuvenate the village in three complementary trajectories—water, agriculture technology, and culture. Phase II of the Open SourceVillage program generated many mini initiatives. One was led by Jo Ashbridge, a young maker from the UK and a participant of the Hello Shenzhen Project. Her conversations with Xinguang villagers led to the discovery of many abandoned buildings left behind by villagers when they moved to new modern dwellings. A competition challenge was launched by Ashbridge, summoning designers all over the world to redesign those forgotten buildings. Thirty-two proposals from twelve countries were received. An exhibition of those proposed ideas turned into a big event, drawing Xinguang villagers into discussions about the feasibility of what was submitted (Shenzhen Open Innovation Lab 2017a).

The second phase was also accompanied by an in-depth investigation into the cultural life and land use of Xinguang villagers. The conversations between maker visitors, villagers, and the village committee led to the discovery of many outstanding problems the village elders hoped to resolve. Large-scale farming has resulted in the rampant use of pesticides whose containers are piled up on the roadside unattended; vast tracts of banana plantations are deserted due to low yield and low selling price; the annual yield of lychee fruits which every household grew is uneven and not predictable. Last but not least, there is a lack of communal activities for village children. Included on the expanding wish list are expectations for a richer cultural life and increased income (Shenzhen Open Innovation Lab 2017b). Those interactions and explorations continued to evolve through regularly held maker camp activities, which triggered the villagers' curiosity about the possibilities of change.

According to David Li, the conversation with Xinguang village has just begun. The contact made thus far is part of a long and open process of getting to know the village and villagers. The spirit underlying the experiment is less about showcasing a village than witnessing the community-driven process unfolding itself. There is less media fanfare about this project than Village Vision, but it enjoys one clear advantage over the latter: key participants involved in the Open Source Village project live in Shenzhen, only 92 km from the village, which makes this model much more sustainable than the Village Vision's roadmap and the Louna experiment. What can we learn from a maker model that prizes process over product? That's the question that engages me the most.

Back to the Minqin Challenge and the civic hackathon NGO2.0 held in 2017. We already completed the first phase, providing Rescue Minqin with four possible solutions to tackle the problem of manually planting suosuo in the desert. While the prototypes of those four hackathon solutions were being made, David Li came up with the idea that Minqin could serve as another candidate for the Future Village project. Truly, since Xinguang is a South China village, it would take a village in North China to validate the replicability of Li's vision. He sought partnership and persuaded me that NGO2.0 should join the experiment. So, the Minqin Challenge continues.

I am not oblivious to the barriers of cultivating Minqin as the next Xinguang. It is a much poorer village, one that was abandoned by its younger residents. There are, however, several advantages that make it worth a try. Ma Junhe, the founder of Rescue Minqin, is an activist with significant social media influence; Han Jierong, his closest ally and an antidrought engineer as well as the secretary-general of the NGO, lives nearby in Lanzhou; the county leadership is conscientious in its effort of planting vegetation in the desert; and the heroic fight of Minqin against desertification has become a well-celebrated national legend and its reputation has gone far beyond the circle of environmental activists. More importantly, every March for over three successive weeks, volunteers come from all over the country to Minqin to help Ma Junhe plant suosuo seedlings. I have witnessed Ma's skillful use of Weibo and other social media in the last ten years, which has made his hometown increasingly visible and attractive to millennial volunteers. Out they travel to the county town in March, by plane and train or by car, participating in the annual planting fest year after year. The other human factor that could turn the Minqin Challenge into a sustained effort is the trust and bond between Ma and NGO2.0. He is one of our earliest trainees, one of the savviest social media user, and one of the most curious students in pursuit of new knowledge.

I could imagine the following: In spring 2019, SZOIL, NGO2.0, the hackathon participants, and a train of volunteers—hundreds of them, Minqin's annual planting team—congregate in the desert with food and camping gear. During the day, we plant suosuo trees together, and in the evenings, we visit village elders over the sorghum wine, talking about their fears about water shortage and expectations for a better future. We inspect the suosuo planting ground cultivated by the county authorities themselves and discuss with them the government's plan of rescuing Minqin. We speak to small children and find out about their dreams and listen to their grandparents reminiscing about a greener Minqin generations ago.

The vision lingers on, and along its path, hopes are raised and friendships made. Nobody can tell whether Minqin can transform itself into a "future village." But isn't that what activism is all about? It is about process, not short-term impact. It is about trying to change and thinking with optimism. It is like watching the weak suosuo seedlings grow against the odds.

Conclusion

This chapter on makers started with situating the maker movement as a missing piece in the puzzle of Chinese innovation policies. Whether we are speaking of maker-entrepreneurs or makers as change-making citizens, it is obvious that the government has now discovered the value of the individual, creative self-expression, and grassroots energy in transforming Chinese economy and society. Creative industry clusters came under the spotlight more than a decade ago, and it is now evident that they are not key to building a robust creative economy. Li Keqiang's maker slogan reminds policy pundits that a national innovation system is an ecosystem that needs to accommodate both the top-down superhighway approach and the messy centrifugal, bottom-up pathways that fall outside the purview of central planners. Where this new trend of democratized innovation will lead is unclear. Whether the maker policy will succeed in reducing the high unemployment rate of college graduates is also unpredictable.

Meanwhile, the intrusion of an official discourse into an organic cultural phenomenon inevitably provokes anxieties, especially in the minds of purists. I have examined the conceptual trap of dichotomous thinking in analyzing China in Chapter 1 and elsewhere. Binary pairs such as domination versus resistance, state versus society, communism versus capitalism, power versus subjugation, and last but not least, the official versus the grassroots, carry limited analytical weight when they are applied to the Chinese case (Wang 2001, 98–99). We have already seen how Cinnovate and Enactus, both international entities, thrive in China in spite of, or perhaps because of, their formal partnership with governmental organizations.

One thing is certain: makerspaces have proliferated in China thanks to the government's blessings. Nobody can tell if a hundred potent ideas—and successful start-ups—will spring out of those state-funded creative spaces. Will these suffer the same fate as the hundreds of lackluster creative industry clusters all over the country? But that's beside the point. Perhaps we should all look elsewhere, to education and activism, for clues about how to assess the productivity of a state-cosigned maker movement. On the education front, there is ample evidence that something dynamic is happening in places out of media reach. Enthusiastic members of Chaihuo Makerspace set up colorful pop-up stations in shopping plazas, attracting kids and curious families. Universities are by no means the only privileged venues where makerspaces can systematically spread. Rudimentary makerspaces emerged long before 2015 in elementary schools, middle schools, and high schools representing a less publicized grassroots effort initiated by tech enthusiast schoolmasters committed to "teaching children skills needed in a makerspace and let[ting] children build what they want" (Xie 2014; Wang Yu 2015, 81). Most surprisingly, the prototypes of "maker education" are found not only in prestigious schools but also in schools of less developed regions (81). This phenomenon appears to be an attempt started by maker-teachers voluntarily.

Chinese students are now given various creative means to improve their educational capital.[26] Imagine a motion-sensing software "Rap Tech" that targets preschoolers. If Chinese makers continue the speed of producing innovative online education aids, and if primary and secondary school pupils are drawn to campus makerspaces, creative education will be a trend hard to stop even in the kingdom of rote learners. One has to wonder, if those erstwhile bookworms are transforming themselves into happy learners and creative thinkers, can a creative China be far from reach? One can also wonder how many of those creative minds will grow up to be change makers, using their coding skills and DIY ethos to help villages like Xinguang and Minqin create a transformative future.

Surely, the maker has a double personae—an entrepreneurial self and an activist self. In 2011, Michael Keane asked: "How can we understand creativity in a way that accommodates policy and business while still engendering a sense of change, of variety, or value?" (Keane 2011, 169). The answer to Keane's prescient question lies in the steady rise of change-maker communities in urban China. Perhaps given time, China's premier will be advocating a new maker culture that commends not only maker-entrepreneurs but the numerous change makers and their happy emulators who are seizing opportunities to make the crown jewels of a creative society—social wealth and social good.

6

Participatory Action Research
and the Chinese Challenge

This chapter addresses the method question and investigates the relationship between social action and action research in the larger context of participatory action research (PAR). Using NGO2.0 as an example, I examine the myth about "scaled participation" when PAR practices meet social media and ask how we begin to understand PAR practices in authoritarian countries where there is little equation between action and resistance. An overview of the development of PAR in both English and Chinese writings serves to unravel my reluctance of affiliating myself with PAR squarely.

First, what is PAR?

> At its best, participatory action research is a social process of *collaborative learning* realized by groups of people who join together in changing the practices through which they interact in a shared social world in which, for better or worse, we live with the consequences of one another's actions. (Kemmis and McTaggart 2005, 563, italics mine)

> PAR seeks to understand and improve the world by *changing it*. At its heart is collective, *self reflective inquiry* that researchers and participants undertake, so they can understand and improve upon the practices in which they participate and the situations in which they find themselves. (Baum, MacDougall et al. 2006, 854, italics mine)

Participatory action research is an umbrella term for action-driven methods and approaches and provides an alternative to the positivist thinking entrenched in traditional social science paradigms. These two quotes capture the main features of PAR—a social process that is collaborative, self-reflective, participatory, life-changing, and hence empowering. Underlying the various schools of PAR is a deeply engrained faith in the emancipatory potentials of experiential knowledge, which requires that researchers walk out of the study into the field and tear down the boundary separating the investigator from the investigated. Kurt Lewin, the social psychologist who first coined the term *action research*, famously proclaimed, "If you want to truly understand something, try to change it" (Tolman et al. 1996, 31). This conceptual shift transforms the researcher from a distant observer in pursuit of knowledge for its own sake to a participant self-consciously involved in solving real-life problems. Practice is allegedly prioritized over theory. Turned into a critical social practice, knowledge production would never be the same for those committed to PAR.

Several presumptions underlie the basic tenets of participatory action research. No matter how much weight is given to practice and how convincing the dialectics of action and theory may sound, the great majority of Western PAR practitioners are socially concerned *scholars* rather than activists on the ground.[1] In that tradition, activism is rarely the starting point of the process but a means of overcoming positivism and subjectivism in research—what Stephen Kemmis calls the "dead ends that both 'objectivist' and 'subjectivist' philosophy and science has been led into" (Kemmis 2008, 129). I saw in PAR an earnest attempt of social scientists to make a paradigm shift even though PAR handbook editors Peter Reason and Hilary Bradbury define the ultimate goal of action research as the liberation of "the human body, mind and spirit in the search for a better, freer world" (Reason and Bradbury 2001, 2). Regardless of such aspirations, the PAR carried out by European and North American academics impresses me more as an overdue critique of Western epistemology than an emancipatory project in pursuit of social justice.

This chapter investigates the relationship between social action and action research in a variety of contexts. There is no better way of opening up the inquiry than turning to the identity of NGO2.0 and asking, is it an academic inquiry or a social practice? The easiest solution is to go eclectic by claiming both identities and arguing for a straightforward methodological affiliation with PAR. That would be a cop-out. As demonstrated in the Introduction and Chapter 2, NGO2.0 was launched as an activist project originating in my critique of the blind spot of Creative Commons.

Questioning the movement's assumption about universal digital literacy, I introduced digital and social media literacy training into the hinterland of China. There was no research agenda to speak of, only a simple desire to dive into a social practice that helps grassroots NGOs in West China to build their social media communication capacity.

The question about research emerged very slowly over the years as I started giving talks about NGO2.0 on university campuses in the US and Western Europe. Surely, I give similar talks in China to audiences made up of NGO staffers, foundation officers, CEOs and corporate citizenship program managers, techies in IT companies, angel investors, and founders of social innovation incubators. The type of questions raised by those audiences hinges on the social value of NGO2.0 and the project's long-term impact on the nonprofit sector. Delivering talks to nonspecialists was often liberating. Not only was I not obliged to fit my work into theoretical pigeon holes, I was building, unwittingly, a network of change makers from different sectors. The academic audiences, on the other hand, responded differently. I was often quizzed hard about theory and methodology. Despite my insistence on my activist persona, NGO2.0 was perceived as an undertheorized academic project. A typical response is, "What does NGO2.0 have anything to do with research?" In response to those constant queries, I embarked on a search for methodology and came very close to finding an answer in participatory action research.

What is at stake by hairsplitting the identity of NGO2.0? I am curious to discover what happens when the activation process of PAR is reversed, that is, when activism is set in motion by an agent whose research agenda is overwritten by her activist agenda. In such a transformed context, to what degree does PAR and its methodological assumption still make sense? Instead of affiliating myself with PAR, I take a step back and ask what insights can be gained from understanding a research tradition committed to undermining dualism but which ultimately fails to overcome the stubborn divide that separates the dispassionate research from passionate but weakly theorized action. This incorrigible divide is probably one of the main reasons why nonacademic writings by activists are rarely spotted in PAR handbooks published in the Western hemisphere. That is also the reason why I hesitate to pledge full allegiance to PAR.

This chapter not only addresses those issues but also examines PAR as an evolving field in China where academics, social workers, and activists are blended more productively and seamlessly than their Western counterparts. Interestingly, contrary to the androcentric drift of PAR in the English-speaking world, the Chinese pioneers evoke Western feminism—black feminism in particular—as a crucial source of inspiration. Not only is the credo of "the personal is political" fully embraced, the best Chinese PAR scholarship is built on the first-person narrative written with an intense confessional fervor that differs noticeably from the second-person inquiry mode that characterizes the PAR literature written in English (Bradbury and Reason 2008, 437–38). One more difference is noteworthy: because of the political taboo revolving around social action in autocratic countries, the Chinese PAR devotees practice nonconfrontational activism, a brand of social action that doesn't fit well into the dichotomous thinking of domination versus resistance—the golden principle of Western liberalism which even the most dedicated dualism slayer dare not defy. Best practices of nonconfrontational action and an inquiry of its challenge to the theorization of PAR are largely absent in seminal PAR essays and handbooks whose vantage point is hitherto monopolized by practitioners schooled in the Western liberal tradition. Indeed, how do we begin to understand PAR practices in authoritarian societies where the default Western equation between action and resistance is the exception rather than the rule?

The Politics and Problems of Participatory Action Research

Before we turn to China, it is useful to briefly examine the lineage of PAR and its journey from the Global South to North America, ending with PAR's reconstitution into a tool of capitalist accumulation serving the Western neoliberal agenda. Steven Jordan epitomizes the passage as a process of depoliticization and co-option that was "at odds with the emancipatory and revolutionary principles on which PAR was originally founded in the Global South" (Jordan 2009, 18, 22). Nostalgic for the visionary call to action by anticolonial scholars such as Paulo Freire and Orlando Fals Borda, Jordan elicits the best practices of PAR from popular education movements implemented through national literacy campaigns launched by Castro in Cuba and the Sandinistas in Nicaragua in 1961 and 1980, respectively. Those campaigns were not merely literacy focused, they fostered new forms of popular consciousness and solidarity that were critical and emancipatory. Jordan goes on to distinguish "participatory research" from "action research," identifying the former with the living revolutionary legacy of the Global South, and the latter with the increasing institutionalization of a multidisciplinary field taken root in European and North American universities. Once migrated from the South to the North, PAR researchers have focused on improving professional practices in education and business organizations, a development which Jordan deplored, for he saw in it the subjugation of a liberatory project to socioeconomic and political forces of neoliberal governmentality that systematically compromised PAR's emancipatory legacy (17). The "change-making" vision in the original PAR framework is downgraded to effecting organizational changes in factories and businesses where participatory research is leveraged to boost workers' productivity and competitiveness, spark innovation, and strengthen the relationships between labor and management (Ludema and Fry 2008, 280; Whyte 1991).

What impresses me the most is not Jordan's criticism of PAR's appropriation by neoliberalism but his questioning of some of the most fundamental methodological premises about PAR that we take for granted. For example, the discourse of participation assumes that the power relationship between researcher and the researched can be equalized once the latter is empowered through the act of participation. Citing the example of PAR's intervention in Xerox, Jordan warns us that participation is not only bound to technologies of normalization and control but its deployment is closely linked to neoliberal development institutions like the World Bank (Jordan 2009, 21–22, 25). Jordan is not alone in problematizing the romanticism attached to the discourse of participation. Davydd Greenwood and his research partners treat PAR as a protracted, emergent process because it is impossible to impose participation on a research process that constitutes a continuum from expert research to participatory research (Greenwood, Whyte et al. 1993, 1). To be exact, participation is a process that must be generated, with no sure guarantee for success.

Jordan's evocation of the Cuban and Nicaraguan literacy campaigns triggered my reflection on NGO2.0's social media literacy campaign. Like all such campaigns, the end goal of NGO2.0 goes beyond the eradication of illiteracy. As described in Chapter 2, through our Web 2.0 literacy workshops, we train grassroots NGOs to learn how to collaborate online, design advocacy projects, promote their social cause, and recruit volunteers and other resources digitally. Most interestingly, our trainings have yielded, over the years, a number of close-knit online communities that cross provincial boundaries and NGO issue areas. Did we plan for this from the very start? Absolutely not. The web generates scalable societies whether we planned it or not. It is politically sensitive enough to train NGOs persistently and systematically in China on a large scale, not to mention intentionally building a nationwide community infrastructure for change makers based in multiple locales. This is an excellent example illustrating how the androcentric Western PAR that focuses on a purposely goal-driven agenda falls short of explaining what NGO2.0 is all about. In countries ruled by censors, open-ended (non)action stands the best chance of evading governmental intervention. There is no doubt that as literacy trainers, we are committed to a specific goal: transforming our students into social media literates that can create, share, and redistribute the online content of their own making. But a crucial value of NGO2.0 are those open-ended virtual communities established on Weibo, WeChat, and QQ, online collectives made up of past trainees coming from the 1,600-plus NGOs we have taught since 2009.

During the first three years after I founded NGO2.0, I spent four hours daily (two in the morning and two in the evening) conversing with our trainees on QQ, a popular instant messaging hangout built by Tencent .com. I was *not* consciously engaged in relationship building, a process known to be crucial to collaborative learning and research emphasized by PAR theorists. What drove me to QQ at the beginning was the joy of discovering fellow activists and a teacher's intuitive concern about her students' progress. I soon found what our NGO trainees really wanted to chat about were not topics related to technology and new media but what they were doing and how they were feeling day in and day out. They congregated on QQ to empathize and sympathize with one another, to complain about society's discrimination against AIDS patients or the left-behind children in villages, to discuss capital-labor conflicts in factories, to debate about LGBTQ issues or a newly published policy that could impact the future of nonprofits, to promote a crowdfunding campaign set up to help an NGO leader suffering from cancer, or to simply pat each other's virtual shoulders, share resources, and provide moral support to one another. It is energizing to bond with those young, altruistic, resource-starved but passionate NGO workers. Most of them are not aware that the teacher-student hierarchy has already been destabilized. Truly, as Fidel Castro said, "You are going to teach, but at the same time you will learn" (Castro 1961). What I learned from those NGO students reinforced my scholarly conviction that small, incremental changes made persistently in the long haul are comparable to the evolutionary effect of a long tail. The total volume of energy generated by tens and thousands of grassroots niches in the tail can collectively rival or even exceed explosive but short-lived street revolutions.

Take for example, the online communities NGO2.0 has built. They are open-ended communities with no political or organizational tasks intended or assigned. Not only do I have no interest in promoting extreme action, but like Myles Horton, the founder of the Highlander Research and Education Center in Tennessee (Greenwood and Levin 2007), I strongly believe that communities are capable of organizing themselves to produce social good. Simply by providing NGOs with a platform and encouraging them to share their problems and engage in conversations together, a collective identity is already in the making and the process of self-empowerment triggered. The collective learning in which those NGOs are engaged daily is one obvious benefit to speak of, the less obvious is the comradeship built across NGO issue areas, which is a necessary foundation for developing an inclusive, area-crossing, and multifaceted civil community. The mission of NGO2.0—strengthening the communication capacity of grassroots—is in itself an action fraught with enabling possibilities. There is infinite space for action and activism even in an authoritarian country, if we do not confine ourselves within the set ideology of action qua resistance. The majority of the grassroots NGOs we trained practice nonconfrontational activism in which action is decompressed purposefully to divert the gaze of censors.

The Myth about "Participatory" Practice: NGO2.0's Crowdsourced Map

The open-ended civil communities foreground one more critical issue which PAR scholars have yet to examine. When social action meets the digital and the social, is scalable participation a given? As the name of NGO2.0 indicates, the project was born from the ethos of Web 2.0 culture that signaled a shift of web usage from the passive consumption of content by users to their active participation in creating, sharing, and redistributing peer content. As a result, both our curriculum and practice is anchored in participatory design. Although NGO2.0 grew outside of the PAR framework, our experience with collaborative design and crowdsourcing can perhaps shed light on Steven Jordan's and Davyyd Greenwood's argument about the "emergent character" of participatory practice mentioned earlier.

From the outset, NGO2.0 team members made the assumption that our teaching on Web 2.0 thinking and Web 2.0 tools would be sufficient to motivate our NGO students to participate in collaborative practices. That's not the case. Involving them in building common projects for good with NGO2.0 turned out to be much more difficult than teaching them how to make and spread their own digital content. The problem did not simply reside in the students' insufficient grasp of Web 2.0 thinking; it just took NGO2.0 a number of years to design a crowdsourcing model that had the potential to scale up NGOs' participation.

One of our participatory projects is the crowdsourced philanthropy map (www.ngo20map.com) that aims to connect the NGO sector with the CSR (corporate social responsibility) sector so that each can find out what the other has accomplished in producing social good. Cynics would ask: Why involve the corporate sector?

Theoretically, there are four major sources of funding Chinese NGOs can aspire to—the government, foundations, the corporate sector, and the public. The first two funding resources are hard to obtain because grass-roots cannot compete with government-affiliated nonprofits for those funds. What about the public? Unlike much of the rest of the world, scaled and sustainable public fundraising for grassroots is difficult to achieve in China, either online or offline. A significant number of China's grassroots are not registered with the Ministry of Civil Affairs, and even those that have acquired the legal status are not allowed to do public fundraising on their own websites. As Chapter 3 indicates, to solve that problem, both Tencent.com and Sina.com have rolled out crowdfunding platforms enabling grassroots to raise public funds on them. But the income stream from individual giving is unstable, to say the least. Even the most suc-cessful NGO crowdfunding campaigns eventually rely on the same group of supporters made up of family members and relatives, close friends, and NGO peer workers. Every September after Tencent's 9.9 Giving Day—China's internet philanthropy day inaugurated in 2015—it takes a long while for the public to recover from the mental fatigue with crowdfunding.

With all those funding bottlenecks, it is important that grassroots NGOs learn how to build partnerships with corporations. But it takes two to tango. What made Chinese companies willing partners with NGOs?

Chapter 3 foregrounds a Weibo scandal that broke out in 2010, which revolved around Guo Meimei, a Paris Hilton-like woman.[2] To cut a long story short, in the wake of the scandal, not only did public donations to big foundations bottom out in subsequent years, it paved the way for a reconfiguration of the funding pathways that governed the flow of corporate giving. Previously, the corporate sector donated to big state-run foundations as a rule. The scandal pushed the former to restrategize corporate philanthropy. There is now a shift away from the traditional social giving model that is, giving exclusively to big foundations, to diversifying charity investment. We began to witness examples of small donations and resources flowing directly from the corporate sector to grassroots NGOs, skipping the foundations in the process.

The shift of the corporate social investment aside, the central government has published a series of mandate since 2004, requiring all state-run corporations to publish annual CSR reports. Like the rest of the world, social responsibility gained an increasingly important role in Chinese corporate branding. All those developments plus the importation of foreign CSR models have taught me one thing: that corporations are an overlooked gap in the funding loop for NGOs. NGO2.0's acknowledgment of this materialized, as early as 2010, into a crowdsourced map built to link NGOs with CSR managers. Nonprofits can use this map to find each other and post their projects to attract CSR managers who are looking for worthy programs to fund. There are now approximately 24,799 NGOs on our map and more than 3,119 CSR case studies for NGOs to explore. As a crowdsourced project, the map (see Map 3.1 in the "Grassroots NGOs and Activism 2.0" section of Chapter 3) is simultaneously a live database of Chinese NGOs across issue areas and across geographical boundaries.

What can a crowdsourced map accomplish? NGOs come and register themselves voluntarily. The larger the volume of the data, the better chance the grassroots stand in drawing interested CSR managers to the map. This mode of collective sourcing had precedents prior to the digital era, but the arrival of internet-mediated communication and the interactive capacity of Web 2.0 technology has sped up the outsourcing process to the crowd and driven the so-called open collaboration in the process. The logic goes: computer generated crowdsourcing can break down the labor required to undertake a complex task to pieces and distribute them to the participating crowd through an open call for contribution. In the case of NGO2.0's philanthropy map, the crowd in question are grassroots NGOs in need of resources. Each NGO's content entry into the map combined with that of others can achieve a cumulative effect that in turn stimulates more content creation, attracts more visitors and contributors to the map, and further enhances its value to CSR managers. By design then, this map, like all Web 2.0 projects, should in theory trigger a bottom-up participatory process and ignite the network effect with little effort.

But a Web 2.0 platform is easier built than run. Participation doesn't happen overnight simply because we launched a participatory project. It was no easy task to convince NGOs that the greater good would eventually serve the interests of each participant. Our challenge is to convince the NGOs that they have to continuously update the content they initially entered on the map to make it a successful crowdsourced project. Through numerous trials and errors, we found out that "participatory practices," especially scaled participation, is at best a myth in the networked era. What do we do next then to sustain our map project?

We designed an intermediary model of participation involving ten provincially based support-type NGOs as the middlemen to enlist local grassroots to register on the map. That alone is not enough. A number of incentives is provided by NGO2.0 to individual grassroots, which include opportunities to enroll in online and offline training courses, discount for subscriptions to CRM tools and other software featured in our Web 2.0 toolbox, free project design for crowdfunding campaigns, and other bonuses.

This shows that open participation is never cost-free. Behind the veneer of crowdsourcing, there are layers of trade-in mechanisms and incentive schemes. Not only is "developing the participatory dimension a responsibility that is never completely fulfilled [by the researcher]" (Greenwood, Whyte et al. 1993, 175), but bottom-up, scalable participation can never be fully sustained without top-down maneuvering and the intervention of middlemen organizations. *Unmediated, end-to-end, open participatory practice is a myth.* In the context of NGO2.0, full-scale participation has a price tag attached to it. As we are developing a collaborative model based on provincial partnership, the crowdsourced map is managed regionally by multilevel leadership composed of support-type NGOs based in ten provinces (Shaanxi, Gansu, Guizhou, Shandong, Yunnan, Sichuan, Hunan, Anhui, Henan, and Heilongjiang).

At NGO2.0's bidding, this multilayered provincial collective is now working with Syndao, a Beijing based CSR consultancy company, to establish an NGO rating system (http://www.ngo20map.com/Rating/view), which is a quantifiable multitiered evaluation structure that helps classify and rank the NGO data submitted to the map—a crucial, concrete step toward matching NGOs and CSR donors. Starting in 2015, we have also held a series of offline meetings, bringing NGO leaders to brainstorm, face to face, with CSR mangers in long and intense debates about the criteria for assessing the credibility of an NGO seen from the corporate vantage point. This endeavor is challenging not least because the evaluation system has to get the buy-ins from both the grassroots (the party to be evaluated) and corporations (the donor-evaluator). To my surprise, a basic blueprint for the ranking system was completed within four hours. After five years of many false starts and endless experiments, NGO2.0 finally turned the crowdsourced map into a collaborative project. By inviting NGOs to the negotiation table, we made a modest step toward changing the power dynamics between these two sectors.

This evolving story about NGO2.0's map project serves to undermine our simple belief in the crowdsourcing power of the internet. It tells us that the true challenge of participatory design lies in community building, which may or may not require technological means. Granted that a crowdsourced platform like NGO2.0's philanthropy map may have amplified the voices of marginalized communities and helped grassroots NGOs to bypass mainstream media and governmental gatekeepers to represent their own interests. Yet no matter how efficiently we harness tech-powered platforms to catalyze human action, the core principle of community organizing remains unchanged. Thus social movement scholars like Sasha Costanza-Chock emphasize that social media enhance, rather than replace, face-to-face organizing, to wit, the revolution will be tweeted, but tweets alone do not make the revolution (Costanza-Chock 2014). Networking as a participatory act is ultimately dependent on the human will to connect, which can't always be generated or controlled by automated machinery. *Voluntary, scalable participation is not a given even in the age of amazing technology.*

To demystify technological determinism, however, is not the same as writing technology off of the agenda of activism and action research. As postulated by the authors of the Center for Media Justice Report, the understanding of technology "must be integrated into every civil rights agenda, not treated separately, precisely because technology is getting integrated into every issue that activists are working on" (Center for Media Justice et al. 2015). This brings me to observe that the first and second generations of PAR scholars have fallen behind in responding to the challenges and opportunities opened up by the World Wide Web. The Center for Media Justice Report provides a quote from Free Press's president and CEO Craig Aaron, in whose vision "activists and technologists, the grassroots and the netroots" are called upon to break the silos and work hand in hand in the broader human struggle for a better world (Kroin 2015). Will the third generation of PAR scholars answer the call and engage with digital media and reinvent the theory of participatory practices enabled by Web 2.0 culture and technology?

Chinese Participatory Action Research

Generally speaking, scholars lag far behind activists in playing with new tools of communication. Whether PAR researchers in the first world will feel compelled to answer the digital call is not a question I can tackle here. But in a field of study deeply rooted in academia, Western PAR practitioners are destined to be confined within the ivory tower and be subject to the stakes of tenure and other measurements of meritocracy that accompany the professionalization of knowledge—a trademark of Western higher institutions. Truly, as the academy became a self-sufficient industry in itself, the priority of scholars is to publish works appealing to a small circle of peers and highly specialized readers who have low tolerance for research results deviating from mainstream discourses. Researchers devoted to hands-on activism are scarce. For social action is time consuming and a poor theory generator. Not surprisingly, the scholar-activist is an endangered species in the American and Western European academy. Very few Western PAR theorists practice what they preach. Here we come across the key to understanding the PAR practices in developing countries vis-à-vis those undertaken in the first world. In a country like China, where the evaluation of scholarship is less standardized, many activists and public intellectuals hold academic posts, and their involvement on the ground is likely deeper than strictly academic professionals in the West. The most inspiring Chinese participatory action research is often conducted by activists or scholars involved in the discipline of sociology and social work.

This section begins with a quick review of Chinese PAR and then focuses on the social work collective affiliated with Xia Linqing, a Taiwanese PAR scholar-activist who introduced to China a branch of action research that emphasizes the transformation of the lives of participants, rather than knowledge itself, as the end goal of PAR. She foregrounds the self-emancipatory potential of the researcher herself and prioritizes agency over knowledge, the emotional over the analytical. The personalization of Xia's methodology made a significant impact on those trained in what is now called the Xia School of Chinese participatory action research. Many of her teachings are comparable to those of John Heron, Peter Reason, Donald Schön, and Orlando Fals Borda. The difference lies in her invocation of "desire" and its separation from the exercise of the mind, and her priority of foregrounding impassioned practice over dispassionate discoursing on practice. While Heron and Reason are engaged in hairsplitting the four ways of knowing (Heron and Reason 2008), Xia emphasizes the importance of generating the subject's desire for self-emancipation. Granted Fals Borda also preaches the necessity of shifting the quest of knowledge to the "transformation of individual attitudes and values, personality and culture" of the researchers and the researched, but Fal Borda's emancipatory project is in essence an epistemological one, that is, freeing himself from the all-encompassing Enlightenment heritage of rationality (Fals Borda 2001, 31–32). In contrast, Xia speaks from the gendered position of a female for whom liberation is always both a personal and political project. Exactly because women's liberation is an ongoing, incomplete historical project, the burden is *emotionally* charged. Behind her subjectivity stands successive generations of oppressed women fighting for equality in all spheres of life. It is not surprising then that, although trained in the classical androcentric tradition of PAR, Xia evokes feminist thinking unequivocally in her perception of human emancipation. She acknowledges specifically the influence of black feminists bell hooks and Patricia Hill Collins on her framework. Those teamed up with Xia are called upon to respond to the question of desire, pain, and subjectivity, an urgent invocation reminiscent of all equal rights movements. Acutely aware of the "hegemony of specialized knowledge" (*zhuanye baquan*) and the pitfalls of academic knowledge production, she built a network in China made up of social workers and activists rather than professors from prestigious universities. The title of the Chinese PAR handbook, *Action Research and Social Work* (which she co-edited with a researcher in the department of social work at a small Chinese college), speaks volumes about where her priorities lie.

Early Experiments of Chinese Action Research

Xia Linqing was not the first person to bring Western PAR into China. Kurt Lewin's doctrines were imported to the mainland as early as 1977. In subsequent years, PAR-styled methodology—activating a spiral of self-reflective cycles consisted of planning-acting-reflecting-replanning—has flourished in the field of education where university-based professionals collaborated with primary school teachers to experiment with new educational theories. In those early days, the researchers sat in the driver's seat, and the school teachers were enlisted to validate the former's theories through classroom practice.

A large-scale, officially endorsed promotion of action research took place in 2001. That year, China initiated a curricular reform of education, prompting elementary and middle-school teachers to transform themselves from passive knowledge transmitters to researchers actively exploring new educational theories and initiatives, and thus began a decade-long popularization of action research on campuses. University-based PAR evangelists held regular teacher training workshops in primary and secondary schools. In theory, action research built on teacher participation was an indispensable first step toward developing new educational platforms. But those two groups fought constantly over priorities. University researchers downplayed the application value of theories. Elementary and high school teachers valued practice and showed little interest in theories that could not meet pedagogical demands. The expert-practitioner divide was insurmountable, and the campaign ended with most teachers gradually receding to the background as school principals took over the role of agenda setter working closely with action researchers. What was meant to be an interactive, participatory project changed into the execution of a unilateral, top-down research mandate. Skeptical results notwithstanding, the 2001 governmental decree marked the beginning of the school teachers' self-reflection on their own practice in the classroom. For the enlightened few, this triggered the process of the conscious transitioning of them from teachers to teacher-researchers. From then on, engagement in education research became an integral part of the teachers' pedagogical practice itself. Action research in China entered a new phase of localization, driven by grassroots teacher-practitioners all over the country (Zhou 2012).

I am less interested in following the development of education action research in China because it falls short of representing grassroots activism in my definition. Moreover, Chinese practitioners in the subfield of education were prone to replicate Western theories and produce highly formulaic work. It is only when action research intersects with social work can we spot the most creative practices. Popular action research in that domain includes mentorship projects for autistic children (Song 2006), social programs of integrating migrant workers into cities (Huang 2011), social work intervention in problems encountered by left-behind children in rural China (Zhang 2011), empirically based research such as the impact of mobile technologies on the making of working-class network society (Qiu 2009), and various other projects closely tied to traditional NGO issues.

In fact, some of the most innovative action research projects did not originate in academia; they were generated by NGOs themselves. An exhilarating example of Chinese PAR is the post-Sichuan earthquake disaster relief project Green Farming (*lugeng*) funded by the Narada Foundation and executed by a Guangdong based NGO specializing in rural-urban community interaction. Green Farming covered several villages hardest hit by the Wenchuan earthquake and extended to adjacent urban areas. Social workers teamed up with villagers and urban residents to set up rural ecology tours that drove a modest local bed-and-breakfast cottage industry. Subscribing to the principle of fair trade, the project was designed to help rural producers in the disaster area to rebuild sustainable livelihoods and reconstruct the community economy. Those goals could only be achieved through the mobilization of rural and urban collaboration, the strengthening of family and community relations, rediscovery of local customs and culture, and the restoration of the ecosystem of plants and other living organisms in the quake regions covered by the project. In a three year period, Green Farming aimed to create a mutually supportive network of those living in the disaster area, get them engaged in participatory farming, help them revive the local Qiang embroidery culture, and start an oral history project complete with the villagers' participation in writing the history of their own villages (Narada Foundation 2012).

Zhang Heqing, the "Stirrings of the Heart," and Mao Zedong's Legacy of Revolutionary Romanticism

I learned about the Green Farming project from Zhang Heqing, a professor of sociology and social work at Sun Yat-sen University. A pioneer in the field, his theory of *zhixing heyi* (unity of knowing and doing), is widely cited in Chinese PAR literature. My brief review of action research in China would be incomplete without including his contribution to the field. In an effort to redress the instrumental rationality that underlies much of Western PAR scholarship, Zhang sought the origin of "action" (*xingdong*) in the "stirrings of the heart" (*xindong*). At a single stroke, this ingenious wordplay enables him to drive a third term "feelings" into the dichotomy of *Mens et Manus* (mind and hand), theory and practice.

To be touched in the heart (*xindong*) by local customs and local sentiment of a culture different from ours, I gain the cultural sensitivity required for fieldworkers. It is this curiosity that drives me to get to the bottom of things (i.e., observation) and to ask an infinite number of questions (i.e., conducting in-depth interviews). I then sit down and write up a thick description of what I saw and what I heard and turn it into a meaningful story that makes up firsthand research material for a living, exciting action research. Acting in the ways I summed up [above] defines what "action research" is all about. (Zhang 2014; also see Zhang 2015, 99)

From the bottom of my heart, I want to stop their suffering. Acting together with them, I want to bring changes to their life! This is what I meant by the "structure of deep feeling underlying my community practice." This deep feeling has generated in me not only the desire to act, but the impulse to change society. (Zhang 2015, 99)

Juxtaposing Zhang's discursive style with Kemmis's and Lewin's, we can immediately grasp his mode of operation. The starting point of PAR for him is the compassion of the researcher and his heart-felt impulse (*chongdong*) to relieve the suffering of the oppressed. And the relationship between the researcher and the researched has to be built on empathy and noncognitive resonance, at least at the beginning of their encounter.

Does this mean Zhang Heqing runs the risk of emotionalizing his scholarly agenda? The answer is no. A good sociologist at heart, he leaves ample room for the play of "sociological imagination," a term coined by C. Wright Mills, to depict a "quality of mind" that allows one to critically grasp "history and biography and the relations between the two within society" (Mills 2000, 6). He considers this analytical capacity the foundation of all participatory practices. More specifically, only when the researcher and the researched insert sociological imagination into the dyad of action (*xingdong*) and the stirrings of the heart (*xindong*) can the agents of change get to the bottom of the structural shortfalls that account for individual suffering. An analysis of the personal cannot but start with a critique of the social and historical (6). Ultimately, it is the linking of situated personal experience with the larger critique of the sociopolitical structure of our times that enables us to explore the possibilities of emancipation.

This last bit of Zhang Heqing's interpretation of Mills' sociological imagination sounds extremely familiar to the Chinese ear, especially to those who lived through the 1930s and 1940s and bore witness to the 1949 Chinese Revolution. In a long stroke, the Communist ideology of class struggle enacted a historical imagination not too far apart from Mills's sociological imagination, by which the suffering of the proletariat was given a longer and larger context and connected to the corrupt, ailing feudal society. It was Mao's belief that only when the poorest and the oppressed were taught to grasp that equation were they able to topple the old social, political structure and liberate themselves. Mao Zedong himself was a supreme practitioner of the great emancipatory project called the Communist Revolution.

I mentioned Mao because Zhang Heqing is one of the very few Chinese PAR researchers openly evoking the Chairman's name and quoting from his red classic "On Practice" (Zhang Heqing 2015, 101–102). Zhang's evocation of Mao is hardly accidental. Historical amnesia may be a common malaise for the Chinese obsessed with the catch-up game with the post-affluent modern West, but the legacy of the revolution and Mao's impassioned approach to social transformation is nonetheless deeply embedded in the Chinese understanding of practice (*shijian*)—with or without the awareness of those brought under its influence. Precisely because it is all too common for young scholars in post-1978 China to ignore indigenous legacies,[3] Zhang's effort of returning the concept of the "unity of knowing and doing" to Mao's exegesis of the dialectical-materialist concept of theory and practice is much appreciated. Launching into a discussion of Mao's historical merits and mistakes falls outside the agenda of this book. But "On Practice" sheds new light on the predilection of Chinese researchers for accentuating the emotional undertone in PAR practices, and it thus provides a missing link to my analysis of the mixed tradition of current Chinese PAR practices. Revolutionary romanticism lives long after the failure of Mao's vision.

Zhang Heqing did us a good service by reminding us of the familiar Chinese slippery rhymes and adages revolving around the word *practice*. From Mao's "a fall into the pit, a gain in your wit" to Deng Xiaoping's "feeling for the stones while crossing the river," Chinese communist literature is a bible on practice.

> Discover the truth through practice, and again through practice verify and develop the truth. Start from *emotive discerning* (*ganxing renshi*) and actively evolve it into rational discerning, and next, guide revolutionary practice with rational discerning in order to

change both the subjective and objective world. Doing, knowing, and knowing and doing again. The cycle repeats itself infinitely, and with the start of each new cycle, practice and theory rises to a higher level. (Mao 1967, 271, translation mine, italics mine)

My long quote of "On Practice" is meant to emphasize the dialectical-materialist root of Chinese participatory action research. By stressing the primary role of the emotive and a precognitive empathy with those awaiting liberation, Zhang Heqing drives home the crucial difference of the Chinese methodology from its Western counterpart. The spiral of cycles looks the same, but the starting point of the Chinese cycle is "emotive knowing" and for the Western cycle it is "planning," which points to a logocentric mode of inquiry (Kemmis and McTaggart 2005, 6).

The Xia Linqing School—Emancipation of the Self and the Evocation of Black Feminism

Like Zhang Heqing, the founder of the Taiwanese Action Research Association, Xia Linqing, is equally enthusiastic in tracing the ignition point of an agent's *nengdongxing* (capacity to act). A Taiwanese national, Xia was no stranger to activism herself. She was deeply involved in the Taiwanese labor movement during the 1980s. In the late 1990s, she joined a movement against the abolition of licensed prostitution and even ran as a candidate for the legislative election in Taipei in 2012. In Xia Linqing we saw the paragon of a scholar-turned-activist. I mentioned earlier that the eventual transformation of human lives through action is what mattered the most to her. As she grew older, her priority about action research seemed to shift more and more toward social action. Frankly speaking, Xia's writings could be self-consciously jargonistic when her activist voice was overtaken by the theorist's. Her teachings come alive only when she succeeds in translating abstract Western PAR formulations such as the "collective self-reflective inquiry" into experiential insights: "The potency of action-based knowledge is double edged. It impacts society and other people's living reality on the one hand, and turns the researcher's reflective inquiry inward to reconstruct and *emancipate her own self*, on the other (*fanshen chonggou zishen*) (Xia 2013, 4, italics mine).

Xia Linqing is an excellent mediator between the Chinese PAR and Western PAR researchers. Between 2007 and 2013, upon the invitation of a mainland Chinese social work researcher Yang Jing, Xia led a series of Youth Action Research workshops in China through which she initiated Chinese participants into the methodologies of Lewin, Schön, Argyris, Kemmis, and Habarmas and began exerting an important influence on the convergence of social work scholarship and action research in China. Perhaps Xia knew very well that the best applications of PAR would not be found in traditional social science disciplines but in social work studies and practices.

Xia's influence in China is important on several grounds. First, post-1970s Taiwan was a fertile ground for indigenous activism. The forty years of the Taiwanese experience in social action provides China-based activists and intellectuals invaluable lessons. Second, Xia inculcates in her disciples a critical consciousness about the merits and flaws of imported teachings. Although the Western masters' experience might be helpful for beginners, her position is that we cannot copy exactly what they did. Critical of the logocentric orientation of standard PAR scholarship, she emphasizes the subject's desire for self-liberation and echoes Zhang Heqing's insistence that the researcher position herself historically and reflect continuously on the situatedness of her own action. She urges the PAR researcher to scrutinize and see through her own personal history to find out where her life experience intersects with the social and with the lifeworld of the people she vows to serve. "Where are you? Where am I? And where are *we?*" (Xia 2013, 8, italics mine). Only when I, the researcher, truly understand the origin of my own desire for social action can I plunge myself into a participatory project that will change *my* destiny, *yours, and ours.* The transforming of the separate entities of the "I" and "you" into the "we" cannot simply be a leap of faith but a cognitive process of self-discovery fraught with yearnings for epiphany.

This impassioned and almost intuitive self-reflection is a hallmark of the Xia School. Together with Zhang Heqing's emphasis on the stirrings of emotional empathy (with the oppressed), it characterizes a Chinese PAR practice that is generative of soulful, personal stories written in the first-person narrative.

I feel stronger and stronger that I am already involved as a participant in the making of a social process in which knowledge is produced by concrete action. When you throw yourself into a social practice for some time, when you find yourself *feeling compelled* to tell others what you have done and what has happened, and when you are *driven* to narrate a complex story, you have already situated yourself in the locale based, contextualized knowledge production itself. (Xia 2004, 13, 8, italics mine)

This quote is significant in two ways. It was taken from Xia's critical autobiography "A Useful Light," a long essay tracing her journey as a scholar-activist in the format of "narrative reflection," a genre of her own invention. Combining poetry with argumentative prose, she creates a confessional but cerebral, self-critical but soul-searching style that makes up much of the Chinese action research tradition her numerous disciples in Taiwan and China would later follow. While most Western PAR scholarship is written in the third person with a cold and distanced scholarly voice, Xia's measured attempt of penning first-person narration reveals a choice made by her activist self. Scholars write in the third person, activists in the first. No matter how much emphasis is given to action and practice, the scholar-activist's double personae is easier said than made in Western academia. Only in countries where knowledge production is less specialized and the system of meritocracy less normalized can academic intellectuals afford to take a more active role in practicing what they preach.

The paragraph quoted from Xia Linqing's autobiography carries yet another point of connection. It was frequently cited by Xia Linqing's disciples. I turn momentarily to Yang Jing, the editor of *Action Research and Social Work*, Xia's closest ally-cum-student in China. Yang reiterates many of Xia's teachings and reinterprets them in mainland Chinese context. For example, "The process unfolded through action research is one and the same as the process of [a researcher's] life changing the lives [of the researched]" (Yang Jing 2013, 50). How do we begin to initiate that process? Here Yang fills the gap of her teacher's mantra (and redresses the Western PAR's blind spot) by coining the term *yushui guanxi* (a perfect fusion like fish in the water), which foregrounds the organic relationship building of the researcher with those served by her—an understudied topic in PAR literature.

Yang warns Chinese social work researchers against a wholesale acceptance of Western PAR theories because specialized knowledge should not overshadow local experiences and because, to her chagrin, the traveling PAR theory often prescribes a cold, professional relationship between the researcher and the researched that "fails to connect life with life" (Yang

Jing 2013, 55). It is a kind of manufactured relationship guided through textbook-based pedagogies and a loosely built network of weak ties, not a natural bond made of shared destiny like the dharma of fish swimming in the water. As a social worker engaged in women's empowerment projects, Yang Jing returns to the history of Chinese women's liberation in search of indigenous precedents of organic relations built between the activist and those acted upon:

> The women comrades engaged in women's liberation in those years penetrated deep into the backwaters. Their seamless connection with the (female) populace was the result of a number of combined factors that included the system design made by the state, day-to-day mobilization of social movements, and the accompanying numerous educational campaigns, and no less important, *the deep feelings of the women liberators and the liberated women for each other.* (Yang Jing 2013, 50, italics mine)

The last sentence of the quote nails down the kind of fish-in-the-water relationship that precludes the habitual *othering* practice of researchers. But Yang fell short of articulating in full what feminist PAR scholars Bev Gatenby and Maria Humphries put so eloquently, "Our emotions are invested in the research and in the women involved, and that some of the moments of illumination happen precisely because of that investment" (Gatenby and Humphries 2000, 11). The feminist consciousness embedded in the Xia School is a topic I will address in the next section. Here I want to emphasize that Yang Jing's focus is not on feminism per se but on unearthing the historical examples of potent relationship building, a contribution she believes Chinese social work researchers can make to the world literature of PAR.[4] Truly, as both the mentor and the student are committed to "decolonizing" imported knowledge and traveling theories, there is no better way of achieving the task than learning from locally bound and pivotal local-historical experiences. Perhaps that's why Yang looks back at Chinese women's liberation in Mao's era, while Xia is drawn to the lifeworlds inhabited by black feminists. Both are preoccupied with the question of an agency fully embodied in history, without which action can never be purposefully self-transformative.

Xia Linqing was never vocally critical of her mentor Donald Schön's and other PAR pioneers' rationalist approach. But those closely affiliated with her are less discreet. Xia's Taiwanese colleague Lian Xi openly critiques the lack of attention paid by Schön and Argyris to the question of human sensibility, the "living desire" (*shengming yuwang*), and its relationship to conscious action (Lian 2013, 16). In fact, the mode of scholarship is markedly different even when the Taiwanese and Western theorists discuss similar concepts such as the "living desire" and "relationship building." Translated into Western theoretical discourse, those concepts correspond to Habermas's "lifeworlds" and the "space of the intersubjective communicative space" (Habermas 1987). Yet those who bring Habermas to enrich the theoretical framework of PAR—Steven Kemmis comes to mind (Kemmis 2008, 126–129)—have handed over to us lifeworlds without inhabitants and an intersubjective space emptied of human relationships. On the question of agency and subjectivity in particular, there is little in the androcentric PAR literature from which Xia and her followers can borrow. In the early years of her involvement in Taiwanese social movements, Xia turned constantly to bell hooks for inspiration.

Thus, we hear Xia invoke hooks's practice of "intimate understanding" achieved through the black feminist's personal involvement in mainstream feminist movements and the American civil rights movements (South End Press Collective 1999, 39–52; Xia 2002, 151). She marvels at hooks's idea of finding the "nodes of resistance spread across the power grid of society" (hooks 2000, 138, 163; Xia 2010) and utilizes it to the fullest in her own fight for the cause of licensed prostitution (Xia 2002, 152–154). Thinking through and working through our own subjectivities in the act of resistance is the fastest route to nurturing critical consciousness. Xia's exposure to hooks drove home a lesson her male mentors could not teach: that action researchers sit at the edge between public knowledge and private lived experiences and that the emotional agenda of the researcher is an overpowering driver of action:

> When I see how many of the people who are writing about domination and oppression are distanced from the pain, the woundedness, the ugliness . . . I say remember the pain because I believe true resistance begins with people confronting pain, whether it's theirs or somebody else's, and wanting to do something to change it. (hooks 1990, 215)

This latter reference of the motivating power of pain in action research is found in Lian Xi's article in which she attributes to hooks her understanding of the "emancipatory meaning of personal pain" (Lian 2013, 18). Taiwanese action researchers are known to pursue radical, passionate politics. What Xia started—evoking the embodied, feminist subjective practice—has spread to her circle of colleagues who dive even deeper into Western feminist literature. In Patricia Hill Collins's intersecting systems of oppression, Maxine Greene's educational philosophy, and Donna Haraway's cyborg theory, Taiwanese and Chinese female researchers found kindred spirits who helped them transcend the androcentric thinking and practice dominant in the orthodox tradition of PAR.[5]

Nonconfrontational Activism: Strategies of Gaming the System

Xia Linqing's mainland disciples live with one obvious constraint that the Taiwanese experience cannot help remedy. Mainland Chinese PAR practitioners are engaged in nonconfrontational activism. How do we begin to understand PAR practices in authoritarian countries where there is little equation between action and resistance? What kind of action are we talking about when we speak of participatory action research in the Chinese context? *Action Research and Social Work* (Yang and Xia 2013) provides an excellent entry point for us to address those questions. In this volume, two examples attracted my attention especially: feminist researcher Gao Xiaoxian's project on rural women's political participation in a Shaanxi village and Guo Weihe's report on a social work experiment with construction workers in Beijing. Both participatory projects are aimed at empowering the disenfranchised, and both are led by intellectuals who have cultivated close relationships with the government. Their success is especially worth noting not least because we have seen similar efforts censored and failing elsewhere.

Gao Xiaoxian was trained as a historian. She founded one of the first nongovernmental organizations in the northwestern Shaanxi Province and started her social work on gender equality as early as 1986. Gao's organization, Research Association for Women and Family, developed a flagship program named after the village where the experiment took place—the Heyang Project. In six years, she succeeded in increasing the total number of the Shaaxi women village officials from 184 to 1,193 (Gao 2013, 196). Her interventionist approach was triple-pronged. She worked with the provincial and county-based Women's Federation to develop a series of consciousness-raising campaigns. First, they identified capable village women and then attracted them to participate in gender equality and leadership training workshops on a regular basis. Next, to neutralize the prejudice deeply rooted in the village against female leadership, Gao and her team developed a multipronged popular education program involving the entire village in participatory self-education. With the help of pervasive media campaigns, a network effect was quickly triggered. "The husbands, mothers-in-law, and male village officers who were previously opposed to women's participation in village election and governance had all changed their attitude" (203). But these first two steps of mobilization would have achieved nothing but a short-term effect if they were not reinforced by official policy provisions supporting the political participation of the "female sex" (*funu canzheng*). The third prong thus refers to the establishment of a quota system issued by the Shaanxi provincial government, which codifies the minimum number of women representing each village in an official capacity.

This experiment is a hybrid in which the influence of global feminism is seamlessly mingled with action research on one hand and the Maoist strategy of social mobilization on the other. Asked if the Heyang Model is replicable to the rest of China, Gao Xiaoxiang was doubtful. She reminded us that her NGO is closely affiliated with the Chinese Women's Federation in Shaanxi. The success of her project was highly dependent on the strong networks she built with local authorities, a variable hard to reproduce in other locales and by other practitioners. For pessimists, the nonsystematic, personalizing aspect of Chinese activism should have rendered even the most winning model unsustainable in the long haul. But for those who know how Chinese society works, this is not an issue. Old networks come and go, eroded relationships are continuously replaced by new ones. The whole country is engaged in weaving the right *guanxi* to get things done—a daily practice by no means confined to activists alone. As long as there is *guanxi,* there are possibilities for action and incremental change. It is safe to proclaim that the instability of Chinese sociopolitical networking is both a liability and an opportunity for activists. As Chapter 1 illustrates, Chinese activists excel in gaming the system, a process that invariably starts with identifying enlightened members in the government and building a personal relationship with them. It is not exactly a covert operation but an unwritten rule people living in cultures highly dependent on *guanxi* ethos understand and practice intuitively. *Activists who operate by utilizing guanxi are already practicing nonconfrontational social action.* This is not only true for grassroots NGOs but for anybody engaged in participatory action in China.

The second PAR example is politically more sensitive than the first. As we know, women's liberation has been on the state agenda since Mao's time. It is a politically "correct" ideology even if feminist practice and rural self-governance are considered controversial in parts of rural China. In contrast, the rights protection of construction workers is a political landmine. How did Professor Guo Weihe (a PAR researcher) and his collaborators succeed in dodging governmental censorship while implementing a labor justice project?

Professor Guo works with a Beijing-based nonprofit organization that provides cultural and educational services and legal assistance to migrant workers in the construction sector. In a year-long period, his team designed a training curriculum, teaching laborers about their basic rights as stipulated in the Chinese Labor Law, building an alliance of politically confident workers and cultivating their negotiating skills in labor disputes. The participatory momentum kicked in even more powerfully when trained construction workers relocated elsewhere or returned to their rural homes. Once there, they were turned into trainers themselves, propagating the same messages in which they were previously inculcated. The mobilization did not stop at construction sites. A lecture series on the topic and a traveling exhibition of migrant workers' living condition was held on university campuses all over Beijing as part of a themed consciousness-raising campaign meant to attract more student volunteers to participate in the project. Well-known progressive intellectuals like Sun Liping and Shen Yuan at Tsinghua University were on board as lecturers. Sometimes, the programmatic use of the language of "struggle" and "exploitation of capital" brought us back to the historical time when the proletariat was holding up the sky. In less than a year, the nonprofit organization visited six construction sites and came into contact with more than 10,000 workers (Guo 2013, 278). One cannot but wonder whether the awakening of class consciousness and the strengthening of the organizational capacity of workers will lead them to concrete forms of self-organization.

Organized labor *is* the plan. In Guo Weihe's blueprint, the first step to achieve that end is to build a mobile-phone mediated network of the core members of politically awakened workers. That is the backbone of the worker community targeted by Professor Guo's advocacy project. Workers hired as divisional foremen (*xiao baogong tou*) are expected to take the lead in managing subordinates in their own small divisions. Sporadic worker unions organized at the grassroots level would follow. Of course, those grassroots "unions" would observe the legal specifications spelled out in PRC's Trade Union Law.

I am especially drawn to this project because it navigates so tactfully between what is lawful and what is illegitimate. We now arrive at the heart of Chinese nonconfrontational activism:

> In China, the socialist ideology is continually being rejuvenated and solidified. It serves not only as a regime legitimation tool by the [Communist] rulers, but a weapon used by grassroots actors to withstand oppression and control. (Guo 2013, 285)

How does this work? There is no better strategy of fighting against the censors than borrowing the official ideology to seal their tongues. The construction workers were fed not ideas of Western democracy and social justice but old socialist propaganda that glorifies the struggle of workers against oppressive labor conditions. They were taught to sing the 1947 revolutionary song "Our Workers Are Powerful." From one construction site to the next, workers joined by university volunteers gathered to sing "AiHeiAiHeiHeiYa! Our face is lit up in red light, our sweat keeps flowing. Why are we laboring so hard? To liberate ourselves!" The spectacle was ironic, but it sent a powerful signal to the state that the radical mobilization of construction workers coincided with the state project of reviving the Red legacy of the Communist revolution. Touting the ideological line endorsed by the state is a protective shield that never fails. Indeed, throughout the mobilization campaign, the labor NGO took care to stress over and over again that the problems resulting in the exploitation of construction workers had not originated in the central government. The culprit was said to be the iniquitous capital and corrupt local officials (Guo 2013, 283). In fact, the mission of this project was to teach worker participants how to resort to a "reasoned and legitimate collective action" in their fight for labor interests, whereby the "informal, traumatic resistance can be channeled into formalized, positive, and constructive social action" (275).

These strategies, like all the other nonconfrontational tactics treated throughout the book, are helping activists to legitimate social actions in China. Networking with friendly forces within the Party is one, hiding in plain sight is another. Both strategies allow activists to make incremental changes without taking huge personal or organizational risks. As I argued in Chapter 1, Chinese activists have choices other than becoming martyrs or brainwashed dummies. Asking whether they are co-opted by the state—

whether they are inside or outside the system—is beside the point. In my previous work, I caution against treating all planned spaces in contemporary China as devoid of transformative potential. This is not just a theoretical issue. In real life, the Chinese have a saying, "The most invisible place is the spot right underneath the light." Translating this metaphoric saying into plain language, it means that no place is safer than the place of danger. That is because, paradoxically, under the surveillance of the Party-state, it is easier to carve out "breathing spaces" (*shengcun de kongjian*) within the planned space than to create them outside it. Activists as well as ordinary Chinese people pride themselves in finding their own space and place in what seems to be an exquisitely planned space (Wang 2005, 28). No wonder Xia Linqing is optimistic about the future of social action in China (Xia 2013, 7). It is a fascinating playground where no rules absolutely rule.

Conclusion

This chapter investigated the complex relationship between social action and action research in a number of contexts. I started with a methodological provocation that NGO2.0 could not pledge full allegiance to participatory action research. Via a discussion about the project's crowdsourced philanthropy map, the ideology of participation and its methodological implications were put under the microscope. Not only did scaled participation not happen overnight simply because we launched a participatory project, it could not be fully unraveled from top-down maneuvering and hierarchical relations. This case study of NGO2.0's experiment with collaborative design was followed by a discussion of the Chinese challenge to some of the fundamental assumptions underlying PAR. What happens when social action does not lead to resistance, as is commonly seen in the day-to-day comings and goings in an authoritarian regime? How have Chinese and Taiwanese women scholars critiqued the androcentric tradition of Western PAR? The rest of the chapter pursued this double plot. It discussed the short history of Chinese action research, detailing the influence of a Taiwanese action researcher, Mao's revolutionary tradition of practice, and the impact of black feminist theories on the development of Chinese PAR. At the same time, two important strategies of nonconfrontational activism were closely examined to conclude that there is infinite space for action and activism in countries where the neoliberal tradition is weak. The mountains are high and the emperors far away. In Xia Linqing's terms, the mainland is a huge living laboratory for those wishing to collectively experiment with radical social practice (Xia 2013, 7). Change agents are spread in every corner of the land, busy knitting collaborative relationships with each other. Isn't that the ultimate goal PAR aspires to?

Conclusion

Between Star Trek and Brave New World?

The Other Digital China: Nonconfrontational Activism on the Social Web is devoted to social media and digital practices emerging from China's social sector caught at a transformative moment, thanks largely to the arrival of Web 2.0 technology and its accompanying cyberutopianism, and partly due to a coordinated series of policies that opened up a space for change makers in China to experiment with open tools and open platforms to serve social good. Among those policies are official decrees directly relevant to the haunting question of the "social." Side by side with the ideological tightening of Xi Jinping's regime is the emergence of a body of governing strategies that is reshaping the social sector in the name of "separating the government from society"—a policy course said to define the next thirty years of "social reform." Other details of implementation soon followed. The new Philanthropy Law sets up a legal infrastructure for charity activities and organizations while the policy of "social governance" heralds in the era of consultative politics based theoretically on nonconfrontational interactions between the community, social organizations, and local authorities. Is China's future dark or bright? Are those new policies benefiting censors or change makers? This book challenges binary questions and binary answers. The pendulum, I argue, has rarely swung to one end for very long in the past three decades. Nor will it do so in the next thirty years. That's because both government authorities and activists are engaged in the balancing act of maintaining a harmonious society. Directing our attention to the middle ground, where various kinds of nonconfrontationalism are operating, is crucial. Networking with friendly forces within the Party is one kind of nonconfrontational action, hiding in plain sight is another. Both strategies and a host of other strategies discussed in the book allow Chinese activists to make incremental change without taking huge personal or organizational risks. What emerges is an ever-expanding networked activism at a grand scale.

NGOs are not the only change makers in China. *The Other Digital China* unveils less visible channels of change making. The Internet Plus policy, for example, together with state laws reinforcing corporate citizenship, have galvanized the commercial sector to think about how to integrate digital and new media practices into corporate social responsibility programs. Meanwhile, the Maker Movement and Internet Plus have not only turned Chinese millennials into feverish digital entrepreneurs but also pushed the idea of tech4good deep into a social sector pressured to innovate itself through technology. We began to witness a growing number of civic hackathons held by young techies. No less significant is the emergence of a small cluster of nonprofit tech start-ups manned by the most civic-minded of the post-1980s and post-1990s generations. Together, those various policy discourses have started making a long-term impact on the activities of change makers in contemporary China. Within that larger context, this book fleshes out the mutually transformative processes of social agents and constraining structure while mapping out the emerging Chinese ecology of social media activism that traverses multiple sectors and communities—the NGO sector, the corporate sector, the IT sector, the millennials, and the software developer and maker communities.

Why is it important to highlight the connection of state policies to the diverse practices of tech4good and social media for social good in contemporary China? The shorthand answer is: precisely because the majority of Chinese activists opt for neither revolution nor inertia, state policy offers them critical clues to carve out *the middle ground*. In illiberal societies in which open resistance is not the norm, social action unfolded in gray areas is by default nonconfrontational, and social change occurring there is by definition incremental and largely invisible to the outside world. For those operating in the massive middle ground, policy serves as an indispensable marker that helps change makers draw the boundary of the legitimate. In Reform China especially, policy signals not so much what is forbidden as what it is enabled (Wang 2008b, 249–59, 265). It is not surprising that savvy activists feel compelled to scrutinize policies with diligence so as to better detect what is permissible, which in turn allows them to better draw or expand the designated gray area where noncontentious social action takes place.

Hackers and programmers responded to the policies of the Maker Movement by channeling their social energy into civic hackathons and activities revolving around the ideology of tech4good. IT corporations like Tencent.com and Sina.com found justification in China's CSR regulations to create crowdfunding platforms for grassroots NGOs, a double-win strategy that benefits not only the nonprofits but the two conglomerates themselves. Thus, the series of registration reform policies in the NGO sector freed the majority of the grassroots from worrying about status legitimation. The new policy emphasis on the dialogue between the (local) government and social organizations further opened up a theoretical possibility of collaboration between the two. Indeed, tangible two-way dialogues could lead to better understanding if not immediate trust. This is already happening with support-type NGOs based in every province, whose relationship with the local government is a strong one by default. I myself have taken part in exploratory dialogues with officials in the Ministry of Civil Affairs, the regulatory body governing China's NGOs and other social organizations. All that doesn't mean constraints and censorship have disappeared. It simply means that leveraging those policies enables us to dance around constraints with resilience and that there is ample space for action and activism in countries where the neoliberal tradition is weak. Laying bare the myriad ways with which Chinese change makers are creating social good, this book teases out the proposition that despite blatant censorship, activists in China are practicing activism that is making impactful social change over time. Not only should we talk about the agency of change makers in authoritarian regimes, but by reckoning with their existence and breaking the absolute link between activism and outright resistance, we pose a challenge to the mainstream definition of *social action* and *activism*, and in so doing, we cannot but problematize the neoliberal framing of illiberal political cultures and the people living in those cultures. This argument runs through *The Other Digital China* and is treated from multiple vantage points, complete with case studies and an analysis of nonconfrontational strategies, all of which are couched in the context of participatory action and viral communication. Social media is a crucial enabler that provides nonconfrontational activists with a means of innovating the strategy of gaming the system.

Against this backdrop, I addressed two sets of questions in six chapters. First, what are the key trends that are converging to reshape the

Chinese social sector and facilitating the emergence of an activism 2.0 culture? Second, how are free agents, grassroots NGOs, CSR mangers, IT corporations, and socially responsible techies and millennial makers utilizing social media and Web 2.0 technology to carry out their social mission?

Writing this book would be impossible if I were not an activist myself. As I laid out at the beginning, this book grew out of my own practice as the founder and secretary-general of NGO2.0, a grassroots organization specializing in ICT-powered activism in China. During the process of NGO2.0's evolution into a full-fledged organization, I was exposed, bit by bit, to a gradually unfolding, captivating landscape of social media activism, in which multiple groups of players—NGO2.0's multisectoral collaborators—are leveraging the network effect of Web 2.0 to make change in a country where rampant problems of poverty, injustice, and inequality are challenging its emergent status as a developed country. What gave impetus to the genesis of this book is thus my own experience as an activist practicing social media activism on the ground.

While the experiential does not always carry value in academic discourse, a conceptual framework devoid of personal testimonies can be anemic. I have written *The Other Digital China* as a scholar, but I would like to end it in an activist voice, spelling out the highs and lows of my ten years' experience in running NGO2.0. But before delivering my concluding remarks, there is one big elephant in the room that I saved until the end to unveil: the debate on ICT4D, tech4good, and other issues related to technological determinism. First, is ICT4D (information and communication technology for development) a relevant conceptual frame for this book?

My immediate answer is a no, not least because I chose to anchor my account of activism 2.0 in two other frames—social media for social good (for the information and communication components in ICT) on one hand, and tech4good (for the technology component in ICT) on the other hand. I steer away from ICT4D or social media for development for a number of reasons.

Information and Communication Technology for Development

Underlying the old discourse of ICT4D is the deep conviction that information and communication technology is an effective means of poverty alleviation and that it allows developing countries to leapfrog to the wealth level of modern industrial societies (Thapa and Saebø 2014). In such a frame, the main problem of the world is seen as the digital divide, the lack of access to ICTs, and an ensuing information and knowledge deficit that prevents the poor and the disadvantaged from entering the era of the knowledge economy. Proponents of ICT4D argue, sometimes rightfully, that ICT increases interactivity and knowledge sharing at such fast speed and low cost that it allows the integration of different types of media, which makes censorship more difficult to be thoroughly enforced, not to mention that such technologies are powerful tools for social inclusion (Weigel 2004, 20–21, 24). Truly, as we enter the twenty-first century, the digital and mobile revolution has so deeply infiltrated the daily lives of both the rich and the poor that it is possible to argue that "bread or computers" is no longer a moot question. In this view, since technology is already part of the broader context for the poor, digital rights matter to all social groups and the right to communicate is as important as the bread-and-butter issues (Center for Media Justice et al. 2015; Weigel 2004, 18). Even middle-of-the-road scholars like Gerard Raiti have noted that although technologies may not be a cure-all for developing countries, it is important to recognize the many well-documented success stories in which ICTs helped rural farmers increase their literacy and facilitate communal communication (Raiti 2006, 3). What then is the problem with ICT4D as a practice?

On the other side of the debate, critics of ICT4D focus on the neoliberal discourse of *development*. The term itself is contentious not only because it is seen as an overly optimistic, GDP-driven Western-centric ideology (Raiti 2006; Heeks 2010; Qureshi 2013; Harriss 2014; Walsham 2017), but because it also reveals an agenda with "a historical bias toward project-based and economic outcomes" (Nicholson, Nugroho, and Rangaswamy 2016, 358). A staple of modernization theory, the concept of *development* is emblematic of the instrumental rationality underpinning a positivist definition of *progress*. Furthermore, ICT4D projects an epistemological vision about knowledge production dominated by researchers specializing in information systems, computer science, and development studies, fields whose top-down and supply-side driven trajectory turns a blind eye to the design-reality gap, with the result that ICT4D projects often fail to deliver human-centered perspectives on "growth."

A critical intervention in development studies occurred in 1999 when Amartya Sen, a Harvard professor and Indian economist and philosopher, formulated a new paradigm known as "development as freedom" that humanizes ICT4D studies, at least in theory. What he brings to the front burner is an argument that freedom, with its "thousand charms," should be seen as the ultimate goal of development for all unfree citizens in the world. This entails a shift of neoliberal development strategy from the pursuit of economic productivity to unleashing individual capabilities and creating a society where such liberating potentials can be fully realized. Putting *people* at the center of the development process, Sen attempts to link values, development, and individual freedom in an analytical framework that prioritizes the relationship between individual well-being and economic wealth (Sen 1999). But "development as freedom" remains an alluring abstract philosophy. How to implement it in ICT4D projects poses a daunting challenge.

Other alternative discourses emerged in succeeding decades, for example, ICT4D2.0 (Heeks 2009) and social media for development (Nicholson, Nugroho, and Rangaswamy 2016). Both propositions represent efforts of pouring new wine in old bottles. In the end, neither alternative looks viable not only because the term *development* carries too much historical and ideological baggage to be resuscitated, but these new visions fall short in two regards. First, just like ICT4D1.0, the 2.0 edition fails to incorporate multidisciplinary thinking, which would entail the inclusion of disciplines like media studies, cultural studies, and other adjacent humanities disciplines that are suspicious of development theory and critical of its underlying ideological thinking precisely because they are tied closely to the logocentric tradition of the Enlightenment. Second, ICT4D2.0 will not be able to transform itself thoroughly until it cuts its umbilical cord from the agenda of bilateral and multilateral development agencies such as the World Bank whose subscription to the universal applicability of neoclassical economic theory has contributed to the ongoing controversy surrounding such discourses (Williams 2014). These two shortcomings are interrelated as they invariably touch upon the issue of the shaky disciplinary foundation of ICT4D.

During the 1980s and 1990s, the twin research arms of ICT4D projects consisted of information systems studies and development studies. According to Richard Heeks, each discipline failed to adequately understand and appreciate the other's priorities, which led to a technocentric approach dominated by an informatics worldview, on one hand, and an economics-focused development vision highly skeptical of new technology, on the other hand (Heeks 2009, 19–24). To what extent ICTs are contributing to development is a question hotly debated to this day. At best, the assessment of the impact of ICT intervention on development remains inconclusive (Dey and Ali 2016). In plotting the future course for ICT4D, Heeks proposes ICT4D2.0 as the new catchword and asks how the old field can be opened up for "broader world views" (Heeks 2009, 23). He goes so far as to nominate "communication studies" as the "fourth world-view" and reformulates the old question by asking: can social media be transformative to "human development"? To respond to his own call for action, Heeks turns to the task of reframing the beneficiaries of ICT4D by restoring agency to the poor as "active producers and active innova-tors" (31), turning the supply-driven focus of ICT4D1.0 on its head.

The mere replacement of 1.0 by 2.0 within the aging framework of ICT4D is, however, doomed to fail for as long as the multidisciplinary al-liance in question—a collaboration between the humanities (especially media studies and cultural studies), communication studies, computer sci-ence, information systems, and development studies—remains a distant dream. All other attempts would only end in rhetorical makeovers. Heeks is right about one intractable task at least, that the very nature of ICT4D-styled participation is difficult because it requires multiple divides be bridged, among them disciplinary partitions, the divide between the ICT designer and the user, techies and nontechies, the rich and the poor, and the Western and non-Western mind-set (Heeks 2009, 16).

Tech4Good and Social Media for Social Good

As a scholar of the humanities, I opt out of the ICT4D framework and choose an open-ended substitute term *social good* for three reasons. First, "social media for social good" immediately broadens the identity of change makers beyond that of techies, researchers, and development agen-cies, for it is within the capacity of *every* human being to do social good. Indeed, the change makers in this book include individual free agents and common folks as well as NGOs, universities, tech companies, and other commercial organizations. Second, *social good* flings the door open to other definitions of social change beyond that of development. Third, ac-tivists need not be entangled in jargon or acronyms. The vernacular value of "social media for social good" is an additional boon. It is a frame ac-cessible to all and well understood by practitioners on the ground.

As mentioned earlier, digital media transformed the ways people communicate, and social media changed the ways people network. And networking fundamentally changed the way work is defined and organized. Throughout *The Other Digital China,* we saw how different sectors in China use social media to serve the public good. On Weibo and WeChat, grassroots NGOs are able to broadcast their mission, create spreadable content, interact with the public, recruit volunteers, and launch social media enabled advocacy campaigns. The corporate sector is rolling out an increasing number of CSR 2.0 initiatives that trigger mass mobilization online. Free agents, many of whom are social media influencers, are shaping networked fundraising campaigns for those in dire need, at little sweat. University students—the post-1990s millennials in particular—are at the forefront of the domestic Chinese and global volunteer initiatives driven by Web 2.0 thinking and interactive media. The tech sector, of course, is another crucial participant in building the social tableau where creating scalable impact through ICTs remains a deep commitment to which makers and hackers are drawn. Today's tech4good practices in China have evolved beyond the old top-down approach, and under the banner of collaborative design, the most gifted techies are learning to work with NGOs as peers. Last but not least, an empowered mass audience—the average Wangs and Zhangs—are now given a chance to take part in social good 2.0 campaigns that have mushroomed all over China, whether we are talking about planting trees via virtual reality to curb global warming or multicity peer measurement of PM2.5 and polluted waters.[1] All those energies and resulting synergies are released precisely because social media have percolated into our daily lives regardless of which sector we belong to. This is how proponents of Web 2.0 trumpet its virtue. Surely, social media speed up scaled participation in social causes and the public airing of diverse perspectives. And yet, just as many contest the democratizing potential of social media by arguing that such content is still controlled by a privileged few.

Like ICT4D and other utopian visions, social media for social good has its detractors. NGO leaders with a more traditional mind-set harbor skepticism about the efficacy of social media to generate systemic change on the ground. There are other critics who suspect that the social good in question is nothing more than personal charity and that social media for social good easily falls into the feel-good fluff to which slacktivists and FOMOs[2] mindlessly gravitate. "Do-gooders" and "feel good marketing" are a few derogatory epithets older generations of activists heap upon corporate champions of cause marketing 2.0 as well as NGOs heavily invested in social media communication strategies. Meanwhile, questions about the Internet as a whole are raised to challenge social media as a change agent. "Are social media emancipatory or hegemonic?" (Miranda, Young, and Yetgin 2016). This question keeps resurfacing whenever a new scandal about social media goes viral.

It doesn't help that increasing negative press about Facebook and company further undermines the fairy tale that social media is a silver bullet for democracy. Headlines such as "Something Has Gone Wrong with Facebook, Google, and Twitter," "Do Social Media Threaten Democracy?" and "Facebook, Twitter, and Google Grilled by MPs over Hate Speech" are just a few examples that illustrate how the cult of social media can just be as illusory as the cult of technology.

In fact, the social media and all things digital backlash has triggered new critical discourses and new social cravings. The seamless connectedness of lives and devices has given rise to the return of our yearning for "simple pleasures, farm-to-table food, homemade meals, [and] handwoven items" (Andjelic 2017). The offline lifestyle is the new luxury. A slow and handmaking culture is on the rise to resist the accelerating overdrive of a digital lifestyle consumed by relentless velocity and hyperconnectivity. JOMO, "the joy of missing out," has emerged to trump the once-popular FOMO, "fear of missing out."[3] A slew of mobile features, designed by Google and Apple to make our phones a little less addictive, turned "digital well-being" into the talk of the Silicon Valley. (Waite 2018; Gurman 2018). The vogue of digital detox unveils new consumer categories such as the smart "dumbphone." An emerging analog revolution has brought back to the market vinyl records, paper notebooks, and old board games (Chun 2017). Similarly, the demise of FilmStruck, a well-curated digital collection of acclaimed classic and cult movies, shows just "how ephemeral streaming is" (Raftery 2018). We are witnessing the renaissance of Blue-ray culture bolstered by the niche community of art house film enthusiasts. In the meantime, critical neologisms like *cyberbalkanization* and *homophily*—the syndrome of "selective exposure" in psychologists' parlance—have driven home the arrival of a dystopia where like-minded people attract each other, flock together, and insulate themselves from viewpoints different from their own. Social networks like Facebook and WeChat are in effect made up of hundreds of millions of echo chambers that wall off diverse opinions and reinforce social and political schisms, a trend detrimental to the growth of democratic culture (Van Alstyne and Brynjolfsson 2005; McPherson, Smith-Lovin, and Cook 2003). All this defies Mark Zuckerberg's expectation that universal connectedness would unite rather than divide (Packer 2013). The list of the critiques of cyber-optimism goes on and on. No book better articulates this rising wave of antidigital angst than Evgeny Morozov's *To Save Everything, Click Here: The Folly of Technological Solutionism*.

Is the Internet, and its sibling social media, at a crossroads? The answer eventually depends on who is sitting in the driver's seat. Tech utopianists and cybercynics could be both partially right and partially wrong. Nobody can contest the fact that the movement of peer progressivism has fundamentally changed the way decisions are made and collaboration is forged. Problem solving in dynamic workplaces and classrooms today unfolds incrementally through the decentralized activity of countless interconnected equals (Johnson 2012). Scalable participation as well as the subversion of top-down hierarchy merits our attention as much as the critiques of what is lacking in the egalitarian discourse of peer networks. Although Marshall McLuhan would likely frown at Alex Pentland's idea that a "responsible society" can be engineered through the statistical modeling of digital data,[4] McLuhan himself did predict that "the computer can be used to direct a network of global thermostats to pattern life in ways that will optimize human awareness" (McLuhan 1969). The notion of artificial intelligence and machine-learning being capable of making ethical decisions may sound outlandish if not downright disturbing to advocates of analog culture. Lawrence Lessig, Harvard professor and the founder of Creative Commons, has delineated for us the hackers' design-4good worldview in which humans can build computer codes and architecture to serve ethical purposes, while the law, the market, and social norms—the three other forces that constrain our actions—are absolutely beyond our control. He goes on arguing that algorithms at least can be designed to serve human good and make pernicious values disappear (Lessig 1999).

Lessig's coders and hackers are not imaginary creatures, for our cyberspace is already filled with stories that illustrate the power of coding to protect the values we hold sacrosanct. Twitter, for example, is developing metrics to distinguish between incivility—which plays a crucial role in political dialogue—and intolerance (like hate speech and racism) that threatens democracy; machine-learning algorithms are tasked to "reduce toxic conversations" and crack down on spam and fake accounts (Wang 2018). New technological norms, in short, could be a force for good or for evil. On one hand, Silicon Valley trumpets the value of "responsible disruption," one that incorporates inclusion and diversity (Teinmetz and Vella 2017); on the other hand, we could argue that the high tech libertarians may just be seen as another special interest group (Packer 2013, 8). While we are greeting the good news that developers are working on AI to help people with autism to make sense of other people's emotions (Yonck 2017), the once-technoholic Kentaro Toyama, author of *Geek Heresy* and now a disillusioned tech-activist, confesses with regret that throwing gadgets at social problems is a dead end (Toyama 2015). Similarly, the miraculous CRISPR, a gene editing tool that holds the potential of curing all genetic disease, may just likely turn out to be a game changer for terrorists or rogue states that could deploy it as a weapon of mass destruction (Park 2016, 44). For every inspiring innovation, there is a danger lurking behind it, and for every tech4bad example, there are counterexamples. Just like all the media and technologies that preceded the Web 2.0 era, social media are not inherently liberatory. It depends upon who the user is and for what purpose they are deployed.

Amidst all the rage and cheers, it is unlikely that we will throw the social web out with the bath water. Toyama is skeptical of social media cheerleaders like Clay Shirky, and he deplores that a generation ago when young people said they wanted to change the world or make an impact, they joined the Peace Corps, but now they move to Silicon Valley (Toyama 2015, 21). In reality though, the youth today, and the average Joes and Janes we know, are not obliged to make a *singular* choice between two polarized ideals of serving the world. Each one of us operates both online and offline and pursues a lifestyle neither purely digital nor purely analog. I bring my iPhone to access my music playlist while I travel, and on a snowy night, I curl up on my sofa sipping tea and listening to old vinyl records. Like many others, I am both a clicktivist and an on-site activist. Am I torn in conflict every day? Not at all. Clicking to seed a virtual plant and participating in offline advocacy campaigns are *not* mutually exclusive; they are part of my growing portfolio of social actions. Only purists and devotees of binarism would ask whether our life today is virtual or material, as if such choice can be made. Even Kentaro Toyama, the tech dissident, has come to reckon with the complex interaction between technology and people, and he concludes that its impact can be both positive and negative. "The truth is neither *Star Trek* nor *Brave New World*" but a mixture of both (Toyama 2015, 24). For me at least, Lessig is too optimistic, but Morozov is too dark. The truth, as always, lives in between.

The Mother of All Questions

I started this book with a chapter on NGO2.0 that is now ten years old. On the eve of its anniversary, many critics as well as supporters of NGO2.0 have asked me to evaluate the success or failure of my decade-long engagement in ICT-powered activism. While it is too early to assess our tech4good efforts and predict the destiny of our vision for the Future Village project, this is the opportune moment to examine the results of our social media training workshops and contemplate the mother of all questions: Is social action spurred by social media helping NGOs and other change agents to become more capable of self-transformation, and thus, more transparent, innovative, and collaborative? Fully addressing this ambitious question is difficult as it requires regular and vigorous follow-up studies of the 1,600 organizations we have trained, a workload too heavy for a small organization like NGO2.0 to take on. The following tables and figures, however, provide a partial glimpse of how we tackle that question at the moment. Each chart speaks to a major criterion— transparency, collaboration, and innovation—with which we evaluate the impact of our social media workshops on trainee organizations.

Transparency Index. One hundred NGOs joined the 2013 social media follow-up survey (NGO-SM Survey 2, 2013), which we sent to 200 trainee organizations, with a 50 percent response rate. We established three evaluative categories—transparency, collaboration, and innovation—each corresponding to what is raised in the "mother question"—the impact of social media on NGO work. We then define performance indicators for each category. Table C.1 is the transparency model. On the left are all the tools we have taught that can help NGOs enhance transparency. An NGO's transparency score is decided by two factors: (1) whether the organization has used those designated tools and (2) the number of transparency tools each organization has used since the training.

Figure C.1 illustrates how well participating NGOs scored in the survey results. Among the 100 respondents, 5 used all seven transparency tools, 15 NGOs used six tools, 21 NGOs used at least 5, and 25 used 4. Overall, 66 NGOs used four or more tools to publish organizational content and achieved what we considered satisfactory transparency. Only one NGO used none of the tools, which indicates how little its staff had learned from our literacy training.

Table C.1. NGO Transparency Indicator (NGO-SM Survey 2, 2013)

Transparency Index	Impacting Factor	Score
Have set up an organizational Weibo account	Yes	1
	No	0
Have built an official blog or official website	Yes	1
	No	0
Have used e-newsletter subscription services	Yes	1
(such as QQ News Letter open subscription)	No	0
Have uploaded to a video-sharing website videos	Yes	1
made by your organization	No	0
Have used wikis (e.g., Baidu Wiki or Wikipedia) to	Yes	1
publicize information about your organization	No	0
Have shared pictures of organization's activities	Yes	1
on photo-sharing platforms (e.g., Weibo, QQ	No	0
Space, FlowerPetals, NetEase Album, etc.)		
Have updated organization's project information	Yes	1
on NGO2.0 philanthropy map	No	0

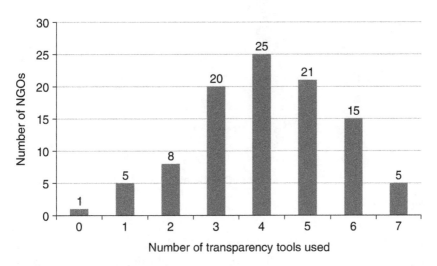

Figure C.1. Transparency Scores (NGO-SM Survey 2, 2013)

Table C.2. NGO Collaboration Indicator (NGO-SM Survey 2, 2013)

Collaboration Index	Impacting Factor	Score
Have used multiparty online meeting/chatting	Yes	1
tools (e.g., YY or Skype)	No	0
Have used desktop sharing tools	Yes	1
	No	0
Have used cloud note-taking tools (e.g., Evernote,	Yes	1
Onenote, Youdao Cloud Note)	No	0
Have used cloud storage (e.g., Sina Vdisk, Gold	Yes	1
Mountain WPS Quick Disk)	No	0
Have used collaborative editing tools (e.g.,	Yes	1
Baihui, GoogleDocs, etc.)	No	0
Have looked up CSR projects and information	Yes	1
on NGO2.0 philanthropy map	No	0

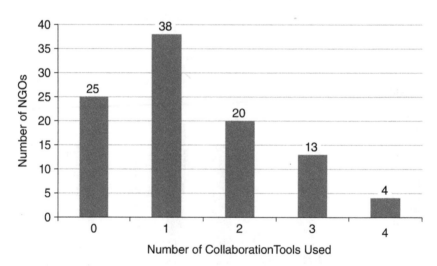

Figure C.2. Collaboration Scores

Collaboration Index. We also set up a model for collaboration performance. Table C.2 shows all the tools we taught that are relevant to enhancing the collaborative potentials of an organization.

Based on this set of criteria and relying on the simple indicator of whether each organization has used each designated tool, we derived the statistics presented in Figure C.2

Figure C.2 indicates that only thirty-seven organizations used two or more collaboration tools, which we set as the bar for passing. This indicates that using online tools for collaboration was a relatively weak area of competency for our NGOs in 2013, but it was encouraging that thirty-eight organizations had used at least one collaborative tool.

Innovation Capability Index. How could we measure the potentials of NGOs for technological innovation? The fourteen tools and methods listed in Table C.3 indicate an NGO's interest in and the degree of their acceptance of tech-enabled solutions. By "innovation capability," we mean an NGO's ability to adopt cutting-edge tools to complete tasks such as identifying partners, communicating with them, and finding opportunities for new philanthropy practices. Tool adoption and digital action only represent one small step toward the creative use of social media and ICTs. But these criteria provide us with a useful starting point to delve deeper into the innovation inquiry.

As shown in Figure C.3, only two organizations learned little. Twenty-nine NGOs surveyed used at least two innovation tools. The strongest performance came from twenty-two organizations that used five or more tools.

So, is action spurred by social media helping NGOs and other change agents become more capable of self-transformation and more transparent, creative, and collaborative? Are they more transparent? Absolutely yes. Transparency involves a concentrated effort on the part of a grassroots NGO to transform itself from its previously self-enclosed and haphazard presence to a trustworthy entity highly conscious of public scrutiny. Those findings are impressive, given the participating NGOs' ability to understand what "openness" means and their attempt to professionalize despite scarce resources. Looking at the lists of the difficult tools we taught our trainees, I sometimes wonder if they do better in ICTs than my colleagues in the humanities.

Are our NGOs creative? I think so, whether they achieved it through digital means or not. Looking at the data sets, I feel confident that more exemplary cases like Greening Han River will emerge as we continue our educational mission. NGO2.0 will continue to experiment with new ways of turning our students from passive learners of new technology into actors collaborating with us teachers to co-design a creative curriculum both for our social media workshops and Design Thinking trainings.

Next, the collaboration data deliver a lesson that goes beyond ICTs: It is not easy to ascertain to what degree new media tools stimulated grassroots

Table C.3. NGO Innovation Indicator (NGO-SM Survey 2, 2013)

Innovation Capability Index	Impacting Factor	Score
Have used keyword search services (such as	Yes	1
Google News Alert)	No	0
Have used web analytics tools (e.g., Baidu	Yes	1
Analysis, Google Analytics, etc.)	No	0
Have used WeChat	Yes	1
	No	0
Have used online survey tools (such as Wendao,	Yes	1
Survey Monkey, etc.)	No	0
Have used desktop sharing tools (such as JoinMe,	Yes	1
Team Viewer, etc.)	No	0
Have used cloud note-taking tools	Yes	1
	No	0
Have used cloud storage services (Baidu, Gold	Yes	1
Mountain, etc.)	No	0
Have used collaborative editing tools (e.g.,	Yes	1
Baihui, Google Docs, etc.)	No	0
Have used visual discovery and visual curating	Yes	1
tools (e.g., Petals, Pinterest, etc.)	No	0
Have used Weibo analytics (Zhiwei Analytics, etc.)	Yes	1
	No	0
Have established social media communication	Yes	1
strategies for your organization	No	0
Have hands-on experience of making logs for	Yes	1
organization or activities	No	0
Have searched for corporate social responsibility	Yes	1
projects on NGO2.0 map	No	0
Have used Douban.com and Renren.com to plan	Yes	1
and hold offline activities	No	0

collaboration and helped grow translocal causes. After all, revolution-izing organizational thinking and changing communication patterns may not be the key reasons why most NGOs joined our workshops and col-lectively produced more than 25,000 pages of conversation in NGO2.0's QQ instant messaging forum during the first two years of the founding of the project. It has been a delight to visit our QQ group where ICT-related informal instruction took place (yes, we teachers are available for chats) along with hearty discussions of NGO-related issues. Above all, this is a cross-issue NGO community self-conscious of its vanguard position in

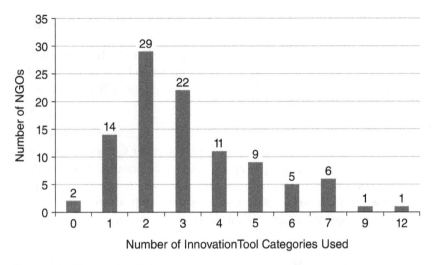

Figure C.3. Innovation Scores

creating a new NGO tech culture in China. The spirit of sharing, which is central to the culture of Web 2.0, is already boosting the morale of resource-deprived NGO workers. The bonding of like-minded idealists is an achievement as precious as improved ICT and social media proficiency.

We stopped conducting follow-up surveys after 2013 since we can cull needed data from our regular NGO Internet Usage surveys. Among the 531 organizations surveyed in 2016, approximately 48.4 percent have used telecom application software for multiparty meetings (NGO20-IU Survey 5 2017). The percentage climbed to 60.94 in the sixth survey conducted in 2017 (NGO20-IU Survey Report 6 2018). The growing culture of collaboration is also revealed in the increasing number of grassroots resorting to multiparty online editing tools, screen sharing software for online meetings, and digital calendar tools for time management. The usage of collaborative software such as OneNote, Shimo, and EverNote jumped from 22.49 (NGO20-IU Survey Report 4 2015a) to 34.5 percent in 2017 (NGO20-IU Survey Report 6 2018). It looks like, however slowly, Chinese grassroots are developing the practice of sharing, a characteristic crucial to the flourishing of a vibrant social media culture. Also worth noting is the number of grassroots—50 percent of the 489 organizations participating in the sixth survey—that answered the call for online project contests and tournaments initiated by venture capital investment programs

(NGO20-IU Survey Report 6 2018), a symptom underpinning the grass-roots' potential and desire for innovation.

All this provide a glimpse of our self-evaluation. As the editing of *The Other Digital China* was drawing to an end, a new book *Internet Philanthropy in China*, written by Charles Chen (cofounder of Tencent), summed up the contributions of NGO2.0:

> NGO2.0 was born from a critique and evolved through innovation. It followed a path different from the other Chinese NGOs in its inquiry on internet philanthropy. It was because of the existence of NGO2.0 and its persistent advocacy for the model and concept of "Internet plus public good" that China's internet philanthropy flourished to the degree we witnessed today. (Chen 2018, 145)

That encouraging assessment came at the moment when NGO2.0 was struggling to continue our operation and break out of a growth bottleneck. We are having a difficult time not because of censorship but because Chinese foundations, who hold the money bag, lag far behind NGOs in understanding the significance of tech4good and social media for social good.

The Joy and Fear of an Activist

One of the most convincing arguments brought forth in Toyama's *Geek Heresy* (2015) is the idea that positive or negative outcomes of tech and media use are not absolute but context dependent. When we turn to the context of China and discuss the destiny of the NGOs there, we encounter the inevitable question: Why are digital media and social media indispensable to the survival of grassroots NGOs? Chinese NGOs have sprung up rapidly in the past twenty years across thematic fields. Under the current political climate, however, small, mid-sized, and emerging NGOs encounter a severe bottleneck of growth for predictable reasons. Giving a free rein to nongovernmental organizations has never been a priority of the Chinese government. Second, NGOs are crippled in acquiring resources in a country where size is what matters the most to foundations and donors. Third, grassroots cannot compete with government-affiliated NGOs for the attention of state-owned and state-controlled media, which leads to the difficulty of increasing public awareness of the social cause they are promoting. Lack of media exposure is a death knell for the disadvantaged. Social media is one of the few options left for resource-deprived organizations to solicit volunteers, funding, and other resources. That is the context out of which an organization like NGO2.0 evolved. That is why we dedicate ourselves to the cause of ICT-powered activism.

The practices of NGO2.0 in the past decade yielded both intangible and quantifiable benefits for the grassroots NGOs in our network. The data presented in the tables and figures in this chapter point to some tangible results. Most of the time, however, learning is not quantifiable. All educators are familiar with the impalpable nature of knowledge we impart to our students, lessons that trickle down into the mind and heart bit by bit like water flowing into the ocean, ceaselessly. The NGOs we train learn how to navigate the social web with a focused purpose, take their equal place in cyberspace as media creators, understand the importance of self-positioning and self-representation, build online communities to enable scalable collaboration, and in the process, they gradually overcome their fear about technology and become a member of the digital commons we set up on Weibo and WeChat. Comradeship and self-confidence are invisible trophies, but priceless.

On the other hand, we also reaped quantifiable benefits for participating NGOs. For example, in 2015, NGO2.0 rolled out 101 crowdfunding projects in collaboration with 80 grassroots organizations and raised 4,463,735.10 yuan for them; in the following year, 7,948,480 yuan was raised for 54 grassroots projects; in 2017, we raised 8,376,964.2 on behalf of 137 NGOs for 160 grassroots projects altogether. Those are not mere numbers to brag about but evidence of social media proficiency acquired by participating grassroots organizations and achieved under the painstaking, step-by-step guidance provided by our NGO2.0 staff. By implementing viral communication strategies skillfully, participating NGOs mobilized as many as 111,437 individual donors on a variety of social media platforms in 2015, a total of 80,585 the following year, and 122,952 contributors in sum in 2017. An astounding number of 45,170 donors gathered online to support NGO2.0-mentored projects in the short span of three days during the 2017 Tencent Giving Day. These numbers are a clear indication of effective viral communication, a result of assiduous teaching and successful learning.

But data itself is not the best trophy. How shall I count the intangible moments of gratification? There was the joy of bonding with youthful grassroots leaders at our three-day intensive workshops, my admiration for the inexhaustible altruism they hold on to, and the happiness of watching the videos they produced for a storytelling contest after offering them a two-hour crash course on video making. There were the indelible memories of the group playing Assassin—the workshop icebreaker—from late night till dawn, and the day-to-day postworkshop Weibo marathon chats I had with them into the wee hours. And how could I forget the eureka moment when I discovered the UK platform Impossible,[5] which I transformed into an offline game for team building? I remember watching the thirty-two NGO leaders enact the best scenarios of Impossible by trading favors with each other and in so doing, meeting each other's needs. I recall the collective joy while playing that game, for we realized the sharing economy works for the NGO community too and that in mobilizing our own resources to help each other out, our utopia seems within reach. Let me also celebrate the happy moments of spotting our fellow travelers, whether they are devoted techies, angelic volunteers, or CSR vanguards with a vision. Last but not least, I am continuously amazed by the perseverance of our NGO2.0 teammates—the nine musketeers I call them—who have been Skyping with me every Sunday, Beijing time from 8:30 pm to midnight, year in and year out, over the past decade. Those long weekly team meetings are the lifeline of NGO2.0. It is during those three hours that our digital surveys are crafted and finalized, detailed hackathon plans ironed out, interface upgrades for our philanthropy map reviewed and confirmed, collaboration with multiple sectors sealed, future strategies and annual budgets concocted, and learning sessions of what's new in social media are held—all this is accomplished in a peer-to-peer decision-making process. One year, unaware that the autumn moon festival fell on a Sunday, I held a regular meeting at the designated time, with nobody calling in absent.

Surely there were low moments in the past ten years? Yes, but they hardly made a dent on the will of resilient change makers. Those were very different kinds of memories: being kicked out of a university training venue and chased around town by local public security officers; the unbearable suspense about the future of NGO2.0 when the crackdown on foreign foundations cast a shadow on an important source of our funding; dealing with callous university financial officers who kept our grant without processing reimbursements for years; begging for attention and funding from corporations that showed less interest in social causes than what the MIT brand name could offer them; suffering setbacks from a prestigious Chinese university that tricked us into "collaboration" talks when all they wanted was for me to appear at a gala event as an MIT professor and then pulled the carpet from under our feet without notice; enduring the many broken promises of would-be collaborators and learning to take their merry words with a grain of salt; and passing sleepless nights worrying if I could find money to pay for employee salaries.

All those ordeals came and went because I have found an infallible way of regalvanizing myself and my team—holding more workshops in China's hinterland and renewing our close encounter with grassroots activists on Weibo and WeChat. When our morale is waning, I remind myself and my teammates of the mission we are committed to—balancing the ecology of the philanthropy sector by strengthening the capacity of disfranchised grassroots organizations to solve their communication, resource, and technology needs.

Truly, if I have any fear about the future, it would not just be the resurgence of inimical state policies, but the rise of elitism and the unequal allocation of discursive power and financial resources in China's philanthropy sector—an ironic scenario not least because this is supposedly a sector that makes commitments to treating the symptoms of social inequality. This concern of mine has grown over the years as I experienced firsthand the increasing domination of big nonprofit organizations at the expense of the grassroots, with the result that the philanthropy sector is now ruled by the economy of scale, mirroring exactly the unequal power relations plaguing other sectors.

The social, economic, and political life in the twenty-first century will be increasingly digital, and those without ICTs will be increasingly marginalized. The big fish need not worry too much. They can stick to their static Web 1.0 ways of communication without suffering much repercussion. For the grassroots, however, building the proficiencies of social media and digital media become crucial. Eventually, I would argue that we need to shift the terms of debate from whether free and open source software can make the world a better place to what are the means of helping disadvantaged change makers accumulate their social capital. No one can gainsay the proposition that social media remains vital to media justice and that the right to communicate is an inalienable right of the marginalized. I deem myself extremely fortunate to be able to serve thousands of NGOs that belong to the network of NGO2.0 and cross paths with like-minded activists from diverse sectors. Together, our practice in walking around obstacles and our faith in incremental change is turning digital China into a seed bed sown with a myriad of possibilities.

Notes

Bibliography

Acknowledgments

Index

Notes

1. The spokespeople of the James Irvine Foundation raised the same question in a 2009 report titled "Convergence: How Five Trends Will Reshape the Social Sector."

2. The initial group of collaborators were the Chinese University of Science and Technology, NGOCN, ICS at Sun Yat-sen University, Friends of Nature, and Ogilvy & Mather China. Among them, my own lab "New Media Action Lab" at MIT, the University of Science and Technology of China, and Ogilvy China remain important partners in succeeding years.

3. The concept of "Web 2.0" began with a conference brainstorming session between O'Reilly Media and MediaLive International in 2004. It was later described in fuller detail in Tim O'Reilly's article "What Is Web 2.0: Design Patterns and Business Models for the Next Generation of Software" on September 30, 2005. Apart from collective intelligence and interactive communication, many other concepts are associated with Web 2.0, for instance, the Web as platform, the end of software release cycle, and rich user experiences.

4. Compare that data with another developing country, India, where internet penetration hovered only at around 10–15 percent in 2014; see Shah 2014, 58.

5. The Chinese internet is filled with advocacy proposals made by representatives of the National People's Congress (NPC). Typical examples can be found in https://www.lookmw.cn/fanwen/qxauini.html (July 3, 2017). Not all proposals were sound ones, however. China's spoof platform *Longyan dayue* (The Emperor Must Be Pleased) showcased a few that provoked public outrage (please see Chapter 4 for examples). But this is undeniably a recent trend—NPC representatives began to search eagerly for meaningful advocacy projects to present at the NPC sessions.

6. As a long-time grant recipient of Ford Foundation in Beijing, NGO2.0 was repeatedly lectured by local officials and fellow NGOs to seek funding elsewhere. I began a plan of diversifying our funding structure in 2015.

7. According to a report published by Caixin, the funding of Chinese NGOs from overseas sponsors has sharply dropped by 40 percent. The number of foreign foundations that has funded more than five NGOs has also decreased from eight to six since 2013. See "Sharp Drop in NGO Sponsorships from Overseas," Caixin Net, http://china.caixin.com/2015-11-12/100873331.html, Nov. 12, 2015.

8. 1995 was the year when the Fourth World Conference on Women was held in Beijing. It marked the beginning of the flourishing of grassroots NGOs in China.

9. The making of Philanthropy Law involved teams of legislators working closely with university researchers, leaders of charity and nonprofit organizations, and media. The draft was made open for public discussion for several rounds before it was finally published in 2016.

10. Wang Ping's emphasis is placed on the collaborative process through which multiple social partners engage in identifying and solving problems. Instead of being treated as the last link on the chain of problem solving, social organizations need to partake in the process from the very beginning so that they can play a pivotal role in designing, supervising, and evaluating public interest related projects.

1. Nonconfrontational Activism and the Chinese "Social"

1. "Internet Plus" is a Chinese state policy promoting the digitalization of the manufacturing sector economy. Released by the State Council in 2015, the initiative focuses on deepening the integration of digital technologies (i.e., the internet, cloud computing, smart hardware, and big data) into traditional manufacturing. The end goal of the policy is to resuscitate the sectoral economy, moving it from labor-intensive manufacturing to the digital value chain, and in the process, spur the growth of the domestic Chinese technology industry. The implementation of Internet Plus has infiltrated every sector such as transportation, food, finance, and even the nonprofit sector. For details, see Chen 2015.

2. This is a quote from a conversation I had with Elizabeth Knup in March 2018.

3. The South China Tiger incident, known as the Tigergate, was one of the earliest internet incidents in China. In 2007, Chinese netizens exposed a hoax staged by the Forestry Department of Shaanxi province that released online images of a South China tiger that was said to be an endangered species. Netizens soon discovered that the photographed tiger looked identical to the one in popular Chinese New Year posters. A hunt for truth was set off. A panel including a conservationist, a zoologist, a photographer, an image graphics specialist, and a criminal detective convened by Netease (a Chinese IT company) analyzed the images and declared them fake. This incident bore testimony to the power of netizens to challenge governmental authority. In 2008, the Forestry Department made a public apology for the mistake, marking the Tigergate the first incident of governmental accountability achieved through a public debate on the Chinese Web.

4. Sun Zhigang was a migrant worker in Guangzhou. In 2003, while strolling on the street, he was accosted by the police and detained for not being able to show his ID card and temporary living permit in the city. He died in the medical clinic of

the Detention Center. An autopsy report ordered by his family showed that he was beaten severely a few days before his death, which was announced by the authority as the result of a stroke. A furor broke out online, with legal scholars declaring China's Custody and Repatriation (C&R) Law unconstitutional. Those directly responsible for the "murder" of Sun were sentenced to death, accomplices were sent to prison, and several civil servants also served sentences for malpractice. The C&R Law was abolished by the central government. From then on, Chinese netizens were emboldened to redress social injustice through the internet.

5. "Nail houses" refer to households that refuse to move and make room for new development projects. Several such incidents led to confrontation with the local authority and resulted in self-immolation, whereby residents burned themselves alive to protest forced demolition. One of the most famous cases was the Yihuang incident that took place in Yihuang County, Jiangxi province in 2010. The Zhong family were confronted by police officers seeking to carry out the forced demolition of their home to make room for new construction. Three family members set themselves on fire at the top of the house, and the process was streamed by onlookers and published online. In the immediate wake of the tragedy, the two daughters of the Zhong family set off to Beijing to make a petition to higher authorities. Chased by local police and government officers, they locked themselves in an airport lavatory and sent out mobile text messages to local reporters. A number of blogging journalists like Deng Fei began to livecast the ordeal of the two sisters on Weibo. Those tweets quickly spread over online platforms. The local authorities were forced to the negotiation table with the grieving family. Under the tremendous pressure from the public, the higher authorities stepped in and punished those held accountable for the tragedy. Although there were other similar incidents occurring in different parts of the country, this incident stood out in its impact because of the network effect triggered by microblogging. For more details, see Oiwan Lam's "China: Yihuang Self-Immolation Incident and the Power of Microblogging" in GlobalVoices, https://globalvoices.org/2010/09/21/china-yihuang-self-immolation-incident-and-the-power-of-microblogging/.

6. Xiamen PX refers to an environmental protest staged by the residents of Xiamen (also known as Amoy) in Fujian province against the building of a petrochemical plant proposed by the government. The incident was triggered by a mobile text message sent anonymously by a resident, which mobilized residents to take to the streets to oppose the proposal. A spontaneous rally involving at least a thousand protesters occurred even though the city government made a concession to temporarily halt the construction of the PX plant. It was seen as a peaceful demonstration with participants discreetly leveraging nonconfrontational tactics to negotiate with the local government. Guangzhou-based *Southern Weekly* named the people of Xiamen as the Person of the Year.

7. The spoof video can be found at https://www.youtube.com/watch?v=Dr3JVaebZWI.

8. The technique is also known as the "human flesh search engine" (*renrou sousuo*), which refers to actions initiated by righteous Chinese netizens to track down, expose, and stalk the "offenders" through web searches. Their personal information will be posted online. Those offenders could be corrupt officials, mistresses suspected of breaking up families, or individuals committing morally

unacceptable deeds. Once identified, they are subject to cyber and offline bullying and harassment.

9. The rewriting of *Journey to the West* started as early as the Ming Dynasty. *Xiyou Bu* (A Supplement to the Journey to the West) was written by Don Yue around 1640 A.D., which pioneered the deconstruction of the master-disciple relationship in the parent novel. Fast forward to the 1990s, Jeffrey Lau directed the modern classic, *A Chinese Odyssey* in which Stephen Chow played Monkey in the well-celebrated two-part fantasy comedy. In the mid-2010s, Chow codirected *Journey to the West: Conquering the Demons* (2013) and rolled out a sequel *Journey to the West: The Demons Strike Back* (2017) in collaboration with Tsui Hark.

10. This is not the place to investigate the historical and political processes underlying culturally operative concepts like *yinren*. Is it an epiphenomenon of the cultural unconscious, or a political practice and affect triggered by what Althusser called ideological "interpellation"? While critics can argue robustly that culture and ideology are inseparable, *yinren* was, in fact, not assimilated or incorporated into official discourses either in imperial China or in today's Communist China, which makes the answer to the above question a rather difficult one. Nonetheless, I fully recognize that the ideological nuances of collectivism are variables that cannot be captured by foundational terminology. A whole book is called for to unravel the culture, practice, and politics of *yinren*.

2. NGO2.0 and Social Media Activism

1. 1995 was the year when the Fourth World Conference on Women was held in Beijing. It marked the beginning of the flourishment of grassroots NGOs in China. During the conference period, many self-organized groups and scholars, formally organized social groups, and government officials participated in the NGO Forum of the conference. The Forum enabled the Chinese participants to meet foreign NGOs face-to-face, establish contacts with foreign NGOs, especially with foreign foundations that had grant-making capacity. The convening of the conference and the media reports of the event not only promoted knowledge about NGOs in China, but also incentivized many socially concerned elites to create change organizations similar to foreign NGOs. Many of the first-generation grassroots NGOs in China were set up shortly after 1995.

2. As of July 2014, 895 grassroots NGOs among 1,492 that appeared on the NGO2.0 philanthropy map did not own Weibo accounts.

3. My Chinese collaborators at the University of Science and Technology include Professor Rongting Zhou and Dr. Xie Dong at the Department of Sci-Tech Policy and Communication.

4. At the beginning, the map was completely crowdsourced, meaning users came to the map voluntarily to register their data. At the end of 2017, we started to incorporate crawled data into the map to facilitate the launch of a new program—the NGO Evaluation Databank. Approximately, before December 2017, a total of 4,296 NGOs were crowdsourced users. From then on, users are mixed, some are voluntary entrants, others are not.

5. A scandal—known as the Guo Meimei Incident—involving China's Red Cross broke out in 2011. Known as the atomic bomb of the Chinese nonprofit sector, the incident blew away the last shred of the public's trust in the state-monopolized philanthropic structure. Multisectoral collaboration began to take shape in renewing the philanthropy sector. Please see Chapter 3 for details of this scandal.

6. The Chinese government backed up the IT sector's dabbling in social media to promote a new brand of philanthropy that would involve the participation of average netizens. In 2011 and 2012, Beijing hosted the summit of "Global Social Media and Social Good," which involved a host of international and domestic Chinese luminaries. For details, see http://news.56.com/sp/zt2012 and http://gongyi.qq.com/a/20111203/000010.htm.

7. In mid-November of 2018, MIT held its first summit in Beijing, a mega event that brought together not only academics and leaders in industry, but also Chinese government to explore topics at the frontiers of science and technology in shaping the future of the globe. An official reception of MIT's president and the Institute's Board of Trustees by Wang Qishan, the vice president of the People's Republic of China, sent a clear signal that technology is a safe area for collaboration even in the era of turbulent US-China relations. For details of the summit, please see http://chinasummit.mit.edu/home.

8. Tencent.com launched a crowdfunding platform in October 2011 to enable NGOs and volunteer communities to raise public funds. Sina.com established its MicroCharity platform soon after. Chapter 3, "WeChat versus Weibo," will detail such developments.

9. The unregistered number dropped around the mid-2010s when the Chinese government revised the strict regulations governing NGO registration. By 2016 when NGO2.0 conducted our fifth survey on the internet usage of Chinese NGOs, only 8.66 percent of the 531 organizations surveyed were not registered. Please see NGO-IU Survey 5, 2017.

10. The University of Science and Technology of China has been the closest ally to NGO2.0 since 2009. Professor Rongting Zhou and Endy Xie have been steadfast supporters. And Endy especially, has worked with me shoulder to shoulder over the decade on things big and small.

11. My research relationship with Ogilvy & Mather in the 2000s led to my writing of *Brand New China: Advertising, Media, and Commercial Culture* (Wang 2008a).

12. The surviving partners are the University of Science and Technology and Ogilvy & Mather, thanks to the unswerving support of Professor Rongting Zhou at UST, and Scott Kronick and Mikko Lan at Ogilvy Public Relations/Beijing.

13. One interaction design team involved a team based at the School of Communication and Design at Sun Yat-sen University, led by Professor Liao Hongyong. A more permanent team is made up of Wan Weixiang and Chen Bobing, two designers based in Shanghai, led by Xiang Fan, a professor at Tsinghua University.

14. NGO2.0 collaborates routinely with IT companies such as SAP, Tencent.com, ThoughtWorks, Frog, and software developer and maker communities in Beijing, Shanghai, Guangzhou, and Shenzhen. We recruit makers from those companies to participate in hackathons held to connect NGOs with techies. Details of hackathons can be found in Chapter 5, "Makers and Tech4Good Culture."

15. The first nonprofit technology conference in the US was held in 2002. Beth Kanter, one of the most passionate American advocates of nonprofit technology started working in the field in 1992.

16. See "*Nongcun diqu xinxi xiaofei qianli buke xiaoxu*" (The Potential of Information Consumption in Rural Regions Cannot Be Underestimated), Xinhua Net, July 23, 2013, http://news.xinhuanet.com/info/2013-07/23/c_132565097_2.htm. Accessed December 2013.

17. The statistics were provided by Li Jianbo, the chief technology officer of NGOCN in 2009.

18. This number is pure speculation based on NGO2.0's survey experience in the past ten years. As a result of the influx of community NGOs (C-NGOs) in recent years, it is difficult to distinguish grassroots organizations with a change agenda from those grown out of neighborhood communities whose raison d'être is to serve community needs. By "stable" grassroots organizations, I meant organizations that have at least three full-time employees and sustainable funding for at least three years. The number of those grassroots NGOs fluctuates between 6,000 and 10,000. The number of 8,000 is a median.

19. For details of the new Philanthropy Law, please visit http://www.npc.gov.cn/npc/dbdhhy/12_4/2016-03/21/content_1985714.htm for the Chinese edition, and http://www.ngocn.net/news/2016-04-12-db0a48c60a8b1c67.html for the English edition.

20. For details of the law, please visit http://news.xinhuanet.com/legal/2016-04/29/c_1118765888.htm for the Chinese edition, and http://www.xzgat.gov.cn/zcfg/5376.jhtml for the English edition.

21. Please visit www.ngo20map.com, click on "NGO Issue Areas," and choose the category of "policy advocacy" to find the self-identified policy-advocacy NGOs.

22. Minqin County is known to be the *next* Lop Nur, which was formerly a salt lake, now largely dried up, located in the southeastern portion of Xinjiang Uygur Autonomous Region.

23. First-tier cities refer to Shanghai, Beijing, Guangzhou, and Shenzhen.

24. For details about this hackathon, see NGO2.0, "Gongyi jiketuan Guangzhou dier ci Hackathon huodong yuanman chenggong" (NGO-Tech Network Successfully Held Its Second Hackathon in Guangzhou), http://www.ngo20.org/?p=1808, August 17, 2013. Accessed December 2013.

25. For details about the grassroots organization, please visit https://user.qzone.qq.com/123196150/infocenter. Accessed January 2018.

3. WeChat versus Weibo

1. Mu Zimei was a journalist and blogger from Guangzhou. She kept a blog where she described her sexual encounters with men. Her blog did not attract much attention until 2003 when she posted a recording of her lovemaking sounds online and embedded the link in her blog. She single-handedly popularized blogging culture in China. More than 50,000 people simultaneously tried to download her

twenty-five-minute podcast, crashing the host server. Her sex blogs were so popular that *Muzimei* was intermittently the most searched keyword on China's top search engines.

2. This question was raised by Pramond K. Nayar in his edited anthology *The New Media and Cybercultures Anthology* (Nayar 2010, 25). Other scholars raised similar inquiries, for example, Robert W. Williams scrutinizes both the potentials and the perils of cyberdemocracy in his treatise "Democracy, Cyberspace, and the Body" (2006). He concludes that cyberpolitics is disembodied, and as such, it leaves untouched the social relationships in which the computer technology is embedded and embodied. It is the embodied social relations of production rather than the disembodied cyberpolitics that provide the material bases for our emancipatory projects. Zizi Papacharissi questioned the potential of the internet to revive the public sphere in "The Virtual Sphere: The Internet as a Public Sphere," *New Media and Society,* February 1, 2002. See http://journals.sagepub.com/doi/abs/10.1177 /14614440222226244.

3. IKG More in China and Charity: Water in the USA are two prime examples. 1KG More is cited and analyzed later in this chapter. "Water: Charity" is a US-based NGO that provides safe drinking water to people in developing nations. It has rolled out various social media strategies to build its community. Please see http://tools .ngo20.org/index.php/post/24 for a crowdsourcing example of the organization.

4. I would like to acknowledge my source of inspiration in penning this particular sentence—Lin Chun. Her original sentence is "The experimental project of Chinese socialism has the potential to encompass the intrinsically interconnected ideas of the commons, community, communism, communication and common culture" (Lin Chun 2013, 166).

5. Those who complete the challenge name three other people who then have a day to dump a bucket of ice water over their heads or donate $100 to the ALS Association.

6. After the Asian Games, in order to preserve the beautifully lit scenery surrounding the Pearl River, the Guangzhou municipal government undertook a renovation project to light up the river banks. The project was planned to cover the Guangzhou Baihetan area, Ershadao area, and Haixinsha area.

7. Our tech team—programmers based in the Chinese University of Science and Technology, my former MIT graduate student Wang Yu, and two interface designers located in Shanghai, joined by a hired techie—have been heroic in their efforts to develop the map as it continues to evolve.

4. Millennials as Change Agents on the Social Web

1. The Chinese Jasmine Revolution refers to a series of public assemblies in a dozen cities all over China starting in February 2011. Those local events were triggered by the spontaneous response of Chinese youths to anonymous calls on the internet to stage a Tunisia-style Jasmine Revolution in China. During that time, those small assemblies were crushed by local authorities and the words *jasmine* and *flower* were censored online.

2. "Grass Mud Horse" or *caonima,* a homonym of the Chinese obscene expression "fuck your mother," was an internet meme that ridiculed and defied Chinese censors. The fictional horse was popularized in 2009 and turned into a mascot for Chinese netizens fighting for free expression. Grass Mud Horse themed merchandise appeared in the toy and clothing markets for a short while.

3. "River Crab" or *hexie,* is a homonym of "harmony" and "being harmonized." It is an internet slang that satirizes the Party's signature ideology of "harmonious society." A river crab society is one where censorship rules and the freedom of speech is sacrificed to maintain a society without unrest. The meme has been popular since 2007.

4. The May Fourth Movement broke out on May 4, 1919. It started off as an anti-imperialist, patriotic movement staged and led by students from Peking University in protest against the weak response of the government to the Treaty of Versailles, which transferred the Chinese territories of Shandong, a province previously occupied by Germany, to Japan, upon a secret agreement made among the Allied Powers without the consent of China. May Fourth soon evolved into a full-fledged culture and political movement known as the "New Culture Movement," which gave birth to a new intellectual class that emerged as leaders in both the Communist and Nationalist parties. The legacy of May Fourth is a controversial topic for both parties even today.

5. This expression is found in O'Brien and Li's *Rightful Resistance in Rural China,* 2. "Rightful resistance" is a tactic adopted by the weak and the powerless to "work" a political system that leaves little room for confrontational action. Rightful resisters game the system by resorting to "a form of popular contention that operates near the boundary of authorized channels" and utilize the regime's own policies and legitimating myths to justify their challenge. For details about this tactic, please see Chapter 1.

6. The Wukan Incident refers to the mass protests of villagers against the illegal seizure of farm land by corrupt officials in Wukan Village, Guangdong Province. Several rounds of protests broke out between 2011 and 2016. At the climax of the incident in December 2011, protesters seized the village and expelled the entire local government and local Communist Party leadership out of the village. Clashes between villagers and local authorities erupted again in 2016 but were eventually quashed by riot police.

7. The Foxconn Suicides refers to the escalating rate of workplace suicides at Foxconn facilities in Shenzhen and other locations in 2010. Foxconn, one of the world's largest high-end electronics manufacturers, was condemned by labor activists and other critics as a "labor camp" subjugating employees to illegal overtime practices. Small-scale protests broke out in Shenzhen, Hong Kong, and Taipei.

8. The Watch Brother was an internet nickname given to Yang Dacai, the head of the provincial Bureau of Work Safety in Shaanxi. On August 30, 2012, Yang was photographed grinning broadly at the scene of a deadly traffic accident in Yan'an. Annoyed netizens posted on Weibo photographs showing Yang wearing as many as eleven luxury watches which government officials could not afford. He was later disciplined by the Party for being corrupt.

9. The Yihuang Self-Immolation Incident took place in September 2010 in Yihuang County, Jiangxi Province. Two members of the Zhong family, whose home was about to be forcefully torn down by a demolition crew sent by the government, climbed to the roof and burned themselves in protest. Two female members of the family decided to travel to Beijing to air their grievances. They were chased by local police and government officials at the airport. In desperation, they locked themselves in a restroom and sent mobile messages to local reporters for help. The event was live-broadcast on Sina Weibo and Tencent Weibo, stirring up media attention and ignited a furor of public response on the internet.

10. Steamed Buns refers to a spoof made in 2005 by Hu Ge, an amateur media artist, to satirize Director Chen Kaige's blockbuster film *The Promise* (*Wuji*). Hu considered the film a huge disappointment. To vent his frustration, he remixed original footage from the film with other images taken liberally from other productions and produced a short internet video titled "A Murder Caused by a Steamed Bun." The video became a viral phenomenon, kicking off China's *kuso* trend online. Hu was sued by the director for violating intellectual property rights. The video is available at https://www.youtube.com/watch?v=xIU4udZRKEY.

11. The main website of the Talking Tree is http://talking-tree.com/. A video about the campaign is on http://theinspirationroom.com/daily/2010/the-eos-talking -tree/. Accessed May 2011.

12. The Facebook site of the Talking Tree had another 11,963 friends as of May 7, 2011.

13. Crowdsourcing in advertising campaigns points to a variety of definitions and practices. Although the meaning of crowdsourcing may shift from sector to sector, lying at the very heart of this concept is a consistent set of values that revolves around a vocal, creative amateur instilled with the DIY ethos, armed with advanced digital literacy, and a self-empowered sense of being a proactive stakeholder of a brand community.

14. FreeRice is a multiple-choice quiz platform that allows netizens all over the world to play the game while donating to the cause of hunger alleviation. Players can choose any quiz category to play, including English vocabulary, human anatomy, geography, and literature. After the game was popularized in the rest of the world, the category of "foreign language vocabulary for English speakers (French, German, Italian, Latin, and Spanish)" was added to the inventory. For every question answered correctly, ten grains of rice are donated via the World Food Programme to relieve hunger in underdeveloped countries. Teams can be formed to play the game collaboratively. Team scores are ranked in real time on a bulletin board embedded in the site. Please see the main website at http://www.freerice.com/.

15. Coleman and Ross emphasize that "there is no *a priori* public that is 'captured' or 'recorded' by the media."

16. Nonprofit technology or technology for nonprofit organizations is a subsector that has grown steadily in the last two decades in the US. TechSoup (founded in 1987) and NTEN: The Nonprofit Technology Enterprise Network (founded in 2000) are two of the most important organizations (themselves NGOs) that promote the use of technology to scale up the social impact of change makers. TechSoup

provides technical support and technological tools to nonprofits. It launched its website TechSoup.org in 2002 that serves as a platform for providing training webinars, community forums, and other resources about the use of technology in the nonprofit sector. The annual conventions of NTEN are attended by NGOs, technologies, IT corporations, and researchers. Many of the conference panels address the issues of hardware and software tools for NGOs.

Apart from TechSoup and NTEN, other important players in this young sector are Beth Kanter and Idealware. Kanter is one of the pioneers of tech trainers of NGOs. She identified herself as a "Master Trainer & Nonprofit Innovator in networks, learning, and social media." She travels around the globe to provide those trainings. Idealware, an NGO, provides tech training and helps nonprofits make technology decisions. Most notably, it publishes field guides to software for nonprofits.

Generally speaking, the thriving social enterprise culture in the US offers fast-growing space for young tech entrepreneurs to experiment with technological innovations that can benefit nonprofits. Increasingly, the dividing line between the for-profit and nonprofit sectors is eroding. The business of nonprofit technology is considered business, period.

17. The statistics were provided by YiNongDai on January 2, 2019.

5. Makers and Tech4Good Culture

1. See discussions about this TV serial on Chinese social media platforms. There are some lone defenders of the grandpa's action, but the majority of public opinions are partial to Qian Qian.

2. The average number of employees per US firm (with or without payroll) is just four! (See Rabb 2010, 1).

3. Beijing Maxpace on Douban, http://site.douban.com/124037/. Accessed June 2015.

4. Chaihuo Makerspace, http://maker.eefocus.com/makerspace-orgnization /chaihuomakerspace. Accessed June 2015.

5. Xin Che Jian, http://xinchejian.com/about-2/?lang=zh. Accessed June 2015.

6. This embryonic system developed as China acceded to the World Trade Organization and subsequently modernized its corporate governance structure, shifted investments from an industrial to knowledge-based economy, and improved key framework conditions for innovation, including making a commitment to enforcing intellectual property rights protection.

7. Since 2001, Beijing and many local governments have published a "steady stream of Blue Books (*lanpi shu*)" that report and examine the state of the art of the cultural and creative industries of China in different locales. For a critical analysis of the Blue Book syndrome, see Zitong Qiu 2016.

8. http://v.youku.com/v_show/id_XNTM0MDA0OTIw.html?from=y1.2-1-105 .3.4-2.1-1-1-3; http://v.youku.com/v_show/id_XMTEyMDM0ODYw.html; http://tv .sohu.com/20141105/n405785309.shtml; http://v.youku.com/v_show/id_XMTgwOT cwNTMy.html

9. It is worth noting that Plan 2011 is an extension of Project 211 and Project 985, reform projects that focus on the development of talents and other innovation elements confined within the university.

10. One of the grant recipients is the Future Media Collaborative Innovation Center set up jointly by Shanghai Jiaotong University and Peking University in 2012, with partners spanning across the broadcasting, TV, information and communication, and internet service sectors. It pulled in resources from a number of ministries—the Ministry of Education, Ministry of Science and Technology, State Administration of Radio, Film, and Television, National Development and Reform Commission, and Standardization Administration of China. The resource sharing among ministries on such a grand scale speaks to its own symbolism—cross-sector collaboration is no longer a theory, and it also underscores the future direction of China's innovation plan. (See Mai Qi 2014).

11. "Unicorns" are privately held start-ups that are valued at over USD$1 billion.

12. Chinese people are rather loose about the definition of makers, which include both hardware and software makers. Please see the definition of maker in http://baike.baidu.com/subview/371405/11140298.htm.

13. You can find the description of Night Edge on the website for China-US Young Maker Competition, http://www.chinaus-maker.org/en/staff/visible -interactive-electric-instrument/2014.

14. This crab was highlighted on the website for Shenzhen Maker Faire, http://www.shenzhenmakerfaire.com/szmf2014/post/category/workshop.

15. In April 2015 after receiving $6,000,000 from investors, his company grew from four founding members to a team of eighty employees.

16. See http://smellme.cn/index.html.

17. Pet owners can create profiles for their cute animals on the site, post fun snapshots and videos of their furry creatures, set up forum communities for pet-related topics, consult veterinarians on the site, and brainstorm with specialists on pet food, pet nutrition, pet fashion, and pet training. Most interestingly, users can initiate offline activities to plan pet walking in groups or orchestrate breeding schemes. The platform also incorporates features of e-commerce, rewarding dedicated users with in-site currency to purchase pet gifts on Taobao.com.

18. Not all China-originated start-ups are founded and owned by indigenous Chinese inventors, for example, Origins, whose Mandarin-speaking Swiss founder announced a palm-sized solution to affordable air pollution monitoring. I did not include those foreign start-ups in the catalog listed because my research focus is on homegrown innovation.

19. The spoof "A Murder Caused by a Steamed Bun" satirizes Director Chen Kaige's blockbuster film *Wuji* (The Promise). After watching the film, Hu Ge, an electronic musician in Shanghai, was so disappointed that he remixed footage from the film and turned it into a spoof that arguably became better known than the original movie. The spoof started China's remix culture.

20. See Qiangxiu bangfu zhongxin 2013.

21. Enactus has a partnership with the Chinese People's Association for Friendship with Foreign Countries (CPAFFC), and Innovate's governmental partner is the

Ministry of Civil Affairs. The depoliticized nature of CPAFFC made it much easier for Enactus to expand.

22. For details of Baidu's Micro-School Project, please see "Baidu xieshou qing-jihui" 2016. The project aims to solve water and electricity shortage problems in the five elementary schools. School children will enjoy a smart campus that will save water and energy. The campuses are driven by Baidu's internet-of-things technology that provides "smart electricity management system" and "smart water management system."

23. The Alibaba platform is called *Mashang gongyi* (coding for good). The term *mashang* is a pun, referring to "instantaneous" and "coding" at the same time. See https://greencode.aliyun.com/.

24. The Fab Lab program began as a collaboration between the Grassroots Invention Group and the Center for Bits and Atoms at MIT's Media Lab with a grant from the National Science Foundation in 2001. The model soon became a movement spread to other creative venues in the rest of the world. Today, a fab lab is "typically equipped with an array of flexible computer-controlled tools that cover several different length scales and various materials, with the aim to make 'almost anything.'" For more details, see Gershenfeld 2005.

25. "Peach Blossom Spring" was a poetic fable created by Tao Yuanming of Chin Dynasty in the fourth century. A fisherman gets lost while fishing. While searching for his way home, he follows a stream lined with peach blossom trees and stumbles upon an idyllic village where villagers have lived for generations a happy and peaceful life, unaware of the outside world and untouched by wars and political upheavals for centuries. He eventually takes his leave, and reports his discovery to the emperor. But when he tries to find the stream again, it has vanished mysteriously. "Peach Blossom Spring" has since then become a coded term for "wonderland" with a utopian touch.

26. Creative education software is flooding into the market: among these are Yuantiyk (a mobile test-prep software), Vipkid (an English learning app), Xueba (a homework answering tool), Mofangge (a crowdsourced learning app), and Geek Academy, a virtual IT university that exposes students in middle high and universities to playful learning routines.

6. Participatory Action Research and the Chinese Challenge

1. The identity of the authors in the two Sage handbooks on PAR supports this observation. The great majority of the contributors in the two handbooks are university lecturers and professors.

2. The Guo Meimei scandal and the crisis of the China Red Cross led to the bankruptcy of the public's trust in state-run foundations. A pretty but vain twenty-year-old, Guo posted a series of microblogs and selfies on Weibo, flaunting her designer handbags and luxury sports cars day in and day out. Much to her regret, she escalated Chinese netizens' righteous anti-new-rich sentiment to a boiling point. And worst of all, she identified herself as the "General Business Manager of the China

Red Cross Society." This incident sank the reputation of the Chinese Red Cross and fanned the public fury about the corrupt ways with which state-owned foundations managed the funds raised in public and from corporations. No matter that it was revealed later that Guo Meimei made a false claim about her affiliation with the Red Cross. The damage was done. For more details, see Chapter 3.

3. Chinese economic reform, also known as *gaige kaifang* (reform and opening up), started in 1978 when Deng Xiaoping regained his power. He deviated from the orthodox Maoist policies by advocating the Four Modernizations, including a thought reform program. The following decade witnessed the importation of foreign ideas and theories. A nationwide debate on the future of China spurred the discussions of tradition versus modernity and the indigenous culture versus foreign culture. For a detailed account of that era, see Wang 1996.

4. This line of thinking is picked up again by Ji Jiaxin, a contributor to *Action Research and Social Work* (Yang and Xia 2013) and the deputy director of a Guizhou-based NGO specializing in rural community development. He is critical of the Western development discourse and its characteristic approach of participatory farming that emphasizes improving the livelihood of rural people rather than revolutionizing their way of thinking as the primary means of intervention. Relationship building that inevitably triggers the process of self-reflection and the villagers' reeducation, should, in Ji's activist vantage point, play a far more important role than changing rural economic infrastructure. See Ji Jiaxin in Yang and Xia 2013, 439–441.

5. Lian Xi, one of Xia Linqing's Taiwanese disciples, published the syllabus of her course on the pedagogy of feminism taught at Taiwan's Hualian Education University. It gives us a fascinating glimpse of the required readings made up of a mixed repertoire of white, black, and brown feminist literature. See http://www.mce .ndhu.edu.tw/~gimewww/_private/program/96-1/96-1-3-1.doc.

Conclusion

1. Please see http://tools.ngo20.org/index.php/case for more examples of social good 2.0 campaigns in China.

2. FOMO is an acronym for "fear of missing out."

3. On September 5, 2018, MIT and the Atlantic held a cosponsored conference titled Humanity+Tech" at the MIT Media Lab. One of the panels I attended was called "From FOMO to JOMO: Building Towards Digital Well-Being" presented by Google.

4. MIT professor Alex Pentland published *Social Physics: How Social Networks Can Make Us Smarter* in 2014, in which he claims that computers can mine social data to determine the mathematical underpinnings of civic behavior. Underlying his argument is the faith that an ideal society can be engineered through model building.

5. Impossible is "an altruism-based social network which invites people to give their services and skills away to help others." It was created by Lily Cole, a British model and actress. She set up the platform with the purpose of creating a giving

culture based on the idea of a sharing economy, linking those in need with those wanting to give. Every user on the platform can be both a giver (responding to other people's needs) and a taker (posting the need). Through constantly practicing giving and taking without involving the middlemen, she hopes that citizens in society will be able to work together and progress toward their utopian goals. The Impossible platform has been rolled out in the UK and the US. For details, please see https://www .impossible.com/.

Bibliography

A Qiang. 2018. "Tongxinglian qinyouhui xin meiti changdao anli" (Supporter for Gay Love Uses New Media for Advocacy). January 18, 2018. *NGO2.0 Field Guide to Software for NGOs*. http://tools.ngo20.org/index.php/post/330.

Aalai, Azadeh. 2018. "What Is the Real Impact of Hashtag Activism?" *Psychology Today*. April 26, 2018. https://www.psychologytoday.com/us/blog/the-first -impression/201804/what-is-the-real-impact-hashtag-activism.

"Abei zhou funu Qiang xiu jiuye bangfu zhongxin: Qiangxiu bangfu jihua" (Abei County's Qiang Embroidery Occupation Help Center: The Qiang Embroidery Project). March 30, 2010. Sohu.com, http://gongyi.sohu.com/20100330 /n271211916.shtml. Accessed December 2013.

Alibaba Research Center. 2015. "Hulianwang + yanjiu baogao" (Internet Plus: A Research Report). http://i.aliresearch.com/img/20150312/20150312160447 .pdf.

All-China Youth Federation. 2009. "Voluntary Work." December 25, 2009. http://www.acyf.org.cn/2009-12/25/content_3314913.htm. Accessed in August, 2017.

Anderson, Chris. 2012. *Makers: The New Industrial Revolution*. New York: Crown Business.

Andjelic, Ana. 2017. "The New Nondigital Divide." *Ad Age*, February 21, 2017. http://adage.com/article/digitalnext/digital-divide/308018/.

Ant Forest (mayi senlin). 2016. https://zh.wikipedia.org/wiki/%E8%9A%82%E8 %9A%81%E6%A3%AE%E6%9E%97. Accessed in December 2018.

Apollo Group. 2015. "Taiyang shen di shisi jia 'Delin shuwu" luohu Fuling" (The Apollo Group's 14th "Delin Classroom" Landed in Fuling). June 19, 2015. http://www.dsbaike.com/article/view/id/23664.html.

Arnett, J. J. 2010. *Adolescence and Emerging Adulthood: A Cultural Approach*. 4th ed. Boston, MA: Prentice Hall.

Arnold, Daryl. 2011. "Protecting People, Planet and Profit." *Ad Age.* January 19, 2011. http://adage.com/china/article/viewpoint/protecting-people-planet-and -profit/148263/. Accessed May 2011.

Ash, Alec. 2017. "How the Rise of a Liberal, Social Media-Savvy Generation Is Changing Chinese Society." Vox, March 26, 2017. https://www.vox.com /world/2017/3/26/15035702/china-social-media-youth-society-culture -politics-government.

Assange, Julian et al. 2016. *Cypherpunks: Freedom and the Future of the Internet.* New York: OR Books.

Atkinson, P., and M. Hammersley. 2012. "Ethnography and Participant Observation." In *Handbook of Qualitative Research,* edited by N. K. Denzin and Y. S. Lincoln, 110–136. Thousand Oaks, CA: Sage.

Atwood, Margaret. 2018. "Am I a Bad Feminist?" *The Globe and Mail,* January 15, 2018. https://www.theglobeandmail.com/opinion/am-i-a-bad -feminist/article37591823/.

Baidu Baike. 2010. "Fanke ti" (The Fanke Style). http://baike.baidu.com/view /4055632.htm. Accessed May 2011.

"Baidu xieshou qingjihui, quanguo shouge 'zhineng weixiao' xiangmu qidong" (Baidu Collaborated with China Youth Development Foundation to Launch the Micro-School Project). May 17, 2016. http://tech.huanqiu.com/launch /2016-05/8942454.html.

Baum, Fran, Colin MacDougall et al. 2006. "Participatory Action Research." *Journal of Epidemiology & Community Health* 60, no. 10: 854–857.

Benkler, Yochai. 2007. *The Wealth of Networks: How Social Production Transforms Markets and Freedom.* New Haven and London: Yale University Press.

Bennett, W. Lance. 2008. "Changing Citizenship in the Digital Age." In *Civic Life Online: Learning How Digital Media Can Engage Youth,* edited by W. Lance Bennett, 1–24. Cambridge, MA: The MIT Press.

Berlatsky, Noah. 2015. "Hashtag Activism Isn't a Cop-Out." *The Atlantic,* January 7, 2015. https://www.theatlantic.com/politics/archive/2015/01/not -just-hashtag-activism-why-social-media-matters-to-protestors/384215/.

Bian Jiaojiao. 2010. "The People's VANCL." *LEAP: The International Art Magazine of Contemporary China.* October 3, 2010. http://leapleapleap.com /2010/10/the-people%E2%80%99s-vancl/#7. Accessed May 2011.

Bradbury, Hilary, and Peter Reason. 2008. "Introduction to Exemplars: Varieties of Action Research." In *The Sage Handbook of Action Research: Participative Inquiry and Practice,* edited by Peter Reason and Hilary Bradbury, 435–438. Los Angeles: Sage.

Brainbrighter. 2011. *Wangyi boke* (NetEase Blog). "Zhengji guangtou zhaoliang Guangzhou: Meiti baodao zonghui" (A Call for Shaved Heads to Brighten up Guangzhou: A Summary of Media Reports). May 7, 2011. http:// brainisbrighter2.blog.163.com/blog/static/18597121720114735097 9/. Accessed May 2011. NetEase shut down its blog business on November 30, 2018.

British Council China. 2014. "China-UK Social Innovation and Social Enterprise Seminar." https://www.britishcouncil.cn/en/programmes/society/news/si -seminar.

Buckley, Chris. 2013. "Crackdown on Bloggers Is Mounted by China." *The New York Times,* September 11, 2013, A4.

Carnesecca, Cole. 2015. "Voice of the Masses: The Internet and Responsive Authoritarianism in China." In *Urban Mobilization and New Media in Contemporary China,* edited by Lisheng Dong et al., 117–131. Burlington, VT: Ashgate.

Carty, Victoria. 2015. *Social Movements and New Technology.* Boulder, CO: Westview Press.

Castells, M. 1996. *The Rise of the Network Society. The Information Age: Economy, Society, and Culture.* Vol. 1. Oxford: Blackwell.

Castells, M. 2009. *Communication Power.* Oxford and New York: Oxford University Press.

Castro, Fidel. 1961. "Castro Pledges 100 Percent Literacy." *Castro Speech Data Base: Speeches, Interviews, Articles 1959–1966.* http://lanic.utexas.edu /project/castro/db/1961/19610514.html. Accessed January 2018.

Center for Innovation and Social Responsibility (CISR). 2010. Brochure on "The Center for Innovation and Social Responsibility." School of Public Policy and Management, Tsinghua University.

Center for Media Justice et al. 2015. "The Digital Culture Shift: From Scale to Power." http://centerformediajustice.org/wp-content/uploads/2015/08/digital _culture_shift_report.pdf.

Center on Philanthropy, Sun Yat-sen University. 2011. "Quanmin gongyi: 2011 niandu fazhan baogao" (Universal People's Philanthropy: The 2011 Development Report).

Center for Psychology of the Chinese Academy of Sciences, Sina Weibo Data Center, et al. 2013. "2013 nian Zhongguo daxuesheng 'Weibo' fazhan baogao" (The 2013 Development Report on the Weibo Usage of Chinese College Students). September 1, 2013. http://data.weibo.com/report /reportDetail?id=126.

Chao, Eveline. 2017. "How Social Cash Made WeChat the App for Everything." *Fast Company,* January 2, 2017. https://www.fastcompany.com/3065255 /china-wechat-tencent-red-envelopes-and-social-money.

Chase, Michael, and James Mulvenon. 2002. *Chinese Dissident Use of the Internet and Beijing's Counter-Strategies.* Santa Monica, CA: RAND.

Chen, Charles Yidan. 2018. *Zhongguo hulian wang gongyi* (Internet Philanthropy in China). Beijing: Renmin University Press.

Chen Guojia. 2015. *Hulianwang+: Chuantong hangye kuajie moshi yu zhuanxing shengji xin moshi* (Internet Plus: The Cross-Sectoral Integration of Traditional Manufacturing and the New Model of Sectoral Transformation and Upgrade). Beijing: People's Posts and Telecommunications Publishing House.

Chen Shihua. 2016. *Weibo canyu shehui zhili yanjiu* (A Study of Weibo Participation and Social Governance). Beijing: Zhongguo shehui kexue chubanshe.

Chen Tian. 2013. "Cash Donations Flood in on Weibo." *Global Times*, April 22, 2013. http://www.globaltimes.cn/content/776522.shtml.

Chen Wenhong, and Stephen D. Reese. 2015. "Introduction: A New Agenda: Digital Media and Civic Engagement in Networked China." In *Networked China: Global Dynamics of Digital Media and Civic Engagement: New Agendas in Communication*, edited by Chen Wenhong and Stephen D. Reese, 1–16. New York and London: Routledge.

Chin, Josh. 2016. "The Good—and Bad—about China's New Charity Law." *Wall Street Journal*, March 16, 2016. https://blogs.wsj.com/chinarealtime/2016/03/16/the-good-and-bad-about-chinas-new-charity-law/.

China Development Brief. 2011. Special Issue: *New Trends in Philanthropy and Civil Society in China*. http://www.chinadevelopmentbrief.cn/?p=333.

China Financial and Economic News (*Zhongguo caijing bao wang*). 2017. "Beijing jiedao goumai shehui fuwu jin'e yue 10 yi" (Beijing Street-Level Social Service Purchasing Amounts to Approximately One Billion Yuan). *Caijing.com*. July13, 2017. http://www.cfen.com.cn/cjxw/zfcg/201703/t20170307_2548121.html

China Internet Development Foundation. 2016. "Rang hulianwang chengwei ai de haiyang: Fazhan wangluo gongyi changyishu (Let the Internet Evolve into an Ocean of Compassion: A Proposal for Developing a Web-based Social Good Sector). January 11, 2016. http://it.sohu.com/20160111/n434119061.shtml.

China Internet Network Information Center. 2016. "Di sanshiba ci Zhongguo hulianwang fazhan zhuangkuang tongji baogao" (The 38th Survey Report on the Statistics of Chinese Internet Development). August 3, 2016. https://www.cnnic.net.cn/hlwfzyj/hlwxzbg/hlwtjbg/201608/t20160803_54392.htm.

China Merchants Group. 2010. "Yixin YiNongDai huode shoujie 'Zhaoshangju fupin chuangxin xingdong jiang" (CreditEase's YiNongDai Received the First Innovative Action Award for Poverty Alleviation Sponsored by China Merchant Group). December 15, 2010. http://www.cmhk.com/main/a/2015/k13/a25438_25493.shtml?2.

Chinese People's Political Consultative Committee in Chongqing, ed. 2017. *Xieshang minzhu lilun gaiyao* (The Essentials of the Theory of Consociational Democracy). Beijing: Zhongguo fazhan chubanshe.

China-US Young Maker Competition. 2015. "Night Edge." http://maker.xmu.edu.cn/index.php/home/index/article/gtype/19.html. Accessed July 2017.

Christensen, Henrik Serup. 2011. "Political Activities on the Internet: Slacktivism or Political Participation by Other Means?" *First Monday* 16, no. 2. https://firstmonday.org/article/view/3336/2767.

Chun, Rene. 2017. "If You Need a Digital Detox, You'll Love this Smart Dumbphone." *Wired*, June 22, 2017. https://www.wired.com/story/need-a-digital-detox-youll-love-this-very-smart-dumbphone/.

Cinnovate. 2010. "Xin shijie' gongyi chuangxinjiang pingxuan huodong jieshao' (Introduction to Cinnovate's Social Innovation Contest). January 14, 2010. http://gongyi.sohu.com/20100114/n269582374.shtml.

Cinnovate Center. 2013a. Promotion pamphlet.

Cinnovate Innovation Week. 2013b. http://www.huodongxing.com/go/siw.

Coleman, Stephen, and Karen Ross. 2010. *The Media and the Public: The "Them" and "Us" in Media Discourse.* Hoboken, NJ: Wiley-Blackwell.

Committee of the Chinese People's Political Consultative Conference (CPPCC). 2011. "Zhengxie weiyuan Wang Ping cheng 'bie guli nongcun haizi nian daxue' yin reyi" (CPPCC Member Wang Ping's Statement "Don't Encourage Rural Youths to Attend College" Stirred Up Controversy). March 9, 2011. http://cppcc.people.com.cn/GB/45579/14097713.html. Accessed August 2017.

Communist Party Central Documentation Research Center, ed. 2004. *Deng Xiaoping nianpu* (The Deng Xiaoping Chronicle: 1975–1997). Vol. 2. Beijing: The Central Documentation Publishing House.

Cone Communications Inc. 2017. "2017 Cone Communications CSR Study." http://www.conecomm.com/research-blog/2017-csr-study. Accessed July 2018.

Corera, Gordon. 2016. *Cyberspies: The Secret History of Surveillance, Hacking, and Digital Espionage.* New York: Penguin Books.

Costanza-Chock, Sasha. 2014. *Out of the Shadows, Into the Streets!* Cambridge, MA: MIT Press.

CPC Central Committee of the Chinese Communist Party. 2001. "Zhonghua renmin gongheguo guomin jingji he shehui fazhan di shige wunian jihua gangyao" (The Essentials of the 10th Five-Year Plan of the National Economic and Social Development of the PRC). http://www.china.com.cn/ch-15/15p8/2.htm.

CreditEase. 2016. "CreditEase Releases Report on Inclusive Finance." *PR Newswire,* November 18, 2016. http://www.prnewswire.com/news-releases/creditease-releases-report-on-inclusive-finance-300365819.html.

Cubbitt, Sean. 2006. "Tactical Media." In *Ideologies of the Internet,* edited by Katharine Sarikakis and Daya Thussu, 35–46. New York: Hampton Press.

Cui Zheng. 2015. "Xin huanbao fa shishi hou NGO daying shouli gongyi susong" (After the Implementation of the New Environmental Law, NGO Won the First Public Lawsuit). Caixin Net. October 30, 2015. http://china.caixin.com/2015-10-30/100868387.html.

Dangpu. 2018. "Haiyou shei?" (Who else is [a sex offender]?). WeChat Public Account. July 23, 2018. https://matters.news/forum/?post=cc67ac69-df19-46ea-8cc3-fc2d6b5751f5.

Derogatory Scholar (Fubi shushing). 2014. "Ganxie Guo Meimei, wanjiu le shanxin, wanjiu le Honghui" (Thank You, Guo Meimei, for Rescuing Our Compassion, for Rescuing the Red Cross). Tianya Forum. August 4, 2014. http://bbs.tianya.cn/post-worldlook-1215358-1.shtml.

Dey, B., and F. Ali. 2016. "A Critical Review of the ICT for Development Research." In *ICTs in Developing Countries,* edited by B. Dey, K. Sorour, and R. Filieri, 3–23. London: Palgrave Macmillan.

Ding Min, and Xu Jie. 2015. *The Chinese Way.* New York and London: Routledge.

Ding Wei. 2014. *Liudong de jiayuan (Mobile Homelands)*. Beijing: Social Science Academic Press.

Downing, J. 2008. "Social Movement Theories and Alternative Media: An Evaluation and Critique." *Communication, Culture & Critique* I, no. 1: 40–50.

Du-jitang. 2017. "Buyao zai zuo pengyouquan de 'muzhi gongyi' le" (Don't Engage in the Fingertip Philanthropy Circulated in Your Friends' Circles). August 10, 2017. *Baijiahao* (Baidu Public Account). https://baijiahao.baidu.com/s?id=1575268871983277&wfr=spider&for=pc.

E Fan. 2014. "Disanzhong liliang 'zhili' shehui" (The Third Social Governing Force). *Xiaokang* (Insight China) no. 203: 44–47.

The Economist. 2013. "Made in China." November 30, 2013. http://www.economist.com/news/technology-quarterly/21590756-technology-and-society-china-has-its-own-distinctive-version-maker-movement.

"Ecotonoha Tree." 2008. https://www.youtube.com/watch?v=7qHLtx5_hkQ. Accessed June 2015.

Eikeland, O. 2006. "Condescending Ethics and Action Research." *Action Research* 4, no. 1: 37–47.

Enactus. 2013. "Finding Value in Discarded Oyster Shells." http://enactus.org/project/finding-new-value-in-discarded-oyster-shellls/.

Enactus. 2014. "Enactus China Program: 2013–2014." Promotion pamphlet.

Enactus. 2015. "Ryegrass Helps Fish Farmers Net a Better Business." http://enactus.org/project/project-2/. Accessed June 2015.

Enactus China. 2017. "China." http://enactus.org/country/china/. Accessed July 2017.

Enactus China. 2018. "About Enactus." http://www.enactuschina.cn/AboutEnactus. Accessed July 2018.

Ertas, Nerbahar. 2016. "Millennials and Volunteering: Sector Differences and Implications for Public Service Motivation Theory." *Public Administration Quarterly* 40, no. 3: 517–558.

Fals Borda, Orlando. 2001. "Participatory (Action) Research in Social Theory: Origins and Challenges." In *Handbook of Action Research: Participative Inquiry and Practice,* edited by Peter Reason and Hilary Bradbury, 27–37. Thousand Oaks, CA: Sage.

Fang Gang. 2008. "Huoju jihua yao chengwei jianshe chuangxinxing guojia de yindao liliang" (Torch Will Become the Guiding Force for Building an Innovation Nation). December 26, 2008. http://scitech.people.com.cn/GB/126054/141612/141614/8585872.html.

Feng Jing, and Zhang Hong. 2016. "Qian Liqun: Dangdai qingnian zhong, yizhong xiang Wusi de dongxi zheng fasheng" (Qian Liqun Says: Something Like May Fourth Is Emerging Among Contemporary Youths). *Fenghuang Wang* (Phoenix Net). May 4, 2016. http://culture.ifeng.com/niandaifang/special/qianliqun/.

Ferguson, M., and Golding, P. 1997. *Cultural Studies in Question*. New York: Columbia University Press.

Fine, Allison. 2008."Social Citizens BETA." Case Foundation. May 8, 2008. http://www.casefoundation.org/case-studies/social-citizens. Accessed June 2009.

Finley, Klint. 2012. "Robotics Hacker Erects Open Source 'Lego for Adults.'" *Wired*. December 13, 2012. http://www.wired.com/2012/12/makeblock/.

Fish, Eric. 2015. *China's Millennials: The Want Generation*. Lanham, MD: Rowman & Littlefield.

Fiske, John. 1989. *Understanding Popular Culture*. London and New York: Routledge.

Forgas, David, and Geoffrey Nowell-Smith, eds. 1985. *Antonio Gramsci: Selections from Cultural Writings*. Cambridge, MA: Harvard University Press.

Friends of Nature. 2014. "'Wo wei chengshi liang tiwen: xingdong zhinan" (Action Manual for "Measuring the Temperature of My City"). http://fon .org.cn/uploads/attachment/42401403764571.pdf.

Friends of Nature. 2017. #Wo wei chengshi liang tiwen# (Measuring the Temperature of My City). May 12, 2017. http://www.fon.org.cn/index.php ?option=com_k2&view=item&id=10294:2017-05-12-08-11-35&Itemid =111. Accessed December 19, 2018.

Fu, Diana. 2017. "Disguised Collective Action in China." *Comparative Political Studies* 50, no. 4: 499–527.

Fuchs, Christian, Kees Boersma et al., eds. 2012. *Internet and Surveillance: The Challenges of Web 2.0 and Social Media*. New York: Routledge.

Future+Academy. 2017. http://www.futureplus.net.cn/.

GamesThatGive. 2011. http://gamesthatgive.net/about/. Accessed May 2011.

Gao Xiaoxiang. 2013. "Cong Heyang moshi dao Shaanxi moshi: Tuidong nongcun funu canyu cunzhuang zhili de xingdong yanjiu" (From the Heyang Model to Shaanxi Model: An Action Research That Promotes Village Women to Participate in Rural Governance). In *Xingdong yanjiu yu shehui gongzuo* (Action Research and Social Work), edited by Yang Jing and Xia Linqing, 195–213. Beijing: Social Sciences Academic Press.

Garcia, David, and Geert Lovink. 1997. "The ABC of Tactical Media." *Tactical Media Network*. May 16, 1997. http://www.nettime.org/Lists-Archives /nettime-l-9705/msg00096.html.

Gatenby, Bev, and Maria Humphries. 2000. "Feminist Participatory Action Research: Methodological and Ethical Issues." *Women's Studies International Forum* 23, no. 1 (Jan.–Feb.): 89–105.

Gershenfeld, Neil. 2005. *Fab: The Coming Revolution on Your Desktop—from Personal Computers to Personal Fabrication*. New York: Basic Books.

Giddens, Anthony. 1984. *The Constitution of Society: Outline of the Theory of Structuration*. Cambridge, UK: Polity Press.

Goldkind, Lauri. 2015. "Social Media and Social Service: Are Nonprofits Plugged In to the Digital Age?" *Human Service Organizations: Management, Leadership & Governance* 39, no. 4: 380–396.

Greenwood, Davydd, and Morten Levin. 2007. *Introduction to Action Research: Social Research for Social Change*. Thousand Oaks, CA: Sage.

Greenwood, Davydd J., William Foote Whyte et al. 1993. "Participatory Action Research as a Process and as a Goal." *Human Relations* 46, no. 2: 175.

Grossberg, Lawrence. 1993. "The Formations of Cultural Studies: An American in Birmingham." In *Relocating Cultural Studies: Developments in Theory and Research,* edited by Valda Blundell, John Shepherd, and Ian Taylor, 21–66. London and New York: Routledge.

Grossberg, Lawrence. 1996. "History, Politics and Postmodernism: Stuart Hall and Cultural Studies." In *Stuart Hall: Critical Dialogues,* edited by David Morley and Kuan-hsing Chen, 151–173. London and New York: Routledge.

GTZ (Deutsche Gesellschaft fur Technische Zusammenarbeit) et al. 2008. "Qiye shehui zeren: Qiye zai quanqiu shichang shang de jingzheng youshi" (Corporate Social Responsibility: Competitive Advantages for Enterprises in the Global Marketplace). Pamphlet.

Guo Jing, Liu Fei et al. 2017. "90 hou quanguo renda daibiao shi yizhong shenmeyang de tiyan?" (How Did the Post-1990s Representatives on the National People's Congress Feel about the Experience?). March 10, 2017. http://www.sohu.com/a/128501883_115420.

Guo Weihe. 2013. "Gongping shehui zhuanxing de weiguan jichu: Jianzhu gongren de shehui gongzuo fuwu" (The Microscopic Basis for the Transition of a Just Society: Social Work Service for Construction Workers). In *Xingdong yanjiu yu shehui gongzuo* (Action Research and Social Work), edited by Yang Jing and Xia Linqing, 268–287. Beijing: Social Sciences Academic Press.

Gurman, Mark. 2018. "Apple Announces Slew of New Anti-Addiction iPhone Controls." *Bloomberg,* June 4, 2018. https://www.bloomberg.com/news/articles/2018-06-04/apple-announces-slew-of-new-anti-addiction-iphone-controls.

Habermas, Jürgen. 1987. *The Theory of Communicative Action. Vol. 2: Lifeworld and System: A Critique of Functionalist Reason.* Boston: Beacon Press.

Hagey, R. 1997. "Guest Editorial: The Use and Abuse of Participatory Action Research." *Chronic Diseases in Canada* 18, no. 1: 1–4.

Hai Yin. 2011. "Cong 'guangtou ge' dao 'zhimu mei'" (From the Bare-Head Brother to the Thumbs-Up Sister). NetEase Blogs, August 10, 2011. http://yangrongzhen1010.blog.163.com/blog/static/5035564201171013611873/. Accessed July 2017.

Hall, S. 1990. "The Emergence of Cultural Studies and the Crisis of the Humanities." *October* 53: 11–23.

Han Jing. 2015. "Zuoge you wendu de luren jia" (Be A Warm-Hearted Pedestrian). *Sina.com.* April 2, 2015. http://finance.sina.com.cn/hy/20150402/175121875594.shtml.

Han Miao, and Xu Xingtang. 2011. "'Wo wei zuguo ce kongqi: Zhongguo gongzhong huanbao yishi jinru 'lizi shidai'" ("Let's Do Air Monitoring for My Homeland": Chinese Environmental Consciousness Entered the Era of "Particle Movement"). *China Development Brief,* December 6, 2011. http://www.chinadevelopmentbrief.org.cn/news-4452.html.

Han Qing. 2015. "99 gongyi zhaji: Cong choukuan dao chouren, cong gongyi dao gongmin" (Notes on 9.9 Giving Day: Thoughts on Raising Funds versus Hunting Down Donors and Philanthropy Engagement versus Citizen Engagement). *NGOCN Blog.* September 16, 2015. http://ngocn.blog.caixin.com/archives/134189.

Hanleng tiyan guan (Cold Day Experience Volunteer). 2015. *Sina Weibo*. https://s
.weibo.com/weibo/%25E5%25AF%2592%25E5%2586%25B7%25E4%25
BD%2593%25E9%25AA%258C%25E5%25AE%2598?topnav=1&wvr
=6&b=1. Accessed January 7, 2017.

Harriss, John. 2014. "Introduction: What Development Theories Are About." In
International Development: Ideas, Experience, and Prospects, edited by
Bruce Currie-Alder et al., 35–49. Oxford: Oxford University Press.

Hartley, John. 2010. "Foreword: Whose Creative Industries?" In *China's Creative
Industries: Copyright, Social Network Markets and the Business of Culture
in a Digital Age*, edited by Lucy Montgomery, vi–xxvii. Cheltenham, UK:
Edward Elgar.

Hasmath, Reza. 2016. "The Pros and Cons of China's NGO Laws." *The Di-
ploma*. March 23, 2016. https://thediplomat.com/2016/03/the-pros-and-cons
-of-chinas-ngo-laws/.

Hatton, Celia. 2015. "Is Weibo on the Way Out?" BBC News. February 24, 2015.
http://www.bbc.com/news/blogs-china-blog-31598865.

He Yilian. 2011. "Wangluo weiguan xianxiang yanjiu" (A Study on the Phenomenon of Online Crowd Gazing). *Sheke zongheng* (Social Sciences Review) 26,
no. 12: 140–143.

Heeks, Richard. 2009. "The ICT4D 2.0 Manifesto: Where Next for ICTs and
International Development?" *Development Informatics Working Paper
Series*, Paper No. 42: 1–35.

Heeks, Richard. 2010. "Do Information and Communication Technologies (ICTs)
Contribute to Development?" *Journal of International Development* 22,
no. 5: 625–640.

Herbst, Jeffrey. 1989. "How the Weak Succeed: Tactics, Political Goods, and
Institutions in the Struggle over Land in Zimbabwe." In *Everyday Forms of
Peasant Resistance*, edited by Forrest D. Colburn, 198–220. Armonk, NY:
M. E. Sharpe..

Hernandez, Javier C. 2016. "Across China, Walmart Faces Labor Unrest as
Authorities Stand Aside." *The New York Times*, November 17, 2016.
https://www.nytimes.com/2016/11/17/world/asia/across-china-walmart-faces
-labor-unrest-as-authorities-stand-aside.html. It appears under a different
title "As Employees Battle Walmart, China Warily Holds Its Tongue" in the
print edition of *The New York Times*, November 17, 2016, A1.

Heron, John. 1996. *Cooperative Inquiry: Research into the Human Condition*.
London: Sage.

Heron, John, and Peter Reason. 2008. "Extending Epistemology within a
Co-operative Inquiry." In *The Sage Handbook of Action Research: Participative Inquiry and Practice*, edited by Peter Reason and Hilary Bradbury,
366–380. Thousand Oaks, CA: Sage.

Hildebrandt, Timothy. 2013. *Social Organizations and the Authoritarian State in
China*. Cambridge: Cambridge University Press.

Ho, Peter, and Richard Edmonds, eds. 2012. *China's Embedded Activism:
Opportunities and Constraints of a Social Movement*. New York and
London: Routledge.

hooks, bell. 1990. *Yearning, Race, Gender, and Cultural Politics*. Boston: South End Press.

hooks, bell. 2000. *Feminism Is for Everybody: Passionate Politics*. New York: South End Press Classics.

Howe, Jeff. 2009. *Crowdsourcing: Why the Power of the Crowd Is Driving the Future of Business*. New York: Crown Business.

Howell, J. 1994. "Striking a New Balance: New Social Organizations in Post-Mao China." *Capital and Class* 54: 89–111.

Hsing, You-Tien, and Ching Kwan Lee. 2010. "Social Activism in China: Agency and Possibility." In *Reclaiming Chinese Society: The New Social Activism*, edited by You-Tien Hsing and Ching Kwan Lee, 1–13. New York: Routledge.

Hu Yong. 2010a. "Weiguan de liliang" (The Power of "Weiguan"). *Zhongguo qingnian bao* (China Youth Daily), December 27, 2010. http://zqb.cyol.com /content/2010-12/27/content_3470031.htm.

Hu Yong. 2010b. *Wangluo conglin shidai de xinren weiji* (The Trust Crisis in the Era of the Digital Jungle). *Wenhua zongheng* (Beijing Cultural Review) no. 4: 98–104.

Hu Yong, and Chen Qiuxin. 2017. "Yuqing: Bentu gainian yu bentu shijian" (Public Opinion as Intelligence: A Local Concept and Practice). *Chuanbo yu shehui xuekan* (Journal of Communication and Society) no. 40: 33–74.

Huang Xiaoyan. 2011. "Chengshi xinyimin shehui rongru de xingdong yanjiu: Yi Tianjin shi huazhang li shequ weili" (An Action Research of Social Inclusion of New Immigrants: Taking the Huazhang Neighborhood in Tianjin as an Example). *Jinyang Xuekan* (Jinyang Journal) no. 1: 52–56.

Huanqiu Wang (Global Net). 2017. "Chuangxing Zhongguo shehui chuangxin dasai zai Jing chenggong juban" (Enactus China's Social Innovation Competition Was Held Successfully in Beijing). May 19, 2017. http://lx.huanqiu .com/roll/2017-05/10701284.html.

Hubbard, Jessica. 2016. "Millennials: Self-Starters or Just Selfish?" *Finweek*, May 5, 2016, 40–41. http://www.fin24.com/Finweek/Featured/millennials -self-starters-or-just-selfish-20160511.

Huo Weiya. 2014. "The Rise and Challenges of Public Environmental Testing." In *Public Action and Government Accountability, Vol. 3: Chinese Research Perspectives on the Environment*, edited by Jianqiang Liu, 45–53. Leiden: Brill.

iCenter. 2017. "Chuangke gongyi jishu malasong zai iCenter juban: Cuangke zhuli Zhengjiu MInqin guimohua zhongzhi suosuo" (Maker Civic Hackathon Held in iCenter: Makers Helped "Rescue Minqin" Plant Suosuo at Scale). December 27, 2017. https://mp.weixin.qq.com/s /PPIIDMlW0z5YnPP71XYb6w.

Invisible Children. 2012. "The Results of Kony 2012." https://invisiblechildren .com/kony-2012/. Accessed July 5, 2018.

Ji Jiaxin. 2013. "Wode NGO zhi 'dao'" (The Dao of My NGO Journey). In *Xingdong yanjiu yu shehui gongzuo* (Action Research and Social Work), edited by Yang Jing and Xia Linqing, 433–445. Beijing: Social Sciences Academic Press.

Jiang Min. 2010. "Authoritarian Deliberation on Chinese Internet." *The Electronic Journal of Communication* 20, nos. 3 and 4. http://www.cios.org/EJCPUBLIC/020/2/020344.html.

Jiao Yujie. 2012. "'Wo wei zuguo ce kongqi': Fang Daerwen ziran qiuzhi she faqiren Feng Yongfeng" ("Let's Do Air Monitoring for Our Homeland": An Interview with the Founder of Green Beagle Feng Yongfeng). *Shijie huanjing* (World Environment), no. 1. http://d.wanfangdata.com.cn/periodical/sjhj201201013.

Johnson, Bobby. 2010. "Shanzai." *Wired UK*. December 7, 2010. http://www.wired.co.uk/magazine/archive/2011/01/features/shanzai.

Johnson, Christopher K., and Scott Kennedy. 2015. "China's Un-Separation of Powers: The Blurred Lines of Party and Government." December 25, 2015. https://www.foreignaffairs.com/articles/china/2015-07-24/chinas-un-separation-powers.

Johnson, Steven. 2012. *Future Perfect: The Case for Progress in A Networked Age*. New York: Riverhead Books.

Jordan, Steven. 2009. "From a Methodology of the Margins to Neoliberal Appropriation and Beyond: The Lineages of PAR." In *Education, Participatory Action Research and Social Change,* edited by Dip Kapoor and Steven Jordon, 15–27. New York: Springer.

Kanter, Beth. 2014. "Has the Ice Bucket Challenge Spawned Charity Jacking?" *Beth's Blog*. August 28, 2014. http://www.bethkanter.org/icebucket-challenge3/.

Kanter, Beth, and Fine, A. H. 2010. *The Networked Nonprofit: Connecting with Social Media to Drive Change*. San Francisco, CA: Jossey-Bass.

Keane, Michael. 2011. *China's New Creative Clusters: Governance, Human Capital and Investment*. London and New York: Routledge.

Keane, Michael. 2016. "The Ten Thousand Things, the Chinese Dream and the Creative←→Cultural Industries." In *Handbook of Cultural and Creative Industries in China,* edited by Michael Keane, 27–42. Cheltenham, UK: Edward Elgar.

Keating, Joshua. 2014. "The Less You Know." *Slate*. May 20, 2014. http://www.slate.com/blogs/the_world_/2014/05/20/the_depressing_reason_why_hashtag_campaigns_like_stopkony_and_bringbackourgirls.html.

Kemmis, Stephen. 2008. "Critical Theory and Participatory Action Research." In *The Sage Handbook of Action Research: Participative Inquiry and Practice,* edited Peter Reason and Hilary Bradbury, 121–138. Thousand Oaks, CA: Sage.

Kemmis, Stephen, and Robin McTaggart. 2005. "Participation Action Research: Communicative Action and the Public Sphere." In *The Sage Handbook of Qualitative Research,* edited by Norman K. Denzin and Yvonna S. Lincoln, 559–603. Thousand Oaks, CA: Sage.

Ken zhijia jiu xiniu (Nail Biting Rescues Rhinos). 2015. Sina Weibo. https://s.weibo.com/weibo?q=%23%E5%95%83%E6%8C%87%E7%94%B2%E6%95%91%E7%8A%80%E7%89%9B%23&page=2. Accessed January 7, 2017.

King, Gary, and Jennifer Pan et al. 2017. "How the Chinese Government Fabricates Social Media Posts for Strategic Distraction." April 9, 2017. https://gking.harvard.edu/files/gking/files/50c.pdf.

Klandermans, Bert. 1997. *The Social Psychology of Protest*. Oxford: Blackwell.

Kline, David. 2017. "Behind the Fall and Rise of China's Xiaomi." *Wired*. December 22, 2017. https://www.wired.com/story/behind-the-fall-and-rise-of-china-xiaomi/.

Kroin, Amy. 2015. "Report: Why Organizers of All Stripes Need to Fight for Digital Rights." *Free Press*. August 18, 2015. https://centerformediajustice.org/2015/08/18/report-why-organizers-of-all-stripes-need-to-fight-for-digital-rights/.

Lam Oiwan. 2010. "China: My Father Is Li Gang." *Global Voices*. October 22, 2010. https://globalvoices.org/2010/10/22/china-my-father-is-li-gang/.

laoyu201703. 2017. "80% de Weixin gongzhonghao dakailu buzu 5%, ruhe zuo caineng poju" (80% of WeChat Public Accounts Have Less Than 5% Open Rate, What Can Be Done to Break through the Dilemma). Sohu.com. April 6, 2017. http://www.sohu.com/a/132272613_118786.

Lawless, Jennifer, and Richard L. Fox. 2015. *Running from Office: Why Young Americans Are Turned Off to Politics*. Cambridge: Oxford University Press.

Le Bon, Gustav. 1897. *The Crowd: A Study of the Popular Mind*. 2nd Edition. New York: MacMillan. First edition, 1896.

Lei Yu. 2015. 'Guangdong guli gaoxiao chengli chuangxin chuangye xueyuan' (Guangdong Province Encouraged Colleges to Establish Innovation and Entrepreneurship Schools). April 1, 2015. http://tech.southcn.com/t/2015-04/01/content_121305369.htm.

Leng, Lim Teng. 2014. "Overview of Social Governance in China." Working Paper, Singapore Civil Service College. June 18, 2014. https://www.cscollege.gov.sg/Knowledge/Documents/Website/Overview%20on%20China%20Social%20Governance.pdf. Accessed July 2017.

Lessig, Lawrence. 1999. *Code: And Other Laws of Cyberspace*. New York: Basic Books.

Li, David. 2014. "The New Shanzhai: Democratizing Innovation in China." *ParisTech Review*. December 24, 2014. http://parisinnovationreview.com/articles-en/the-new-shanzhai-democratizing-innovation-in-china.

Li Feng, and Zhang Yiqi. 2014. "The Field of Philanthropy: The Duo-Variation of Administration and De-Administration." Huamin Research Center, Rutgers University. https://socialwork.rutgers.edu/sites/default/files/2014_observation_report_on_chinas_third_sector.pdf. Accessed March 2016.

Li Keqiang. 2015. "Chinese Premiere Li Keqiang's Speech at 2015 Davos: Uphold Peace and Stability, Advance Structural Reform and Generate New Momentum for Development." *World Economic Forum*. January 21, 2015. https://agenda.weforum.org/2015/01/chinese-premier-li-keqiangs-speech-at-davos-2015/.

"Li Keqiang zongli wusi qingnian jie gei Tsinghua daxue xuesheng chuangke huixin" (Premiere Li Keqiang Replies to the Makers of Tsinghua University on May Fourth). 2015. http://www.tsinghua.edu.cn/publish/thunews/9649/2015/20150504162305504431629/20150504162305504431629_.html.

Li Li. 2011. "Micro Blogs Saves Abducted Children." *China Daily USA,* February 15, 2011. http://usa.chinadaily.com.cn/china/2011-02/15/content _12010771.htm.

Li Miao. 2015. *Xin wangmin de saibo kongjian* (The Cyberspace of the New Netizens). Beijing: Jingji ribao chubanshe.

Li Wuwei. 2011. *How Creativity Is Changing China,* ed. Michael Keane. New York: Bloomsbury Academic.

Li Xiaoyun. 2016. "Ma Huateng tongguo zhijian ba gongyi wenhua chuantou le zhongchan jieceng" (Pony Ma Brought Philanthropy Culture Penetratingly to the Middle Class through Slactivism). *Nandu guangcha* (The Nandu Observer), September 9, 2016. http://nandugongyiguancha.blog.caixin.com /archives/151244.

Li Zheng, Luo Hui, and Zhang Li. 2016. "Zhongmei chuangke bijiao yanjiu: Ronghe, hubu, fenxiang" (A Comparative Study of Chinese and American Makers: Integration, Complementarity, and Sharing). *Quanqiu keji jingji liaowang* (A Review of the Global Tech Economy) 31, no. 6: 20–28.

Lian Xi. 2013. "Cong geren dao gonggong: Dikang yu zhuanhua de jiaoyu xingdong yanjiu" (From the Individual to the Public: Resistance and Transformative Education Action Research). In *Xingdong yanjiu yu shehui gongzuo* (Action Research and Social Work), edited by Yang Jing and Xia Linqing, 10–30. Beijing: Social Sciences Academic Press.

Liang Yitao. 2011. "Nuhai hua 49 tian zhuiwen 1.5 yi guangliang gongcheng" (Young Girl Took 49 Days to Chase [after City Government] for Information about the 150 Million-Yuan Night Illumination Project). *Yangcheng wanbao* (Yangcheng Evening News). July 6, 2011. http://news.sina.com.cn/s/2011-07 -06/144522767136.shtml.

Lievrouw, Leah. 2011. *Alternative and Activist New Media.* Cambridge, UK: Polity Press.

Lin Chun. 2013. *China and Global Capitalism: Reflections on Marxism, History, and Contemporary Politics.* London: Palgrave Macmillan.

Lin Guanxun. 2010. "Tiaoxi Vancl zhaodian le: Yichang shangye guanggao yinfa de caogen kuanghuan" (Flirting with VANCL, Looking for Pleasure: A Grassroots Carnival Triggered by a Commercial). *Guoji pinpai guancha* (Advertising Age: Chinese Edition), no. 9: 80–81.

Lin Shangli. 2014. "Political Consultation and Consultative Politics." In *China's Political Development: Chinese and American Perspectives,* edited by Yu Keping, 156–162. Washington DC: Brookings Institute Press.

Lindtner, Sylvia, 2014. "Hacking Shenzhen." *The Economist.* January 18, 2014. .http://www.economist.com/news/special-report/21593590-why-southern -china-best-place-world-hardware-innovator-be-hacking.

Link, Perry, and Xiao Qiang. 2013. "From Grass-Mud Equestrians to Rights-Conscious Citizens." In *Restless China,* edited by Perry Link, Richard P. Madsen, and Paul G. Pickowicz, 83–107. Lanham, MD: Rowman & Littlefield.

Liu Changchun. 2015. "Li Xiaoyun: Dang qian gongyi wenhua shi 'jingyinghua' de" (Li Xiaoyun Says That Today's Philanthropy Culture Is Elitist). ShandaNet, May 13, 2015. http://www.shanda960.com/shandaguan/article/3505.

Liu Jinfa. 2014. "From Social Management to Social Governance: Social Conflict Mediation in China." *Journal of Public Affairs* 14, no. 2: 93–104.

Liu, Melinda. 2014. "China's Underground Railroad." *Newsweek,* June 13, 2014, 34–41.

Liu Shifa. 2006. "Shishi chuangyi shiji jihua, kaizhan chuangyi Zhongguo xingdong" (Implementing the Creative Century Plan, Developing the Creative China Campaign). http://blog.sina.com.cn/s/blog _506135de01008hgr.html.

Liu Tao. 2014. "Dazao you Zhongguo tese de gongmin shehui" (Establishing a Civil Society with Chinese Characteristics). *China Development Brief,* no. 62: 8–10. Beijing: Zhishi chanque chubanshe.

Liu Xiaobo. 1992. "That Holy Word, 'Revolution.'" In *Popular Protest and Political Culture in Modern China,* edited by Jeffrey N. Wasserstrom and Elizabeth J. Perry, 309–324. Boulder, CO: Westview Press.

Liu Zhongtian. 2018. "Quanguo shehui zuzhi shuliang tupo 80 wan" (The Number of Social Organizations in the Country Exceeded 800,000). *Xinhua Net.* March 4, 2018. http://www.he.xinhuanet.com/xinwen/2018-03/04/c _1122483633.htm.

Liu Zhouhong. 2015. "Duihua Liu Zhouhong: Zhongyao de shi peiyang gongyi rencai shengtai" (A Dialogue with Liu Zhouhong: The Important Issue Is Nurturing the Ecology of Talents in the Philanthropy Sector). *Shanda Net.* September, 29, 2015. http://www.shanda960.com/shandaguan/article/14697.

Longyan Dayue. 2011. "Longyan kan lianghui" (Dragon's Take on NPC). No. 39. April 10, 2011. https://www.youtube.com/watch?v=LljzCdGlsjw. https://www.youtube.com/watch?v=2kXMVLFFvB4 (with English subtitles).

Lovejoy, Kristen, and Gregory D. Saxton. 2012. "Information, Community, and Action: How Nonprofit Organizations Use Social Media." *Journal of Computer Mediated Communication* 17: 337–353.

Lovink, Geert. 2016. *Social Media Abyss: Critical Internet Cultures and the Force of Negation.* Cambridge: Polity.

Lu Xun. 1926. "Daoshi" (Mentor). In *Huagai ji,* 52–54. Beijing: Beixin Book Store.

Lu, Y. 2009. *Non-governmental Organizations in China: The Rise of Dependent Autonomy.* London and New York: Routledge.

Ludema, James D., and Ronald E. Fry. 2008. "The Practice of Appreciative Inquiry." In *The Sage Handbook of Action Research: Participative Inquiry and Practice,* edited by Peter Reason and Hilary Bradbury, 280–296. Thousand Oaks, CA: Sage.

Luege, Timo. 2015. "When Disaster Strikes: Social Media That Drives Self-Recovery." *NTEN: Change Quarterly,* June. https://www.nten.org/change -quarterly-june/june2015/#social-media-drives-self-recovery-in-emergencies.

Luo, Tina. 2012. "Grassroots Mobilization of Internet NGOs in China: The Cases of www.1kg.org and www.geshanghua.org." Proceedings of the Fifth International Conference on Information and Communication Technologies and Development, Atlanta, GA, March 12–15, 2012. New York: ACM Publications.

Lu Lanqing. 2018. "2018 nian zhongchuang kongjian chanye fazhan xianzhuang fenxi (The 2018 Analysis of the Current Development of the Maker and Makerspace Sectors). February 9, 2018. https://www.qianzhan.com/analyst /detail/220/180209-e38f895b.html.

Ma Haiyan. 2017. "Baogao zhi 80 hou, 90 hou cheng wangluo geren juanzeng zhuli" (A Report Says the Post-80s and Post-90s Generations Became the Backbone of Individual Donors Online). *ChinaNews.* January 21, 2017. http://www.chinanews.com/sh/2017/01-21/8131424.shtml.

Macnamara, Jim. 2010. *The 21st Century Media (R)evolution: Emergent Communication Practices.* New York: Peter Lang.

Mahapatra, Sudip, and Kumar Visalaksh. 2012. *Emerging Trends in Corporate Social Responsibility: Perspectives and Experiences from Post-Liberalized India.* National Academy of Legal Studies and Research, University of Law, Hyderabad, India.

Mai Qi. 2014. "Shanghai jiaoda weilai meiti wangluo xietong chuangxin zhongxin huo guojia rending" (Shanghai Jiaotong University's Future Media Network Cooperative Innovation Center Received Recognition from the State). October 22, 2014. http://bc.tech-ex.com/2014/exclusivenews/57780.html.

Makeblock. 2015. "Makeblock di shiwu jie malasong: Mangwen dayinji" (The 15th Hackathon Held by Makeblock: Braille Typewriter). August 17, 2015. https://v.qq.com/x/page/v0162noef5a.html.

Maker Sustainability Consulting. 2017. "Buke buzhi de CSR redian" (CSR Hotspots We Have to Know). July 19, 2017. http://msc-world.com/news /detail/id/211. Accessed August 1, 2017.

Mao Gangqiang. 2014. "Shehui zhili zhong de shehui zuzhi peiyu ji shequ zuzhi fazhan" (The Development of Social and Community Organizations in the (Policy of) Social Governance). December 3, 2014. http://www.lvngo.com /ngo-41614-1.html.

Mao Zedong. 1967. "Shijian lun" (On Practice). In *Mao Zedong xuanji* (The Selected Works of Mao Zedong). Vol. 1, 259–273. Beijing: Renmin chubanshe.

Marcuse, Herbert. 2005. "Liberation from the Affluent Society." *The New Left and the 1960s.* London and New York: Routledge.

Martinez, Sylvia Libow, and Gary Stager. 2013. *Invent to Learn: Making, Tinkering, and Engineering in the Classroom.* Torrance, CA: Constructing Modern Knowledge Press.

McCann, Laurenellen. 2015. "Tools, Not Tech." *Smart Chicago Collaborative.* May 4, 2015. http://www.smartchicagocollaborative.org/tools-not-tech/.

McClelland, J. S. 2010. *The Crowd and the Mob: From Plato to Canetti.* 2nd ed. London and New York: Routledge.

McDonald, Kadi. 2014. "Cause Marketing and Millennials." *Third Sector Today.* February 18, 2014. http://thirdsectortoday.com/2014/02/18/cause-marketing -and-millennials/.

McLuhan, Marshall. 1969. "Marshall McLuhan Interview." *Playboy Magazine.* March 1969. http://web.cs.ucdavis.edu/~rogaway/classes/188/spring07 /mcluhan.pdf.

McPherson, Miller, Lynn Smith-Lovin, and James M. Cook. 2001. "Birds of a Feather: Homophily in Social Networks." *Annual Review of Sociology* 27, no. 1: 415–444.

Meng Zhaoli. 2014. "Cishan dashuju dui gongyi de daoxiang" (Big Data in Philanthropy Made an Impact on the Nonprofit Sector). *Xinlang gongyi* (Sina Philanthropy). September 29, 2014. http://gongyi.sina.com.cn/2014-09-29/154650404.html.

Milan, Stefania. 2013. *Social Movements and Their Technologies: Wiring Social Change.* London: Palgrave Macmillan.

Mills, C. Wright. 2000. *The Sociological Imagination.* 40th anniversary ed. Oxford: Oxford University Press.

Ministry of Civil Affairs. 2017. "2016 nian shehui fuwu fazhan tongji gongbao" (The 2016 Social Service Development Statistical Communique). August 3, 2017. http://www.mca.gov.cn/article/sj/tjgb/201708/20170815005382.shtml. Accessed June 2018.

Ministry of Civil Affairs and State-owned Assets Supervision and Administration Commission of the State Council. 2015. "Minzhengbu guoziwei guanyu zhichi zhongyang qiye jiji toushen gongyi cishan shiye de yijian" (Opinions on the Two Governmental Departments' Support of the Active Participation of State-Owned Enterprises in Public Welfare and Philanthropy Activities). June 2, 2015. http://cppcc.people.com.cn/n/2015/0602/c34948-27088302.html.

Ministry of Education. 2010. "Jiaoyu bu guanyu dali tuijin gaodeng xuexiao chuangxin chuangye jiaoyu he daxuesheng zizhu chuangye gongzuo1d1yijian" (Opinions on the Work by the Ministry of Education in Advancing the Education Programs of Innovation and Entrepreneurship in Universities and in Facilitating Self-Employment of College Students). May 4, 2010. http://www.moe.edu.cn/publicfiles/business/htmlfiles/moe/s4531/201105/120174.html.

Ministry of Education and Ministry of Finance. 2011. "2011 xietong chuangxin zhongxin jianshe fazhan guihua" (The Development Guidelines for the Construction of the 2011 Cooperative Innovation Center Plan). http://www.moe.edu.cn/publicfiles/business/htmlfiles/moe/s7062/201404/167787.html. Accessed June 2015.

Miranda, Shaila M., Amber Young, and Emre Yetgin. 2016. "Are Social Media Emancipatory or Hegemonic? Societal Effects of Mass Media Digitization in the Case of the SOPA Discourse." *MIS Quarterly* 40, no. 2: 303–329.

Morozov, Evgeny. 2009. "From Slactivism to Activism." *Foreign Policy.* September 5, 2009. http://foreignpolicy.com/2009/09/05/from-slacktivism-to-activism/.

Morozov, Evgeny. 2011. *The Net Delusion: The Dark Side of Internet Freedom.* New York: PublicAffairs Books.

Morozov, Evgeny, 2013. *To Save Everything, Click Here: The Folly of Technological Solutionism.* New York: PublicAffairs Books.

Mouffe, Chantal. 2013. "Artistic Strategies in Politics and Political Strategies in Art." *Dissidence* 10, no. 2. http://hemisphericinstitute.org/hemi/en/e-misferica-102/mouffe.

Nanfang de Feng. 2014. "Ganwen lu zai hefang? 'Woba shi Li Gang'" (May I Ask Where I Should Be Headed? My Dad Is Li Gang). *Sina Weibo*. July 26, 2014. http://blog.sina.com.cn/s/blog_ed302c1b0102uxx7.html.

Narada Foundation. 2012. "Zaihou shehui sunshi pinggu yu jieru xingdong yanjiu xiangmu" (Research Project on the Evaluation of Post-Earthquake Social Loss and Participatory Action Research). September 6, 2012. http://www.naradafoundation.org/content/3863.

Narada Foundation. 2016. "He pingtai" (The Togetherness Platform). www.narada foundation.org/content/5455. December 31, 2016.

National People's Congress. 2015. "Quanguo renmin daibiao dahui changwu weiyuanhui guanyu shouquan zuigao renmin jiancha yuan zai bufen diqu kaizhan gongyi susong shidian gongzuo de jueding" (Decisions of the Standing Committee of the People's Congress on Implementing Pilot Projects on the Supreme People's Procuratorate Initiating Public Interest Litigation in Parts of the Country). July 1, 2015. http://www.npc.gov.cn/npc/xinwen/2015 -07/01/content_1940395.htm.

Nayar, Pramod K. 2010. *The New Media and Cybercultures Anthology.* Hoboken, NJ: Wiley-Blackwell.

NEC. 2003. "Ecotonoha." http://www.nec.co.jp/ecotonoha/index_en.html. Accessed May 2011.

Nelson, Phil, Anthony Gao, and Yinuo Li. 2015. "Does China Have a 'Giving Season'?" *Medium*. November 19, 2015. https://medium.com/biacs -publication/does-china-have-a-giving-season-52430990e729#.q4kbda45q.

Neurogadget Staff. 2015. "WeChat Adds WeRun to Monitor Your Daily Move- ment." September 6, 2015. http://neurogadget.net/2015/09/06/wechat-adds -werun-to-monitor-your-daily-movement/14636.

Ng, Eddy S. W., Charles Gossett, and Richard Winter. 2016. "Millennials and Public Service Renewal: Introduction on Millennials and Public Service Motivation." *Public Administration Quarterly* 40, no. 3: 412–428.

NGO2.0. 2009. "NGO-Internet Usage Survey 1: Report." http://www.ngo20.org /6. Stored in https://pan.baidu.com/s/1hscCbzu.

NGO2.0. 2010. "NGO-Internet Usage Survey 2: Report." http://www.ngo20.org /6 . Stored in https://pan.baidu.com/s/1dEHJ3uL.

NGO2.0. 2012. "NGO-Internet Usage Survey 3: Report." http://www.ngo20.org /6. Stored in https://pan.baidu.com/s/1gfjzHVP.

NGO2.0. 2013. "NGO-SM Survey 2." *NGO2.0 Survey Reports*. https://pan .baidu.com/s/1nwmBAJ3.

NGO2.0. 2015a. "NGO-Internet Usage Survey 4: Report." http://www.ngo20.org /6. Stored in https://pan.baidu.com/s/1dFgLXN7.

NGO2.0. 2015b. Workshops. http://www.ngo20.org/3. Accessed June 2015.

NGO2.0. 2016. *Gongyi ditu jianbao* (NGO2.0 Philanthropy Map Newsletter) no. 38. August 22, 2016. https://mv.lingxi360.com/m/ojx278.

NGO2.0. 2017. "NGO-Internet Usage Survey 5: Report.". http://www.ngo20.org /6. Stored in January 2017. https://pan.baidu.com/s/1eS7jBTg.

NGO2.0. 2018. "NGO-Internet Usage Survey 6: Report." http://www.ngo20.org /6. Stored in https://pan.baidu.com/s/15RW7MGn9M9FIqwfsT2TyEg.

NGO2.0map. 2009. "Zhongguo Yidong 2009 nian kaizhan bangzhu Aizibing zhigu ertong he liushou ertong" (China Mobile Brought Aid to Orphans of AIDS Patients and Left-Behind Children in 2009). http://www.ngo20map .com/Event/view/id/28.

NGO2.0map. 2010. "Zhongying Renshou: Xingxing diandeng guanai liushou erting jihua yuanman luomu" (Aviva-COFCO Life Insurance Co.: The "Star Light Left-Behind-Children Project" Was Successfully Accomplished). http://www.ngo20map.com/Event/view/id/714. Accessed on August 1, 2017.

NGO2.0map. 2017. "Shoujie Foshan gongyi cishan xiangmu dasai" (The Inaugurating Contest of Philanthropy Projects Created by the Foshan-Based NGOs). http://www.ngo20map.com/Event/view/id/6129.

Ngok, Kinglun. 2016. "Social Policy Making in China." In *China's Social Policy: Transformation and Challenges,* edited by Kinglun Ngok and Chak Kwan Chan, 12–30. New York and London: Routledge.

Nicholson, Brian, Yanuar Nugroho, and Nimmi Rangaswamy. 2016. "Social Media for Development: Outlining Debates, Theory and Praxis." *Information Technology for Development* 22, no. 3: 357–363.

Novaretti, Simona. 2014. "Social Governance vs. Social Management: Towards a New Regulatory Role for Social Organizations in China?" (CDCT Working Paper). *Comparative and Transnational Law* 11: 1–29. http://www.cdct.it/wp -content/uploads/2014/10/Master-Wp-Novaretti.pdf.

O'Brien, J. Kevin, and Lianjiang Li. 2006. *Rightful Resistance in Rural China.* Cambridge: Cambridge University Press.

OECD. 2007. *OECD Reviews of Innovation Policy China Synthesis Report: Synthesis Report.* OECD Publishing.

Ogreenworld, 2011. "My Dad Is Li Gang." *KnowYourMeme.* https:// knowyourmeme.com/search?q=my+dad+is+li+gang.

One Foundation. 2015. "Shouge 'hanleng gongyi ri', Yi Jijin zhaomu 'hanleng tiyan guan'" (Our First Winter Solstice Day Philanthropy: One Foundation Calls for Volunteers to Experience Cold Weather). December 22, 2015. http://www.onefoundation.cn/index.php?m=article&a=show&id=863.

Orwell, George. 1998. "Funny but Not Vulgar." In *Funny, But Not Vulgar and Other Selected Essays and Journalism,* 118–123. London: The Folio Society. The article was originally published in 1945.

Packer, George. 2013. "Change the World: Silicon Valley Transfers Its Slogans—and Its Money—to the Realm of Politics." *The New Yorker,* May 27, 2013: 44–55.

Palfrey, John, and Urs Gasser. 2008. *Born Digital: Understanding the First Generation of Digital Natives.* New York: Basic Books.

Palser, Barb. 2010. "Beneath the Tattoos." *American Journal Review,* June/July 2010. http://ajrarchive.org/article.asp?id=4882.

Pan Jiaen, Luo Chia-Ling, and Wen Tiejun. 2017. "Three 'Centuries': The Context and Development of Rural Reconstruction in China." *Inter-Asia Cultural Studies* 18, no. 1: 120–130.

Park, Alice. 2016. "Life, the Remix." *Time,* July 4, 2016, 42–48.

Paulin, Michele, and Ronald J. Ferguson et al. 2014. "Motivating Millennials to Engage in Charitable Causes through Social Media." *Journal of Service Management* 25, no. 3: 334–348.

Peng Lan. 2008. "Xian jieduan Zhongguo wangmin dianxing tezheng yanjiu" (A Study of the Current Characteristics of Chinese Netizens). *Shanghai Normal University Journal: Philosophy and Social Sciences* 37, no. 6: 48–56.

Peretz, Marissa. 2017. "Want to Engage Millennials? Try Corporate Social Responsibility." *Forbes,* September 27, 2017. https://www.forbes.com/sites/marissaperetz/2017/09/27/want-to-engage-millennials-try-corporate-social-responsibility/#1c83fffe6e4e.

Perry, Elizabeth. 1994. "Trends in the Study of Chinese politics: State-Society Relations." *China Quarterly* 139: 704–713.

"Qiangxiu bangfu zhongxin: Zhuiqiu youxian lirun jiejue shehui wenti" (In Pursuit of Limited Profits to Solve Social Problems). *Huanqiu Net.* October 1, 2013. http://hope.huanqiu.com/exclusivetopic/2013-10/4395825.html. Accessed December 2013.

Qin Hui. 2004. "NGO in China: The Third Sector in the Globalization Process and Social Transformation." http://web.mit.edu/newmediaactionlab/www/seminars/4_21_04_ngo.pdf. Accessed March 2016.

Qiu, Jack Linchuan. 2008. "Wireless Working-Class ICTs and the Chinese Informational City." *Journal of Urban Technology* 15, no. 3: 57–77.

Qiu, Jack Linchuan. 2009. *Working-Class Network Society: Communication Technology and the Information Have-Less in Urban China.* Cambridge, MA.: The MIT Press.

Qiu, Jack Linchuan, and Bu Wei. 2013. "China ICT Studies: A Review of the Field, 1989–2012." *The China Review* 13, no. 2: 123–152.

Qiu, Zitong. 2016. "Doing Chinese Cultural Industries: A Reflection on the Blue Book Syndrome and Remedy Paradigm." In *Handbook of Cultural and Creative Industries in China,* edited by Michael Keane, 15–26. Edward Elgar Publishing: Cheltenham, UK, and Northampton, MA.

Qureshi, S. 2013. "Information and Communication Technologies in the Midst of Global Change: How Do We Know When Development Takes Place?" *Information Technology for Development* 19, no. 3: 189–192.

Rabb, Chris. 2010. *Invisible Capital: How Unseen Forces Shape Entrepreneurial Opportunity.* San Francisco: Berrett-Koehler.

Raftery, Brian. 2018. "Streaming Isn't Everything, and Blue-Rays Are Back to Prove It." *Wired.* December 12, 2018. https://www.wired.com/story/blu-ray-resurgence-collectors/.

Raiti, Gerard C. 2006. "The Lost Sheep of ICT4D Research." *ITD: Information Technologies & International Development* 3, no. 4: 1–8.

Ramo, Joshua Cooper. 2004. *The Beijing Consensus.* London: Foreign Policy Centre.

Reason, Peter. 1994. "Three Approaches to Participative Inquiry." In *Handbook of Qualitative Research,* edited by N. K. Denzin and Y. S. Lincoln, 324–339. Thousand Oaks, CA: Sage.

Reason, Peter, and Hilary Bradbury. 2001. *Handbook of Action Research: Participative Inquiry and Practice.* Thousand Oaks, CA: Sage.

Reason, Peter, and Hilary Bradbury. 2008. "Introduction: Inquiry and Participation in Search of a World Worthy of Human Aspiration." In *The Sage Handbook of Action Research: Participative Inquiry and Practice,* edited by Peter Reason and Hilary Bradbury, 1–10. Thousand Oaks, CA: Sage.

Ren Meina. 2018. "Woerma bagong shijian: laogong NGO yu Zhongguo gongren guanxi de zhuanzhe dian"(The Incident of Walmart Labor Strikes: A Turning Point in the Relationship between Labor NGOs and Chinese Workers). *Shelun qianyan* (The Vanguard of Editorials), February 10, 2018. Republished in *China Development Brief,* February 11, 2018. http://www.chinadevelopmentbrief.org.cn/news-20955.html.

Reynolds, Justin. 2013. "The Promise and Limits of Civic Hacking." *Impact48.* September 17, 2013. https://impact48.org/2013/09/17/the-promise-and-limits-of-civic-hacking/.

Rheingold, Howard. 2002. *Smart Mobs: The Next Social Revolution.* Cambridge, MA: Perseus.

Rheingold, Howard. 2005. "The New Power of Collaboration" TED Talk. February 2005. https://www.ted.com/talks/howard_rheingold_on_collaboration.

Ryan Singel. 2008. "ETech: Text Messages, not Web 2.0, Will Dominate Africa Tech Future." *Wired.* March 6, 2008. https://www.wired.com/2008/03/etech-text-mess#previouspost.

Saich, Anthony. 2000. "Negotiating the State: The Development of Social Organizations in China." *China Quarterly* 161: 124–141.

SASAC (State-owned Assets Supervision and Administration Commission of the PRC's State Council). 2008. "Guanyu zhongyang qiye luxing shehui zeren de zhidao yijian" (Regarding the Guidance on Social Responsibility of State Enterprises). January 2, 2008. Pamphlet distributed by SASAC.

SASAC. 2011. "Zhongyang qiye 'shier wu' hexie fazhan zhanlue shishi gangyao" (The Implementation Plan of the Harmonious Development Strategy of the State Enterprises). October 8, 2011. Pamphlet distributed by SASAC.

Schell, Orville. 2016. "Crackdown in China: Worse and Worse." *The New York Review of Books,* April 21, 2016; 12–14.

Scott, James C. 1985. *Weapons of the Weak: Everyday Forms of Peasant Resistance.* New Haven and London: Yale University Press.

Selyukh, Alina. 2015. "A Click Too Far: Why Using Social Media Isn't That Great for Fundraising." *NPR All Things Considered.* December 2, 2015. https://www.npr.org/sections/alltechconsidered/2015/12/02/458008461/a-click-too-far-why-social-media-isnt-that-great-for-fundraising.

Sen, Amartya. 1999. *Development as Freedom.* Oxford: Oxford University Press.

Shah, Hasit. 2014. "Devices, Design, and Digital News for India's Next Billion Internet Users." *Internet Monitor 2014: Reflections on the Digital World: Platforms, Policy, Privacy, and Public Discourse.* December 15, 2014. Berkman Center Research Publication No. 2014–17. https://ssrn.com/abstract=2538813.

Shanghai Jiaotong University. 2015. "Ynjiu cheng shehui zuzhi GDP gongxian yuan gaoyu guanfang shuju" (Research Proved That the GDP Count of Nonprofit Organizations Far Exceeded the Official Statistics). *Caixin Net.* July 30, 2015. http://china.caixin.com/2015-07-30/100834493.html.

Shell, Hana Rose. 2012. *Hide and Seek: Camouflage, Photography, and the Media of Reconnaissance.* Cambridge, MA: MIT Press.

Shenzhen City Committee of IT Innovation. 2015. "Shenzhen shi renmin zhengfu guanyu yinfa cujin chuangke1 fazhan ruogan cuoshi (shixing) de tongzhi" (Shenzhen City Government's Announcement of Experimental Policies Regarding the Acceleration of the Development of Makers). July 1, 2015.

Shenzhen Open Innovation Lab (SZOIL). 2017a. "Xinguang cun, yige zouxiang guoji de kaiyuan cun"(Xinguang Village, An International OpenSource Village). May 22, 2017. http://www.sohu.com/a/142699652_742704.

Shenzhen Open Innovation Lab (SZOIL). 2017b. "Kaiyuancun: Chuangke yundong x xinnongcun jianshe" (An OpenSourceVillage: Maker Movement Multiplies New Rural Reconstuction).October 24, 2017. https://meta.tn/a/5a b3c42c207a1b8ac510cdc1a2d61b31688c827430e3fc4a6867ae3319b14098.

Shenzhen Open Innovation Lab (SZOIL).2017c. "Ziji dongshou tanmi Zhu Jiang" (DIY, Exploring the Secret of the Pearl River). December 14, 2017. http://mp.weixin.qq.com/s/gLPik6nYG9ROXQO3lCtejg.

Shi Can. 2017. "Luhan he Guan Xiaotong ganbong le Weibo, Weiguan buzai gaibian Zhongguo" (Luhan and Guan Xiaotong Crashed Weibo, Virtual Spectatorship Could No Longer Change China). *36 Kr.* October 9, 2017. https://36kr.com/p/5096319.html.

Shirky, Clay. 2008. *Here Comes Everybody: The Power of Organizing without Organizations.* New York: Penguin.

Shue, V. 1994. "State Power and Social Organization in China." In *State Power and Social Forces: Domination and Transformation in the Third World,* edited by J. S. Migdal, A. Kohli, and V. Shue, 65–88. Cambridge: Cambridge University Press.

Shunfeng Foundation. 2017. http://www.sfgy.org/project/introduce?moduleId=27.

Sina Weibo. 2015. "Han Jing: Zuo ge you wendu de luren jia" (Han Jing: Be a Compassionate Pedestrian). *Sina Finance and Economics.* April 2, 2015. http://finance.sina.com.cn/hy/20150402/175121875594.shtml.

Sina.com. 2015. "Wei gongyi san zhounian, mukuan tupo 2.4 yi" (On the Third Anniversary of MicroCharity, Donations Broke through 240 Million Yuan). January 14, 2015. http://gongyi.sina.com.cn/gyzx/2015-01-14/115951212 .html.

Singel, Ryan. 2008. "ETech: Text Messages, not Web 2.0, Will Dominate Africa Tech Future." *Wired.* March 6, 2008. https://www.wired.com/2008/03/etech -text-mess#previouspost.

Song, Bing. 2018. "The West may be wrong about China's social credit system." *The Washington Post.* November 29, 2018. https://www.washingtonpost.com /news/theworldpost/wp/2018/11/29/social-credit/?noredirect=on&utm_term= .e086999db6e0.

Song Yongning. 2006. "Yige zibizheng ertong fudao de xingdong yanjiu" (Action
    Research on Mentoring Autistic Children). *Zhongguo teshu jiaoyu* (Chinese
Journal of Special Education) no. 4 (serial no. 70): 58–61.

The South End Press Collective. 1999. *Talking about a Revolution*. New York:
    South End Press.

Spencer, David. 2017. "Calls to Loosen Chinese Online Censorship Are Cen-
    sored." March 15, 2017. https://www.vpncompare.co.uk/calls-to-loosen
    -chinese-online-censorship-are-censored/.

Spires, A. J., L. Tao, and K. M. Chan. 2014. "Societal Support for China's
    Grass-Roots NGOs: Evidence from Yunnan, Guangdong and Beijing." *The
    China Journal*, no. 71: 65–90.

Stanley, Jay, and Barry Steinhardt. 2003. "Bigger Monster, Weaker Chains: The
    Growth of an American Surveillance Society," American Civil Liberties
    Union. https://www.aclu.org/report/bigger-monster-weaker-chains-growth
    -american-surveillance-society?redirect=technology-and-liberty/bigger
    -monster-weaker-chains-growth-american-surveillance-society.

The State Council of PRC. 2006. "Guojia zhong chang qi kexue he jishu fazhan
    guihua gangyao (2006–2020)" (The Essentials of China's Fifteen-Year Plan
    for Science and Technology). February 9, 2016. http://www.gov.cn/jrzg/2006
    -02/09/content_183787.htm.

The State Council of the PRC. 2012. "Jiaoyubu deng shiwu bumen guanyu
    yinfa 'Nongcun yiwu jiaoyu xuesheng yingyang gaishan jihua shishi xize'
    deng wuge peitao wenjian de tongzhi" (Regarding the Publication of the
    Five Supporting Documents Including "the Detailed Implementation of the
    Plan of Improving Nutrition of Rural Students Schooled under Compul-
    sory Education"). June 14, 2012. http://www.gov.cn/zwgk/2012-06/14
    /content_2160689.htm.

The State Council Information Office of the PRC. 2015. "Jixu zuohao nongcun
    yiwu jiaoyu xuesheng yingyang gaishan jihua" (Continue to Excel in
    Implementing the Project of Improving the Nutrition of Rural Students
    Schooled under Compulsory Education). January 30, 2015. http://www.scio
    .gov.cn/32344/32345/32347/20150130/zy32526/Document/1393746
    /1393746.htm.

The State Council Information Office. 2016. "Zuigao jian tongbao jiancha jiguan
    tiqi gongyi susong shidian gongzuo tuijin qingkuang fabuhui" (Press
    Conference on the Outcome of Implementing the Pilot Project on Procura-
    torates Initiating Public Interest Litigation). January 6, 2016. http://www.scio
    .gov.cn/xwfbh/qyxwfbh/Document/1463261/1463261.htm.

Stein, Joel. 2016. "Tyranny of the Mob." *Time*, August 29, 2016, 27–33.

Sullivan, Daniel, Mark Landau, and Aaron Kay. 2016. "When Enemies Go Viral
    (or Not)—A Real-Time Experiment during the 'Stop Kony' Campaign."
    Psychology of Popular Media Culture 5, no. 1: 15–26.

Sun Huan. 2013. "The Hidden Activism: Media Practices and Media Opportunity
    in Chinese Politics of Resistance. Comparative Media Studies thesis, MIT,
    October 22, 2013. https://cmsw.mit.edu/sun-huan-hidden-activism-chinese
    -politics-of-resistance/.

The Supreme People's Procuratorate (SPP) of the People's Repbulic of China. 2013. "Lianggao fabu banli guanyu banli wangluo feibang deng xingshi anjian shiyong falu ruogan wenti de jieshi" (The Explanatory Notes on Appropriate Legal Treatment of the Criminal Cases Related to Online Rumor Mongering and Other Offences). September 10, 2013. http://www .spp.gov.cn/zdgz/201309/t20130910_62417.shtml.

Svensson, Marina. 2016. "Connectivity, Engagement, and Witnessing on China's Weibo." In *The Internet, Social Media, and a Changing China*, edited by Jacques deLisle, Avery Goldstein, and Guobin Yang, 49–70. Philadelphia: The University of Pennsylvania Press.

Talking Tree. 2012. *Facebook.* http://www.facebook.com/pages/Talking-Tree /119345101452789?sk=wall. Accessed May 2011.

Taylor, Paul. 2016. "The One Way Millennials Could Still Change the World." *Time.* February 11, 2016. http://time.com/4217071/millennials-could-still -change-the-world/.

Teets, Jessica. 2014. *Civil Society under Authoritarianism: The China Model.* Cambridge: Cambridge University Press.

Teinmetz, Kat, and Matt Vella. 2017. "Uber Fail: Upheaval at the World's Most Valuable Startup Is a Wake-Up Call for Silicon Valley." *Time,* June 15, 2017, 22–28.

Tencent Foundation (Tengxun jijin hu). 2012. "Tengxun jijinhui dashi ji" (The Chronicle of Important Events of Tencent Foundation). http://gongyi.qq.com /jjhgy/index.htm.

Tencent Foundation (Tengxun jijin hui). 2014. "Tengxun cishan dashuju? (Big Data from Tencent Foundation). September 28, 2014. http://gongyi.qq.com/a /20140928/034429.htm.

Tencent Foundation. 2015. Tengxun Wei'ai (Tencent MicroCompassion). May 21, 2015. http://gongyi.qq.com/a/20150521/002328.htm. Accessed January 9, 2017.

Tencent Foundation. 2016–2017. Tengxun lejuan (Tencent Happy Donation). http://gongyi.qq.com/succor/project_list.htm. Accessed January 9, 2017.

Tencent Foundation (Tengxun jijin hui). 2017. "2017 nian Weixun shuju baogao fabu" (The 2017 Report on WeChat [User] Data). First published on WeChat Moment. Sohu.com. November 10, 2017. http://www.sohu.com/a /203492754_481775.

Tencent Philanthropy (Tengxun gongyi). 2015. "Tengxun gongyi lianhe duofang faqi '9.9 gongyiri' dazao Zhongguo shouge quanmin gongyi lichengbei" (Tencent Philanthropy Launched the 9.9 Giving Day in Collaboration with Multiple Partners to Make the First Milestone of Everyone a Donor Charity Movement). Tencent News. September 8, 2015. http://news.qq.com/a /20150908/011203.htm.

Tencent Philanthropy (Tengxun gongyi). 2016. "99 gongyiri santian shankuan po liuyi" (Donations on 9.9 Giving Day Exceeded 600 million yuan). September 10, 2016. http://news.qq.com/a/20160910/003827.htm.

"Tencent's Report on the Result of 9.9 Giving Day" (Tengxun huibao 99 gongyiri 'zhankuang'). 2017. Sohu.com. September 12, 2017. http://www.sohu.com/a /191572708_648461.

Thapa, Devinder, and Østein Saebø. 2014. "Exploring the Link between ICT and Development in the Context of Developing Countries: A Literature Review." *Electronic Journal of Information Systems in Developing Countries* 64, no. 1: 1–15.

Tolman, Charles W. et al., eds. 1996. *Problems of Theoretical Psychology*. North York, Ontario: Captus Press.

Toyama, Kentaro. 2015. *Geek Heresy: Rescuing Social Change from the Cult of Technology*. New York: PublicAffairs Books.

Tufekci, Zeynep. 2018. "The Road from Tahrir to Trump." *MIT Technology Review* 121, no. 5: 10–17.

Twenge, J. M. 2006. *Generation Me: Why Today's Young Americans Are More Confident, Assertive, Entitled—And More Miserable Than Ever Before*. New York: Free Press.

"2018 nian Zhongguo Weixin denglu renshu, Wexin gongzhonghao shuliang ji Weixin xiaochengxu shuliang tongji" (The Statistics of the Number of Chinese WeChat Users, WeChat Public Accounts and WeChat Micro Apps in 2018). May 30, 2018. *Zhongguo Chanye Xinxi* (Chinese Industry Information). http://www.chyxx.com/industry/201805/645403.html.

Ushahidi. 2017. "Ushahidi." *Wikipedia*. https://en.wikipedia.org/wiki/Ushahidi#Crowdmap. Accessed January 10, 2017.

Van Alstyne, Marshall, and Erik Brynjolfsson. 2005. "Global Village or Cyber-Balkans? Modeling and Measuring the Integration of Electronic Communities." *Management Science* 51, no. 6: 851–868.

Village Vision. 2016. "Village Vision weilai xiangcun, tujing 'taohua yuan'" (Village Vision, The Future Village: Visualizing "The Peach Blossom Spring"). November 25, 2016. http://www.archcollege.com/archcollege/2016/11/29727.html.

Waite, Emily. 2018. "Google and the Rise of 'Digital Well-Being." *Wired*. August 22, 2018. https://www.wired.com/story/google-and-the-rise-of-digital-wellbeing/.

Wakeman, Fredric. 1993. "The Civil Society and Public Sphere Debate: Western Reflections on Chinese Political Culture." *Modern China* 19, no. 2: 108–138.

Walsham, Geo. 2017. "ICT4D Research: Reflections on History and Future Agenda." *Information Technology for Development* 23, no. 1: 18–41.

Wang Daoyong. 2007. "Niming de kanghuan yu renxing de xianxian (Invisible Carnival and the Revelation of Human Nature). *Qingnian yanjiu* (Youth Studies) no. 3: 21–27.

Wang, Jing. 1996. *High Culture Fever: Politics, Aesthetics, and Ideology in Deng's China*. Berkeley: University of California Press.

Wang, Jing. 2001. "Culture as Leisure and Culture as Capital." In "Chinese Popular Culture and the State," ed. Jing Wang, special issue, *Positions: East Asia Cultures Critique* 9, no. 1: 69–104.

Wang, Jing. 2004. "The Global Reach of A New Discourse." *International Journal of Cultural Studies* 7, no. 1: 9–19.

Wang, Jing. 2005. "Introduction: The Politics and Production of Scales in China: How Does Geography Matter to Students of Local, Popular Culture?" In *Locating China: Space, Place, and Popular Culture,* edited by Jing Wang, 1–30. London and New York: Routledge.

Wang, Jing. 2008a. *Brand New China: Advertising, Media, and Commercial Culture.* Cambridge: Harvard University Press.

Wang, Jing. 2008b. "CCTV and the Advertising Media." *Brand New China: Advertising, Media, and Commercial Culture,* 247–287. Cambridge: Harvard University Press.

Wang, Jing. 2012. "Triggering a snowball effect." *China Daily Europe,* May 11, 2012. http://europe.chinadaily.com.cn/epaper/2012-05/11/content_15268257 .htm.

Wang, Jing. 2015a. "NGO2.0 and Social Media Praxis: Activist As Researcher." *Chinese Journal of Communication* 8, no. 1: 18–41.

Wang, Jing. 2015b. "TV, Digital, and Social: A Debate," *Media Industries* 1, no. 3. https://quod.lib.umich.edu/m/mij/15031809.0001.311/--tv-digital-and-social -a-debate?rgn=main;view=fulltext.

Wang, Jing. 2016a. "The Makers Are Coming! China's Long Tail Revolution." In *Handbook of Cultural and Creative Industries in China,* edited by Michael Keane, 43–63. Cheltenham, UK and Northampton, MA: Edward Elgar Publishing.

Wang, Jing. 2016b. "Shehui hua meiti chuanbo celue" (Social Media Communication Strategy). In *Hulianwang jia gongyi: Wanzhuan xin meiti* (Internet Plus Public Good: Playing with New Media), 3–30. Beijing: Electronics Industry Press.

Wang, Jing, and Zhou Rongting. 2016. *Hulianwang jia gongyi: Wanzhuan xin meiti* (Internet Plus Public Good: Plying with New Media). Beijing: Electronics Industry Press.

Wang Kala, Jin Yu et al. 2012. "'Lvse guonian' changyi shao fangpao wei kongqi jianfu" (Have a Happy "Green New Year," Shoot off Fewer Firecrackers to Alleviate Air Pollution). *Xin jingbao* (Beijing News), January 20, 2012. http://epaper.bjnews.com.cn/html/2012-01/20/content_311675.htm?div=-1. Also see http://www.bjep.org.cn/pages/Index/39-39?rid=2239.

Wang Liping, and Guo Fenglin. 2016. "Zhongguo shehui zhili de liangfu miankong: Jiben gonggong fuwu de shijiao" (The Two Faces of Social Governance in China: From the Perspective of Basic Public Service). *Nankai xuebao: Zhexue shehui kexue ban* (Nankai Journal: Philosophy and Social Science) no. 3: 93–107.

Wang Ming. 2014. "Zhili chuangxin zhongzai zhengshe fenkai" (The Innovation of Governance Consists of the Separation of Government from Society). CPC News. April 1, 2014. http://theory.people.com.cn/n/2014/0401/c40531 -24796890.html.

Wang Ping. 2015. "Tantao shehui fazhan he jingji fazhan jiehe de dingceng sheji he weiguan shijian" (Investigating the Superstructural Design and Microscopic Implementation of the Integration of Social Development and

Economic Development). April 29, 2015. http://www.charityalliance.org.cn
/membernews/4723.jhtml.

Wang Ruohan. 2011. "Chen Danqing: Weiguan yu minzhu de juli" (Chen
Danqing Says, The Distance Between Crowd Spectatorship and Democracy).
Tengxun Pinglun (Tencent Review), July 15, 2011. http://view.qq.com/a
/20110716/000011.htm.

Wang, Selina. 2018. "Twitter to Measure Echo Chambers, Unruly Comments on
Service." July 30, 2018. *Bloomberg.* https://www.bloomberg.com/news
/articles/2018-07-30/twitter-to-measure-echo-chambers-unruly-discussion-on
-service.

Wang Shuang. 2012. "Zhenhou chongsheng qiangxiu, baqian xiuniang liaode"
(The Rebirth of Qiang Embroidery after the Earthquake: A Thumbs up to
the Eight Thousand Embroiderers). April 6, 2012. http://sichuan.scol.com.cn
/dwzw/content/2012-04/06/content_3572849.htm?node=968. Accessed
December 2013.

Wang, Y., Zhe, X., and Sun, B. 1993. *Shehui Zhongjian Ceng: Gaige yu
Zhongguo de Shetuan Zuzhi* (The Social Intermediate Stratum: Reform and
China's Social Associations). Beijing: Development Publishing House. Cited
in Yiyi Lu's *Non-Governmental Organizations in China,* 20.

Wang Yiming. 2015. "Tiyanshi gongyi huodong de youxiao chuanbo" (Effective
Communication of Experiential Philanthropy). *Shanda Net.* December 17,
2015. http://www.shanda960.com/shandaguan/article/5865.

Wang Yu. 2015. *Heike, Jike, Chuangke:* Creativity in Chinese Technology
Community. Master of Science thesis, MIT. http://cmsw.mit.edu/heike-jike
-chuangke-creativity-chinese-technology-community/.

Waters, Richard D., and Kristen LeBlanc Feneley. 2013. "Virtual Stewardship in
the Age of New Media: Have Nonprofit Organizations Moved beyond Web
1.0 Strategies?" *International Journal of Nonprofit and Voluntary Sector
Marketing* 18, no. 3: 216–230.

Weigel, Gerolf. 2004. "ICT4D Today: Enhancing Knowledge and People-Centered
Communication for Development and Poverty Reduction." In *ICT4D:
Connecting People for a Better World,* edited by Gerolf Weigel and Daniele
Waldburger, 16–31. Berne, Switzerland: Swiss Agency for Development and
Cooperation & Global Knowledge Partnership.

Weilai zhi cun (Future Village). 2004–2015. http://www.future-village-nepal.org.
Accessed December 2017.

Wertime, David. 2014. "It's Official: China Is Becoming a New Innovation
Powerhouse." *Tea Leaf Nation (Foreign Policy).* February 7, 2014. http://
foreignpolicy.com/2014/02/07/its-official-china-is-becoming-a-new
-innovation-powerhouse/.

WeRun. 2017. "Staying Fit with WeRun on WeChat." *The Official WeChat Blog.*
May 5, 2017. http://blog.wechat.com/2017/05/05/staying-fit-with-werun-on
-wechat/.

Wessler, Rainer. 2013. "Shanzhai's Role in Innovation Strategy." *Insights China,*
Collection No. 1. https://designmind.frogdesign.com/2013/04/shanzhais-role
-innovation-strategy/.

White, Micah. 2010. "Clicktivism Is Ruining Leftist Activism." *The Guardian*. August 12, 2010. http://www.guardian.co.uk/commentisfree/2010/aug/12/clicktivism-ruining-leftist-activism. Accessed in May 2011.

Whyte, William Foote, ed. 1991. *Participatory Action Research*. Thousand Oaks, CA: Sage.

WildAid. 2015. "Yesheng jiuyuan: 'Ken zhijia jiu xiniu' gongyi huodong" (WildAid: "Nail Biter Rescue Rhinos" Nonprofit Campaign). December 23, 2015. http://www.digitaling.com/projects/16358.html.

Williams, David. 2014. "The Study of Development." In *International Development: Ideas, Experience, and Prospects*, edited by Bruce Currie-Alder, Ravi Kanbur et al., 21–34. Oxford, UK: Oxford University Press.

Williams, Robert W. 2006. "Democracy, Cyberspace, and the Body." *Cultural Logic*. Vol. 9 (2006). Online e-journal. http://clogic.eserver.org/2006/williams.html.

Woetzel, Jonathan, Jeongmin Seong et al. 2017. "Digital China: Powering the Economy to Global Competitiveness." *McKinsey Global Institute*. https://www.mckinsey.com/global-themes/china/digital-china-powering-the-economy-to-global-competitiveness.

Wong, Winnie Won Yin. 2015. "Lantern Slide Moments and the Taught Subject, 1906 and 2006." In "Reconsidering the 2006 MIT Visualizing Cultures Controversy," eds. Winne Wong and Jing Wang, special issue, *Positions: Asia Critique* 23, no. 1: 91–114.

Xi Jinping. 2014. Speech given at the 65th anniversary of the Chinese People's Political Consultative Conference. *Xinhua Net*. September 21, 2014. http://news.xinhuanet.com/politics/2014-09/21/c_1112564804.htm.

Xia Linqing. 2002. "'Yuchang tongxing, fanqiang yuejie' luntan baogao shilu" (The Truthful Recording of the Forum on 'Traveling with Prostitutes and Transcending the Boundaries'). *Yingyong xinli xue yanjiu* (Applied Psychology Research) no. 13 (spring): 147–197.

Xia Linqing. 2004. "Yizhan gouyong de deng: Bianzheng faxian de lujing" (A Useful Light: Identifying the Path of Discovery). *Yingyong xinli xue yanjiu* (Applied Psychology Research), September 2004: 131–156.

Xia Linqing. 2010. "Shehui lichang zhong de duikangdian: Qidong ren de fazhan wancheng shi" (The Nodes of Resistance in the Power Grid of Society: Triggering the Completion of Human Development). http://www.psychspace.com/psych/viewnews-2299.html. Accessed January 2018.

Xia Linqing. 2013. "Xingdong yanjiu de shuangmian zuoyong" (The Double-Edged Nature of Action Research). In *Xingdong yanjiu yu shehui gongzuo* (Action Research and Social Work), edited by Yang Jing and Xia Linqing, 3–9. Beijing: Social Sciences Academic Press.

"Xiaodu nongzhuang" nuanxin shangxian: Baidu ditu yong gongyi lianjie wangyou yu huangmo" ("Baidu Eco-Farm" Project Went Online: Baidu Map Links Netizens with Desert). 2018. *China Daily.com*. February 7, 2018. http://tech.chinadaily.com.cn/2018-02/07/content_35664174.htm.

Xiao Shu. 2010. *Guanzhu jiushi Liliang, weiguan gaibian Zhongguo* (Giving Attention Is Power, Online Spectatorship Is Changing China). *Nanfang zhoumo* (Southern Weekly), January 14, 2010, F29.

Xiao Xi. 2018. "Wei gongyi tequan xia de xing gaochao (The Orgasm under the Privilege of Pseudo Philanthropy). WeChat Public Account "Cingergongyi." July 24, 2018. https://mp.weixin.qq.com/cgi-bin/loginpage?t=wxm2 -login&lang=zh_CN. Accessed in August 2018.

Xie Baohui. 2014. *Media Transparency in China: Rethinking Rhetoric and Reality.* Lanham, MD: Lexington Books.

Xie Meng. 2011. "Guangzhou Wangyou qianren ti guangtou chaofeng Guang-zhou 1.5 yi shengji guangliang gongcheng" (A Guangzhou Netizen Mobi-lizing a Thousand People to Shave Heads in Opposition to the 150 Million Night Illumination Project). *Nanfang Ribao* (South China Daily), April 29, 2011. http://news.qq.com/a/20110429/000696.htm.

Xie Pu. 2010. "Fanke ti de dansheng" (The Birth of the Fanke Style). Sep-tember 26, 2010. http://tech.ifeng.com/internet/detail_2010_09/26/2630687 _0.shtml?_from_ralated. Accessed May 2011.

Xie Zuoru. 2014. "Zhongxiaoxue chuangke kongjian liebiao" (List of Elementary and Middle School-Based Makerspaces). Sina microblog. November 9, 2014. http://blog.sina.com.cn/s/blog_6611ddcf0102v7qt.html.

Xinhua Net. 2017. "Quanguo yi rending cishan zuzhi 916 jia" (China Has Recognized 916 Nonprofit Organizations as 'Charity Organizations"). July 14, 2017. http://news.xinhuanet.com/gongyi/2017-07/14/c_129655453 .htm.

Xu Jian. 2016. *Media Events in Web 2.0 China: Interventions of Online Activism.* Eastbourne, UK: Sussex Academic Press.

Xu Ming. 2016. "Xin shiqi shehui zhili chuangxin yu shehui dongyuan jizhi yanjiu" (Studies of the Innovation of Social Governance and Social Mobiliza-tion in the New Era). Dalian: Dongbei Caijing daxue chubanshe.

Xu Yongguang. 2015. "Gongyi jingji cong chaohui diushi de GDP kaishi" (Let's Start with the Search for the Lost GDP Points If We Want to Talk about Philanthropy Economy). Narada Foundation. May 10, 2015. http://www .naradafoundation.org/content/4484.

Xu Yongguang. 2016. "Caogen NGO kaishi zhudao gongyi hangye de fangxiang" (Grassroots NGOs Began to Guide the Direction of the Nonprofit Sector). *Zhongguo caifu* (China Fortune). Republished in Shanda Net. January 7, 2016. http://www.naradafoundation.org/content/4787.

Xuan Feng. 2011. "Shayu mei, shiwusui" (The Shark Sister, A Fifteen-Year-Old). *Nandu zhoukan* (Nandu Weekly), June 3, 2011. http://city.sina.com.cn/focus /t/2011-06-03/105118509.html.

Yan Xia. 2015. "Wenwen wo Sun Yan: yizhi gou yinfa de chuangye gushi" (SmileMe's Sun Yan: A Story about Entrepreneurship Triggered by a Dog). May 12, 2015. http://www.chinaz.com/start/2015/0512/405312.shtml.

Yang Guobin. 2009a. "Historical Imagination in the Study of Chinese Digital Civil Society. In *China's Information and Communications Technology Revolution,* edited by Zhang Xiaoling and Zheng Yongnian, 17–33. London and New York: Routledge.

Yang Guobin. 2009b. *The Power of the Internet in China: Citizen Activism Online.* New York: Columbia University Press.

Yang Guobin. 2016. "Narrative Agency in Hashtag Activism: The Case of #BlackLivesMatter. *Media and Communication* 4, no.4: 13–17.

Yang Guobin. 2017. "Qing zhi shang: wangluo ganqing dongyuan de wenming Jincheng" (Killing Emotions Softly: The Civilizing Process of Online Emotional Mobilization). *Chuanbo yu shehui xuekan* (Journal of Communication and Society) no. 40: 75–104.

Yang Jing. 2013. "Huigu lishi, bianshi jingyan, xunzhao bian de liliang: Yige shehui1gongzuozhe de xingdong yanjiu" (Look Back at History, Identify Experiences, and Seek the Power of Transformation: The Action Research of a Social Worker). In *Xingdong yanjiu yu shehui gongzuo* (Action Research and Social Work), edited by Yang Jing and Xia Linqing, 48–63. Beijing: Social Sciences Academic Press.

Yang Jing, and Xia Linqing, eds. 2013. *Xingdong yanjiu yu shehui gongzuo* (Action Research and Social Work). Beijing: Social Sciences Academic Press.

Ye Xueli. 2017. "Qingnian zhiyuanzhe xingdong" (Young Volunteers Operation). *Qingyun shi* (The History of Youth Movement) 407, no. 1: 47–49.

Yongshi yongshi. 2015. "Zhongguo gongyi ren women mei zige tan Bijie beiju" (Chinese Nonprofit Workers, We Don't Have the Right to Discuss the Bijie Tragedy). *Xici hutong.* June 17, 2015. http://www.xici.net/d218206920.htm.

Yonck, Richard. 2017. *Heart of the Machine: Our Future in a World of Artificial Emotional Intelligence.* New York: Arcade Publishing.

Yu Jianbin, and Deng Wei. 2015. "'Chuangke' yuanhe yin zongli dianzan" (Why Did Makers Receive Endorsement from the Premiere?). March 19, 2015. http://politics.people.com.cn/n/2015/0319/c1001-26715378.html.

Yu Jianrong. 2010. "Everyone Has a Microphone." *China Digital Times,* December 10, 2010. http://chinadigitaltimes.net/2010/12/yu-jianrong-%E4%BA%8E%E5%BB%BA%E5%B5%98-everyone-has-a-microphone/.

Yu Keping. 2011. "A Shift towards Social Governance in China." *East Asia Forum.* September 9, 2011. http://www.eastasiaforum.org/2011/09/09/a-shift-towards-social-governance-in-china/.

Yu Keping. 2014. "What Political Reform Looks Like in China." *The Huffington Post*, October 29, 2014. http://www.huffingtonpost.com/keping-yu/china-political-reform_b_6075464.html.

Yu Keping. 2016. *Democracy in China: Challenge or Opportunity.* Singapore and Beijing: World Scientific Publishing Co. and Central Compilation and Translation Press.

Yuan, Elaine J. 2015. "The New Political of Mediated Activism in China." In *Networked China: Global Dynamics of Digital Media and Civic Engagement,* edited by Wenhong Chen and Stephen D. Reese, 214–230. New York and London: Routledge.

Zhang Heqing. 2014. Sina Blogs, March 25, 2014. http://blog.sina.com.cn/s/blog_6310d2290106nnal.html.

Zhang Heqing. 2015. "Zhixing heyi: Shehui gongzuo xingdong yanjiu de lichen" (The Unity of Knowing and Doing: The Journey of Social Work Action Research). *The Journal of Zhejing Gongshang University* 4: 98–103.

Zhang Jian. 2011. "Shehui gongzuo jieru nongcun liushou ertong wenti de xingdong yanjiu" (An Action Research on Social Work Intervening in Left-behind Children). *Shehui gongzuo* (Journal of Social Work) no. 9: 23–26.

Zhang Jie. 2012. "90hou de qunti kangzheng" (The Collective Contention of the Post-1990s Generation). *Caijing wenzhai* (Financial Digest) no. 8.

Zhang Qiang. 2017. "NGO2.0 zai Qinghua juban gongyi jishu malasong, chuangke zhuli Zhengjiu Minqin guimohua zhongzhi suosuo" (NGO2.0 Held a Civic Hackathon at Qinghua University, Makers Helped Rescue Minqin Scale Up the Planting of Suosuo Trees). December 17, 2017. http://www.ngo20.org/blog/ngo2-0-6c65bab8-c27e-4088-b85f-0394fd1867b0.

Zhang Ruwei. 2016. "Yong Weibo yingxiao gongyi" (Using Weibo to Market Public Good). In *Hulianwang+gongyi: Wanzhuan xin meiti* (The Internet + Public Good: Playing with New Media), edited by Jing Wang and Zhou Rongting, 60–92. Beijing: Publishing House of Electronics Industry.

Zhang Weisheng. 2015. "Ren xiaomi: Yili xiaomi beihou de gongyi chuangxin" (A "Responsible" Millet: The Story about Philanthropy Innovation behind Xiao Mi). *Zhongguo cishan jia* (Chinese Philanthropists) no. 2 (March 3). http://www.icixun.com/2015/0303/4848.html.

Zhang Yaxin. 2014. *Gonggong shijian de weibo "weiguan" yanjiu* (A Study on the "Casual Witnessing" of Public Incidents on Weibo). Master's thesis, Hunan University.

Zhang Yi. 2015. "Mingxing weibo yingxiao de 'Mingxing xiaoying fenxi" (Analysis of the Celebrity Effect of Weibo's Celebrity Marketing). *Daguan* (Panoramic View) no. 6. http://wenku.baidu.com/view/d3ccd07619e8b8f67c1cb9ed.html?re=view.

Zhao Dingxin. 2012. "Weibo, zhengzhi gonggong kongjian he Zhongguo de fazhan" (Weibo, Political Public Sphere and the Development of China). April 26, 2012. *Guanchazhe* (The Observer). https://www.guancha.cn/ZhaoDingXin/2012_04_26_71174.shtml.

Zhao Guo, and Gregory D. Saxton. 2014. "Tweeting Social Change: How Social Media Are Changing Nonprofit Advocacy," *Nonprofit and Voluntary Sector Quarterly* 43, no. 1: 57–79.

Zhao Yuezhi. 2008. *Communication in China: Political Economy, Power, and Conflict.* Lanham, MD: Rowman & Littlefield.

Zhao Yuezhi. 2012. "Understanding China's Media System in a World Historical Context." In *Comparing Media Systems Beyond the Western World*, edited by D. C. Hallin and P. Mancini, 143–173. Cambridge: Cambridge University Press.

Zheng Yongnian. 2007. *Technological Empowerment: The Internet, State, and Society in China.* Stanford, CA: Stanford University Press.

Zhengrong Foundation. 2015. "He pingtai xiangmu jieshao" (Introduction to He Platform). http://www.zrgy.org/project.asp?cid=99.

Zhou Hongyun. 2013. "Shehui guanli tizhi gaige: xianzhuang, chuangxin, yu zhanwang" (Social Management System Reform: The Current State, Innovation, and Prospects for the Future). In *Shehui guanli chuangxin* (Social

Management Innovation), edited by Zhou Hongyun, 1–41. Beijing: Central Compilation and Translation Press.

Zhou Jun. 2012. "Xingdong yanjiu zai woguo de fazhan: Huigu yu fansi (The Development of Action Research in China: A Review and Reflection). *The Journal of Tianjin Normal University* 13, no.1: 1–4.

Zhu Jiangang. 2016. "Jiedu 'Cishan fa': Gongyi cishan zhuanxing tuidong guojia zhili zhuanxing" (The Philanthropy Law: Public Good Governance in Transition Propels the Transformation of State Governance). Caixin.com. May 4, 2016. http://www.icixun.com/2016/0504/5406.html.

Zhu Qianwei. 2016. "Zhengshe fenkai de luoji ji qi kunjing" (The Logic and Dilemma of Separation of Government and Society). *Jiangsu xingzheng xueyuan xuebao* (Journal of Jiangsu Administration Institute) 87, no. 3: 96–102.

Zhu Wenqian. 2015. "Bill Gates Launches Institute Focused on Philanthropy." *China Daily.* December 3, 2015. http://www.chinadaily.com.cn/kindle/2015 -12/03/content_22618104.htm.

Zuckerman, Ethan. 2013. *Rewire: Digital Cosmopolitans in the Age of Connection.* New York: W. W. Norton.

Acknowledgments

The Other Digital China: Nonconfrontational Activism on the Social Web was written as a testimony to my decade-long involvement in social media activism in China. In 2009 when I founded NGO2.0, I had no idea it would later evolve into a full-fledged nonprofit organization based in Shenzhen. Nor would I have guessed I would write a book on nonconfrontational activism and publish it on the tenth anniversary of the founding of NGO2.0.

I would like to thank Lindsay Waters at Harvard University Press for appreciating my subversive ways of thinking and for shepherding this manuscript to fruition at such a quick pace. Although this book is not an ethnography of NGO2.0, I am indebted to the Ford Foundation in China, whose decade-long support (2009–2019) of NGO2.0 made it possible for me to build alliances and develop collaboration with social actors from diverse sectors, whose actions inspired my writing of *The Other Digital China*. I would not have embarked on an activist career without the steadfast support of Dr. Kate Hartford, a former Ford-in-China project officer, whose decision to fund NGO2.0 in 2009 changed my intellectual life for good. Dr. Elizabeth Knup, the foundation's current China representative, and Dr. John Fitzgerald, a former chief operating officer at Ford, have both contributed to the buildup of my NGO work through which I gained invaluable insights about nonconfrontational activism in China. And without a fellowship awarded by the Radcliffe Institute for Advanced Study at Harvard University between 2015–2016, I would not have been able to wrap up the writing.

Professor Rongting Zhou at the University of Science and Technology of China, cofounder of NGO2.0, is a comrade who weathered all kinds of risks to help me set up our organization. I would not have been able to juggle between Beijing, Shenzhen, and Cambridge, Massachusetts, without the backing of my dedicated team—current and erstwhile NGO2.0 staffers and volunteers: Endy Xie Dong, Zhang Qiang, Shi Song, Xiao Ruifeng, Wang Yu, Wan Weixiang, Chen Bobing, Han Zongchuan, Deng Ping, Xiao Zhihua, Zhang Qian, Wang Man, Sun Huan, Zhou

Feng, Li Jianbo, and Yang Weihe. They are my fellow travelers from whom I learned a great deal about teamwork and vision making, and whose companionship lit up the winding passage of our collective effort to create a better digital ecosystem for Chinese NGOs. I have watched Zhang Qiang, the executive director of NGO2.0, grow from a grassroots worker with minimal knowledge of the internet to an able instructor of all the courses offered in our Web 2.0 training curriculum. I took great pleasure in playing a part in his chance encounter with Xiaohui, who ended up being his wife. The patient presence and wise counsel provided by Endy Xie, our CTO, made it possible for me to forge ahead and survive occasional meltdowns. There are many stories to tell and memories to share, especially the group outings in the night markets in West China.

I am also grateful to the members of the Board of NGO2.0—Xiang Fan (Tsinghua University), Mikko Lan (Ogilvy Beijing Public Relations), Peiyuan Guo (syntao.com), Zhang Song (ThoughtWorks), and Maggie Liu (Nvidia)—for their great wisdom and encouragement of our endeavor.

My ten-year-long immersion in ICT activism gained a lot of backing from colleagues in China—Zhao Zizhong at the Communication University of China, Li Wenjun, Hu Shuli, Liao Hongyong, Wang Qing, and Li Yanhong at Sun Yat-sen University, Zhang Ruwei, a former employee at Sina.com, and Qiu Zhijie at the China Central Academy of Fine Arts. Dou Ruigang, Lin Hong, and Chen Yueguang are thought leaders in China's foundation sector to whom I turned for guidance and inspiration. I also learned a great deal about the sustainable models of civic hackathons from Matt Jung, program director for TechSoup Asia-Pacific. Tang Ning, the founder and CEO of CreditEase, helped our crowdsourced philanthropy map gain a new life.

MIT is a powerful brand name that helped me establish my credibility in China with speed. I benefited from my ongoing conversations about the "agency versus structure" debate with Paloma Duong, a young Latin American Studies colleague in the Global Studies and Languages (GSL). T. L. Taylor, Lisa Parks, and William Uricchio, my colleagues at Comparative Media Studies/Writing (CMS/W), brainstormed with me about the title of this book. James Paradis in the department tapped me on the shoulder when a word of encouragement was needed. Although I was not always present at the weekly meetings of the MIT Center for Civic Media led by Ethan Zuckerman, my exposure to the work at the center enriched my understanding of ICT-powered activism. I am also indebted to Emma Teng and Ian Condry for their support of my NGO work while they were heads of GSL.

Louisa Schein at Rutgers University met me offline, in New York, where we mulled over alternative titles for this book. I have given talks about my activism in China on numerous campuses since 2010 and benefited a great deal from conversations with students and faculty at those universities. Stephen Sheehi at William and Mary, Mayfair Yang and her colleagues at UC Santa Barbara, and Stanley Rosen at UCSC raised provocative questions that helped me clarify my conceptual framework. The sparkling intelligence of my students at MIT and their love for hands-on collaborative work is a constant reminder to me of the pedagogical value of fun-making and experiential learning, which I applied to my teaching of NGOs in China.

Colleagues in the field (Tani Barlow, Jack Linchuan Qiu, Anthony Fung, Michael Keane, Lin Chun, Qin Shao, Michael Dutton, and Elisa Oreglia) and my old friends in Beijing (Liang Li, Lola Zhang, Dawei Li, Eric and Echo Liao, Sarah Xu, Chunyan Wang, Weihua Wu, and Ye Ying), as well as my local "families" in Boston (Don and Julie DeSander, Sister Lian, Justin Life, Liwen Jin, and Dawei Shen) may not know they are also present in *The Other Digital China*. Their kindness is a constant reminder that life is simple and abundant when I am weighed down by real and imaginary obstacles. I am also grateful to the four anonymous readers of the manuscript. Their sharp questions, comments, and critiques strengthened the argument of this book. The production of this book went smoothly thanks to Joy Deng at Harvard University Press, and Sherry Gerstein and Catherine Mallon at Westchester Publishing Services.

I would like to acknowledge the reprint of the following copyrighted materials: Chapter 2 incorporates, with some deletions and additions, the text of "NGO2.0 and social media praxis: activist as researcher," published online in *Chinese Journal of Communication* at http://wwww.tandfonline.com/[10.1080/17544750.2014.988634 and is reprinted here with permission of Taylor & Frances Group. Chapter 5 reprints, with some deletions and additions, "The makers are coming! China's long tail revolution," published in 2016 in *Handbook of Cultural and Creative Industries in China* edited by Michael Keane. I thank Edward Elgar Publishing for permission to reprint portions of that text here.

This book is dedicated to my NGO students who are also my teachers, among them Ban Aihua, Chen Ci, Chen Hongyan, Chen Zhimei, Cheng Wenbin, Du Yujin, Fan Yuze, Fu Qiang, Gao Qiang, Guo Bin, Han Jierong, Huo Minhao, Li Zunwei, Liang Xiaomei, Lin Jun, Liu Kui, Ma Junhe, Ni Kaizhi, Peng Weifeng, Peng Yanhui, Qi Yongjin, Ruan Huanjun, Tian Shuai, Wang Jun, Wang Wei, Wu Fengyun, Xu Yanjie, Yang Ke, Yin Hang, Yu He, Zhang Bo, Zhang Jie, Zhang Yi, Zhang Yucai, Zhang Zhengwen, Zhao Donglin, Zhao Lin, and Zhong Xiangming—a list that is simply too long to complete. I share their faith in changing China for the better, one inch at a time.

Index

Note: Page numbers followed by *f* or *t* indicate figures or tables, respectively. Page references including n indicate endnotes.